W9-AJT-188

The Stephen King
Companion

921
KI

Stephen King
companion

$10.95

DATE			
MR 26 '90	MY 10 '13		
AP 27 '90			
JE 12 '90			
JY 16 '90			
JY 28 '90			
JA 12 '91			
AP 14 '93			
SE 13 '93			
DEC 02 '97			
JAN 18 '97			
DE 28 '06			

EAU CLAIRE DISTRICT LIBRARY

© THE BAKER & TAYLOR CO.

Photo courtesy of the *Bangor Daily News*

King holding mounted head of a rattlesnake in a crystal ball.

The Stephen King Companion

Edited by
George Beahm

EAU CLAIRE DISTRICT LIBRARY

WITHDRAWN

B+T 3/1/90 #10.85

74795

Andrews and McMeel
A Universal Press Syndicate Company
Kansas City · New York

The Stephen King Companion copyright © 1989 by George and Mary Beahm

All rights reserved.

Printed in the United States of America.

No part of this book may be used or reproduced in any manner
whatsoever except in the context of reviews.

For information write Andrews and McMeel, a Universal Press Syndicate Company,
4900 Main Street, Kansas City, Missouri 64112.

Library of Congress Cataloging-in-Publication Data

The Stephen King companion / edited by George Beahm.
   p.   cm.
  Includes bibliographical references.
  ISBN: 0-8362-7978-6 : $10.95
  1. King, Stephen, 1947–   —Criticism and interpretation.
I. King, Stephen, 1947– . II. Beahm, George W.
PS3561.I483Z88   1989
813′.54—dc20   89-17811
                                               CIP

See page 362 for continuation of copyright notice.

Cover photograph by Carroll Hall,
courtesy of the *Bangor Daily News*

Book Design: Edward King
Typography: Connell-Zeko Type & Graphics

ATTENTION: SCHOOLS AND BUSINESSES

Andrews and McMeel books are available at quantity discounts
with bulk purchase for educational, business, or sales
promotional use. For information, please write to:
Special Sales Department, Andrews and McMeel,
4900 Main Street, Kansas City, Missouri 64112.

To our parents, and to
Anne Hearth, Don and Jacqueline Wescott,
and Howard and Maria Wornom.

George and Mary Beahm

Contents

Appendices

Acknowledgments

I am grateful to the many people who gave generously of their time and effort to assist me on this book project.

I am especially indebted to my wife, Mary, who performed many duties, both editorial and secretarial, in addition to reading the manuscript and providing many ideas that enhanced the book. Without her help, the book would not have been written.

Similarly, I am greatly indebted to Howard ("Rusty") Wornom, who assisted in innumerable ways to shape the manuscript: assisting in interviewing, contributing articles, proofreading, and providing many ideas incorporated herein. Rusty's editorial acumen is present throughout this book.

Timothy O'Shaughnessy deserves special mention for his artistic input. I am grateful for his invaluable assistance.

I also wish to express my gratitude to those at Andrews and McMeel who have worked hard to bring this project to fruition: Thomas Thornton, who encouraged me to write it; Donna Martin, my book editor, whose draconian cuts and suggestions greatly improved the manuscript; Patty Dingus, who managed somehow to keep the letters, packages, phone calls, and FAX transmissions coming and going; Jean Lowe, who oversaw the editing; and Lisa Shadid, who midwifed the production. To all my friends at Andrews and McMeel, I am greatly indebted.

I am especially grateful to the following individuals: Charlie Campo (the librarian at the *Bangor Daily News*) for photographs, microfilmed copies of articles, letters, and assistance during my visits to the newspaper; Eric S. Flower (head of the Special Collections Department at the Fogler Library of the University of Maine at Orono) for the phone calls, letters, and personal assistance while doing research at the library; Barry R. Levin for his invaluable work on the price guide; Paul Reynolds (managing editor at the *Bangor Daily News*) for generously allowing me to reprint photographs and excerpts from articles from King's hometown newspaper; and Stephen King and his professional staff and business associates: Shirley Sonderegger (secretary), Christopher Spruce (editor/publisher of *Castle Rock* newsletter), Kirby McCauley (of the Kirby McCauley agency), and King's literary agent, Arthur B. Greene.

To numerous persons and organizations that provided invaluable assistance in many ways, my thanks: Michael Autrey for bibliographic information, photographs, and copies of publications; the Bangor Historical Society for copies of research material; Paul Burke for advice and support; May Castleberry (of the Whitney Museum) for information and updates on *My Pretty Pony;* Michael R. Collings for advice and critical insights; Colleen Doran for encouragement and advice; Ted Ditky for information and copies of Starmont books; Donald M. Grant for taking time out of his busy schedule to revise his humorous article about King; Karen and Pat Killough; Patrick Piper, the producer of "The Larry King Show," for permission to reprint from the King interviews; Martha J. Sims (library director for the Virginia Beach public library system) for background information and assistance in putting together a detailed picture of King's speech at the Virginia Beach Pavilion; Sandy Spencer (of Recorded Books) for copies of King audiotapes and permission to reprint at length from an interview with King; Carroll Terrell (a professor at the University of Maine at Orono) for personal insights and critical observations about King; Michael and Audrey Whelan, who gave generously of their time to allow me to interview them and reprint art; and Herb Yellin (of Lord John Press) for information on specialty publishing, advice, and encouragement.

I am especially indebted to those who granted interviews: Clive Barker, Michael R. Collings, Harlan Ellison, Terry Steel, Michael and Audrey Whelan, Nye Willden, Douglas E. Winter, and Berni Wrightson.

Thanks are also due those who allowed me to reprint from their publications: John F. Baker (of *Publishers Weekly*), Dara Tyson (of Waldenbooks), Grace Darby (of the *New Yorker*), Fran Arminio (of Taunton Press, Publishers), Marcia Terrones (of *Playboy*), and Avis Weatherbee (of *Cinefantastique*).

I also thank those people who sent copies of requested publications and other material: American Express, Bowling Green University's Popular Press, Carolee Brockway (of ZBS Foundation), New American Library, the Public Relations office of the University of Maine at Orono, and Stephen Spignesi.

To anyone whose work was solicited but not used, or anyone overlooked who deserved mention, I extend my sincere apologies.

GEORGE BEAHM

Newport News, Virginia
July 1989

The Stephen King
Companion

**I think with the best writing you actually
feel the writer's joy, the writer's vision,
or something like that. God,
it's a strange way to make a living.
It's a child's activity, really.**

Stephen King, excerpted from an interview, "The Author Talks: Stephen King,"
Copyright© 1987 by Recorded Books, Inc.,
reprinted with permission.

Photo courtesy of the *Bangor Daily News*

Stephen King in downtown Bangor, Maine.

Part One

The Real World of Stephen King

What is King *really* like?

When Douglas E. Winter interviewed horror writers for *Faces of Fear,* that question came up several times from the interviewees. Later, in pondering the question, Winter concluded that if he had found an easy answer, he wouldn't have had to write an entire book, *Stephen King: The Art of Darkness.*

What is King really like? That question, for most, will remain unanswered. Early in his writing career, King was accessible—he went on national publicity tours, attended conventions, appeared at many book signings, and made himself available for interviews. In an early interview, King remarked that he felt guilty about saying no. Soon, however, he realized it was a necessity because of the endless demands that would leave him no time for writing.

Today, King is insulated from his fans (by his secretary, who screens his mail and answers the phone), from the business community at large (by his business manager/agent), and from his readers (public appearances and talks are, at best, infrequent).

This section shows you the real world of Stephen King, the boogeyman of Bangor, Maine.

An overview of King's career gives you the big picture, setting the stage for the remainder of the book.

To give you a personal insight into his work, the *Playboy* interview—the best of the many interviews he has given over the years—is reprinted.

You'll be front row center in Virginia Beach, where King delivered a lecture in 1986 on the occasion of Banned Books Week—a lecture that appears in print for the first time in this book.

You'll view his home in Bangor, the historic William Arnold house, easily recognizable with its custom-made wrought-iron fence.

You'll read of the King roast at which Donald M. Grant tells of his fictional journey to Maine to visit King.

A chronology, a brief profile of writer Tabitha King, and King trivia complete the section.

1

Chronology

Personal Life

1947   Born, September 21, in Portland, Maine

1949   Father leaves and is never heard from

1949–58   Family moves to Fort Wayne, Indiana, then to Stratford, Connecticut

1958   Family moves to Durham, Maine

1959–60   Turning point: discovers box of horror and science-fiction books at aunt's house

1962–66   Lisbon Falls high school

1966–70   University of Maine at Orono (UMO); graduates with B.S. in English, a minor in speech, and a side interest in drama; meets wife to be, Tabitha Spruce

1971   Marries Tabitha Spruce

1971–73   Teaches English at Hampden Academy (Hampden, Maine), lives in trailer in Hermon, Maine

1973   Becomes writer full-time with sale of *Carrie* to Doubleday in hardback, and NAL in paperback

    Mother dies of cancer

    Moves family to North Windham, Maine

1974   Moves to Boulder, Colorado

1975   Moves to Bridgton, Maine, and purchases house

1977   Extended visit to England, but returns after three months to purchase home in Center Lovell, Maine (summer residence)

1978   Writer-in-residence at UMO; rents home in Orrington, Maine

1979   Returns to Center Lovell after teaching stint

1980   Buys Victorian mansion in Bangor (current residence)

Published Books

1974   *Carrie* (Doubleday)

1975   *'Salem's Lot* (Doubleday)

1977   *Rage,* a Bachman book (NAL)
        The Shining (Doubleday)

1978   *Night Shift* (Doubleday)
        The Stand (Doubleday)
1979   *The Dead Zone* (Viking)
        The Long Walk, a Bachman book (NAL)

1980   *Firestarter* (Viking)

1981   *Cujo* (Viking)
        Danse Macabre (Everest House)
        Roadwork, a Bachman book (NAL)

1982   *Creepshow* (NAL)
        The Dark Tower: The Gunslinger (Donald M. Grant, Publisher)
        Different Seasons (Viking)
        The Running Man, a Bachman book (NAL)

1983   *Christine* (Viking)
        Cycle of the Werewolf (Land of Enchantment)
        Pet Sematary (Doubleday)

1984   *The Eyes of the Dragon* (Philtrum Press)
        The Talisman (Viking & G.P. Putnam's Sons)
        Thinner, a Bachman book (NAL)

1985   *The Bachman Books* (NAL)
        Skeleton Crew (Putnam)

1986   *It* (Viking)

1987   *The Dark Tower II: The Drawing of the Three* (Donald M. Grant)
        The Eyes of the Dragon (Viking)
        Misery (Viking)
        Silver Bullet [see *Cycle of the Werewolf*] (NAL)
        The Tommyknockers (Putnam)

1988   *The Dark Tower: The Gunslinger* (NAL, trade paperback)

1989   *The Dark Half* by Stephen King (Viking)
        The Dark Tower II: The Drawing of the Three (NAL, trade
            paperback)

The Dark Tower: The Gunslinger (NAL, mass-market paperback)
Dolan's Cadillac (Lord John Press)
My Pretty Pony (Whitney Museum)
My Pretty Pony (Whitney Museum and Alfred A. Knopf)

1990   *The Dark Tower II: The Drawing of the Three* (NAL, mass-market
      paperback)
    The Stand, revised edition (Doubleday)
    An untitled collection of two novellas: "Secret Word, Secret
      Garden" and "Sun Dog" (Viking)

1991   *Needful Things* (Viking) [reported title but not confirmed]

1992   *Dolores Claiborne* (Viking) [reported title but not confirmed]

Books About King

1981   *Teacher's Manual: Novels of Stephen King* (NAL)

1982   *Fear Itself: The Horror Fiction of Stephen King*
      (Underwood–Miller)
    Stephen King (Starmont Reader's Guide 16)

1984   *Stephen King: The Art of Darkness* (NAL)
    Stephen King at the Movies (NAL)

1985   *Discovering Stephen King* (Starmont House)
    The Many Facets of Stephen King (Starmont House)
    The Shorter Works of Stephen King (Starmont House)
    Stephen King as Richard Bachman (Starmont House)

1986   *The Annotated Guide to Stephen King* (Starmont House)
    The Films of Stephen King (Starmont House)
    Kingdom of Fear: The World of Stephen King (Underwood–Miller)

1987   *The Gothic World of Stephen King: Landscape of Nightmares*
      (Bowling Green State University Popular Press)
    Stephen King Goes to Hollywood (NAL)
    The Stephen King Phenomenon (Starmont House)

1988   *Bare Bones* (McGraw-Hill)
    Landscape of Fear: Stephen King's American Gothic
      (Bowling Green State University Popular Press)
    Reign of Fear: Fiction and Films of Stephen King
      (Underwood–Miller)
    Stephen King: The First Decade, Carrie to Pet Sematary
      (Twayne Publishers)

1989   *Feast of Fear* (Underwood–Miller). A companion book to *Bare Bones,* this book collects 47 interviews with King.
The Moral Voyages of Stephen King (Starmont House). Scheduled for fall.
"The Shining" Reader (Starmont House). Scheduled for fall.
The Stephen King Companion (Andrews and McMeel)
The Unseen King (Starmont House)

1990   *Infinite Explorations: Art and Artifice in Stephen King's It, Misery, and The Tommyknockers* [working title] by Michael R. Collings (Starmont House). A scholarly examination of King's more recent novels. Possibly "early 1990," according to the publisher. Tentatively priced at $11.95 in trade paperback, and $21.95 in hardback.
In the Darkest Night: A Student's Guide to Stephen King by Tim Murphy (Starmont House). A bibliography. Possibly "early 1990," according to the publisher. Tentatively priced at $11.95 in trade paperback, and $21.95 in hardback.
The Shape Under the Sheet: The Complete Stephen King Encyclopedia by Stephen J. Spignesi (Popular Culture, Ink.). A fall release.
The Stephen King Bibliography by Douglas E. Winter (Donald M. Grant, Publisher, Inc.). An exhaustive primary and secondary bibliography—updated, revised and expanded from the version in *The Art of Darkness.* Annotations by King. (Perhaps 1990).
The Stephen King Quiz Book by Stephen J. Spignesi (NAL). In paperback, an August release.

Movies, TV Shows, Audiotapes

1976   *Carrie*

1979   *'Salem's Lot* (TV miniseries)

1980   *The Shining*

1982   *Creepshow I*

1983   *Christine*
The Dead Zone
Cujo

1984   *Cat's Eye*
Children of the Corn
Firestarter

1985　　*Silver Bullet*
　　　　"The Boogeyman" and "The Woman in the Room," *Two Mini-
　　　　　　Features from . . . Stephen King's Night Shift Collection*
　　　　　　(videotape)
　　　　"The Word Processor of the Gods" (TV adaptation)

1986　　"Gramma" (TV adaptation)
　　　　Maximum Overdrive
　　　　Stand by Me

1987　　*Creepshow II*
　　　　Return to 'Salem's Lot
　　　　"Sorry, Right Number" (TV adaptation)

1988　　*The Running Man*

1989　　*Pet Sematary*

Original Screenplays and Teleplays

Cat's Eye

Creepshow I

Maximum Overdrive

Pet Sematary

Silver Bullet

"Sorry, Right Number"

The Long, Strange Trip of Stephen King
An Overview

*Writers are made, not born. Most people have a talent to write.
To develop that talent into a salable commodity takes a lot of work.
You write a lot, sharpening your writing skills, honing the edge,
until you can cut your own bread and butter.*

Stephen King, in *Bangor Daily News,* October 15, 1980

1. The Books

To paraphrase the Grateful Dead, what a long, strange trip it has been for Stephen King.

After publishing *The Tommyknockers*—the last book in the four-book King firestorm, totaling *four million* copies sold in hardback—King went on record and, in an interview with *Publishers Weekly* in February 1988, said of his next novel, *The Dark Half:* "It won't be published for a long, long time."

King was on a break—from publishing, not writing—and although some King fans expected a dry spell, most never even noticed: In 1988 King published the second *Dark Tower* book, a trade edition of the long-awaited first *Dark Tower* book, and "authored" a book of photographs, *Nightmares in the Sky* (King fans who saw the oversized book assumed it was by King; but a quick look inside proved otherwise, and King's general readership put the book back on the shelf).

Within months of King's announcement that he was on an extended break, in a front-page story in the February 1989 issue of *Castle Rock,* the King newsletter, editor/publisher Christopher Spruce reported that King had signed a four-book deal. The first book was scheduled for publication in the fall of 1989 (*The Dark Half*), to be followed by the three others, each released a year apart. The break, short-lived, was clearly over. King was cranking up the word processor.

Immediately, rumors began to fly about the art of the deal. How much did King earn? David Streitfeld, writing in "Book Report" for the *Washington Post,* reported:

> Details are sketchy, but the consensus is that King will get around $32 million for the North American hardcover and paperback rights.

The sum may even be greater than this: one source in a position to know says it was $40 million—a nice, even $10 million per book. Even before you add in foreign language rights, movie options and various other angles, you're talking about the richest publishing deal ever. . . . Most "literary" novelists, remember, make between $10,000 and $20,000 from each tale.

It's the kind of praising with faint damns that King has had to endure almost from the beginning of his meteoric career. *If it's that popular, it can't be good. But look at how much he's getting paid—isn't it incredible?*

As King explained in 1976 in "The Guest Word," the opinion column of the *New York Times Book Review,* he felt guilty when a book like David Madden's *Bijou* earned its author only $15,000 over a six-year period—while his own second novel, *'Salem's Lot,* then recently published in paperback, and written in less than a year, was on its way to making a small fortune.

King further explained that although he feels guilty when that happens, because *Bijou* is better than *'Salem's Lot,* he also does *not* feel guilty, because he's written the best book he can, an honest book, and in the end that's all that matters.

It's a perceptive comment, one that strikes at the heart of the question: Why does King sell so well?

Harlan Ellison—a contemporary fantasist who called King "one of the most accomplished storytellers the twentieth century has produced"—offers one answer in his film criticism column, "Harlan Ellison's Watching":

It is because he is as honest a popular writer as we've been privileged to experience in many a year. He writes a good stick. He never cheats the buyer of a King book. You may or may not feel he brought off a particular job when you get to page last, but you *never* feel you've been had. He does the one job no writer may ignore at the peril of tars and feathers, he *delivers.*

It's a fairly accurate assessment. With an estimated *eighty million* books in print worldwide, King's fiction obviously strikes a responsive chord in today's book-buying public—an audience that snaps up over a million copies of a new novel at $21.95 retail, and three million of its paperback edition at $4.95 (or more).

King's work is unquestionably popular. But what his critics tend to overlook, fixated as they usually are by the dollar signs in his contracts, is that his books are, on the whole, good, *honest* books. He is a writer with a vision who writes to please himself, and in doing so pleases millions of others. That is what I call success, and what King called in his foreword to *Night Shift* a "marketable obsession."

While writing short stories and selling them to magazines like *Cavalier,* King was virtually unknown except to those who accidentally ran across his work and noticed how good he was. (One such casual reader was Douglas E. Winter, who later became King's Boswell, the official biographer and bibliographer, and wrote *Stephen King: The Art of Darkness.*)

It wasn't until King published a novel in 1974 that he came to the attention of the book-reading public at large, making his part-time obsession full time and profitable. While King undoubtedly benefited from exquisite timing—publishing *Carrie* in the wake of *Rosemary's Baby, The Exorcist,* and *The Amityville Horror*—the real boost came from the tale itself, a nakedly honest story about a sympathetic girl named Carrietta White, a social misfit and ugly duckling with whom many readers could identify. But then, unlike the rest of us, she had a strange power and got even, a revenge of the paranormal nerds, so to speak.

During the initial writing of *Carrie,* King thought so little of the effort that he threw the first few pages into the trashcan. Plagued with self-doubt and experiencing what appeared to be a writer's block brought on by the usual writer's worries—financial woes, marital stress, and the inability to make a living at what one does best—King had little confidence in *Carrie.*

Fortunately for King, those in the publishing community felt differently. Doubleday's Bill Thompson bought the book for $2,500, but when a copy of the manuscript found its way to the offices of New American Library, King hit the long-awaited jackpot. The paperback rights to *Carrie* sold for $400,000. King's writing career had begun its meteoric climb.

Carrie is one hell of a good novel. Harlan Ellison, in fact, considers it to be uniquely King: "*Carrie* is pure Stephen King. It is Stephen King before any self-consciousness, before any attention was paid. It's Stephen writing for himself."

Carrie was no fluke. King followed up with *'Salem's Lot*—a brilliantly textured horror novel that has inspired many writers in the genre—and proved that lightning can strike twice. Winter, in *Stephen King: The Art of Darkness,* wrote

King's Ten Favorite Fantasy-Horror Novels*

Ray Bradbury, *Something Wicked This Way Comes*
Ramsey Campbell, *The Doll Who Ate His Mother*
Jack Finney, *The Body Snatchers*
Shirley Jackson, *The Haunting of Hill House*
T. E. D. Klein, *The Ceremonies*
Robert Marasco, *Burnt Offerings*
Richard Matheson, *I Am Legend*
Anne Rice, *Interview with the Vampire*
Curt Siodmak, *Donovan's Brain*
Peter Straub, *Ghost Story*

*From *How to Write Tales of Horror, Fantasy & Science Fiction,* edited by Jack Williamson.

that *Carrie* and *'Salem's Lot* together sold "some three-and-a-half million copies." The sales were goosed by the critically and financially successful Brian DePalma film adaptation of *Carrie*, released within two months after the paperback of *'Salem's Lot* was published.

Mel Allen, profiling King in the June 1977 issue of *Writer's Digest*, put things in perspective: "Stephen King is only thirty, but few writers sell as many books in a lifetime as he has sold with two novels, *Carrie* and *'Salem's Lot*."

Not until *The Shining*, his third novel, did King have a hardcover bestseller, the first of many. And for the first time, the flap copy reflected King's growing popularity in the horror field. Doubleday, to King's chagrin, billed him as "the undisputed master of the modern horror story."

What most people didn't know then was that he had also published a novel under his pen name, Richard Bachman, *Rage*. It would be one of the best-kept secrets in the publishing world until the fifth Bachman book, *Thinner*, published seven years later, blew his cover.

But by this time King *was* a brand-name writer, whose name conjured up the image of a born storyteller sitting by the campfire telling horror tales late into the night.

Marketing King as a horror writer was for his publishers a convenient marketing device but, ultimately, a little misleading. King would later write other books that were obviously not the kind of horror many people assumed he wrote. But it didn't matter because by that time King's brand name gave people the confidence to take a chance on each new book, regardless of how the publishers packaged it: *Different Seasons*, a collection of novellas, is mainstream fiction; *The Dark Tower* books are outright fantasy; *The Talisman* is a fantasy-quest novel; and *Eyes of the Dragon* is, at heart, a children's story packaged as an adult tale.

King's readers, it turned out, were interested only in reading a tale well told. His accessible prose and honesty in approaching the craft of writing have paid off with his readers; King, as Ellison says, "delivers."

After three novels that could be termed horror fiction (*Carrie*, *'Salem's Lot*, and *The Shining*), King published *The Stand*. The ambitious epic tale was cut by nearly four hundred pages, because of marketing considerations, but still ran over eight hundred pages. The revised edition, to be published in 1990, will probably total over twelve hundred pages, exceeding *It* as King's longest novel.

Following *The Stand* was *Night Shift*, King's first collection of short fiction—the kind of book most writers can't get published unless they have a built-in audience. The book, containing many *Cavalier* pieces, showed that King was that rare writer who could write not only novels but short stories. As his reading public later discovered, King could write at any length, from poetry to short stories, from the novella to the epic (like *The Dark Tower* series, which King estimates will include up to seven books).

As King neared the eighties, he began one of the most productive periods in his writing career. He published *The Dead Zone* and *The Long Walk* in 1979, *Firestarter* in 1980, three books in 1981 (*Danse Macabre, Cujo,* and *Roadwork*), and four books in 1982: *The Dark Tower: The Gunslinger, Different Seasons, Creepshow,* and *The Running Man.*

In 1983 King published two minor books (*Christine* and *Cycle of the Werewolf*) and, for contractual reasons, allowed Doubleday to publish *Pet Sematary,* one of his most powerful novels.

In 1984 King published *The Talisman,* a collaboration with Peter Straub, and self-published *The Eyes of the Dragon,* a delightful children's story and adult tale that surprised those readers who wondered if he wrote anything but horror. He also published *Thinner,* a novel so unmistakably King that readers put on their sleuthing hats and soon discovered that Bachman was King—a fact bookseller Robert Weinberg of Oak Forest, Illinois, publicized in his monthly catalogue to his clients, mostly fantasy and science-fiction fans.

In 1985 King published a second collection of short fiction, *Skeleton Crew,* and *The Bachman Books,* an omnibus collection comprising the first four Bachman novels, most long out of print in their original editions.

Two Letters from "Stephen King"*

Sirs:

Here's the outline you requested for my upcoming novel: Plot, plot, BOO!, plot, plot, fuck, BOO!, plot, BOO!

Stephen King
Acting weird at B. Dalton

Sirs:

Boo!
Were you scared?
Sure you were. Just call me the master of terror.

Stephen King
Owl's Dung, Maine

*From "letters to the editors," in *National Lampoon,* July 1983 and September 1981.

The Author Talks: King on Writing

> For me, if there's pain sometimes it's when I come in to start a new day and I sit down and say, "I gotta pick up this fish again and it's rotted some more and I've got to smell it." It's tough to get going, but there can be times, completely the opposite of pain, when suddenly you'll feel this burst of exhilaration when suddenly you see something with perfect clarity.

In 1986 and 1987 King's publishers, realizing that his fans couldn't be satiated, stepped up their publishing schedule with what they termed a "Stephen King firestorm." *It* was published in 1986. *Misery, The Eyes of the Dragon,* and *The Tommyknockers* were published in 1987. In addition, *Silver Bullet* (see *Cycle of the Werewolf*) was published in 1987. And *The Dark Tower II: The Drawing of the Three* was also published that year, by Donald M. Grant, Publisher.

Exhausted after finishing *The Tommyknockers,* King announced that he was taking a break from publishing, which proved to be short-lived. Most of his fans were unaware of a break. In 1988 *The Dark Tower: The Gunslinger* came out in a trade paperback edition, and a pseudo-King book was published, *Nightmares in the Sky,* an oversized photobook "by" Stephen King, with photos by "f-stop Fitzgerald." The latter had a 250,000-copy print run and sold an astonishing 100,000 copies—remarkable for the fact that King's contribution was only an essay; the bulk of the book was photographs.

The first half of 1989 saw the publication of three King books: the trade paperback edition of *The Dark Tower II: The Drawing of the Three* from NAL, the limited edition of *Dolan's Cadillac* from Lord John Press, and the limited edition of *My Pretty Pony* from the Whitney Museum. The second half of 1989 will see the publication of *The Dark Tower: The Gunslinger* in a mass-market paperback edition from NAL, a trade edition of *My Pretty Pony* (copublished by the Whitney Museum and Alfred A. Knopf), and a novel, *The Dark Half.*

A Look Down the Road

In 1990 the long-awaited unexpurgated edition of *The Stand* will be published by Doubleday, with the Wrightson illustrations. And in the fall the second of four books in King's recent book deal, which is reportedly an untitled novella collection consisting of "Secret Word, Secret Garden" and "Sun Dog," is to be published as a Viking hardcover.

EAU CLAIRE DISTRICT LIBRARY

A year later, in fall 1991, the third book in the contract, reportedly titled *Needful Things,* is to be issued by Viking as a hardcover. Viking will also publish, in 1992 and as a hardcover, the fourth book in the contract, reportedly called *Dolores Claiborne.*

Then there's the controversial *Dark Tower* series, an epic fantasy that King had begun while in college. In the March 1989 issue of *Castle Rock,* Janet Beaulieu interviewed King and reported that "King now projects the completed project to be up to 10,000 pages in about eight volumes, and estimates the next volume is probably two or three years in the future."

One cannot help speculating that one day King may edit a collection of his own nonfiction, which is as entertaining and readable as his fiction. To date, he's had well over a hundred pieces published, some in obscure magazines or small publications. (Ursula K. LeGuin's collection of nonfiction, *From Elfland to Poughkeepsie,* is a good example of how entertaining such a collection can be.)

A Look Back

From 1974 to 1989, King has established an impressive record: thirty-two books, five screenplays, twenty-two TV/film adaptations, and forty-four audiotape adaptations. (In addition, by the end of 1990, there will be twenty-nine books *about* King in print).

2. The Movies

Book publishers love tie-in products, especially movies of which they can issue a tie-in book edition. The assumption is that some will view the movie and then buy the book. But if the movie doesn't live up to the viewer's expectations, then he won't buy the tie-in book edition.

Unfortunately, few of the many film adaptations of King's stories have been translated faithfully on the screen, despite the millions of dollars spent, the famous actors and actresses hired, and the helming of name-brand directors and producers, who, both in and out of the genre, have discovered the difficulties of successfully adapting King's prose to pictures.

In an interview conducted by Jessie Horsting, in the best of the three books examining King's films (*Stephen King at the Movies,* unfortunately out of print), King acknowledges the huge problems in adapting his work to the screen.

Asked "what's missing?" King replied:

> It's between the lines in the books. It's whatever it is, it's whatever flavor that readers come to expect and they come to want, it's the sort of thing that they come to crave. It's the only reason they go back to buy more. . . . And it's the same reason they *don't* go to the movies; they say, "Ah, it's just another shitty adaptation of a King book."

King's assessment is dead-on. His fans simply don't find in his film adaptations what they like in his books. But part of the problem is that the predominantly teenaged audience of horror films prefers a more bloody and ghoulish fare, like that in *A Nightmare on Elm Street*, or in *Friday the 13th* and in its endless sequels. Such fare drive-in movie critic Joe Bob Briggs calls "spam in a cabin"—sudden death, mutilation, and buckets of blood are the primary attractions.

Stephen King—Actor?

If you think King only writes novels from which movies are made, it may come as a surprise to you that he also acts in his movies. He also performed in one television commercial.

In most instances, King makes only a cameo appearance, as in *Nightriders* (appearing with his wife, Tabitha), *Pet Sematary* (as a minister), and *Creepshow II*.

In some cases, his appearance provides comic relief—the kind of thing a guy will do if he doesn't take himself too seriously. In *Maximum Overdrive* he is insulted by an automatic bank-teller machine as he tries unsuccessfully to make an electronic withdrawal. In *Creepshow I* he enacts Jordy Verrill, a country bumpkin who discovers a meteorite in his backyard. (Does the word *meteorshit* ring a bell?)

But King is best at playing himself, which he does to the hilt in an American Express commercial, one of a series produced by the ad agency Ogilvy & Mather, in which celebrities take center stage.

As the thirty-second ad opens, King, dressed in an after-dinner jacket, crosses the balcony. In the background a cloaked figure surreptitiously slinks across the back room. King, holding a single candle, walks down the staircase. The camera cuts to a piano playing music by itself. King comes through a corridor. His passage is lighted by flickering candles—human hands protrude from the wall, grasping candelabra.

A sudden gust of wind blows the window doors open and the candles are extinguished. Lightning flashes as King, his back to a bookshelf, twists the base of a candle fixture. The bookshelf rotates, revealing behind it a cave corridor filled with mist. King then steps back into the cave.

The campy dialogue gets the point across: "When I'm not recognized, it just kills me," says King. So, to make sure he is recognized, he carries (heh heh) the American Express Card. As the ad ends, King whispers his advice: The American Express Card—"Don't leave home without it."

King's movies, for the most part, are pretty conservative as horror films—just as they are in book form. So mainstream an approach is a far cry from the explicit sex and violence that characterize some of the younger horror writers—self-termed Splatterpunks—who have "appointed" Clive Barker as their titular leader, an "honor" Barker quickly disavows.

In the end, King's movies appeal neither to the hard-core horror fan—the typical teenaged movie-goer—nor to his fans. Generally, the latter are disappointed with the adaptations and many have resolved not to see another King film. (The recently released *Pet Sematary,* for which King wrote the screenplay, garnered lukewarm reviews, despite praise in the same reviews for the novel on which it was based.)

My highly subjective list of successful King movies is, unfortunately, short: *Carrie* (directed by Brian DePalma), *The Dead Zone* (directed by David Cronenberg), and *Stand by Me* (directed by Rob Reiner, based on the novella "The Body" from *Different Seasons*).

3. Stephen King

More than just a popular author, King is a publishing phenomenon and thus a celebrity in his own right. Endlessly interviewed and profiled from the beginning of his career to the point now where he has been "interviewed out," as he put it on "The Larry King Show," Stephen is an American success story—from struggling writer who taught school at $6,400 a year to renowned author whose books earn millions of dollars each. Moreover, King is that rarest of writers: a bestselling author who, unlike many that join him atop the bestseller lists, is also very talented.

But there was a price to pay.

The Horrors of Success

At King's famous Bangor, Maine, residence, a custom-built fence surrounds the home. No Trespassing signs are prominently posted. One reads: "THIS IS PRIVATE PROPERTY. Hunting, Fishing, Trapping, or Trespassing, for Any Purpose Is Prohibited Under Penalty of the Law." The signs mean what they say.

At his summer residence in western Maine no signs are needed. The location is a closely guarded secret, and the locals won't direct you to the house.

King's phone number is, of course, unlisted. But even if you obtain that number and call, Shirley Sonderegger answers the phone during normal business hours. A call late in the evening or on weekends gets no answer.

Because of the volume of mail, it is doubtless screened and King sees only what he must. If you receive any response, chances are it will be his form postcard, which says that although he appreciates hearing from his readers, if he spent time writing replies, he wouldn't have time for writing books—the reason people write to him in the first place.

King rarely attends conventions. When he has, he's been mobbed. Occasionally he has barricaded himself in the hotel room as a matter of necessity. Likewise, he seldom promotes his books through book signings. Experience has shown him that the lines may be longer than he can accommodate in a single session, and rather than disappoint his readers, King finds it simpler just to say no.

On business matters, King makes the final decision, but usually after they have passed through his agent or business manager, both of whom do an excellent job of looking after King's best interests.

Without these key people to shelter King from the world at large, no writing would get done. His people are professionals whose allegiance is steadfast, and they do their jobs well. Selma Lanes, writing in *The Art of Maurice Sendak*, expressed what it must be like: "Certainly . . . the man lives a secluded life . . . his days carefully ordered to eliminate unnecessary distractions so that . . . the artist can devote himself uninterruptedly to the relentless pursuit of his mission in life."

To King, the mission is simple: tell the stories, write the books. In succeeding beyond his wildest dreams, he has given up, with greatest reluctance, something that every celebrity cherishes: privacy.

He is a victim of his own celebrity status. King is a household name, a contemporary figure of popular culture. His face is recognizable, in part because of the many book-jacket photos and the media interviews, but mostly because of the campy American Express ad in which he played himself. When you're famous, popular, and rich, he has found out, everyone wants a piece of you. Understandably, that is what King detests the most; he called it in his *Time* profile "the cult of the celebrity."

As a writer, King has arrived in grand style, like few other writers in our time. He was on the cover of *Time* magazine. He has had almost as many books written *about* him as those written by him. He has won numerous awards in the fantasy and science-fiction fields. A university is collecting his work seriously—the Special Collections at the University of Maine at Orono. He commands the enviable position of usually being able to pick and choose his projects. Publishers love him because he's their money machine and keep him happy at all costs. He is, in short, a power unto himself in the comparatively small world of book publishing. As King put it in his essay "The Politics of Limiteds":

> I have grown into a Bestsellasaurus Rex—a big, stumbling book-beast that is loved when it shits money and hated when it tramples houses. . . . I started out as a storyteller; along the way I became an economic force."

Has success changed King?

According to David Bright, a journalist who has known King since their college days together, King is pretty much the same person he always was: talented, fiercely dedicated to the craft of writing, very much a family man, and blissfully untouched by the sirens of success. In his recent interview with King, published in *Portland Monthly* magazine, Bright observed that King is "a bit more worldly—and certainly more wealthy—today than he was in his college days, but beyond that, not much has changed."

It has been a long, strange trip for Stephen King, who at forty-two has many good books left in him. I, for one, am looking forward to the remainder of the trip.

The *Playboy* Interview[1]
Conducted by Eric Norden

Although King has been interviewed endlessly, to the point where he's been "interviewed out," as he said on "The Larry King Show" in 1986, most of the interviews have been, predictably, repetitious. And many have betrayed the interviewers' ignorance about King, his work, the horror genre in general, and the craft of writing. The *Playboy* interview is an exception. In my opinion, it's the best interview to date with King. Conducted by Eric Norden over a two-week period in Maine with King at his winter and summer homes, the interview reads well today, six years after its original publication.

In his introductory comments, Norden sets the scene: "It was a foggy, drizzling morning in late November" when he showed up at King's "fittingly sinister lair for the writer one hostile critic had called the 'Wizard of Ooze.'"

Norden described King as "a strapping 6'4" and weighing in at 200 pounds, a genial bear of a man with an infectious grin and disconcertingly gentle blue eyes behind thick horn-rimmed glasses. His jet-black hair commas over one eyebrow and curls at the nape of his neck, and his beard is thick but neatly trimmed. . . . He was dressed casually in a faded-blue Levi's work shirt, jeans, black-leather motorcycle jacket and scuffed-suede pukka boots—his everyday uniform in Bangor, which he describes affectionately as 'a hard town, a hard-drinking workingman's town.'"

Norden says that most of the interview was conducted at King's "modern 11-room summer house on a hilltop overlooking lonely Lake Kezar in the foothills of the White Mountains." The reason? "[T]o avoid the ubiquitous long-distance telephone calls from publishers, agents, editors and Hollywood producers that plague King in Bangor."

"As banks of autumnal mist rolled in across the lake on the first day of the two weeks I would spend interviewing King, I began by asking him how it felt to see a fantasy fulfilled."

PLAYBOY: The protagonist of *'Salem's Lot,* a struggling young author with a resemblance to his creator, confesses at one point, "Sometimes when I'm lying in bed at night, I make up a *Playboy Interview* about me. Waste of time. They only do authors if their books are big on campus." Ten novels and several million dollars

---

1. From the PLAYBOY Interview: Stephen King, PLAYBOY Magazine (June 1983); Copyright © 1983 by PLAYBOY. Reprinted with permission. All rights reserved. Interview conducted by Eric Norden.

in the bank later, your books *are* big on campus and everywhere else. How does it feel?

KING: It feels great. I love it! And, sure, it's an ego boost to think that I'll be the subject of one of your interviews, with my name in black bold print and those three mug shots crawling along the bottom of the page on top of the quotes where I really fucked up and put my foot in my mouth. It's an honor to be in the stellar company of George Lincoln Rockwell and Albert Speer and James Earl Ray. What happened, couldn't you get Charles Manson?

PLAYBOY: We picked you as our scary guy for this year. The vote wasn't even close.

KING: OK, truce. Actually, I am pleased because when I was trying, without much apparent success, to make it as a writer I'd read your interviews and they always represented a visible symbol of achievement as well as celebrity. Like most writers, I dredge my memory for material, but I'm seldom really explicitly autobiographical. That passage you quote from *'Salem's Lot* is an exception, and it reflects my state of mind in those days before I sold my first book, when nothing seemed to be going right. When I couldn't sleep, in that black hole of the night when all your doubts and fears and insecurities surge in at you, snarling, from the dark—what the Scandinavians call the wolf hour—I used to lie in bed alternately wondering if I shouldn't throw in the creative towel and spinning out masturbatory wish-fulfillment fantasies in which I was a successful and respected author. And that's where my imaginary *Playboy Interview* came in. I'd picture myself calm and composed, magisterial, responding with lucidly reasoned answers to the toughest questions, bouncing brilliant aperçus off the walls like tennis balls. Now that you're here, I'll probably do nothing but spew out incoherencies! But I suppose it was good therapy. It got me through the night.

PLAYBOY: How you got through your nights is going to be a major topic of this interview. Were you intrigued by ghost stories as a child?

KING: Ghoulies and ghosties and things that go bump in the night—you name 'em, I loved 'em! Some of the best yarns in those days were spun by my Uncle Clayton, a great old character who had never lost his childlike sense of wonder. Uncle Clayt would cock his hunting cap back on his mane of white hair, roll a Bugler cigarette with one liver-spotted hand, light up with a Diamond match he'd scratch on the sole of his boot, and launch into great stories, not only about ghosts but about local legends and scandals, family goings-on, the exploits of Paul Bunyan, everything under the sun. I'd listen spellbound to that slow down-East drawl of his on the porch of a summer night, and I'd be in another world. A better world, maybe.

PLAYBOY: Did such stories trigger your initial interest in the supernatural?

KING: No, that goes back as far as I can remember. But Uncle Clayt was a great spinner of tales. He was an original, Clayt. He could "line" bees, you know. That's a quirky rural talent that enables you to trail a honeybee all the way from a flower back to its hive—for miles, sometimes, through woods and brambles and bogs, but he never lost one. I sometimes wonder if more than good eyesight was involved. Uncle Clayt had another talent, too: he was a dowser. He could find water with an old piece of forked wood. How and why I'm not sure, but he did it.

PLAYBOY: Did you really believe that old wives' tale?

KING: Well, wrapping an infected wound in a poultice of moldy bread was an old wives' tale, too, and it antedated penicillin by the odd thousand years. But, yeah, I was skeptical about dowsing at first, until I actually saw it and experienced it—when Uncle Clayt defied all the experts and found a well in our own front yard.

PLAYBOY: Are you sure you just didn't succumb to the power of suggestion?

KING: Sure, that's one explanation, or maybe rationalization, but I tend to doubt it. I was bone-skeptical. I think it's far more likely that there's a perfectly logical and nonsupernatural explanation for dowsing—merely one science doesn't understand yet.

It's easy to scoff at such things, but don't forget Haldane's law, a maxim coined by the famous British scientist J.B.S. Haldane: "The universe is not only queerer than we suppose, but it is queerer than we *can* suppose."

PLAYBOY: Did you have any other psychic experiences as a child?

KING: Well, once again, I'm not even sure that the dowsing was psychic at all—at least, not in the way that term is bandied around today. Was it a psychic experience when people in the early eighteenth century saw stones falling from the sky? It certainly took the scientific establishment another fifty years to admit the existence of meteorites. But to answer your question, no, I never experienced anything else as a kid that smacks of the paranormal.

PLAYBOY: Didn't we read somewhere that your house—where this interview is taking place, incidentally—is haunted?

KING: Oh, sure, by the shade of an old man named Conquest, who shuffled off this mortal coil about four generations back. I've never seen the old duffer, but sometimes when I'm working late at night, I get a distinctly uneasy feeling that I'm not alone. I wish he'd show himself; maybe we could get in some cribbage. Nobody in my generation will play with me. By the way, he died in the parlor, the room we're in right now.

PLAYBOY: Thanks. Can we take it from your experiences with dowsing and such that you're a believer in extrasensory perception and in psychic phenomena in general?

KING: I wouldn't say I believe in them. The scientific verdict's still out on most of those things, and they're certainly nothing to accept as an article of faith. But I don't think we should dismiss them out of hand just because we can't as yet understand how and why they operate and according to what rules. There's a big and vital difference between the unexplained and the inexplicable, and we should keep that in mind when discussing so-called psychic phenomena. Actually, I prefer the term "wild talents," which was coined by the science fiction writer Jack Vance.

But it's too bad that the orthodox scientific establishment isn't more open-minded on those questions, because they should be subjected to rigorous research and evaluation—if for no other reason than to prevent them from becoming the exclusive property of the kooks and cultists on the occult lunatic fringe.

There's a lot of evidence that both the American and Soviet governments take the subject a damn sight more seriously than they let on in public and are conducting top-priority studies to understand and isolate a whole range of esoteric phenomena, from levitation and Kirlian photography—a film process that reveals the human aura—to telepathy and teleportation and psychokinesis.

Sadly, and maybe ominously, neither side is pursuing the subject out of some objective search for scientific truth. What they're really interested in is its espionage and military potential, as in scrambling the brains of missile-silo operators or influencing the decisions of national leaders in a crisis. It's a shame, because what you're talking about here is unlocking the secrets of the human mind and exploring the inner frontier. That's the last thing that should be left in the hands of the CIA or the KGB.

PLAYBOY: Both *Carrie* and *Firestarter* deal with the wild talents of young girls on the threshold of adolescence. Were they fictional reworkings of the poltergeist theme, as popularized by Steven Spielberg's recent film *Poltergeist?*

KING: Not directly, though I suppose there's a similarity. Poltergeist activity is supposed to be a sudden manifestation of semihysterical psychic power in kids, generally girls who are just entering puberty. So in that sense, Carrie, in particular, could be said to be a kind of superpoltergeist. Again, I'm not saying there's anything objectively valid to the so-called poltergeist phenomenon, just that that's one of the explanations advanced for it. But I've never seriously researched the whole subject, and those cases I've read about seem surrounded by so much *National Enquirer*-style hype and sensationalism that I tend to suspend judgment. Charlie McGee, the girl in *Firestarter,* actually had a specific gift, if that's the word, that goes beyond the poltergeist phenomenon, though it's occasionally reported in conjunction with it. Charlie can start fires—she can burn up buildings, or, if her back's against the wall, people.

On this whole subject of wild talents, it was fascinating to discover when researching *Firestarter* that there is a well-documented if totally baffling phenomenon called pyrokinesis, or spontaneous human combustion, in which a man or woman burns to a crisp in a fire that generates almost inconceivable temperatures—a fire that seems to come from inside the victim. There have been medically documented cases from all over the world in which a corpse has been found burned beyond recognition while the chair or the bed on which it was found wasn't even charred. Sometimes, the victims are actually reduced to ash, and I know from researching burial customs for a forthcoming book that the heat required to do that is tremendous. You can't even manage it in a crematorium, you know; which is why, after your body comes out of the blast furnace on the conveyor belt, there's a guy at the other end with a rake to pound up your bones before they pour you into the little urn that goes on the mantelpiece.

I remember a case reported in the press in the mid-sixties in which a kid was just lying on a beach when suddenly he burst into flames. His father dragged him into the water and dunked him, but he continued to burn *underwater,* as if he'd been hit by a white-phosphorus bomb. The kid died, and the father had to go into the hospital with third-degree burns on his arms.

There's a lot of mystery in the world, a lot of dark, shadowy corners we haven't explored yet. We shouldn't be too smug about dismissing out of hand everything we can't understand. The dark can have *teeth,* man!

PLAYBOY: The dark has also been very lucrative for you. Aside from the phenomenal sales of the books themselves, *'Salem's Lot* was sold to television as a miniseries, and *Carrie* and *The Shining* have been made into feature films. Were you pleased with the results?

KING: Well, considering the limitations of TV, *'Salem's Lot* could have turned out a lot worse than it did. The two-part TV special was directed by Tobe Hooper of *Texas Chainsaw Massacre* fame, and outside of a few boners—such as making my vampire Barlow look exactly like the cadaverously inhuman night stalker in the famous German silent film *Nosferatu*—he did a pretty good job. I breathed a hearty sigh of relief, however, when some plans to turn it into a network series fell apart, because today's television is just too institutionally fainthearted and unimaginative to handle real horror.

Brian De Palma's *Carrie* was terrific. He handled the material deftly and artistically and got a fine performance out of Sissy Spacek. In many ways, the film is far more stylish than my book, which I still think is a gripping read but is impeded by a certain heaviness, a Sturm und Drang quality that's absent from the film. Stanley Kubrick's version of *The Shining* is a lot tougher for me to evaluate, because I'm still profoundly ambivalent about the whole thing. I'd admired Kubrick for a long time and had great expectations for the project, but I was deeply disappointed in the end result. Parts of the film are chilling, charged with a relentlessly claustrophobic terror, but others fall flat.

I think there are two basic problems with the movie. First, Kubrick is a very cold man—pragmatic and rational—and he had great difficulty conceiving, even academically, of a supernatural world. He used to make transatlantic calls to me from England at odd hours of the day and night, and I remember once he rang up and asked, "Do you believe in God?" I thought a minute and said, "Yeah, I think so." Kubrick replied, "No, I don't think there is a God," and hung up. Not that religion has to be involved in horror, but a visceral skeptic such as Kubrick just couldn't grasp the sheer inhuman evil of the Overlook Hotel. So he looked, instead, for evil in the characters and made the film into a domestic tragedy with only vaguely supernatural overtones. That was the basic flaw: because he couldn't believe, he couldn't make the film believable to others.

The second problem was in characterization and casting. Jack Nicholson, though a fine actor, was all wrong for the part. His last big role had been in *One Flew Over the Cuckoo's Nest,* and between that and his manic grin, the audience automatically identified him as a loony from the first scene. But the book is about Jack Torrance's gradual *descent* into madness through the malign influence of the Overlook, which is like a huge storage battery charged with an evil powerful enough to corrupt all those who come in contact with it. If the guy is nuts to begin with, then the entire tragedy of his downfall is wasted. For that reason, the film has no center and no heart, despite its brilliantly unnerving camera angles and dazzling use of the Steadicam. What's basically wrong with Kubrick's version of *The Shining* is that it's a film by a man who thinks too much and feels too little; and that's why, for all its virtuoso effects, it never gets you by the throat and hangs on the way real horror should.

I'd like to remake *The Shining* someday, maybe even direct it myself if anybody will give me enough rope to hang myself with.

PLAYBOY: In *The Stand,* which has become something of a cult object to many of your fans, a rapidly mutating flu virus accidentally released by the U.S. military wipes out nine-tenths of the world's population and sets the stage for an apocalyptic struggle between good and evil. That ultimate genocide was presaged on a more modest scale by *Carrie* and *Firestarter,* both of which conclude with the beleaguered heroines raining fiery death and destruction on their tormentors and innocent bystanders alike; by *'Salem's Lot,* in which you burn down the town at the end; and by the explosion and burning of the Overlook Hotel at the conclusion of *The Shining.* Is there a pyromaniac or a mad bomber inside you screaming to get out?

KING: There sure is, and that destructive side of me has a great outlet in my books. Jesus. I *love* to burn things up—on paper at least. I don't think arson would be half as much fun in real life as it is in fiction. One of my favorite moments in all my work comes in the middle of *The Stand,* when one of my villains, the Trashcan Man, sets all these oil-refinery holding tanks on fire and they go off like bombs. It's as if the night sky had been set ablaze. God, that was a gas! It's the werewolf in me, I guess, but I love fire, I love destruction. It's great and it's black and it's exciting. When I write scenes like that, I feel like Samson pulling down the temple on top of everybody's head.

The Stand was particularly fulfilling, because there I got a chance to scrub the whole human race and, man, it was fun! Sitting at the typewriter, I felt just like Alexander lifting his sword over the Gordian knot and snarling, "Fuck unraveling it; I'll do it *my way!*" Much of the compulsive, driven feeling I had while I worked on *The Stand* came from the vicarious thrill of imagining an entire entrenched social order destroyed in one stroke. That's the mad-bomber side of my character, I suppose.

But the ending of the book reflects what I hope is another, more constructive aspect. After all the annihilation and suffering and despair, *The Stand* is inherently optimistic in that it depicts a gradual reassertion of humane values as mankind picks itself out of the ashes and ultimately restores the moral and ecological balance. Despite all the grisly scenes, the book is also a testament to the enduring human values of courage, kindness, friendship, and love, and at the end it echoes Camus' remark: "Happiness, too, is inevitable."

PLAYBOY: There must have been a time, before all this wealth and fame, when happiness didn't seem inevitable to you. How rough were the early days?

KING: Well, let's just say that, like most overnight successes, I've had to pay my dues. When I got out of college in the early seventies with a degree in English and a teaching certificate, I found there was a glut on the teaching market, and I went to work pumping gas in a filling station and later on pressing sheets in an industrial laundry for $60 a week. We were as poor as church mice, with two small kids, and needless to say, it wasn't easy to make ends meet on that salary. My wife went to work as a waitress in a local Dunkin' Donuts and came home every night smelling like a cruller. Nice aroma at first, you know, all fresh and sugary, but it got pretty goddamned cloying after a while—I haven't been able to look a doughnut in the face ever since.

Anyway, in the fall of 1971, I finally got a job as an English instructor at Hampden Academy, just across the Penobscot River from Bangor, but it paid only $6,400 a year, barely more than I had been earning before. In fact, I had to go back and moonlight in the laundry just to keep our heads above water. We were living in a trailer on top of a bleak, snow-swept hillside in Hermon, Maine, which, if not the asshole of the universe, is at least within farting distance of it. I'd come home exhausted from school and squat in the trailer's furnace room, with Tabby's little Olivetti portable perched on a child's desk I had to balance on my knees, and try to hammer out some scintillating prose.

That was where I wrote *'Salem's Lot,* actually. It was my second published book, but the bulk of the writing was completed before *Carrie* was even accepted by Doubleday. And believe me, after a day of teaching and then coming home and watching Tabby gamely juggle her way through a mountain of unpaid bills, it was a positive pleasure to squeeze into that cramped furnace room and do battle with a horde of bloodthirsty vampires. Compared with our creditors, they were a fuckin' relief!

PLAYBOY: Were you selling any of your work at that time?

KING: Yes, but only short stories, and only to the smaller-circulation men's magazines, such as *Cavalier* and *Dude.* The money was useful, God knows, but if you know that particular market, you know there wasn't much of it. Anyway, the payment for my stories wasn't enough to keep us out of the red, and I was getting nowhere with my longer work. I'd written several novels, ranging from awful to mediocre to passable, but all had been rejected, even though I was beginning to get some encouragement from a wonderful editor at Doubleday named Bill Thompson. But as gratifying as his support was, I couldn't bank it. My kids were wearing hand-me-downs from friends and relatives, our old rattletrap 1965 Buick

Special was rapidly self-destructing and we finally had to ask Ma Bell to remove our phone.

On top of everything else, I was fucking up personally. I wish I could say today that I bravely shook my fist in the face of adversity and carried on undaunted, but I can't. I copped out to self-pity and anxiety and started drinking far too much and frittering money away on poker and bumper pool. You know the scene: it's Friday night and you cash your pay check in the bar and start knocking them down, and before you know what's happened, you've pissed away half the food budget for that week.

PLAYBOY: How did your marriage stand up under those strains?

KING: Well, it was touch and go for a while there, and things could get pretty tense at home. It was a vicious circle: The more miserable and inadequate I felt about what I saw as my failure as a writer, the more I'd try to escape into a bottle, which would only exacerbate the domestic stress and make me even more depressed. Tabby was steamed about the booze, of course, but she told me she understood that the reason I drank too much was that I felt it was never going to happen, that I was never going to be a writer of any consequence. And, of course, I feared she was right. I'd lie awake at night seeing myself at fifty, my hair graying, my jowls thickening, a network of whiskey-ruptured capillaries spiderwebbing across my nose—"drinker's tattoos," we call them in Maine—with a dusty trunkful of unpublished novels rotting in the basement, teaching high school English for the rest of my life and getting off what few literary rocks I had left by advising the student newspaper or maybe teaching a creative-writing course. Yechh! Even though I was only in my mid-twenties and rationally realized that there was still plenty of time and opportunity ahead, that pressure to break through in my work was building into a kind of psychic crescendo, and when it appeared to be thwarted, I felt desperately depressed, cornered. I felt trapped in a suicidal rat race, with no way out of the maze.

PLAYBOY: Did you ever seriously contemplate suicide?

KING: Oh, no, never; that phrase was just metaphorical overkill. I have my share of human weaknesses, but I'm also bone-stubborn. Maybe that's a Maine trait; I don't know. Anyway, wasn't it Mencken who said that suicide is a belated acquiescence in the opinion of your wife's relatives? But what did worry me was the effect all that was having on my marriage. Hell, we were already on marshy ground in those days, and I feared that the quicksand was just around the bend.

I loved my wife and kids, but as the pressure mounted, I was beginning to have ambivalent feelings about them, too. On the one hand, I wanted nothing more than to provide for them and protect them—but at the same time, unprepared as I was for the rigors of fatherhood, I was also experiencing a range of nasty emotions from resentment to anger to occasional outright hate, even surges of mental violence that, thank God, I was able to suppress. I'd wander around the crummy little living room of our trailer at three o'clock on a cold winter's morning with my teething nine-month-old son Joe slung over my shoulder, more often than not spitting up all over my shirt, and I'd try to figure out how and why I'd ever committed myself to that particular lunatic asylum. All the claustrophobic fears would squeeze in on me then, and I'd wonder if it hadn't already all passed me by, if I weren't just chasing a fool's dream. A nocturnal snowmobile would whine in the dark distance, like an angry insect, and I'd say to myself, "Shit, King, face it; you're going to be teaching fuckin' high school kids for the rest of your life." I don't know what would have happened to my marriage and my sanity if it hadn't been for the totally unexpected news, in 1973, that Doubleday had accepted *Carrie*, which I had thought had very little chance of a sale.

PLAYBOY: What was more important to you—the money from *Carrie* or the fact that you had finally been recognized as a serious novelist?

KING: Both, actually, though I might question how serious a novelist Doubleday took me for. It wasn't about to promote *Carrie* as that year's answer to *Madame Bovary,* that's for sure. Even though there's a lot I still like and stand behind in the book, I'm the first to admit that it is often clumsy and artless. But both creatively and financially, *Carrie* was a kind of escape hatch for Tabby and me, and we were able to flee through it into a totally different existence. Hell, our lives changed so quickly that for more than a year afterward, we walked around with big, sappy grins on our faces, hardly daring to believe we were out of that trap for good. It was a great feeling of liberation, because at last I was free to quit teaching and fulfill what I believe is my only function in life: to write books. Good, bad, or indifferent books, that's for others to decide; for me, it's enough just to *write.* I'd been writing since I was twelve, seriously if pretty badly at first, and I sold *Carrie* when I was 26, so I'd had a relatively long apprenticeship. But that first hardcover sale sure tasted sweet!

PLAYBOY: As you've indicated, that compulsion to be a writer has been with you since you were a boy. Was it a means of escape from an unhappy childhood?

KING: Maybe, though it's generally impossible even to remember the feelings and motivations of childhood, much less to understand or rationally analyze them. Kids, thank God, are all deliciously, creatively crazy by our desiccated adult standards. But it's true that I was prey to a lot of conflicting emotions as a child. I had friends and all that, but I often felt unhappy and different, estranged from other kids my age. I was a fat kid—husky was the euphemism they used in the clothing store—and pretty poorly coordinated, always the last picked when we chose teams.

At times, particularly in my teens, I felt violent, as if I wanted to lash out at the world, but that rage I kept hidden. That was a secret place in myself I wouldn't reveal to anyone else. I guess part of it was that my brother and I had a pretty shirttail existence as kids. My father deserted us when I was two and David was four and left my mother without a dime. She was a wonderful lady, a very brave lady in that old-fashioned sense, and went to work to support us, generally at menial jobs because of her lack of any professional training. After my father did his moonlight flit, she became a rolling stone, following the jobs around the country. We traveled across New England and the Midwest, one low-paying job following another. She worked as a laundry presser and a doughnut maker—like my wife, twenty years later—as a housekeeper, a store clerk; you name it, she did it.

PLAYBOY: Did living on the edge of poverty leave any lasting scars?

KING: No, and I didn't think of it in terms of poverty, either then or now. Ours wasn't a life of unremitting misery by any means, and we never missed a meal, even though prime sirloin was rarely on our plates. Finally, when I was about ten, we moved back to Maine, to the little town of Durham.

For ten years, we lived a virtual barter existence, practically never seeing any hard cash. If we needed food, relatives would bring a bag of groceries; if we needed clothes, there'd always be hand-me-downs. Believe me, I was never on the best-dressed list at school! And the well dried up in the summer, so we had to use the outhouse. There was no bath or shower, either, and in those icy Maine winters, we'd walk half a mile or so to my Aunt Ethelyn's for a hot bath. Shit, coming home through the snow we'd steam! So, yeah, I guess in many ways it was a hard-scrabble existence but not an impoverished one in the most important sense of the word. Thanks to my mother, the one thing that was never in short supply, corny as it may sound to say it, was love. And in that sense, I was a hell of a lot less deprived than countless children of middle-class or wealthy families, whose parents have time for everything but their kids.

PLAYBOY: Has your father ever contacted you in the years since he walked out, out of either guilt or—in view of your new-found wealth—greed?

KING: No, though I suspect the latter would be his more likely motivation. Actually, it was a classic desertion, not even a note of explanation or justification left behind. He said, *literally,* that he was going out to the grocery store for a pack of cigarettes, and he didn't take any of his things with him. That was in 1949, and none of us have heard of the bastard since.

PLAYBOY: Now that you're a multimillionaire with more resources at your command than your mother could have dreamed of, have you ever considered launching your own investigation to track down your father or, at least, to determine whether he's alive or dead?

KING: The idea has crossed my mind now and then over the years, but something always holds me back. Superstition, I guess, like the old saw about letting sleeping dogs lie. To tell the truth, I don't know how I'd react if I ever did find him and we came face to face. But even if I ever did decide to launch an investigation, I don't think anything would come of it, because I'm pretty sure my father's dead.

PLAYBOY: Why?

KING: From everything I've learned about my father, he would have burned himself out by now. He liked to drink and carouse a lot. In fact, from what my mother hinted, I think he was in trouble with the law on more than one occasion. He used aliases often enough—he was born Donald Spansky in Peru, Indiana, then called himself Pollack and finally changed his name legally to King.

He'd started out as an Electrolux salesman in the Midwest, but I think he blotted his copybook somewhere along the way. As my mother once told me, he was the only man on the sales force who regularly demonstrated vacuum cleaners to pretty young widows at two o'clock in the morning. He was quite a ladies' man, according to my mother, and I apparently have a beautiful bastard half-sister in Brazil. In any case, he was a man with an itchy foot, a travelin' man, as the song says. I think trouble came easy to him.

PLAYBOY: So you're not eager to be taken for a chip off the old block?

KING: Let's hope heredity takes second place to environment in my case. From what I'm told, my father certainly beat the hell out of me in the Lothario department, where I'm monotonously monogamous, though I do have a weakness for booze that I try to control, and I love fast cars and motorcycles. I certainly don't share his wanderlust, which is one among many reasons that I've remained in Maine, even though I now have the financial freedom to live anywhere in the world. Oddly enough, the only point of similarity may be our literary tastes. My father had a secret love for science fiction and horror tales, and he tried to write them himself, submitting stories to the major men's magazines of his day, such as *Bluebook* and *Argosy.* None of the stories sold and none survives.

PLAYBOY: A scrapbook of your vanished father's personal effects is prominent in the study of your summer house. Doesn't that preservation of the memorabilia of a man you never knew suggest that you're still mentally gnawing at the wound?

KING: No, the wound itself has healed, but that doesn't preclude an interest in how and why it was inflicted. And that, I think, is a far cry from picking at some psychic scab. Anyway, the scrapbook you mention isn't some kind of secret shrine to his memory, just a handful of souvenirs: a couple of old dog-eared postcards he'd sent my mother from various ports of call, mainly in Latin America; a few photographs of different ships on which he'd sailed; a faded and rather idealized sketch from a Mexican marketplace. Just the odds and ends he'd left behind, like the corpse in the E. C. horror comics of the fifties—God, I loved those mothers!—who comes back from a watery grave to wreak revenge on the wife and boyfriend who did him in but phones first and whispers, "I'm coming; I'd be there sooner but little bits of me keep falling off along the way."

Well, the little bits of my father that fell off along the way are preserved in that scrapbook, like a time capsule. It all cuts off in 1949, when he took a powder on us. Sometimes, I'll leaf through the pages and it reminds me of a chilly autumn day in the fifties when my brother and I discovered several spools of old movie film my father had taken. He was an avid photography buff, apparently, but we'd never seen much of his handiwork beyond a few snapshots. My mother had stowed the film away in my aunt and uncle's attic. So here you have these two kids—I must have been around eight and David ten—struggling to operate this old dinosaur of a movie projector we had managed to rent.

When we finally got it working, the stuff was pretty disappointing at first—a lot of strange faces and exotic scenes but no signs of the old man. And then, after we'd gone through a couple reels of film, David jumped up and said, "That's him! That's our father!" He'd handed the camera to one of his buddies and there he was, lounging against a ship's rail, a choppy sea in the background. My old man. David remembered him, but it was a stranger's face to me. By the look of the sea, he was probably somewhere on the North Atlantic, so the film must have been taken during the war. He raised his hand and smiled, unwittingly waving at sons who weren't born yet. Hi, Dad, don't forget to write.

PLAYBOY: Considering what you write about, have you ever thought of going to a seance or of finding some other supernatural way to communicate with him?

KING: Are you kidding? I've never even attended a seance. Jesus, no! Precisely because I know a little bit about the subject, that's the last thing I'd ever do. You couldn't drag me to one of those things, and the same thing goes for a Ouija board. All that shit—stay away from it! Sure, I know most mediums are fakes and phonies and con artists, the worst kind of human vultures, preying on human suffering and loss and loneliness. But if there *are* things floating around out there—disembodied entities, spirit demons, call them what you will—then it's the height of folly to invite them to use you as a channel into this world. Because they might like what they found, man, and they might decide to stay!

PLAYBOY: Is your fear of seances an isolated phenomenon, or are you superstitious about other aspects of the so-called supernatural?

KING: Oh, sure, I'm very superstitious by nature. I mean, part of my mind, the rational part, will say, "Come on, man, this is all self-indulgent bullshit," but the other part, the part as old as the first caveman cowering by his fire as something huge and hungry howls in the night, says, "Yeah, maybe so, but why take a chance?" That's why I observe all the old folk superstitions: I don't walk under ladders; I'm scared shitless I'll get seven years' bad luck if I break a mirror; I try to stay home cowering under the covers on Friday the thirteenth. God, once I had to fly on Friday the thirteenth—I had no choice—and while the ground crew didn't exactly have to carry me onto the plane kicking and screaming, it was still no picnic. It didn't help that I'm afraid of flying, either. I guess I hate surrendering control over my life to some faceless pilot who could have been secretly boozing it up all afternoon or who has an embolism in his cranium, like an invisible time bomb. But I have a thing about the number 13 in general; it never fails to trace that old icy finger up and down my spine. When I'm writing, I'll never stop work if the page number is 13 or a multiple of 13; I'll just keep on typing till I get to a safe number.

PLAYBOY: Are you afraid of the dark?

KING: Of course. Isn't everybody? Actually, I can't understand my own family sometimes. I won't sleep without a light on in the room and, needless to say, I'm very careful to see that the blankets are tucked tight under my legs so that I won't wake up in the middle of the night with a clammy hand clutching my ankle. But when Tabby and I were first married, it was summer and she'd be sleeping starkers and I'd be lying there with the sheets pulled up to my eyes and she'd say, "Why are you sleeping in that crazy way?" And I tried to explain that it was just safer that way, but I'm not sure she really understood. And now she's done something else I'm not very happy with: she's added this big fluffy flounce around the bottom of our double bed, which means that before you go to sleep, when you want to check what's hiding under there, you have to flip up that flounce and poke your nose right in. And it's too *close*, man; something could claw your face right off before you spotted it. But Tabby just doesn't appreciate my point of view.

PLAYBOY: Have you ever considered probing under the bed with a broom handle?

KING: Naw, man, that would be pussy. I mean, sometimes we have house-guests staying overnight. How would it look if the next morning, they said, "Gee, we were going to the bathroom last night and we saw Steve on his hands and knees, sticking a broom handle under his bed"? It might tarnish the image. But it's not only Tabby who doesn't understand; I'm disturbed by the attitude of my kids, too. I mean I suffer a bit from insomnia, and every night, I'll check them in their beds to see that they're still breathing, and my two oldest, Naomi and Joe, will always tell me, "Be sure to turn off the light and close the door when you leave, Daddy." Turn off the light! Close the door! How can they face it? I mean, my God, *anything* could be in their room, crouched inside their closet, coiled under their bed, just waiting to slither out, pounce on them and sink its talons into them! Those things can't stand the light, you know, but the darkness is *dangerous*! But try telling that to my kids. I hope there's nothing wrong with them. God knows, when I was their age, I just knew that the bogeyman was waiting for me. Maybe he still is.

PLAYBOY: What, besides your own imagination, scares you?

KING: A movie I'll certainly never forget is *Earth vs. the Flying Saucers*, starring Hugh Marlowe, which was basically a horror flick masquerading as science fiction. It was October 1957, I'd just turned ten and I was watching it in the old Stratford Theater in downtown Stratford, Connecticut—one of those quarter-a-shot Saturday-afternoon matinees for kids. The film was pretty standard stuff, about an invasion of Earth by this deadly race of aliens from a dying planet; but towards the end—just when it was reaching the good part, with Washington in flames and the final, cataclysmic interstellar battle about to be joined—the screen suddenly went dead. Well, kids started to clap and hoot, thinking the projectionist had made a mistake or the reel had broken, but then, all of a sudden, the theater lights went on full strength, which really surprised everybody, because nothing like that had ever happened before in the middle of a movie. And then the theater manager came striding down the center aisle, looking pale, and he mounted the stage and said, in a trembling voice, "I want to tell you that the Russians have put a space satellite into orbit around Earth. They call it Sputnik." Or *Spoot*nik, as he pronounced it. There was a long, hushed pause as this crowd of fifties kids in cuffed jeans, with crewcuts or ducktails or ponytails, struggled to absorb all that; and then, suddenly, one voice, near tears but also charged with terrible anger, shrilled through the stunned silence: "Oh, go show the movie, you liar!" And after a few minutes, the film came back on, but I just sat there, frozen to my seat, because I knew the manager wasn't lying.

That was a terrifying knowledge for a member of that entire generation of war babies brought up on *Captain Video* and *Terry and the Pirates* and *Combat Casey* comic books, reared smug in the myth of America's military invincibility and moral supremacy, convinced we were the good guys and God was with us all the way. I immediately made the connection between the film we were seeing and the fact that the Russians had a space satellite circling the heavens, loaded, for all I knew, with H-bombs to rain down on our unsuspecting heads. And at that moment, the fears of fictional horror vividly intersected with the reality of potential nuclear holocaust; a transition from fantasy to a real world suddenly became far more ominous and threatening. And as I sat there, the film concluded with the voices of the malignant invading saucerians echoing from the screen in a final threat: "Look to your skies. . . . A warning will come from your skies. . . . Look to your skies. . . ." I still find it impossible to convey, even to my own kids, how terribly frightened and alone and depressed I felt at that moment.

PLAYBOY: Kids do, as you say, have active imaginations, but wasn't yours unhealthily overheated?

KING: I think most kids share some of my morbid preoccupations, and there's probably something missing in those who don't. It's all a matter of degree, I guess. An active imagination has always been part of the baggage I've carried with me, and when you're a kid, it can sometimes exact a pretty grueling toll. But many of the fears I had to learn to cope with had nothing to do with the supernatural. They stemmed from the same day-to-day anxieties and insecurities a lot of children have to come to terms with. For example, when I was growing up, I'd think a lot of what would happen if my mother died and I were left an orphan. Now, a kid with relatively little imagination, the kind with a great future in computer programming or the chamber of commerce, will say to himself, "So what, she's not dead, she's not even sick, so forget it." But with the kind of imagination I had, you couldn't switch off the images once you triggered them, so I'd see my mother laid out in a white-silk-lined mahogany coffin with brass handles, her dead face blank and waxen; I'd hear the organ dirges in the background; and then

I'd see myself being dragged off to some Dickensian workhouse by a terrible old lady in black.

But what really scared me most about the prospect of my mother's death was not being shipped off to some institution, rough as that would have been. I was afraid it would drive me crazy.

PLAYBOY: Did you have any doubts about your sanity?

KING: I didn't trust it, that's for sure. One of my big fears as I was growing up was that I was going to go insane, particularly after I saw that harrowing film *The Snake Pit,* with Olivia de Havilland, on TV. There were all those lunatics in a state mental institution tormenting themselves with their delusions and psychoses and being tormented, in turn, by their sadistic keepers, and I had very little trouble imagining myself in their midst. In the years since, I've learned what a tough, resilient organ the human brain is and how much psychic hammering it can withstand, but in those days, I was sure that you just went crazy all at once; you'd be walking down the street and—*pffft!*—you'd suddenly think you were a chicken or start chopping up the neighborhood kids with garden shears. So, for a long time, I was very much afraid of going nuts.

PLAYBOY: Is there any history of insanity in your family?

KING: Oh, we had a ripe crop of eccentrics, to say the least, on my father's side. I can recall my Aunt Betty, who my mother always said was a schizophrenic and who apparently ended her life in a loony bin. Then there was my father's mother, Granny Spansky, whom David and I got to know when we were living in the Midwest. She was a big, heavy-set woman who alternately fascinated and repelled me. I can still see her cackling like an old witch through toothless gums while she'd fry an entire loaf of bread in bacon drippings on an antique range and then gobble it down, chortling, "My, that's *crisp!*"

PLAYBOY: What other fears haunted you in your childhood?

KING: Well, I was terrified and fascinated by death—death in general and my own in particular—probably as a result of listening to all those radio shows as a kid and watching some pretty violent TV shows, such as *Peter Gunn* and *Highway Patrol,* in which death came cheap and fast. I was absolutely convinced that I'd never live to reach twenty. I envisioned myself walking home one night along a dark, deserted street and somebody or something would jump out of the bushes and that would be it. So death as a concept and the people who dealt out death intrigued me.

I remember I compiled an entire scrapbook on Charlie Starkweather, the fifties mass murderer who cut a bloody swath through the Midwest with his girlfriend. God, I had a hard time hiding that from my mother. Starkweather killed nine or ten people in cold blood, and I used to clip and paste every news item I could find on him, and then I'd sit trying to unravel the inner horror behind that ordinary face. I knew I was looking at big-time sociopathic evil, not the neat little Agatha Christie–style villain but something wilder and darker and unchained. I wavered between attraction and repulsion, maybe because I realized the face in the photograph could be my own.

PLAYBOY: Once again, those aren't the musings of your typical Little Leaguer. Weren't you worried even then that there might be something abnormal about your obsession?

KING: Obsession is too strong a word. It was more like trying to figure out a puzzle, because I wanted to know why somebody could do the things Starkweather did. I suppose I wanted to decipher the unspeakable, just as people try to make sense out of Auschwitz or Jonestown. I certainly didn't find evil seductive in any sick way—that would be pathological—but I did find it compelling. And I think most people do, or the bookstores wouldn't still be filled with biographies of Adolf Hitler more than thirty-five years after World War II. The fascination of the abomination, as Conrad called it.

PLAYBOY: Have the fears and insecurities that plagued you in childhood persisted into adult life?

KING: Some of the old faithful night sweats are still with me, such as my fear of darkness, but some of the others I've just exchanged for a new set. I mean, you just can't stick with yesterday's fears forever, right? Let's see, now, updated phobias. OK, I have a fear of choking, maybe because the night my mother died of cancer—practically the same minute, actually—my son had a terrible choking fit in his bed at home. He was turning blue when Tabby finally forced out the obstruction. And I can see that happening to me at the dinner table, and everybody panics and forgets the Heimlich maneuver and I'm polished off by half a Big Mac. What else? I don't like bugs in general, though I came to terms with the 30,000 cockroaches in our film *Creepshow.* But I just can't take spiders! No way—particularly those big hairy ones that look like furry basketballs with legs, the ones that are hiding inside a bunch of bananas, waiting to jump out at you. Jesus, those things petrify me.

PLAYBOY: Since you've mentioned *Creepshow,* which you wrote and starred in, this may be the time to ask you why it bombed so badly at the box office.

KING: We don't know that it did, because the gross receipts from around the country aren't all in and tabulated yet. It had a fantastic first couple of weeks and since then has done badly in some places and quite well in others. But I think the critical drubbing it got might have driven some adults away, though a lot of teenagers have flocked to see the film. I expected bad reviews, of course, because *Creepshow* is based on the horror–comic book traditions of the fifties, not a send-up at all but a recreation. And if the mainstream critics had understood and appreciated that, I'd have known right off that we'd failed miserably in what we were trying to do. Of course, a few big-name critics, such as Rex Reed, did love the film, but that's because they were brought up on those comics and remember them with affection.

PLAYBOY: Even Reed was less than overwhelmed by the bravura of your performance, writing, "King looks and acts exactly like an overweight Li'l Abner." Unjust?

KING: No, right on the mark, because that's the kind of local yokel I was supposed to be depicting, and Romero told me to play it "as broad as a freeway." Of course, my wife claims it was perfect typecasting, but I'll just let that one pass.

PLAYBOY: Back to what still petrifies you—besides bombing at the box office. What's your darkest fear?

KING: I guess that one of my children will die. I don't think I could handle that. There are a lot of other things, too: the fear that something will go wrong with my marriage; that the world will blunder into war; shit, I'm not even happy about entropy. But those are all wolf-hour thoughts, the ones that come when you can't sleep and you're tossing and turning and it becomes quite possible to convince yourself that you have cancer or a brain tumor or, if you're sleeping on your left side and can hear your heart pounding, that you're on the verge of a fatal coronary. And sometimes, particularly if you're overworked, you can lie there in the dark and imagine that you hear something downstairs. And then, if you really strain, you can hear noises coming *up* the stairs. And then, Jesus, *they're here,* they're in the bedroom! All those dark night thoughts, you know—the stuff that pleasant dreams are made of.

PLAYBOY: You've mentioned your insomnia, and throughout this interview, you've been popping Excedrin like jelly beans. Do you also suffer from persistent headaches?

KING: Yes, I have very bad ones. They come and go, but when they hit, they're rough. Excedrin helps, but when they're really out of control, all I can do is go upstairs and lie in the dark till they go away. Sooner or later, they do, all at once, and I can function again. From what I've read in the medical literature, they're not traditional migraines but "stressaches" that hit me at points of tension or overwork.

PLAYBOY: You consume even more beer than Excedrin; and you've revealed that you once had a drinking problem. Do you smoke grass as well?

KING: No, I prefer hard drugs. Or I used to, anyway; I haven't done anything heavy in years. Grass doesn't give me a particularly great high; I'll get a little giggly, but I always feel ill afterward. But I was in college during the late sixties. Even at the University of Maine, it was no big deal to get hold of drugs. I did a lot of LSD and peyote and mescaline, more than sixty trips in all. I'd never proselytize for acid or any other hallucinogen, because there are good-trip personalities and bad-trip personalities, and the latter category of people can be seriously damaged emotionally. If you've got the wrong physiological or mental make-up, dropping acid can be like playing Russian roulette with a loaded .45 automatic. But I've got to say that for me, the results were generally beneficial. I never had a trip that I didn't come out of feeling as though I'd had a brain purgative; it was sort of like a psychic dump truck emptying all the accumulated garbage out of my head. And at that particular time, I needed that kind of mental enema.

PLAYBOY: Did your experience with hallucinogens have any effect on your writing later on?

KING: None at all. Acid is just a chemical illusion, a game you play with your brain. It's totally meaningless in terms of a genuine expansion of consciousness. So I've never bought the argument of Aldous Huxley that hallucinogens open the doors to perception. That's mystical self-indulgence, the kind of bullshit Timothy Leary used to preach.

PLAYBOY: Are you afraid of writer's block?

KING: Yes, it's one of my greatest fears. You know, earlier, we were discussing my childhood fear of death, but that's something with which I've pretty much come to terms. I mean, I can comprehend both intellectually and emotionally that a day will come when I'll have terminal lung cancer or I'll be climbing a flight of stairs and suddenly feel an icy pain run down my arm before the hammer stroke hits the left side of my chest and I topple down the stairs dead. I'd feel a little surprised, a little regretful, but I'd also know that it was something I'd courted a long time and it had finally decided to marry me. On the other hand, the one thing I cannot comprehend or come to terms with is just drying up as a writer.

Writing is necessary for my sanity. As a writer, I can externalize my fears and insecurities and night terrors on paper, which is what people pay shrinks a small fortune to do. In my case, they pay me for psychoanalyzing myself in print. And in the process, I'm able to "write myself sane," as that fine poet Anne Sexton put it. It's an old technique of therapists, you know: get the patient to write out his demons. A Freudian exorcism. But all the violent energies I have—and there are a lot of them—I can vomit out onto paper. All the rage and hate and frustration, all that's dangerous and sick and foul within me, I'm able to spew into my work. There are guys in padded cells all around the world who aren't so lucky.

PLAYBOY: What do you think you'd be today without your writing talent?

KING: It's hard to say. Maybe I'd be a mildly embittered high school English teacher going through the motions till the day I could collect my pension and fade away into the twilight years. On the other hand, I might very well have ended up there in the Texas tower with Charlie Whitman, working out my demons with a high-powered telescopic rifle instead of a word processor. I mean, I *know* that guy Whitman. My writing has kept me out of that tower.

PLAYBOY: You've been candid in discussing your innermost fears and inse- curities, but the one area we haven't touched upon is sexual. Do you have any hang-ups there?

KING: Well, I think I have pretty normal sexual appetites, whatever the word normal means in these swinging times. I mean, I'm not into sheep or enemas or multiple amputees or marshmallow worship or whatever the latest fad is. God, I was walking through a porn shop recently and saw a glossy magazine with a guy on the cover vomiting all over a naked girl. I mean, *chacun à son goût* and all that, but *yucchhh*! I'm not into the sadomasochism trip, either, on which your competitor *Penthouse* has built an entire empire. Hell, you can shoot a photo spread of a nude girl in a diamond-studded dog collar being dragged around on a leash by a guy in leather and jackboots, and despite all the artistic gloss and the gauzy lens and the pastel colors, it's still sleaze; it still reeks corruptingly of concentration-camp porn. There's a range of sexual variations that turn me on, but I'm afraid they're all boringly unkinky.

PLAYBOY: So there are no bogeymen hiding in your libido?

KING: No, not in that sense. The only sexual problem I've had was more functional. Some years ago, I suffered from periodic impotence, and that's no fun, believe me.

PLAYBOY: What brought it on?

KING: Well, I'm really not good enough at clinical introspection to say for sure. It wasn't a persistent problem. Drinking was partially responsible, I guess—what the English call the old brewer's droop. Henry Fielding points out that too much drink will cause a dulling of the sexual appetite in a dull man, so if that's the case, I'm dull, because if I knock them down too fast, I'm just too drunk to fuck. Booze may whet the desire, but it sure louses up the performance. Of course, part of it has to be psychological, because the surest way I know for a guy to become impotent is to say, "Oh, Christ, what if I'm impotent?" Fortunately, I haven't had any trouble with it for quite a while now. Oh, shit, why did I get onto this subject? Now I'll start thinking about it again!

PLAYBOY: Have you found that your sex appeal has increased along with your bank balance and celebrity status?

KING: Yeah, there are a lot of women who want to fuck fame or power or whatever it is. The entire groupie syndrome. Sometimes, the idea of an anonymous fuck *is* sort of appealing; you know, some gal comes up to you at an autograph signing in a bookstore and says, "Let's go to my place," and you're leaving town the next morning and part of you is tempted to say, "Yeah, let's; we'll pour Wesson Oil over each other and really screw our eyes out." But it's better not to start down that slippery slope—no reference to the Wesson Oil intended—and I haven't. My marriage is too important to me, and anyway, so much of my energy goes into writing that I don't really need to fool around.

PLAYBOY: Have you always been faithful to your wife?

KING: Yes, old-fashioned as it may sound, I have been. I know that's what you'd expect somebody to say in print, but it's still true. I'd never risk my wife's affection for some one-night stand. I'm too grateful for the unremitting commitment that she's made to me and the help she's given me in living and working the way I want to. She's a rose with thorns, too, and I've pricked myself on them many times in the past, so apart from anything else, I wouldn't *dare* cheat on her!

PLAYBOY: Did you feel at all threatened when your wife began to pursue her own writing career and published her first novel, *Small World*?

KING: I sure did. I felt jealous as hell. My reaction was like a kid's: I felt like saying, "Hey, these are *my* toys; you can't play with them." But that soon changed to pride when I read the final manuscript and found she'd turned out a damned fine piece of work. I knew she had it in her, because Tabby was a good poet and short-story writer when we started dating in my senior year at college, and she'd already won several prizes for her work. So I was able to come to terms with that childish possessiveness pretty quickly. Now, the first time she outsells me, that may be another story!

PLAYBOY: Why is explicit sex so consciously absent from your work? Are you uncomfortable with it?

KING: Well, Peter Straub says, "Stevie hasn't discovered sex," and I try to dispute him by pointing to my three kids, but I don't think he's convinced. Actually, I probably am uncomfortable with it, but that discomfort stems from a more general problem I have with creating believable romantic relationships. Without such strong relationships to build on, it's tough to create sexual scenes that have credibility and impact or advance the plot, and I'd just be dragging sex in arbitrarily and perfunctorily—you know, "Oh, hell, two chapters without a fuck scene; better slap one together." There is some explicit sex in *Cujo* and in my novella "Apt Pupil" in *Different Seasons,* in which the teenager, seduced by Nazi evil, fantasizes about killing a girl as he rapes her, electrocuting her slowly and savoring every spasm and scream until he coordinates his orgasm with her death throes. That was consonant with the kid's twisted character but about as far as I could ever go in the direction of S&M, because after a point, my mental circuit breakers just trip over.

PLAYBOY: Along with your difficulty in describing sexual scenes, you apparently also have a problem with women in your books. Critic Chelsea Quinn Yarbro wrote, "It is disheartening when a writer with so much talent and strength and vision is not able to develop a believable woman character between the ages of 17 and 60." Is that a fair criticism?

KING: Yes, unfortunately, I think it is probably the most justifiable of all those leveled at me. In fact, I'd extend her criticism to include my handling of black characters. Both Hallorann, the cook in *The Shining,* and Mother Abagail in *The Stand* are cardboard caricatures of superblack heroes, viewed through rose-tinted glasses of white-liberal guilt. And when I think I'm free of the charge that most male American writers depict women as either nebbishes or bitch-goddess destroyers, I create someone like Carrie—who starts out as a nebbish victim and then *becomes* a bitch goddess, destroying an entire town in an explosion of hormonal rage. I recognize the problems but can't yet rectify them.

PLAYBOY: Your work is also criticized for being overly derivative. In *Fear Itself,* a recent collection of critical essays on your novels, author Don Herron contends that "King seems content to rework well-worn material. . . . Rarely in King's stories are there supernatural creations that do not at least suggest earlier work in the genre [and] usually they are borrowed outright." Would you contest the point?

KING: No, I'd concede it freely. I've never considered myself a blazingly original writer in the sense of conceiving totally new and fresh plot ideas. Of course, in both genre and mainstream fiction, there aren't really too many of those left, anyway, and most writers are essentially reworking a few basic themes, whether it's the angst-ridden introspection and tiresome identity crises of the aesthetes, the sexual and domestic problems of the John Updike school of cock contemplators, or the traditional formulas of mystery and horror and science fiction. What I try to do—and on occasion, I hope, I succeed—is to pour new wine from old bottles. I'd never deny, though, that most of my books have been derivative to some extent, though a few of the short stories are fairly *sui generis,* and *Cujo* and *The Dead Zone* are both basically original conceptions. But *Carrie,* for example, derived to a considerable extent from a terrible grade-B movie called *The Brain from Planet Arous; The Shining* was influenced by Shirley Jackson's marvelous novel *The Haunting of Hill House; The Stand* owes a considerable debt to both George R. Stewart's *Earth Abides* and M.P. Shiel's *The Purple Cloud;* and *Firestarter* has numerous science fiction antecedents. *'Salem's Lot,* of course, was inspired by and bears a fully intentional similarity to the great classic of the field, Bram Stoker's *Dracula.* I've never made any secret of that.

PLAYBOY: You also seem intrigued by the phenomenon of Nazism and have written about it at length in both *Different Seasons* and *The Dead Zone,* which deals with the rise to power of an American Hitler and the desperate efforts of one man to stop him before it's too late.

KING: Well, the nature of evil is a natural preoccupation for any horror writer, and Nazism is probably the most dramatic incarnation of that evil. After all, what was the holocaust but the almost literal recreation of hell on earth, an assembly-line inferno replete with fiery furnaces and human demons pitchforking the dead into lime pits? Millions have also died in the gulag and in such places as Cambodia, of course, but the crimes of the Communists have resulted from the perversion of an essentially rational and Apollonian nineteenth-century philosophy, while Nazism was something new and twisted and, by its very nature, perverted. But when it exploded onto the German scene in the twenties, I can see how it exercised a dangerously compelling appeal. That werewolf in us is never far from the surface, and Hitler knew how to unleash and feed it. So, yes, if I had been in Germany in the early thirties, I suppose I might have been attracted to Nazism.

But I've got a pretty sure feeling that by 1935 or 1936, even before the concentration camps and the mass murders got going in earnest, I'd have recognized the nature of the beast, in myself as well as in the ideology, and would have gotten out. Of course, unless you're actually in a situation like that, you never know how you'd respond. But you can see echoes of the mad Dionysian engine that powered the Nazis all around you. I'm a big rock-and-roll fan, and rock has been an important influence on my life and work, but even there you can some-times hear that beast rattling its chains and struggling to get loose. Nothing so dramatic as Altamont, either; just the kind of wild, frenzied mob emotions that can be generated when you get a couple of thousand people blasted out of their skulls on sound and dope in an auditorium.

I love Bruce Springsteen, and recently, my wife and I were at one of his concerts in Toronto, where he suddenly started pumping his arm straight out from his chest with a clenched fist, like a Fascist salute, and all the screaming fans in the audience followed suit, and for a discordant moment, we felt we were in Nuremberg. And there's obviously not the faintest hint of fascism or racism or violent nihilism in Springsteen, such as you'll find in some of the English punkers, but all at once, that mass hysteria you can get at rock concerts had coalesced into a dark and disturbing apparition. Of course, good, strong rock can evoke a powerhouse of emotional reaction, because by nature, it's go-for-broke stuff; it's anarchistic in the most attractive sense of the word; it's all about living fast, dying young, and making a handsome corpse. And horror is like that, too. Both go for the jugular, and if they work, both evoke primal archetypes.

PLAYBOY: You're universally identified as a horror writer; but shouldn't such books as *The Stand,* which is essentially a futuristic disaster novel, really be classi-fied as science fiction?

KING: Yes, technically, you're right. In fact, the only books of mine that I consider pure unadulterated horror are *'Salem's Lot, The Shining,* and now *Christine,* because they all offer no rational explanation at all for the supernatural events that occur. *Carrie, The Dead Zone,* and *Firestarter,* on the other hand, are much more within the science fiction tradition, since they deal with the psionic wild talents we talked about before. *The Stand* actually has a foot in both camps, because in the second half of the book, the part that depicts the confrontation between the forces of darkness and the forces of light, there is a strong super-natural element. And *Cujo* is neither horror nor science fiction, though it is, I hope, horrifying. It's not always easy to categorize these things, of course, but basically, I do consider myself a horror writer, because I love to frighten people. Just as Garfield says, "Lasagna is my life," I can say, in all truth, that horror is mine. I'd write the stuff even if I weren't paid for it because I don't think there's anything sweeter on God's green earth than scaring the living shit out of people.

PLAYBOY: How far will you go to get the desired effect?

KING: As far as I have to, until the reader becomes convinced that he's in the hands of a genuine, gibbering, certifiable homicidal maniac. The genre exists on three basic levels, separate but independent, and each one a little bit cruder than the one before. There's terror on top, the finest emotion any writer can induce; then horror; and, on the very lowest level of all, the gag instinct of revulsion. Naturally, I'll try to terrify you first, and if that doesn't work, I'll try to horrify you, and if I can't make it there, I'll try to gross you out. I'm not proud; I'll give you a sandwich squirming with bugs or shove your hand into the maggot-churning innards of a long-dead woodchuck. I'll do anything it takes; I'll go to any lengths, I'll geek a rat if I have to—I've geeked plenty of them in my time. After all, as Oscar Wilde said, nothing succeeds like excess. So if somebody wakes up screaming because of what I wrote, I'm delighted. If he merely tosses his cookies, it's still a victory but on a lesser scale. I suppose the ultimate triumph would be to have somebody drop dead of a heart attack, literally scared to death. I'd say, "Gee, that's a shame," and I'd mean it, but part of me would be thinking, Jesus, that really worked!"

PLAYBOY: Is there anywhere you'd draw the line—at necrophilia, say, or cannibalism or infanticide?

KING: I really can't think of any subject I wouldn't write about, though there are some things I probably couldn't handle. There *is* an infanticide scene in *'Salem's Lot,* in which the vampire sacrifices a baby, but it's only alluded to, not described in any detail, which I think heightens the obscenity of the act. As far as cannibalism goes, I have written a story about a kind of cannibalism. It's called "Survivor Type" and deals with a surgeon who's in a shipwreck and is washed up on a tiny, barren coral atoll in the South Pacific. To keep alive, he's forced to eat himself, one piece at a time. He records everything meticulously in his diary, and after amputating his foot, he writes, "I did everything according to Hoyle. I washed it before I ate it." People claim I've become such a brand name that I could sell my laundry list, but nobody would touch that story with a ten-foot pole, and it gathered dust in my file cabinet for five years before it was finally included in a recent anthology. I will admit that I've written some awful things, terrible things that have really bothered me. I'm thinking now mainly of my book *Pet Sematary,* and one particular scene in which a father exhumes his dead son. It's a few days after the boy has been killed in a traffic accident, and as the father sits in the deserted graveyard, cradling his son in his arms and weeping, the gas-bloated corpse explodes with disgusting belches and farts—a truly ghastly sound and smell that have been described to me in grim detail by mortuary workers and graveyard attendants. And that scene still bothers me, because as I wrote it—in fact, it almost wrote itself; my typewriter raced like automatic writing—I could see that graveyard and I could hear those awful sounds and smell that awful smell. I still can. *Brrr!* It was because of that kind of scene that Tabby didn't want me to publish the book.

PLAYBOY: Have you ever censored your own work because something was just too disgusting to publish?

KING: No. If I can get it down on paper without puking all over the word processor, then as far as I'm concerned, it's fit to see the light of day. I thought I'd made it clear that I'm not squeamish. I have no illusion about the horror genre, remember. It may be perfectly true that we're expanding the borders of wonder and nurturing a sense of awe about the mysteries of the universe and all that bullshit. But despite all the talk you'll hear from writers in this genre about horror's providing a socially and psychologically useful catharsis for people's fears and aggressions, the brutal fact of the matter is that we're still in the business of selling public executions.

Anyway, though I wouldn't censor myself, I *was* censored once. In the first draft of *'Salem's Lot.* I had a scene in which Jimmy Cody, the local doctor, is devoured in a boardinghouse basement by a horde of rats summoned from the town dump by the leader of the vampires. They swarm all over him like a writhing, furry carpet, biting and clawing, and when he tries to scream a warning to his companion upstairs, one of them scurries into his open mouth and squirms there as it gnaws out his tongue. I loved the scene, but my editor made it clear that *no way* would Doubleday publish something like that, and I came around eventually and impaled poor Jimmy on knives. But, shit, it just wasn't the same.

PLAYBOY: Are you ever worried about a mentally unstable reader's emulating your fictional violence in real life?

KING: Sure I am; it bothers me a lot, and I'd just be whistling past the graveyard if I said it didn't. And I'm afraid it might already have happened. In Florida last year, there was a homosexual-murder case in which a famous nutritionist known as the Junk-Food Doctor was killed in a particularly grisly way, tortured and then slowly suffocated while the murderers sat around eating fast food and watching him die. Afterward, they scrawled the word REDRUM, or murder spelled backward, on the walls, and, of course, that's a word I used in *The Shining.* Not only should the dumb bastards be fried or at least put away for life, but they should be sued for plagiarism, too!

There were two other cases in a similar vein. In Boston in 1977, a woman was killed by a young man who butchered her with a variety of kitchen implements, and the police speculated that he'd imitated the scene in the film version of *Carrie* in which Carrie kills her mother by literally nailing her to the kitchen wall with everything from a corkscrew to a potato peeler. And in Baltimore in 1980, a woman reading a book at a bus stop was the victim of an attempted mugging. She promptly whipped out a concealed knife and stabbed her assailant to death, and when reporters asked her afterward what she'd been reading, she proudly held up a copy of *The Stand,* which does not exactly exhort the good guys to turn the other cheek when the bad guys close in. So maybe there is a copycat syndrome at work here, as with the Tylenol poisonings.

But, on the other hand, those people would all be dead even if I'd never written a word. The murderers would still have murdered. So I think we should resist the tendency to kill the messenger for the message. Evil is basically stupid and unimaginative and doesn't need creative inspiration from me or anybody else. But despite knowing all that rationally, I have to admit that it is unsettling to feel that I could be linked in any way, however tenuous, to somebody else's murder. So if I sound defensive, it's because I am.

PLAYBOY: In a review of your work in *The New Republic,* novelist Michele Slung suggested that the grisly nature of your subject matter may lead some critics to underestimate your literary talents. According to Slung, "King has not been taken very seriously, if at all, by the critical establishment. [His] real stigma—the reason he is not perceived as being in competition with real writers—is that he has chosen to write about . . . things that go bump in the night." Do you think the critics have treated you unfairly?

KING: No, not in general. Most reviewers around the country have been kind to me, so I have no complaints on that score. But she has a point when she touches on the propensity of a small but influential element of the literary establishment to ghettoize horror and fantasy and instantly relegate them beyond the pale of so-called serious literature. I'm sure those critics' nineteenth-century precursors would have contemptuously dismissed Poe as the great American hack.

But the problem goes beyond my particular genre. That little elite, which is clustered in the literary magazines and book-review sections of influential newspapers and magazines on both coasts, assumes that *all* popular literature must also, by definition, be bad literature. Those criticisms are not really against bad writing; they're against an entire type of writing. *My* type of writing, as it turns out. Those avatars of high culture hold it almost as an article of religious faith that plot and story must be subordinated to style, whereas my deeply held conviction is that story must be paramount, because it defines the entire work of fiction. All other considerations are secondary—theme, mood, even characterization and language.

PLAYBOY: *Time* magazine, hardly a high-brow bastion, has condemned you as a master of "postliterate prose," and *The Village Voice* published a scathing attack illustrated by a caricature of you as a gross, bearded pig smirking over bags of money while a rat crunched adoringly on your shoulder. *The Voice* said, "If you value wit, intelligence or insight, even if you're willing to settle for the slightest hint of good writing, all King's books are dismissible."

KING: There's a political element in that *Voice* attack. You see, I view the world with what is essentially an old-fashioned frontier vision. I believe that people can master their own destiny and confront and overcome tremendous odds. I'm convinced that there exist absolute values of good and evil warring for supremacy in this universe—which is, of course, a basically religious viewpoint. And—what damns me even more in the eyes of the "enlightened" cognoscenti—I also believe that the traditional values of family, fidelity, and personal honor have not all drowned and dissolved in the trendy California hot tub of the "me" generation. That puts me at odds with what is essentially an urban and liberal sensibility that equates all change with progress and wants to destroy all conventions, in literature as well as in society. But I view that kind of cultural radical chic about as benignly as Tom Wolfe did in its earlier political manifestations, and *The Village Voice,* as a standard-bearer of left-liberal values, quite astutely detected that I was in some sense the enemy. People like me really do irritate people like them, you know. In effect, they're saying, "What right do you have to entertain people? This is a serious world with a lot of serious problems. Let's sit around and pick scabs; *that's* art."

The thrust of the criticism in the *Time* piece was a bit different. It basically attacked me for relying on imagery drawn from the movies and television, contending that that was somehow demeaning to literature and perhaps even heralded its imminent demise. But the fact is, I'm writing about a generation of people who have grown up under the influence of the icons of American popular culture, from Hollywood to McDonald's, and it would be ridiculous to pretend that such people sit around contemplating Proust all day. The *Time* critic should have addressed his complaint to Henry James, who observed eighty years ago that "a good ghost story must be connected at a hundred different points with the common objects of life."

PLAYBOY: John D. MacDonald, a big fan of yours, has predicted that "Stephen King is not going to restrict himself to his present field of interest." Is he right? And if so, where will you go in the future?

KING: Well, I've written so-called mainstream stories and even novels in the past, though the novels were pretty early, amateurish stuff. I'll write about anything that strikes my fancy, whether it's werewolves or baseball. Some people seem convinced that I see horror as nothing more than a formula for commercial success, a money machine whose handle I'm going to keep pulling for the rest of my life, while others suspect that the minute my bank balance reaches the right critical mass, I'm going to put all that childish nonsense behind me and try to write this generation's answer to *Brideshead Revisited.* But the fact is that money really has nothing to do with it one way or the other. I love writing the things I write, and I wouldn't and *couldn't* do anything else.

My kind of storytelling is in a long and time-honored tradition, dating back to the ancient Greek bards and the medieval minnesingers. In a way, people like me are the modern equivalent of the old Welsh sin eater, the wandering bard who would be called to the house when somebody was on his deathbed. The family would feed him their best food and drink, because while he was eating, he was also consuming all the sins of the dying person, so at the moment of death, his soul would fly to heaven untarnished, washed clean. And the sin eaters did that year after year, and everybody knew that while they'd die with full bellies, they were headed straight for hell.

So in that sense, I and my fellow horror writers are absorbing and defusing all your fears and anxieties and insecurities and taking them upon ourselves. We're sitting in the darkness beyond the flickering warmth of your fire, cackling into our caldrons and spinning out our spider webs of words, all the time sucking the sickness from your minds and spewing it out into the night.

PLAYBOY: You indicated earlier that you're a superstitious person. Do you ever fear that things are going just *too* well for you and that suddenly, some malign cosmic force is going to snatch it all away?

KING: I don't fear it, I *know* it. There's no way some disaster or illness or other cataclysmic affliction isn't already lurking in wait for me just down the road. Things never get better, you know; they only get worse. And as John Irving has pointed out, we are rewarded only moderately for being good, but our transgressions are penalized with absurd severity. I mean, take something petty, such as smoking. What a small pleasure that is: you settle down with a good book and a beer after dinner and fire up a cigarette and have a pleasantly relaxed ten minutes, and you're not hurting anybody else, at least so long as you don't blow your smoke in his face. But what punishment does God inflict for that trifling peccadillo? *Lung cancer, heart attack, stroke!* And if you're a woman and you smoke while you're pregnant, He'll make sure that you deliver a nice, healthy, dribbling baby Mongoloid. Come on, God, where's Your sense of proportion? But Job asked the same question 3,000 years ago, and Jehovah roared back from the whirlwind, "So where were you when I made the world?" In other words, "Shut up, fuck face, and take what I give you." And that's the only answer we'll ever get, so I know things are going to go bad. I just *know* it.

PLAYBOY: With anyone else, this final question would be a cliché. With you, it seems just right. What epitaph would you like on your gravestone?

KING: In my novella "The Breathing Method," in *Different Seasons,* I created a mysterious private club in an old brownstone on East 35th Street in Manhattan, in which an oddly matched group of men gathers periodically to trade tales of the uncanny. And there are many rooms upstairs, and when a new guest asks the exact number, the strange old butler tells him, "I don't know, sir, but you could get lost up there." That men's club really is a metaphor for the entire storytelling process. There are as many stories in me as there are rooms in that house, and I can easily lose myself in them. And at the club, whenever a tale is about to be told, a toast is raised first, echoing the words engraved on the keystone of the massive fireplace in the library: IT IS THE TALE, NOT HE WHO TELLS IT. That's been a good guide to me in life, and I think it would make a good epitaph for my tombstone. Just that and no name.

An Evening with Stephen King

Twice a year the Friends of the Library, a nonprofit group affiliated with the public library system in Virginia Beach, Virginia, holds an annual book sale. In support of the summer sale, which can gross up to $12,000, teenage volunteers assist the group by sorting books, making signs, unpacking books, and carrying books for customers to their cars, according to the library director, Martha J. Sims. In return, the Friends of the Library donates half its proceeds to bring a favorite author to speak to the volunteers.

In 1985 Mary K. Chelton, then the library programming and community services director, enlisted the aid of the local school system. The school polled its students for the author whom they considered their favorite. "By a tremendous margin, Stephen King was designated as the first choice," said Sims.

Chelton wrote a letter in September 1985 to Stephen King in care of New American Library, King's mass-market paperback publisher. Within a month, King responded through his secretary, Shirley Sonderegger, and said that he would appear for expenses only. What date did she have in mind?

Chelton responded immediately, suggesting April 6–12, 1986. That date was not convenient for King, then involved in the summer promotion of *Maximum Overdrive*, the first movie he directed, and in preparations for "the Stephen King firestorm," in which four King novels would be published within a fourteen-month period—an unprecedented publishing event. Would sometime in the fall be acceptable? Chelton responded, suggesting September 21 or 22. The first was declined because it was King's birthday, but September 22 was fine.

Initial Planning

Once the date was confirmed, preparations began in earnest. A promotional poster and a handbill were designed and printed. The poster went up in area libraries and the handbills were distributed freely. Almost immediately, two concerned Virginia Beach citizens wrote a letter to the local paper and asked, "Is [Stephen King] the type of writer we as parents and responsible citizens want to see the library promoting?"

A promotional letter was mailed to the local fan group, HaRoSFA (the Hampton Roads Science Fiction Association), urging its members to pass the word.

Castle Rock, the Stephen King newsletter, published a brief announcement

46

in its July issue about the event: "If you live near Virginia Beach, Virginia, you might want to note Sept. 22, 1986 on your calendar. Stephen King will speak at the Virginia Beach Public Library. Check with them about tickets and time."

Almost immediately, the phone calls began. Devoted fans, many out-of-state subscribers to the newsletter, called in vain for information and tickets. As it turned out, the announcement was premature and unintentionally misleading. Tickets would not be available until late August, and distribution would be limited locally. None would be mailed.

By then, it was clear that the initial plan of booking the largest room in the Pavilion in Virginia Beach, which seats one thousand, would be inadequate for what would obviously be a capacity crowd. The main auditorium of the Pavilion was booked and over four thousand tickets were printed and distributed free of charge through local branches of the library. The Saturday before King's scheduled arrival, a feature story by William Ruehlmann appeared in the local paper, the only one given to the local media. The story set off a continual series of phone calls from frantic King fans who called in vain for tickets to the library branches, agencies, administration, and the Pavilion. To avoid disappointing the local community that wanted to hear him speak, plans were made to videotape the event and after King's visit make it available on cable channel 29—a well-intentioned plan that would later be sabotaged by officials overly concerned about public opinion.

Meanwhile, the details of King's visit were worked out.

The subject of the talk: Chelton wrote to King, suggesting he talk about "how he became a writer and where he gets all his crazy ideas," about experiences with his readers, and about the right to read—subject matter appropriate for teenagers, for whom the evening was intended.

The flight arrangements: Because of the difficulties of flying from Bangor to Norfolk—connecting flights being problematic and layovers time-consuming—King rented a private jet for the flight. Since he had offered to appear for expenses only, he made up the considerable difference between the first-class commercial air fare and the jet rental.

The schedule: King arrived at Norfolk International and was picked up by a small contingent, headed by Chelton. He then checked into Pavilion Towers under an assumed name to prevent harassment from curious fans and celebrity seekers. Earlier that day, a local bookstore delivered to his hotel room over $50,000 worth (retail) of his books to be autographed. At 6:00 P.M. King dined in the hotel with eight teenagers who assisted in the summer sale. At 9:00 P.M. he was scheduled to speak.

The Visit

The carefully laid plans went off almost without a hitch. The books to be autographed arrived in boxes, packed with Styrofoam pellets. Not knowing what to do with the pellets, King put them in the dresser drawer and left a note of apology to the maid. After hours of autographing, his hand froze—temporarily. More worrisome, however, was King's strep throat. King's remedy was to order bottled beer during dinner, store two bottles in his coat pocket, and use as needed to lubricate his throat during the talk.

At 8:00 P.M. the doors to the Pavilion opened and thousands streamed in. The crowd was predominantly middle class: teenagers, college students, yuppies, and middle-age adults. It was obviously King's mass audience, certainly not the cult audience that King's books also attract.

In front of the main auditorium was a table with King books, autographed and for sale at cover price. The books sold out quickly, and understandably: King rarely makes public appearances, and when he does, his books aren't always on hand for sale.

At 9:00 P.M. King walked to the stage, flanked by armed security guards. For security reasons the event was carefully orchestrated so that nobody would be able to get near King. Greeted with a standing ovation, King took his seat. The evening began with a reading from a prepared text, citing the instances of censorship of King's books in public schools. Following a brief introduction by Mary Chelton, King took the podium and spoke for the next ninety minutes.

King began by explaining that he doesn't give speeches. "I just let my jaw fall open and run." It's his standard spiel, similar to what he said when he addressed a group at the Billerica Library in Massachusetts in 1983: "I can't really lecture—I'm not good at that—and I can't speak with any sense from prepared notes. About the most I can do is *chautauqua,* a fine old word that means you babble on for a little while about the thing that you do and then you sit down. . . ."

The chautauqua started with King's comments on censorship, appropriate for Banned Book Week, then moved on to the main event, a reading from his novel *Misery,* which he introduced with an anecdote about a bizarre meeting with his "number-one fan," Mark Chapman. After the reading, King fielded questions, first from a box stuffed by the attendees as they entered the auditorium, then from the floor.

After ninety minutes, when it was obvious that the questions could go on all night, Mary Chelton, concerned about King's strep throat, cut the questions off. She then closed the evening by presenting King with a "Friends of the Library" T-shirt.

The Aftermath

The following day, a local radio show took questions from its listeners about King's visit to Virginia Beach. Not surprisingly, some listeners were concerned about the "negative" image he presented: King drank beer in front of an impressionable crowd of teenagers and also used mature language! In addition, the mayor's office had received one complaint about King's "public drinking and advocacy of sex and drugs" and the library had received one complaint about the beer consumed by King. The ironic upshot: King's talk, presented as part of a Banned Book Week presentation, was banned from appearing on local cable television.

Much later, in the June 1987 issue of *Castle Rock,* an erroneous report appeared, indicating that the videotape was available through the interstate library loan system. "Just have your librarian contact the Virginia Beach Public Library," said the reviewer, who apparently didn't check the facts.

Marcie Sims explained the library's policy: As a general rule, they don't loan out videotapes because, unlike books which can take abuse in shipping, videotapes are fragile and expensive; for these reasons, videotapes are generally excluded from interlibrary loan. In the few cases where videotapes are sent, the requesting library must accept responsibility for the tape; obviously, few are willing to do so.

As expected, the unintentionally misleading story created a flurry of phone calls from King's out-of-state fans, frustrated earlier by the unavailability of tickets and now by the limited availability of the videocassette.

A Princely Gesture

After the lecture, King wrote a thank-you note to Mary Chelton and enclosed a personal check for the royalties on the books sold before the lecture.

Introducing Stephen King
by Kelly Powell

Our guest, Stephen King, is no stranger to most of you. He's taken all of us on some very peculiar trips to a place called Castle Rock on many occasions. It's not a place you want to visit for fun all by yourself, but somehow, you get a kick out of it when you go with him. There's probably nobody here who sees fog without thinking about being trapped in a supermarket in the mist—with Stephen King. I'll bet some of you look at your cars a little funny after riding in Christine—with Stephen King. And nobody wants to sit with Gramma—after meeting Stephen King's. And prom night is just fine without Carrie. Let Stephen King be her date. And just hope when you die of possibly mysterious causes, that somebody can pay for your funeral with a MasterCard like Stephen King did in *Pet Sematary.* He's not exactly unforgettable, this Stephen King.

Unfortunately, some people don't think the rest of us should read him. Stephen King's books have been banned in the following places:

- Las Vegas, Nevada, 1975—*Carrie* challenged at the Clark High School Library as "trash."

From a window display celebrating Banned Books Week, in the window of Rizzoli's Bookstore in Williamsburg, Virginia.

- Vergennes, Vermont, 1978—*Carrie* was placed on a special closed shelf in the high school library because it could "harm" students, especially "young girls."
- Rankin County, Mississippi, 1984—*Cujo* challenged because it was considered "profane and sexually objectionable."
- Bradford, New York, 1984—*Cujo* was removed from the shelves of the school library "because it was a bunch of garbage."
- Campbell County, Wyoming, 1984—*Firestarter* was challenged because of its alleged "graphic descriptions of sexual acts, vulgar language, and violence." *The Shining* was also challenged because "the story contains violence, demonic possession and ridicules the Christian religion."
- Washington County, Alabama, 1985—*Christine* was banned from all school libraries because the book contained "unacceptable language" and was considered "pornographic."
- Hayward, California, 1985—*Cujo* was rejected for purchase for school libraries because of the "rough language" and "explicit sex scenes."
- Vancouver, Washington, 1986—*The Shining* was removed from four junior high libraries because the book's "descriptive foul language" made it unsuitable for teenagers.

Stephen King gives new meaning to the old phrase about "if you're not controversial, you have nothing to offer," so it is especially appropriate that he is the Friends of the Library featured speaker for Banned Books Week, 1986. This event proclaims his right to write the books that he wants to write, and our right to read them if we choose, and obviously, a great many of us do so choose, despite those who would like to keep us from doing so.

Ladies and gentlemen, I present the contemporary master of horror fantasy—Stephen King.

"Banned Books and Other Concerns: The Virginia Beach Lecture"[1] A Public Talk by Stephen King

That's the most uplifting introduction I've ever had. Think of all those places I've been banned.

I've always wanted to start one of these things by coming out and saying, "Hello, I'm Johnny Cash," but I guess I can't do that now. I do have sort of a strep throat, but I brought a little vitamin B along with me to take care of the problem.

How many of you are sort of bored with Banned Books and the whole discussion on Banned Books? Me, too. I don't go out on purpose to talk about it, and I'm not going to talk about it too long tonight.

---

1. Recorded and transcribed by George Beahm, and edited by Howard Wornom.

"I would just say to you as students who are supposed to be learning, as soon as that book is gone from the library, do not walk, *run to your nearest public library or bookseller and find out what your elders don't want you to know, because that's what you* need *to know!*"

I don't lecture because I don't really know how, and I don't make speeches because I don't know how to do that. What I do is sort of let my jaw fall open and let it run by itself. See, I used to be a high school teacher and it's sort of like Pavlov's dogs: the bell rings and your jaw falls open. You continue to talk until another bell rings, so you guys could be here all night if somebody doesn't ring a bell.

But I wanted to tell you a couple of stories about books and the sort of situation you get into with controversial material, or material that some people consider to be controversial.

The first thing happened just after I published 'Salem's Lot, which was well received by my relatives, but not too many other people. This was just before the movie Carrie came out and made me sort of a household name like Spiro Agnew. I went to a ladies' reading group in western Maine where I spoke for a while and ran my jaw for a while and asked for questions, and a lady who was about sixty-five going on eight hundred stood up and said, "Well, you know, I like that story, but I didn't like all that foul language. And I don't know any reason for anyone to tell a good story with all that foul language in it."

And I said, "Well, think of it this way: Think of the way guys talk in the barbershop when there's just a bunch of guys on Saturday morning."

And she said, "Well, I've been in the barbershop on Saturday morning, and they don't talk that way."

And I said, "Madame, I am writing about the Saturday mornings you *didn't* come."

I've written a lot of stories about desperate people in desperate situations, and you know, it gets down to a point where you say to yourself: Here's a guy who's building something in his garage, and he's all by himself, and he's hammering a nail into the board and he misses that nail and he hits his thumb instead. And blood squirts out and everything. Now, does this guy say "Oh, pickles"? Use your imagination. In other words, what I'm talking about is telling the truth. Frank Norris, who wrote The Pit, and he wrote McTeague and a number of other naturalistic novels that were banned in a lot of other places, said: "I don't fear, I don't apologize because I know in my heart that I never lied, I never truckled. *I told the truth.*" And I think that the real truth of fiction is that fiction is the truth; moral fiction is the truth inside the lie. And if you lie in your fiction, you are immoral and you have no business doing it at all.

Of course, the other story about banned books. I did a film called Creepshow a few years ago; I actually got to play a part in that. I had done a thing for George Romero earlier, a little bit part in a film called Nightriders where I played a redneck; and he must have figured I gave good neck, because he offered me the part of Jordy Verrill, and I got to play the part of this farmer who turns into a human weed, and I also did the screenplay.

And when the film was in postproduction, there was a controversy in the Pittsburgh school system. A kid who had been assigned to do a term paper on work picked the steelworking industry. And a book that he took out of the school library was a book called *Working* by Studs Terkel. Now the way that Studs Terkel does books is he sits in bars with working guys after they get off work, and his great genius is he turns on the tape recorder and he doesn't ask them any questions; he just lets them rap on about what they do. And of course steelworkers are the same as the guy who is missing the nail with the hammer and doesn't say "Oh, pickles." [The steelworkers] used a number of words that the lady would have heard on those days she wasn't in the barbershop, and they were all in the book.

Well, [the boy's] mother saw the book and took it and read it and was horrified by some of the language. There were words that rhymed with *shuck* and words that rhymed with—never mind, you know those words. George Carlin calls them the seven words that you can't say on TV. But she was horrified and she demanded that the book be taken out of the Pittsburgh school system, that it be banned because it would be harmful to high school kids to read those books; they might read those words and their eyes might turn to jelly and run down their faces, or possibly by reading those words they might be incited to go out and rape women, children, porcupines, who knows? Anyhow . . . you know how impressionable teenagers are. They can't be trusted to do anything; totally useless human beings who will do anything their friends tell them to do, so they can't have things like that. Give them little Golden Books and they'll grow up to be responsible adults capable of facing the world.

It went to the school board and there was a protracted fight, after which *Working* by Studs Terkel was actually taken for a time out of the Pittsburgh school system.

The real kicker to the story was when the kid who had to do the report took the book out, there was one stamp in that book: it was his. It had been in the library for three years and nobody had taken it out. By the time the school board decided to remove the book, there were sixty-three stamps in that book. (Which reminds me of when I was a kid. There was a book named *Peyton Place.* You didn't have to find the naughty parts; the books just fell open and they were there.)

I was involved with an anti-obscenity referendum in Maine. The referendum question was very simply stated: "Do you want to make it a crime to sell or vend obscene material?" This is sort of like saying, "Do you want to make it a crime to kill Santa Claus?" Well, most people said, "Of course." But when they went in there to the voting booths, I think that they thought a little bit different, and I'm happy to say the referendum was voted down, 70 percent to 30 percent. Because they realized that *obscene* is one of those words that exist in the eye of the beholder. What's obscene, what's not obscene? What's bad, what's not bad? What's moral? What's immoral?

We live in a democracy. We live in a place that limits free will where it's supposed to reign. Democracy is a two-edged sword, which is to say there are all sorts of rock-ribbed Republicans and conservatives who argue that they'll take the gun from my hands when they pry my cold, dead fingers from it. . . . Okay, that's fine, and there are people who say, "You can't make me wear a motorcycle helmet when I ride because it's my God-given right to ride any way that I want, and it's not your business to tell me how to ride." And, man, I love that law. We have a no-helmet law in Maine, and as far as I'm concerned, it gets a lot of the dreck out of the gene pool because these guys hit the wall and they're gone, baby. If they're not smart enough to wear a helmet, all right, screw them, they're gone; they won't have a lot of kids and be on welfare and all this other stuff.

But, okay, we understand that democracy is a two-edged sword. If you give people the right to have guns, sooner or later someone is going to get gut-holed. And we understand that if you give people the right to ride without a helmet, sooner or later somebody's brains are going to get turned into something that looks what's in a Mixmaster. But for a lot of conservatives and fundamentalists, there is a point on the blade of democracy where that double edge becomes a single edge; and that point always occurs when their own personal sensibilities are offended. The greatest offenders are fundamentalist preachers and teachers. There are people like Jimmy Swaggart and Pat Robertson who, if they could jump into a time machine and go back to the Garden of Eden, would point up and say, "God, you've got this tree. It's the tree of good and evil. Now, you are going to put a barbed-wire fence around it *right now!*"

Well, God didn't put any barbed-wire fence around it. Jesus said render unto Caesar those things that belong to Caesar, and render unto God those things that belong to God. And as far as I'm concerned, they can keep their noses out of what I read.

Don't tell me I can't have a gun if I'm a moral, upright citizen. Don't tell me I have to wear a mouthguard when I ride my motorcycle, which was a law that existed for a while in California. And don't tell me what goes on the shelves in my living room. I think what a lot of these people don't realize is that the sewer material that so offends them is such a small percentage of the total sale of all material that these people go in and out of business all the time. It's not the problem that they see it as: *it's built up,* and that's all I want to say about it because it's really sort of boring.

King on Censorship

I was involved with an anti-obscenity referendum in Maine. The referendum question was very simply stated: "Do you want to make it a crime to sell or vend obscene material?" This is sort of like saying, "Do you want to make it a crime to kill Santa Claus?"

From Virginia Beach lecture

I would like to say one other thing, and that has to do with public school libraries, okay? Because when you deal with public school libraries—and this is particularly aimed at those of you who are now in public schools—they are in a situation called *in loco parentis,* which means that they have to adhere very carefully to the idea that *they are the parent.* And if there's a consensus that decides that a book should be taken out of the library, I believe they should take that book out. I have no problem with that at all, if they take *Cujo* or *'Salem's Lot* or *The Shining* out of a public school library somewhere in New York or Vermont or something; or if they take *Working* out of the Pittsburgh system. I would just say to you as students who are supposed to be learning, as soon as that book is gone from the library, do not walk, *run to your nearest public library or bookseller and find out what your elders don't want you to know because that's what you* need *to know!*

Don't let them bullshit you and don't let them guide your mind, because once that starts, it never stops. Some of our most famous leaders have been book-banners, like Hitler, Stalin, Idi Amin. People like that need to be thought about.

Anyway, enough about banned books and all that stuff.

Let me see, what questions I'm most often asked.

Where do you get your ideas? I don't really know; they come.

How does it feel to be famous? No different than anyone else, except when you are at things like this and you see everybody looking at you, and it's a little bit strange. One of the odd things that happens about being famous is that you learn to always button your fly or to zip it because people say, "That's Stephen King and his fly's undone!" Which is always a good time.

The story about being famous is the famous Pittsburgh story. I don't know if you've heard this or not, but I'll give you the abbreviated version.

The first tour that I ever did for a book was for *The Shining,* which Double-day decided to push. And I went on an author tour, which means you do everything in a city that gives you media. And the last thing that I did was a banquet/dinner with Julius Feiffer and [Brendan] Gill and a couple of other writers, and somebody said, "Well, let's go and get drunk after it's all over," which sounded like a very sensible idea at the time. Because when you sit up on a stage, you know that you have to make a speech and two thousand people are watching you eat chicken and seeing which fork you use, it's a little bit unsettling.

So we went up to a sort of bar that was way up on top of a mountain which Pittsburghians call the Incline, and I started to feel what is politely called Montezuma's revenge. And a real sort of earthquake was going on inside me, and I excused myself and ran into the gentleman's facility . . . a fantastic place; it was gold and marble and everything. There was a bathroom attendant who was eight-hundred years old with a bald skull and veins pulsing—you know what I'm talking about—with a towel over his arm and a couple of quarters in a dish to show you what you were supposed to do in case you were unlettered. The only thing that this ornate bathroom didn't have was doors on the stalls, but I was past caring at that point. The situation had reached the redline, so I rushed in and I never felt more sorry for myself in my entire life.

I had been away from home for a week, and I was homesick and I was sick, physically sick, and I thought that things could not get any worse until the attendant approaches me with a silver pen in his hand and says, "Aren't you Stephen King? My mother saw you on the 'Morning' show. She loves all your books. Could I have your autograph for her?" So there I sat with my jeans around my ankles, giving this guy my autograph, and what a good time it was. And that's what it's like to be famous. Now, let me see . . .

Let's reach into the box and see if we have any Lotto winners! [King is holding a handful of papers with questions scribbled on them.] This ought to be enough to take us through tomorrow morning. [From the audience: "Happy birthday!"] Thank you. I turned thirty-nine yesterday. Like Jerry Lee says: thirty-nine and holding onto anything I can. Not really; I don't mind being thirty-nine. I got all this figured out: This midlife crisis business is bull. The actuarial tables say everybody croaks by seventy-two—that's the average—so I figure I passed my midlife crisis around thirty-six and I didn't even notice it when it happened; it just went by. You figure the three stages of life: Being young, being middle-aged, and being old, okay? According to the actuarial tables, you are middle-aged as soon as you turn thirty-five. That's when you should have your midlife crisis. As soon as you are forty-eight, you are an old fart and you can forget it. But, okay . . .

This first question—why, it's Lotto—"What do you think about God and what do you think about Pat Robertson?" And then it says,"PS, When is PBS going to make *The Stand* into a miniseries?" PBS may be the only hope because you can't do it on a network; you can't have the end of the world brought to you by Charmin Toilet Tissue; they just aren't into it. As to what I think about God: I think that He's out there. A more important question is what God thinks about me. As far as what I think about Pat Robertson running for president: Baby, you don't want to know. That's like asking me what I think about if Christ had run for the emperor of Rome. I don't think the place for a preacher is in politics and I don't think the place for a politician is in preaching, and I think that one person who proved that admirably was Jimmy Carter, who at least understood the difference between Caesar and God, and God and Caesar. Maybe he wasn't such a great president, but he was okay.

Here's one that says, "What do you think of Virginia Beach?" Well, I saw a hotel and a hall. The outside of this place [the Virginia Beach Pavilion] has got sort of an interesting construction. It looks sort of like a bunch of huge . . . have any of you read *The Stand*? It looks like something Trashcan Man might burn up. It's all these round things all stuck together. But I think Virginia Beach is great because they asked me to come here, and not everybody does that. Actually, you are very sweet to have me, and you've all sat there while I've run my chops.

This one says, "Who is my favorite comic book character?" The answer is Batman, without a doubt, and Spiderman is in second place, but what I'm really sort of into is G.I. Joe.

I have a word processor which I only use for rewrites, but the brain is called a CPU, which is this great big box that just sits there, and it's a little bit intimidating, so I just cover the top with G.I. Joes fighting each other and sometimes when I'm roadblocked I push them together [sound effect of men fighting] and stuff like that, and people come in that you don't know and you get a little embarrassed, and you say, "I'm just trying to figure out something the kids can do when they get home from school."

But for my birthday yesterday, my youngest son who is nine, Owen, knows the truth. And he gave me a Doctor Mindbender. Doctor Mindbender is so cool.

"Do you scare yourself sometimes?" The answer is [drinks beer]. There's always poor man's Valium when you get too scared; it comes in bottles. Who's going to be at the Silver Bullet tonight? Well, I'm one of them.

The answer is, yes, I've scared myself three times. A lot of times it feels like you've got a bulldozer inside your head and you know that you are going to scare people, but it doesn't feel bad. It feels like—I don't want to say it feels like you are running them down—but my idea about what a really good book is, is when the writer, whether he's alive or dead, suddenly reaches out of the page and grabs you by the throat and says *You're mine, baby! You belong to me! Try to get away! You want to cook some dinner for your husband? Too bad! You want to go to bed? Tough shit! You're mine! You belong to me.*

You know, that's my idea about what it's supposed to be about. You're supposed to go out there and get them. You are not supposed to mess around and be delicate or anything like that; you are supposed to run them down. They live afterwards, you know, but I have scared myself on three occasions, and one of them is in the book I just read to you [*Misery*] where something extremely nasty happens later, and I just passed that point in the rewrite and realized to myself that I've been dragging my feet because I knew when I got up there to the axe and the blowtorch, things were going to be nasty and I didn't want to write that.

And there's one in a book called *The Shining* where this kid goes into this room and there's this dead lady in the bathtub, and he keeps telling himself those things aren't there, and he turns around and, man, she's still there. I got so freaked, I couldn't believe it.

It usually comes up on you the worst in the rewrite when you realize that you've got to face that whole nightmare again.

And, I guess, probably the third time would have been sorta toward the end of *Christine* when I began to see how badly everything would turn out, and I really didn't like it very much because the whole thing started out to be sort of a joke. It was like "Happy Days" gone mad: Boy gets car, boy loses car, boy finds car. I thought it was hilarious until the kid started to run people down. Because sometimes [stories] get out of control and they are like the car itself; they start to run by themselves and they don't always turn out the way you think they are going to turn out.

I'll do a couple more of these and then I'll ask for a couple more from the audience. This is like no interaction whatsoever. I can't stand that. There's got to be some feedback, I think.

"What's the average and the longest hours a day you might spend writing?" Well, let's see, okay, I think the longest I ever spent in front of the typewriter was when I was working on *The Talisman,* which was a book that I did with Peter Straub. And I was writing this thing about the Sunlight Gardner home and all this stuff and realized that seven hours had gone by and that my kidneys hurt like hell, and I could barely get out of the chair. That was a weird experience, but that was [with] the word processor which I've since given up because—have you ever seen that James Bond movie [*Thunderball*] where he gets hooked into the exercise machine and the thing starts exercising him to death? That's what a word processor is like: it's insanity. I've given it up. I used to write six pages and I was out. But with a word processor, it just keeps scrolling up and up and up. There's no end.

"Some of your readers can find a moral story in many of your stories. Do you intend this, and if so, do you intend your stories to be the next set of Mother Goose stories for the coming generations?" The answer is, yeah, I try to be as moral as I can because you walk a fine line in this field. There's too much exploitation. There's too much that is slasher stuff. It's like [the] later *Friday the 13th* movies. My criterion here is that you don't come to see people get away; you come to see people die. And at that point, to me, you've crossed the line into immoral territory. I have always wanted my characters to be alive and I've always wanted my readers to like the characters and to find them good and hopeful, and everything like that, and to want them to live.

I got a lot of letters about the novel *Cujo* when the little boy Tad Trenton died. Well, I didn't think he was going to die. I didn't mean for him to die; I thought he was going to live. So I get these letters saying, "Oh, you son of a bitch . . . the kid died. How could you do that?" And I would write back and say, "I don't know; he died. I was working away and I thought she was going to get him back to life, and the kid just croaked. I couldn't help it." But the fact is, that's the moral ending because kids don't always live—sometimes kids do die. That's the truth: sometimes they die, sometimes they can be saved.

Well, then let him live in the movie because I think we would have been lynched from pillars outside every movie theater in America. Also, I was curious to see what would happen if the kid did live because that's what I had intended. But unfortunately, after the movie ends, I think that in the context of the movie story, the kid dies an even nastier death because after the dog has been bitten by the rabid bat and licks the kid's face, I'm sure he ended up with rabies, so I'm sure he died an even worse death. But that's after the end.

Do you have any other questions? I'll talk for a little while.

[A question from the audience about *The Stand* as a movie.] I hope *The Stand* will come out as a movie. We've been talking about it. There has been a script for a long time, and I think it would make a wonderful movie. To me, it doesn't look that terrible or expensive to do. Luckily, a movie has been made based on "The Body," which has been a success, *Stand by Me.* Maybe that will make a difference and unlock some of the funds. I don't know. The real problem isn't money, it's time. The movie would run probably two and a quarter hours, and with their unfailing vulgarity, Hollywood has a term for that period of time between the end of one showing of a feature and the start of the next one; they call it "spill and fill," and they don't like movies that run longer than two hours because it makes it tough to run three shows a night, and they like that.

Pet Sematary? I don't know. It was scheduled and unscheduled and rescheduled . . . Hollywood people are crazy; they're not like us. [Editor's note: The movie was released in April 1989.]

[A question from the audience about *The Stand.*] He asked me about *The Stand,* and whether or not it was true that it was going to be reissued, and that pages were cut from it. The truth was that *The Stand* was four hundred pages longer than it was when it finally appeared. And the reason that those four hundred pages were cut was that it was the last book with Doubleday and they wanted to publish it at $12.95—it's now $19.95, by the way, in hardcover, which shows you inflation at work—but they were determined that they were going to publish it at $12.95, and they knew I was leaving for various reasons, so I was called into a meeting where they said, "This book is four hundred pages too long. Do you want to cut it or shall we?" So I said, "Well, maybe I better do it," because I didn't know what they would cut, so I made the best cuts that I could. But there was a lot of good stuff in those pages, and so we're going to publish it in about two years and reinstate the stuff that's gone. It's real nice stuff; a lot of it's real cool. Complete with pictures from Berni Wrightson and stuff like that. It's going to be a nice book. It'll be . . . all kinds of gross stuff that you've never seen before. [Editor's note: The revised edition of *The Stand* will be published by Doubleday in 1990.]

[Question from the audience about how much Stephen King was in Bill Denbrough from *It.*] It was to an extent, but when writers write about themselves, they always lie. The thing about writers when they write about themselves—and I've done this a couple of times—is that you think to yourself because you lie for a living, you think to yourself: I know what happened. This happened, this happened, and this happened, but it wasn't too interesting how that turned out, but suppose *this* had happened. So you change things around a little bit.

The actual physical character of Bill Denbrough is based on Peter Straub. The Bill Denbrough character is bald and while I'm at thirty-nine, I've started to show a little snow on top of the mountain, I don't seem to be losing too much of my hair. Some of my marbles, maybe, but not too much of my hair. . . . And Peter—one of the reasons I think Peter stuttered, which is something that he's overcome now—was that when he was three years old [like] the character in *It*, he was struck by a car and driven into the wall. He and his seven-year-old brother had been allowed to go down to the market to get ice cream cones. On their way back a car struck Peter, driven by a drunk driver, and drove him headfirst into a brick wall, at which point his older brother picked up his ice cream cone, walked back to the house, and said, "Peter's dead. He was a good brother." But Peter wasn't dead, and I showed him the manuscript and [asked if] I could use it. It's funny, for instance, in "The Body," which turned into this movie *Stand by Me*, almost every incident in that book actually happened, but I twisted everything around. I have leech scars in several places on my body, some of which could not be shown without really getting Pat Robertson mad. If you see the movie, you'll know what I'm talking about.

But you twist things around to fit the story, that's all.

[From the audience: "*The Talisman* is good. Do you plan on collaborating again?"] Not in the near future. It was tough. Working with someone else was tough, but it was fun, too. It was a good story.

Fanny fatigue seems to be setting in with some people. I'll tell you what: I'll take two more questions. And I do want to say that generally I don't have any problem with autographing as a rule, but this would be like having a wine-and-cheese party for the entire Democratic party. And once you start, you can't stop because you can do about forty people, and the first forty people are insane collectors who have books in these wrappings which they don't even want you to touch without gloves on. And what you end up with is three hundred signed autographs and a hand that looks like one of Jerry's kids, and everyone else is sort of left out and they are not happy about it.

[In response to a question from the audience:] Am I a big Boston Red Sox fan? Do ursine mammals excrete in high foliage inside the woods? I'm such a big Boston Red Sox fan that I can't wait for the Red Sox–Houston World Series. And if they play those wimps, the Mets, it'll be over in four games because the Mets are so soft, and the Houstons are a scrappy little team.

I made a bet with a sportswriter who foolishly declared they would be out by Flag Day and, yes, he ate some chicken in his skivvies. I ate mine in my tuxedo. That was one of the best days—as the guy says in the song—one of the best days of my life.

Rocking in the Dead Zone!

Well, for me, radio, and in particular, music, made me real as a kid.
It's where I discovered my identity. You reach out and find something
that belongs to you and it's yours. It's difficult to explain,
but it's like a pair of shoes that fit you. My first record was a
78 rpm version of Elvis Presley's "Hound Dog." From that moment on I knew
it's what I wanted, and I wanted all I could get.

Stephen King, interview with *Radio and Records,* 1984

In the *Playboy* article "Between Rock and a Soft Place" (January 1982) King tells the story of his drive from Boston to Maine on I-95 where, more than anything else, he "wanted to dial some good rock 'n' roll and turn the volume up until the speakers started to distort."

The rental car had only an AM dial, and he soon discovered that there was no hard rock on the air. "That was when I began to worry—to seriously worry—about rock 'n' roll."

It worried him enough that, a year later, he did something about it—he bought an AM radio station in Bangor, as an investment at the urging of his business manager, but primarily because of his interest in keeping hard rock and roll alive. As King put it in an October 1987 article for *Castle Rock,* "I did it because the cutting edge of rock and roll has grown dangerously blunt in these latter days."

WACZ (originally WLBZ in 1926) became WZON, owned and operated by the Zone Corporation. It currently operates on the AM band at 620 kilohertz.

The investment offers King another benefit. When he sits down to write, he "turns on some hard rock on WZON. He is never dissatisfied with what he hears: after all, he owns the station," said *Time* magazine in its October 6, 1986, cover story on King.

It its March 1988 issue, *Castle Rock* reported that the station would be sold. "King made the decision to offer WZON for sale last year after several months of both ratings and financial decline." But, more recently, in its October 1988 issue,

Castle Rock reported that King had changed his mind. The station would become a noncommercial radio station, with ownership transferred from the Zone Corporation to the Bangor Public Communications, Inc., a not-for-profit corporation, with King as president.

According to *Castle Rock,* the programming would change, with the shift in profit to not-for-profit status:

> The station currently offers classic and album rock, mixed with blues, as its basic format. However, listeners also are apt to hear some crossover country songs and an occasional heavy metal tune as part of the station's varied format. Plans are being made to add other types of music to the programming, including special blocks of gospel and New Age Music.

Castle Rock quoted King as saying, "Commercial AM rock 'n' roll is nearly dead. Resurrecting the Z as a noncommercial rocker may be one way of keeping the format alive on AM."

The sign outside WZON radio station in Bangor.

Stephen King as Breckinridge Elkins?
by Donald M. Grant

If you've ever read Robert E. Howard's stories about Breckinridge Elkins, you'll catch many of the allusions in this roast by publisher Donald M. Grant, who, incidentally, published collections of the Breckinridge Elkins stories with wonderful illustrations by Tim Kirk. (It also helps if you've read Talbot Mundy, whom Grant has also published. Grant has also compiled a bibliography of Talbot Mundy, Talbot Mundy: Messenger of Destiny. *As a publisher, Grant has issued four Stephen King books in eight different editions.)*

The following roast was given at NECON (New England Convention), established in 1980 as an annual convention held each July. The chairmanship has been split between Robert Booth (for the first five or six conventions) and Robert Plante, the current chairman. NECON is a smallish, relaxed, and very affordable affair held on the campus of Roger Williams College in Bristol, Rhode Island. The college overlooks the water and the Island of Rhode Island.

Donald M. Grant, a four-time recipient of the prestigious Howard Award of the World Fantasy Convention, was the first roastee in what has become an annual convention highlight. Charles L. Grant followed in 1981, and Stephen King was the third roastee in 1982.

Note: all notes are by Donald M. Grant.

Two years ago, under similar circumstances, I was barbarously attacked, slandered, brutalized in these same surroundings. The attack was unprovoked and unexpected, and it originated with a motley horde of convicted felons headed by convention chairman Robert Booth. Again, a year ago, Booth engineered an attack upon my poor old defenseless uncle,[1] Charlie Grant [Charles L. Grant]. Therefore, when that designing Brutus—and I refer to the scoundrel who is known throughout Rhode Island as Booth the Betrayer (he's treated even less gently elsewhere)—brained another, a third NECON sneak attack, I resolved to foil the rascal! He's got a lot of gall anyway![2]

In the first place, Booth has an obsession for attacking Grants. And somewhere in his bungling, inept way he has learned that Steve King's middle name is

---

1. Actually, there is no relation, though I have published three of Charlie's books.
2. Robert Booth, convention chairman, had his gallbladder removed about two weeks before the convention.

Grant.[3] Moreover, I have just learned this very morning that he plans to attack Kathy Grant next year.[4]

In the second place, I take great pride in my association with the great state of Maine, and any attack on a Maine resident I take as a personal affront. To abuse Steve King here and now is like asking me to give up my subscription to the *Maine Times* and *Down East* magazine. I'll fight first! Why the state of Maine has been home to such fiction writers as Kenneth Roberts, pulp favorites Hugh Pendexter and George Surdez, Achmed Abdullah who wrote *The Thief of Baghdad*, Clarence E. Mulford who wrote *Hopalong Cassidy*, George Allan England who even ran for governor of the state, and last but not least, Talbot Mundy. Remember that last name.[5]

Steve King belongs in the company of this illustrious group of writers. They're all dead. But let me tell you how I became acquainted with him.

Some years ago I read a novel from the pen of a new writer called Stephen King. I was rather taken with it, but there was something vaguely disconcerting about it, something almost recognizable. Try as I might I couldn't put my finger on it. In good time I forgot about it, but when a second novel appeared, again I was struck by the fact that it was vaguely familiar. This time it bothered me enough so that I phoned that obscure publishing house that represented King and fired a few questions at them. "Where does this fellow King live? What are his credentials? When can I talk to him?"

The answers came evasively at first, but I bullied the rascals a bit and they finally acknowledged that King lived in Maine, and had something to do with the educational system of the state, a teacher or school administrator, perhaps. Now I know the state well—I've even been called a Maineiac on occasion—but the directions they gave me to get to the King Rancho were almost beyond my comprehension. Still, I decided to follow them to the letter. I went so far north into Maine that Hudson's Bay was a day and a half to the southwest—by dogsled. This fellow King lived so far up in the wilderness that the average high temperature for the month, which was July, was 32 degrees Fahrenheit. Anyway, I made it across the mountains and the tundra—there was still plenty of snow around—to this big farmhouse and knocked at the door. A lady appeared who identified herself as King's wife, Tabitha. She was a pleasant young woman who informed me that her hubby was off at school, but would return shortly. Would I come in and wait? I hadn't gone that distance for a view of the northern tundra, so I went in and sat down gratefully. It was cold up there, as mentioned, and there was a great big fire roaring in a massive fireplace. Stretched out in front of it was what I took to be a big dog—one of those huge, white Great Pyrenees, I think you call them. But the creature rolled over and grunted, and it wasn't a dog at all—it was a polar bear!

Tabitha King talked easily about the abundance of game and the absence of

---

3. Not so, of course. (King's middle name is Edwin.)

4. Author "Les Simons" is Kathy Grant (Mrs. Charles L. Grant).

5. All of these authors actually resided in Maine at one time or another.

snow that year, and how Steve wasn't doing so well with his third grade remedial reading class. It was the second time he had taken it, and it didn't look like he'd pass again this year.

From where I was sitting, I could see the whole uncivilized panorama outside the window—the musk oxen nosing through the snow, the Arctic foxes, the snow leopards and all that sort of wildlife. The King kids were outside having a great time around an igloo they had built. Pretty soon a fellow came riding up on horseback. He was on one of those great, draft horses like Marshal Dillon used to ride on "Gunsmoke," a beast capable of carrying the four-hundred-pound hombre that was on its back. Steve King weighed a lot more then; living off the land, I guess he got to eat more than he does today as a starving, full-time writer. He was quite an imposing and giant figure, tramping the snow. When he entered the house, I looked at him closely, and if he had said "Howdy, stranger, I'm Breckinridge Elkins[6] from B'ar Creek, Nevadee," I wouldn't have been surprised. Instead he said: "Howdy, stranger, I'm Steve King from B'ar Creek, Maine. We don't get too many visitors in this here part of the country. Ayuh!"

After some introductions and small talk in which I identified myself as a publisher interested in fantasy, a state of Maine enthusiast, and told him how much I was taken with his first two books, we sat down. He seemed pleased at my interests, genuinely pleased, and the conversation moved along nicely. Eventually, it got around to the two new books that he was writing, but not before he had excused himself and went outside to a little shed next to the igloo. He returned with what I took to be a side of beef. I was about to be invited to dinner.

"Ever et reindeer?" he asked. "I shoots one yesterday."

We talked a little further and seemed to be getting on well. Finally, Steve volunteered to bring out his two new manuscripts, warning me that they were first drafts and in rough form. At this, Tabitha interceded. "I don't think you want to bore our guest by showing him anything so rough." But there was no holding back Steve King. He had never met a real-life reader of fantasy before, and he wanted to show off his wares.

Out came the manuscripts, and after a bit of flourishing they found their way to the apple crate in front of my chair. One look was enough. "Where did you get these?" I exclaimed, jumping to my feet.

"What you mean?" he replied testily, also jumping to his feet. "They's mine!"

"I know that typewriter," I told him slowly and deliberately. "Where did you get these manuscripts?"

"I writes them," he declared defiantly, snatching up the manuscripts and looking very menacing. Even then he had that magical command of English that so typifies his books.

Have you ever had a four-hundred-pound Breckinridge Elkins lookalike snarling in your face? To make matters worse, the polar bear woke up and started

---

6. Robert E. Howard's famous mountain man–superman.

to growl. Now, all of you know that I have been asked to play Tarzan in the movies on two occasions, and Conan on another. And I was still wrestling professionally at the time.[7] I think I could have whipped that bear one on one, but the bear and that Maine mountain together—that was too much for me. Of all the toughs that I know, only Crazy Dick Brisson [of the convention committee, one of the founders of the convention] would have stood up and fought the two of them alone. I got out of there as fast as I could. I'm sure the bear got my share of the reindeer meat.

Out in the car, heading over the tundra at as high a speed as I dared to drive—he'd sicced a pack of wolves (werewolves, maybe) after me—everything fell into place. For years the old-time bookmen in Maine had been floating a tall tale about a legendary lost cache (that's spelled c-a-c-h-e, but in this case it ought to be spelled c-a-s-h) of manuscripts by a resident author. I just plain didn't believe it—up to now. But those so-called first drafts that King had given me a glimpse of were typed on a typewriter that was very familiar. It was Talbot Mundy's type-writer that did the typing, and the manuscripts were written more than sixty years ago when Mundy lived in Maine.[8]

If all of this is true, you may ask, why do I hold Stephen King in such high regard? Simple. Somehow, somewhere, this Maine mountain man had stumbled onto this lost cache of manuscripts and he realized what a find he had! More than that, he or someone close to him—I have reason to believe it was Tabitha King—had the foresight to get these manuscripts rewritten, updated. Again, King deserves the credit. He married Tabitha, didn't he?

One question remained, and I gave it a lot of thought and even did some research. If King didn't update those manuscripts to the point where they could be sold as contemporary pieces, then who did? I have strong evidence now that Tabitha King hired Alan Ryan[9] to work on the Talbot Mundy novels. Alan is a very good, very competent writer. Moreover, he writes fast, but best of all Alan works real cheap.

After this exposé, I may have to run up to Nova Scotia and become a hermit, so before closing I admit publicly that part of what I have disclosed here may be very slight exaggeration. However, there is one carefully guarded secret that I want to reveal for the first time, and this is something that not even King's regular publishers have guessed at. *I published Stephen King's first book!* Impossible! you tell me. Not at all. Consider how many writers use pseudonyms these days. King did with that very first book, and I published it. It's really a first-class tale. I did have to fight with Steve's vanity in titling the book—he has more humility now. After long argument, I printed the story using the title that he had submitted it under. *Almost!* Finally, he agreed to let me print it under a title that dropped only the first word: He had called it: STEPHEN KING—OF THE KHYBER RIFLES.[10]

---

7. Grant stands 6′2″ and weighs slightly more than 160 pounds.

8. Talbot Mundy lived in Norway, Maine, during World War I.

9. Writer Alan Ryan was roastmaster, and later was roastee himself.

10. *King—Of the Khyber Rifles* was Talbot Mundy's best known novel, first published in 1916. Subsequently, Grant published a profusely illustrated edition of this title.

Stephen King Trivia

King's first published story: "I Was a Teenage Graverobber," published in a fan publication, *Comics Review*.

King's first fiction sale: A short story to *Startling Mystery Stories*, for which he received $35.

Oddest accident while reading a King book: While a girl was reading a book late at night during a thunderstorm, her bed was struck by lightning.

King's first book advance: $2,500 for *Carrie*.

King's first hardcover bestseller: His third novel, *The Shining*.

Most expensive King book: *My Pretty Pony*, a limited- edition book published by the Whitney Museum, at $2,200.

Most uniquely bound King books: A limited edition of *Firestarter*, bound in asbestos; and the limited edition of *My Pretty Pony*, bound in stainless steel.

The largest limited-edition print run: 30,000 copies of Donald M. Grant's edition of *The Dark Tower II: The Drawing of the Three*.

Highest price paid for a King letter: $440 for a letter to Forrest Ackerman, offering a story for *Famous Monsters of Filmland* that was not accepted for publication.

Most expensive holographic manuscript: $6,600 for a school notebook containing work in progress and private notes.

Jobs held by King before he became a full-time writer in 1973: According to a press release from NAL, King had a writer's career—"janitor, bagger, dyer and sewer in a mill, a baseball coach, library shelver and stacker, industrial washroom worker, and for a while in a laundromat." King termed these jobs "shitwork." His first professional job was as a teacher.

The largest book advance: A reported (but unconfirmed) four-book deal for approximately $40 million. (The first of four books will be *The Dark Half.*)

Most controversial book: *The Dark Tower: The Gunslinger,* when originally published by Donald M. Grant, Publishers, because of its unavailability in a trade edition until 1988.

Longest King book: *It.*

Only book to be substantially revised in a subsequent edition: *The Stand.*

Worst King film adaptation: *Children of the Corn.*

Best film adaptations: *Carrie* and *Stand by Me* ("The Body" from *Different Seasons*).

Most expensive flop: The Broadway production of *Carrie.*

The only movie King directed: *Maximum Overdrive.*

Estimated books in print: 80 million worldwide.

Projected number of books in print by the year 2000: 100 million worldwide (according to Douglas E. Winter).

Books by King: 32 (including the 1989 releases, which include a limited-edition book, *Dolan's Cadillac,* a short story published by Lord John Press).

Books *about* King: 29 (by the end of 1990).

Total number of visual adaptations based on King's work: 22 (by the end of 1989).

Number of audiocassettes with King's work: 45.

First nonfiction book about King: Underwood–Miller's *Fear Itself.*

First single-author book about King: Douglas E. Winter's *The Art of Darkness.*

Most prolific critic: Michael R. Collings, with six books, and a seventh in the works.

Most frequent occupations of King's characters: They are writers and teachers.

Most frequent locale: Castle Rock, Maine.

Only unauthorized edition of a King book: *Nebel* (*The Mist,* published in Germany; a limited edition of 500 copies).

Best sleuthing: Robert E. Weinberg for discovering and reporting in his book catalogue King's use of the Bachman pen name months before it broke in the news.

Worst sleuthing: A rumor that King wrote a Laser paperback, under the pen name of Aaron Wolfe, which turned out to be a pen name for Dean Koontz.

Funniest hoax: King as the reputed author of a Beeline porno book, *Love's Lessons*, written under the pen name of Helen Purcell.

Most obvious contradiction: King stating that he would not authorize *The Dark Tower: The Gunslinger* to be published in a trade edition.

Most overpriced, artificial limited edition: The signed audiotape sets of the first two *Dark Tower* novels: $100 for *The Gunslinger*, and $125 for *The Drawing of the Three*.

Least attractive King hardbacks: Doubleday's editions.

Most imaginative covers: NAL's mass-market paperback editions.

Best book about King: *Stephen King: The Art of Darkness* by Douglas E. Winter.

Mass-market paperbacks selling over five million copies: *'Salem's Lot, The Shining, The Stand.*

Largest first printing of a King novel in hardback: *The Dark Half* with 1.5 million copies.

A Writer in Her Own Right
Tabitha King

Tabitha King lives in Bangor, Maine, with her husband and their three children.

Jacket copy to *Pearl,* Tabitha King's fourth novel

When Janet O. Jeppson began publishing science-fiction novels, the reviewers, to a person, couldn't resist. Rather than review the work, they reviewed the person. More specifically, they talked about her husband, who just happened to be Isaac Asimov, considered one of the three best science-fiction writers in our time (the two others being Arthur C. Clarke and the late Robert A. Heinlein).

Tabitha King knows how Janet Jeppson must feel. Like Jeppson, Tabitha, a writer in her own right, is married to bestselling novelist Stephen King, a point that reviewers take a special delight in mentioning. (In *Rave Review,* a book-review magazine, *Pearl* was reviewed and, to nobody's surprise, the last comment was that Tabitha's husband's first name is Stephen.)

Despite the inevitable (and oft inane) comparisons of her fiction to her husband's, Tabitha King has garnered praise from fellow writers Douglas E. Winter and Harlan Ellison, who consider her a major regional writer.

Tabitha King: Books in Print

- *Small World* (1981), dedicated to "the Boogeyman, with love" [husband Stephen], available as a paperback from NAL; 311 pages, $4.50.
- *Caretakers* (1983), available as a paperback from NAL; 342 pages, $4.95.
- *The Trap* (1985), available as a paperback from NAL; 349 pages, $4.95.
- *Pearl* (1988), available as a hardback from NAL; 324 pages, $18.95.

71

Tabitha King

Photo courtesy of the *Bangor Daily News*

She has even staked out her own territory. Nodd's Ridge, Maine, is Tabitha King country. The critical assessment? Her work is here to stay. The Special Collections Department of the Fogler Library at the University of Maine at Orono, Tabitha's alma mater, has requested her papers.

Of her four novels, three (including her most recent) use Nodd's Ridge as their settings: *Caretakers, The Trap* (originally titled *Wolves at the Door*), and her latest, *Pearl* (originally titled *Coming to Grief*). In *Pearl* the main character, Pearl Dickenson, returns as a result of an inheritance to Nodd's Ridge and decides to stay, changing the small town (and herself) forever.

Tabitha King is currently at work on her fifth novel, set in Nodd's Ridge. She is very much an author with a distinctive voice, one that tells tales of a Maine not too far from Castle Rock.

Photo courtesy of the *Bangor Daily News*

Tabitha King's home office in the Bangor, Maine, residence.

The House That Horror Built

There's no place like home. Stephen King has spent most of his adult life near Bangor, so Bangor seemed the logical place to settle down. The Kings also maintain a summer residence, in western Maine, but it is the winter residence, the Victorian mansion on West Broadway, that is unmistakably King. In its October 6, 1986, cover story, *Time* magazine described it:

> The family occupies a 23-room, 129-year-old house surrounded by a black iron fence with interwoven designs of bats and spider webs, installed in an excess of whimsy by the owners. The place is within a mile of the down-at-the-heels section of the town where the Kings began their odyssey. It has an eccentric charm appropriate to the tenants: one cupola is conical, the other square.

Known historically as the William Arnold house, King's house stands out from the others on a quiet residential street where King's neighbors respect his privacy. To tourists and his fans, the house is easy to find—and obviously private property. The custom fence is a dead giveaway, but the No Trespassing signs, prominently posted, are a constant reminder that King regards his home as his castle, in which he's King, the private citizen.

Why did King choose Maine and, more specifically, Bangor? As *Time* put it in its cover story on King:

> The five Kings could set their castle anywhere, but Stephen refuses to leave familiar turf, even the family's lakeside summer place is in the state. "Maine is far and away better for a couple of hicks like us," he maintains. "And it's better for the kids."

Bob Haskell, a columnist for the hometown newspaper, the *Bangor Daily News,* reinforced the point:

> Bangor has always seemed an ideal place for Steve King and his family to live. . . . "Now, look," I have told a few people who think I know Steve a lot better than I really do, "he was born in Maine. He lives ten minutes from an airport that can get him anywhere in the world. And he doesn't get hassled like he would if he lived in Boston or New York. Everybody takes him for granted around here. So why should he want to live anywhere else?"

Why indeed?

74

Photo courtesy of the *Bangor Daily News*

A wide-angle view of Stephen King's home office.

King answers the question in his essay "A Novelist's Perspective on Bangor," which appeared only in a limited-edition pamphlet, *Black Magic and Music,* distributed by the Bangor Historical Society at its 1983 benefit.

As King explained, part of the problem is that people have preconceived notions of how they expect him to live, that because of his wealth he should live like a celebrity profiled in Leach's "Lifestyles of the Rich and Famous." But it's not his style, personally or professionally. As King realized—and as many other writers have learned—to develop a milieu means staying close to your roots. Though sometimes restrictive—Maine almost exclusively is the backdrop for his novels— that milieu also imbues his work with a feel and texture that give it an immediacy that rings true with his readers.

The rationale for choosing Bangor, instead of another city in Maine, was not simply put. King explains that in order to write *It* (then titled *Derry*), he had to find the right place to write the book—and the place was Bangor. After he bought the

The left side of the house. (The long, low structure to the left is the swimming pool.)

house in 1980, he told the hometown newspaper, "We're going to make Bangor our winter home for good."

It's been almost ten years since King made Bangor his permanent winter home. True, some folk in town don't consider him local—because he hasn't lived there his entire life—but they have taken to him, and he's taken to them, permanently.

A Girl's Dream Comes True in Mansion Fit for Kings
by Joan H. Smith, of the *News* Staff

You'll never see the place on Robin Leach's television show, "Lifestyles of the Rich and Famous," although its resident, Stephen King, certainly fits that description. King seems perfectly content in living in Bangor, Maine, far from the madding crowd; I suspect he wouldn't have it any other way.

A Victorian mansion set in the historic district, King's winter residence pre-

*sents a conservative front, like the other homes in this well-to-do, quiet neigh-
borhood, but the inside of the house has been modernized to suit its owners. The
most obvious addition is, of course, the indoor swimming pool.*

*In this rare behind-the-scenes tour of the King home in 1984, reprinted from
the* Bangor Daily News, *a hometown reporter talks with Tabitha King and takes
you beyond the front gate flanked with bats and into the home of Bangor's most
celebrated resident.*

As a girl she strolled down West Broadway with a friend and dreamed of living in
one of the mansions. She leaned toward the red one with towers. She certainly
never thought she'd live there one day.

But the wide-eyed girl grew up to be author Tabitha King and married the
man who became the most famous horror author of our time, Stephen King. He
decided the barn-red Victorian mansion at West Broadway replete with towers,
secret passages, and unbeknown to them at the time of purchase, a ghost, was his
kind of place.

"I thought it was destiny," said Tabitha.

The oldest house on the street, built in 1858 for $7,000 by a man who
couldn't afford it, had to go through a transition before it fit the needs of three
children, two writers, and their entourage.

It took a crew of craftsmen from Center Lovell, where the Kings have a
summer home, four years to modernize the mansion on the inside, yet maintain
period architectural integrity on the outside.

"The historical commission is quite pleased with it," she said.

The house proper remained unchanged except for the kitchen and the addition of some closet space and a laundry. The major overhaul took place in the
barn, which had been used to store relatives' old couches, but which is now the
most used living space in their home.

She feels they aren't quite done yet; he's had enough of the constant construction. If the movie version of Stephen's book *Pet Sematary* is filmed in Bangor
this summer—and she believes it will be—Tabitha will be spending the summer
in Bangor and will have time to plan period gardens of peonies and roses to
surround the house.

Through the decades, the 126-year-old house has had many changes, such
as the addition of the front porch and carriage port. Yet, most is original, including
the bright golden oak entry, considered a utility wood at the time, but probably
the best the builder could afford.

The rooms are decorated mostly in cool pastels of green or blue, which
contrast with the warm oak and mahogany woodwork.

King stands in front of his new home in Bangor.

Photo courtesy of the *Bangor Daily News*

The living room is large and beautifully decorated in period furniture. Over a baby grand piano is a photograph of their summer home, which is featured in Tabitha's book *The Caretakers.*

"It was a cold room and for some time after we moved in no one wanted to go in it, the kids, the animals. I added a rug and re-wallpapered, but the vibes were bad. We knew it must be the room with the ghost."

"Bruce [their seal point Siamese cat] likes to sleep on the couch in here; it's his couch," she said.

In the square tower, to the right, is a collection of light oak period furniture, one of Tabitha's many "nests," which are in nooks throughout the mansion.

In this nest she wraps packages and organizes clothes. Parked next to her oak desk is a large orange telescope, which her husband, an amateur astronomer, moves out onto the front lawn on clear nights. This quantum leap in time is a hint of what is to come toward the back of the house.

The Kings combined six small rooms to create a labyrinth of a kitchen. Seated at a lunch bar is a man sipping coffee and chatting with the housekeeper. Tabitha introduces him as the man who maintains their Wang word-processing equipment. Today is a social call. Behind him is another of Tabitha's nests. She calls this one her "concierge nest," where she plans menus and pays bills. A bulletin board plastered with slips of paper and a fast-food restaurant menu is above a small counter covered with books and paper.

On a bar in what was once the butler's pantry is a caged albino guinea pig named Butler. Around the corner is a higher-than-average counter custom-made for 6-foot-3 Stephen to knead his bread. Around another corner is the brick warming oven, where he sets his bread to rise.

"They're Royal River bricks, where Steve grew up," Tabitha said.

The kitchen is a modern room with a brilliant red sink, butcher block counter tops and sleek off-white cabinets trimmed in oak. A red electric dumbwaiter is used to transport clothing to the laundry on the second floor.

"I can show you mistakes all over this kitchen, but the pool is perfect," said Tabitha, who led the way through a long corridor, down a step, which follows the lay of the land, past a number of tiled dressing rooms, which were once box stalls in the pool room, a swimming shrine.

Beyond the 47-foot length of the pool is a window designed by the architectural firm I.M. Pei, which also did the Portland Museum of Art. The mosque-like shapes of the window and pool repeat a motif found in the shape of the front porch floor, a medallion adorning the outside of the house, and a handmade wrought-iron fence added by the Kings.

The small, square windows that once admitted light into the horse stalls remain along the south side of the pool room. From the outside, it appears to be a

Photo courtesy of the *Bangor Daily News*

A shot of the indoor swimming pool. (The soft sculpture hanging from the rafters is sea creatures, creations of Barbara Lambert of Orono, Maine.)

well-maintained 19th-century barn. Inside is Tabitha King's fantasy—a plaster pool 12 feet at its deepest, which she swims in every day.

"For Steve, it's now and then, but the kids and I swim every day and my father, who has a heart condition, uses it, too," said Tabitha, who did not learn to swim until she was 30, but said she then fell in love with it.

She said she "fell insanely in love" with the creations of Barbara Lambert of Orono, whose stuffed cloth sculptures hang from the rafters around the pool. Lambert's fantastical sea creatures are "evolution gone mad," according to Tabitha, who said she reads a lot of biology and believes there is very little in fantasy that does not actually exist.

The sculptures are vividly colored in many shades of blue and green, accenting the pool's color, which changes with the quality of the day and season's light.

Above the pool's dressing rooms is an office with a stained-glass window depicting a bat in flight. A secret entrance to the office is up a narrow low-ceiling staircase, through a foot-thick door that closes and disappears as part of a book-case. Skylights, hanging lights, white walls and white plush carpeting brightly light the writing digs of Stephen King.

He said he wanted a bright office because he doesn't "see all that well." It took two of the largest desks the Kings could find to hold his Wang word-process-ing and printout equipment. Beside the printout machine is a neat stack of paper titled "It" by Stephen King, his latest work. Beside that is a chrome drive-in movie speaker presented to him as King of the Drive-in Horror Movie. The room is rimmed with bookcases. One section has a copy of each of his 18 books, includ-ing those in foreign languages.

Half of King's books have been bestsellers, and eight were made into movies, with three more in the works.

The seating area beyond the office was once a hayloft where the groom slept. Secret passages through the eaves led to the maid's quarters in the attic over the house.

"There was some concern, I was told, of the grooms' getting to the maids . . .," said Tabitha.

A New Hampshire license plate with the word "Cujo" is on one wall. A jigsaw puzzle of Marilyn Monroe and another of Humphrey Bogart hang on the wall above a loose-pillow charcoal gray couch. A plastic model of Frankenstein's mon-ster graces the coffee table.

"The only time I realize it's a barn is in the summer, when I roast in the loft," said Stephen.

Beyond the sitting room is his bath with black jacuzzi tub and black pedestal sink. His secretary's office is in the hayloft, too. Tabitha shares the secretary along with the printout machine, to which the word-processor in her office in the other end of the house is connected.

Tabitha's office in the first floor of the cylindrical tower was Stephen's when they moved in four years ago. Although she had insulated interior wooden shut-ters installed in the massive windows, he found the street sounds too distracting. She enjoys watching the color changes in the original spider web stained-glass windows as the sun floods through them.

"Steve wrote three books here. He never had an office that was really his and he felt he earned it," said Tabitha. "He finally has his own place."

Wrought Iron
by Terry Steel

It's called architectural ironwork, and as Terry Steel, a member of the Artist Blacksmith Association of North America explains in this article, "Only a handful of us are architectural smiths." It's almost a lost art, utilizing techniques that haven't changed over the centuries, but its effects are stunning, as anyone can attest who has seen the wrought-iron, custom-made fence that surrounds the King home in Bangor, Maine.

A fusion of art and artifact, form and function, the 270-foot fence sets the Kings' house apart from all others on West Broadway in the historic district. It also says, in unmistakable terms, that the residents of this particular house have a decidedly macabre tendency, and a touch of whimsy. And for some strange reason, the architectural design of the fence fits in well with the surrounding mansions.

In this excerpt from an article published in Fine Homebuilding, *October/November 1983, about the craft of ornamental ironwork, Terry Steel provides a firsthand account of the story behind the unique fence at the King residence.*

When I tell people I'm a blacksmith, I usually get a blank stare, a disconcerted comment on shoeing horses, or a frank query—"What do you do?" What I "do" is architectural ironwork—I make ornamental wrought iron using traditional blacksmithing methods. The Artist Blacksmith Association of North America (A.B.A.N.A.) lists about 1,800 members, but only a handful of us are architectural smiths.

Blacksmiths are almost as extinct as the dinosaur. The coming of the automobile signaled the end of demand for farriers to shoe horses. And the advent of machine-made, mass-produced parts and hardware, coupled with the development of modern welding methods, made the local blacksmith obsolete. Finally, the styles of 20th-century architecture doomed smiths who produced architectural ornament. The International Style of so-called functional architecture wiped out legions of skilled building craftsmen.

Frank Lloyd Wright labeled the pure functionalist style "flat-chested modern." He understood that a house provided not only seclusion, warmth, shelter and protection, but also an intimate and individual environment. The problem for contemporary architects and homebuilders is to reconcile the need for function with the desire for beauty—to make simple forms attractive and interesting. Decorative wrought ironwork is one way to do it.

. . . [I]f you want both structural integrity and one-of-a-kind design, there is

Three-headed griffin guards the corner of the King residence in Bangor.

only one way to go—ornamental ironwork wrought by an architectural black-smith.

Writer Stephen King and his wife Tabitha recognized this, and in 1981 they commissioned me to make two gates and a wrought-iron fence for their residence in Bangor, Maine. The Kings' house, built in 1855–57 and known locally as the William Arnold house, is located in a designated historic district. It's an Italianate villa with asymmetrical massing, a square hipped roof and a finialed tower. A smaller, octagonal tower is a later addition in the Queen Anne style of the 1880s and 90s.

The Design Process

Wrought ironwork is first and foremost functional—the design must work. Fencing not only defines a property's boundaries, but the pickets must also be spaced to keep animals and children in (or out); hence the inclusion in the pattern of short pickets known as dog bars. Gates must open and close as smoothly as a front door.

The William Arnold House*

The Italianate Villa

Only one stylist Italianate villa was built in Bangor. The William Arnold House . . . dates from 1854 to 1856. It was the first house built in West Broadway on the former Davenport lands, between Hammond and Union Streets.

William Arnold (1806–75) was a prosperous livery stable owner, who lived in Union and Ohio Streets before building this house. Arnold's tax lists show that the low was valued as $1,700 before the house was built; upon its completion in 1856, it was valued at $6,000. Arnold sold the house to William H. Smith of Old Town for $6,148.93 in July 1857.

Though he sold the house for one reason or another, William Arnold continued to prosper. He was later the president of the Penobscot Mutual Fire Insurance Company, and was prominent in the Unitarian and musical circles. When he died his estate amounted to $19,000; this was a comfortable estate but not the fortune of a rich man, which supports the idea that the West Broadway house represented too large an investment for a man of his fortune.

*From *Bangor, Maine, 1769–1914, An Architectural History.*

Close-up of Steel's work on the front gate.

But ironwork is ornamental, too. For the most part it uses linear design motifs that define positive and negative space. Shape and proportion are vital elements. The choice of a double or single gate, for example, depends on the size of the entrance, so that the proportions of the finished product will look right. The design itself must serve a purpose, and the motifs must be expressive.

I brought a lot of magazines showing examples of ironwork to my first conference with the Kings, along with a lot of photographs I'd taken of fence and gate work around Beacon Hill in Boston. The Kings also had books with drawings of ironwork, and we discussed possible designs. It was important for the fence and gates to work with the architecture of the house, to be graceful and attractive, and yet to reflect the personalities of the occupants as well. King, a writer of macabre fiction, wanted bats worked into the design. His wife wanted spiders and webs.

We walked the property line, and I recorded the length of the fencing perimeter and the widths of the sidewalks where the gates would go. We got a survey map and found some old photographs of the property. It looked about 5 feet high, and we decided on the same height for the new fence.

Next I studied the house's architectural details. My eye was caught immediately by the attractive wooden appliqué on the south sidewall of the house, whose design had been borrowed, I was certain, from classic wrought-iron scroll work. I

Bats and Spiders*

The Gate Design

I had a design flash, a moment of creativity, as the design of the gate emerged. I had the concept and drew it on the chalkboard. Then I started making it, putting it together. I was pretty much done when Tabitha drove down to take a look.

Steve initially said he wanted creatures like bats and spiders, so the front gate incorporates them, drawn from the imagery that we as children had of the creatures of the night . . . and fear. That seemed to me to be where King was coming from in his writing. I wanted the gate to say something about the person behind the door.

Also, on my visits, I noticed a lot of comic books lying around, including *Superman* and *Batman*. Remember the bat symbol that is flashed on the clouds in *Batman*? That's what I used for the two bats on the fence: superhero characters, not demonic characters.

*Terry Steel, from interview with George Beahm, 1989.

borrowed it back for the fence design—it shows up in the support sections, and in the side gate design.

The stained-glass windows throughout the house offered another design possibility; their arches and radius lines gave me an idea for the design of the spider webs. The front gate, with its circles and arches, repeat motifs I found over the doors and the back barn's circular windows.

After the initial brainstorming session, I went home and worked up a proposal, including design drawings and cost. Once the Kings approved the picket and fence-section design, I drove back to Bangor to take exact measurements. After consulting with the Bangor Historical Society, we got a building permit.

The commission took a year-and-a-half to finish—270 lineal feet of hand-forged fence, weighing 11,000 pounds, punctuated by two gates composed of spiders, webs, goat heads, and winged bats. The editor of the local paper called the project a major contribution to the architecture of the city of Bangor. A neighbor comes over to tell me the fence is "just what the house needed," and turns to eye her own front yard. One thing's for sure. Anyone touring Bangor trying to pick out the house where Stephen King lives will have little trouble finding it.

Photo courtesy of the *Bangor Daily News*

King holding mounted head of a rattlesnake in a crystal ball.

Part Two

The Unreal World of Stephen King

This section will give you an insider's perspective on what King critic Michael R. Collings termed "the Stephen King phenomenon," the worlds of book and audio publishing, the fans, the critics, and the craft of writing. Also, detailed information is provided on King material available and how to order. (Appendix 6 of this book provides a quick checklist for easy reference.)

• In "Fans" you read King's fan mail, and King's reaction to it. A fun quiz helps you determine just how big a King fan you are. There's information about *Castle Rock*, the monthly newspaper devoted to King and his activities (with subscription information). And if you want to meet other fans, there's Horrorfest, the annual convention for King fans that meet (where else?) at the Stanley Hotel in Estes Park, Colorado, the inspiration for *The Shining*.

• In "Book Publishing" King delivers himself on the phenomenon of best-selling hardback fiction, in a piece appearing in print for the first time since its debut in *Publishers Weekly.* You view the most expensive limited-edition King book ever published—$2,200 for *My Pretty Pony.* You tour the world of limited-edition publishing—companies like Lord John Press, Starmont House, King's own Philtrum Press—and are given a buyer's guide to specialty publishers and dealers (the ones that publish and sell the limited-edition King books).

• In "Audio Publishing" you get the lowdown on all the King audiocassettes available: from the extensive selection of unabridged readings from Recorded Books, to the 3-D "Mist" and *Thinner,* the Bachman book that blew King's cover.

• In "Critics" you meet Michael R. Collings, a major King critic who holds the record for the most books published about King. In an exclusive interview and an article written especially for this book, Collings explains why he loves King's work—and why others hate it. And you get the straight story on King's successful efforts to stop censorship in Maine, reported by *Castle Rock* editor/publisher Christopher Spruce.

• In "Writing" you are privy to what Clive Barker (whom King has called the future of horror fiction) has to say about King—culled from two radio interviews with Larry King. In an interview done exclusively for this book, you find out what Harlan Ellison thinks of King's work. Howard Wornom's article explores the comic deaths of King's characters. And for you who think you know where King gets his ideas, there's a quiz (with answers, of course): Given the germ of an idea, can you identify the book that was later published?

FANS

Fan Letters to Stephen King

*What really knocks me out is a book that, when you're all done reading it,
you wish the author that wrote it was a terrific friend of yours
and you could call him up on the phone whenever you felt like it.
That doesn't happen much, though.*

Holden Caulfield, *The Catcher in the Rye* by J.D. Salinger

If fan mail is a barometer of a writer's popularity, then King is hugely popular indeed. With eighty million books in print, plus millions who have seen his movies, King gets loads of mail from virtually everywhere. Most of it is sent to his publishers, Viking and New American Library, or to magazines where his work has appeared; in these cases, the mail is forwarded. For those who want a more direct route, it is enough, suggests King, to write him at the address "Bangor, Maine." "They know who I am up here," explained Stephen, on a radio talk show with Larry King.

Writing to King is one matter; getting a response is another. Stephen, like any other celebrity, has to deal with volumes of correspondence, from simple letters of thanks from gratified readers to urgent pleas for advice from students writing term papers and from unpublished writers.

If you write to your favorite TV or movie personality, chances are you'll get a response from a company that does nothing but answer celebrity mail; your letter will probably never reach the celebrity. One popular cartoonist has a full-time employee whose job is to answer mail; the cartoonist then signs the letter, which makes it appear personal. If you write again, don't expect a response; he hasn't the time to be your pen pal.

If you write to King, a secretary opens and reads your letter. The chances are good, though, that unless your letter *requires* an individual response you may not get one; or you may get a cheery but apologetic form postcard that says, in effect, thanks for writing, and I appreciate it; but much as I'd like to, if I took time to answer all my mail, I'd never have time to write my books.

In " 'Ever Et Raw Meat?' and Other Weird Questions," an essay originally published in the *New York Times* and subsequently published as "Letters from Hell," a broadside by Lord John Press, King provides amusing examples of letters he received and answers them.

From the files of the Special Collections Department at the University of Maine at Orono, where King has deposited material, one box of correspondence provides ample testimony to the range of letters King receives. Many were what King calls "the old standards," though most people simply wanted to write to express their enjoyment of a particular novel. Most of the letters were handwritten, chatty, and informal; a surprising number were apologetic for taking up his time, and a few took King to task for errors that should have been caught in copyediting.

A sampling of the letters:

A typical letter: "You are only the second author I have ever written to. I wanted to write because I enjoyed the book [*The Shining*] so much and haven't thought about much else since I put it down."

The puzzled thank-you: "How very odd to be writing to thank you for what was really a most unpleasant experience [reading *The Shining*]."

The Author Talks: King on Fan Mail

I'll tell you the truth: A lot of it I don't read because it's repetitive and a little bit scary. If you think too much about [writing] . . . it's like being an actor on the stage: It's all right to know the audience is there; it's all right to sense them as a bulk presence, but never look for faces. They're out there and that's enough. I can't look them in the eye, one by one. It's scary. It's like what I do is very un-selfconscious. I do it for myself, because if you don't like it yourself, if you don't write for yourself, if you write for some hypothetical audience, it's not good—it's fake.

I love the people who read my stuff, and I don't just love them because they support me. I love them because they listen.

There are people who write who believe that the act of putting it down on paper is enough, and I've never felt that was the end of it. I've always felt that to make it complete, it had to go out to some other person. What we're talking about is communication.

The unsolicited commentary: "I've always felt that the author of fearful tales is the most talented because he/she has to be able to take hold of the reader's emotions, and hold them throughout the story."

The reader who knows his limitations: Having read *The Shining,* he felt compelled to read *Carrie* and *'Salem's Lot,* but had misgivings: "Though I consider myself a strong person, I must think of my own mental health."

On King's cinematic style of writing: "While reading, it is almost as if I'm right there when everything is going on."

The plaintive plea for help: "All I want is for that someone to tell me that I'm a lousy writer who should stop wasting his time or that I have some potential and should keep trying. PS: If there is nothing you can do, send money."

The term-paper blues: ". . . due to the fact that I live in a small town, I have been unable to find enough articles and reviews of this novel [*The Shining*]. Therefore, I would appreciate it greatly if you would send me your personal analysis and any other articles and reviews you may have."

The nonbook audience: "My husband, who very rarely reads a book, could not put [*The Shining*] down."

On King's motivations for writing: "Do you write just as a money-making job, for literary value, or in hopes it will be sold for a television or movie screenplay?"

The common questions: "Why did you choose to be a writer? Why do you write horror novels? Where do you get your ideas?"

The affirmation: "I've gotten so that all it takes is the *name* Stephen King on a book and I know it will be good."

The gross-out: "Pardon the phrase, but you scared the shit out of this twenty-year-old [woman]."

A sixteen-year-old writer who needs help: "I've been working (and I really mean *working*) on a novel for close to a year, and it is a lot tougher than I thought writing one would be. It's a pretty good little book but there are so many *problems!!* I really need help! Sometimes I can be writing a very gory blood-and-guts scene that should make a person want to throw up, but when I take the scene from my mind and try to put it down on paper it just doesn't seem scary."

The odd questions: "How come all your books are about something that is possessed? Do you have any suggestions to a sprouting writer?"

And my favorite: "Really, Steve, [*The Shining*] is a masterpiece considering the fact that it was written by an American hack, and I congratulate you."

A Self-Quiz
Rating Yourself as a King Fan

Sometimes it's hard to be objective. Who *are* you? This little quiz will help you find out just how much of a King fan you are. The definitions below, from *The American Heritage Dictionary of the English Language*, 1979 edition, should be kept in mind as you evaluate yourself by the Ten Stages of Fan.

Fan *n. Informal.* An ardent admirer. [< FANATIC.]

Fanatic *n.* One possessed by excessive or irrational zeal. [< Lat. *fanaticus,* inspired by a god.]

Insanity *n.* Persistent mental disorder or derangement. Synonyms: *insanity, lunacy, madness, mania, dementia.*

Nirvana *n. Often capital.* The state of absolute blessedness, characterized by release from the cycle of reincarnations and attained through the extinction of the self.

Obsession *n.* Compulsive preoccupation with a fixed idea or unwanted feeling.

The Ten Stages of Fan

Stage 1: Indifference—"Stephen *who?*"

Stage 2: Mild Contagion—The kind of person who occasionally reads, mostly to kill time when no other alternatives are possible, and accidentally runs across a King book left by someone else, usually a paperback.

Stage 3: "I'm Waiting for the Paperback"—The person who, if he can't get a copy from the library, is perfectly content to wait a year for the paperback edition. This is otherwise known as Annie Wilkes Syndrome, followed by bouts of misery.

Stage 4: A Reader—The person who can't wait for the paperback to come out. When the hardback at twenty bucks hits the bookstores, he is there and ready to buy. (Chances are, he has pestered the bookstore clerks, asking, "When's it going to come out?") Also, if a King story is announced, the reader will track it down in its original hardback or paperback printing. After all, it may not show up in a King collection later.

Stage 5: A Collector—The poor, tormented soul who lives in fear that somewhere, somehow, there exists a King book he can't have. This is otherwise known as the Dark Tower Syndrome.

Stage 6: The Completist—Not content to own a copy of each King book, this person has to have everything in print, in every edition, from every publisher, in every state. (See *fanatic*.)

Stage 7: The Investor—Well heeled, primarily because of "prudent investments" in buying the book at the publication price and selling it for ten times that amount later, the investor prefers not to read the book. It would, then, be no longer in *fine* condition—eye-tracks would mar it. The condition sought for each book is, of course, the condition *beyond* mere fine—the rarefied state of superfine, preferably untouched by human hands and unseen by human eyes. Ideally, the books are purchased directly from the publisher, who has carefully packed and shipped them. These books are never unpacked because they then would not be "as shipped." (One day I'm going to manufacture a blank book, after determining the correct weight, and counterfeit the cardboard shipping container. I'll advertise the copies as "unopened, unread books" and make a mint selling to these suckers. Believe me, they'll never open the books to find out what's inside.)

Stage 8: The Number-Two Fan—The person on the verge of becoming a number-one fan. If a number-two fan—and I pity him because he obviously must *try* harder—he can't live without a King fix. He has everything money can buy. His VISA card has sustained considerable damage because of his abnormal interest in King books. (See *obsession*.) He subscribes to *Castle Rock* and reads every issue religiously. He has, in short, contributed to the apotheosis of Stephen King.

Stage 9: The Number-One Fan—This person is in the dead zone. He is not content to buy all the videotapes, collect all the soundtracks, buy all the books in every edition from every publisher in every printing in every state, including the lettered or signed states of the limited editions. No. His Great Interest is in owning the ultimate King collectible, no matter the cost. If, however, he can't afford everything and must live a life of misery, then he'll settle—reluctantly, agonizingly—for a life as a King groupie, writing fan-boy articles and profiles and reviews and hoping that people will recognize him for what he is: the man who would be King. (See *insanity*.)

Stage 10: Nirvana—The person who thinks he *is* Stephen King.

What stage am *I* at? Wouldn't *you* like to know! Suffice it to say I'd tell you if I had the time, but a snowstorm has choked the roads and I must go out and get the latest Misery Chastain novel—it has just come out in paperback. If I'm lucky, I'll meet someone nice on the way into town.

CASTLE ROCK

The Stephen King Newsletter

November 1988   Bangor, Maine — Vol. 4, No. 11 $1.25

Pet Sematary Film Crews Visit Bangor

by Christopher Spruce

The filming of Stephen King's *Pet Sematary* moved from the Ellsworth area to Bangor during the last week of September. Film crews spent three days and nights filming at Bangor's Mount Hope Cemetery.

Production crews from Laurel Entertainment Inc. set up facilities near the superintendent's office at Mount Hope Sept. 27 and worked through Sept. 29 filming a variety of scenes for their production of *Pet Sematary.*

One of the scenes filmed will feature a cameo appearance by author Stephen King, who also has written the screenplay for the movie based on his best-selling novel.

Among the actors involved in the Mount Hope segments were Fred Gwynn, who plays Jud Crandall, and Dale Midkiff, who plays the part of Louis Creed.

A visit to the set Sept. 28 evidenced literally dozens of people marking time near cemetery offices, waiting for the scene to be filmed to be set up. A number of local people were cast as "mourners," and were carefully dressed and made up for their roles.

Even as cemetery crews went about their regular duties, the film crew set up a graveside scene at the bottom of a hill diagonally facing State Street. Tracks on which to roll one of the cameras were laid, klieg lights erected immediately adjacent to the site and a dozen or more chairs set up next to the fictitious grave for the make-believe mourners. Back on the gravel roadway leading up to the film site, an hydraulic boom truck raised one huge spotlight and its technician 25 feet off the ground.

Eerily, as production workers were setting up the scene under the supervision of Director Mary Lambert, a branch from one of the large, old trees overlooking the set area crashed to the ground. The incident was blamed on the brisk winds racing around the cemetery late Wednesday morning, Sept. 28 but more than a few crew members wondered aloud if supernatural forces were at work.

A quick-witted staffer may have remarked, "It was like something out of Stephen King."

The branch-falling incident caused production assistants to shoo onlookers away from hillside vantage points which offered the clearest view of the filming. A couple dozen curious folk sat on a knoll a half a football field away from the actual filming, observing the proceedings. The sun peaked in and out of the clouds in what was otherwise a perfect fall day. The weather seemed to be just right for the graveside scene being filmed. But Director Lambert waited a couple of hours for just the right cloud cover to occur to shoot a long-distance, wide-angled view of the set from the top of one of the adjacent knolls.

As the actors rehearsed the scene, King was seen clowning with Gwynn. From a distance, it appeared Gwynn fell momentarily into his now-famous Herman Munster character, pulling stiffly with his righthand at the bottom of his suit jacket, and mugging in his best Munsterese.

One of the bizarre scenes at the filming location in the cemetery was a portable table set up parallel to four old weathered gravemarkers. On the table, among other things, were a loaf of bread and jars of

Continued on Page 7

Castle Rock   Second Class Postage
P.O. Box 8183
Bangor, Maine 04401

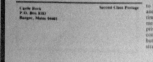

Actor Fred Gwynn, left, confers with Stephen King prior to filming of cameo appearance by SK in the film version of Pet Sematary. *(Tabitha King photo)*

Book Review

Pearl Is 'Engaging Character'

by Janet C. Beaulieu

Pearl by Tabitha King. New American Library, 336 pages, $18.95.

Tabitha King's fourth novel, *"Pearl,"* opens as a newcomer journeys to the familiar territory of Nodd's Ridge, Maine, on the border of the White Mountains, the same setting used in King's earlier novel "The Trap."

Pearl Dickenson has inherited her grandmother's family home and has come to take possession. Our first glimpse of the area is Pearl's:

"One comes upon the skyward folding of the land into the White Mountains as a sudden revelation; all at once the woods open up around the individual houses of the village, standing apart from each other in a community of privacy, their backs to the ancient splendid hills. The lake is a wedge of sapphire in the middle ground between, a blue tear in all that rooted rock and green hallelujah of trees."

When Pearl meets Walter Mackenzie, the caretaker, she remarks: "God had a good day here, didn't She?!"

One of Pearl's first tasks is to see to her grandmother's interment in the cemetery that borders her land, and immediately the reader senses Pearl's instinctive connections to a family and a place she never really knew.

"There was nothing to fear in graveyards, no reason to fear the dead. She had been with both her mother and Gussie at the end. It had been spooky and at the time inexplicably comforting to witness the abandonment of their bodies by their spirits . . . Pearl was surprised to feel a vague but unshakable, odd sensation of connection to relatives in the family plot. Though all but a stranger to them in life, in spite of being a stranger, she was flesh of their flesh."

The kicker, however, is that Pearl is not obviously flesh of their flesh. A thoroughly surprised Walter Mackenzie reports his meeting with their new neighbor to Reuben Styles, owner of the local garage: "Reuben, she's a Negro . . . She's no tarbaby. Lighter'n that. Brown, I mean. Light eyes, too . . . Oo-la-la, I'm telly you. Oo-la-la." In a later conversation, Pearl describes herself somewhat more graciously: "I'm not black. I'm a very nice shade of mahogany."

Though at first her obvious mixed racial ancestry is grist for the local gossip mill, most people seem to quickly forget the color of her skin and concentrate instead on the person inside. Which is not all that difficult, because in Pearl, Tabitha King has created a truly engaging character. Pearl is bright, feisty, determined and irrepressible, the way all women wish they could be. She is also warm and caring, the kind of person who instinctively takes more than one broken stray under her wing — sometimes despite their loud and vociferous objections.

Soon after Pearl settles in and makes herself at home, the sets about making her living, and after much spirited and imaginative dickering, she purchases Needham's Diner from its owner, Roscoe, a man who throughout the story is alternately her friend and her antagonist. One of the more thoroughly entertaining sections concerns the Needham/Dickenson dickering, which is not only funny, but which exemplifies King's enviable talent for natural, authentic dialogue.

The entire novel moves with a quick, lively pace which makes it a real pleasure to read. The characters also make the book pleasureable, because most of them are really likeable people. The reader doesn't want anything bad to happen to anyone — well,

Continued on Page 6

The front page of the November 1988 issue of *Castle Rock.*

If you want straight stuff about me, subscribe to . . . Castle Rock.

Stephen King, March 1985 letter to editor, *Bangor Daily News*

If you have more than a casual interest in Stephen King, you'll want to check out *Castle Rock: The Stephen King Newsletter.* Drawing its name from the fictional town King frequently uses in his books, *Castle Rock* is a monthly newsletter in newspaper format, usually running eight pages an issue, eleven by seventeen inches, and typeset. The newsletter does an admirable job with a skeleton crew.

In the Beginning

It began as a modest six-page letter-size newsletter, set in an almost unreadable old English typeface, and published by King's sister-in-law and then secretary, Stephanie Leonard. Its first issue, published in January 1985, set the tone with its editorial policy:

> Our goal is to keep you up to date on the work of this prolific writer. *Castle Rock* will be a monthly newsletter and we will have, along with all the news, trivia, puzzles, reviews, classifieds, contents, and, we hope, reader contributions.

Inevitable Growth

By its fourth issue, *Castle Rock* had changed from an informal, typewritten newsletter to a professionally designed and typeset tabloid, with photographs and artwork. Veteran journalist Christopher Spruce was responsible for the new look. *Castle Rock,* which started from scratch on a shoestring budget, began to grow through word-of-mouth and house ads in NAL's paperback editions of King's books. At its peak, the newsletter had over five thousand subscribers.

King is not officially or directly involved in *Castle Rock.* He doesn't contribute or benefit financially, nor does he become involved editorially. His presence, however, is always felt. He contributes original fiction and nonfiction, gives advance notice on new projects, dampens the many rumors about his publishing projects fueled by overeager fans, and on occasion uses the publication as a forum for addressing his readers on frequently asked questions about him and his work.

What's in the Newsletter

Castle Rock is not a fan magazine filled with personal gossip about King. Explains Spruce, "There are some people out there who want a fanzine, but we are not interested in King's personal life; I don't feel it's a legitimate concern for us."

Because the news content varies, depending on what King is working on, you should try a few issues to get a feel for what to expect. The best way is a short-term subscription (six issues for $12).

The mainstays in each issue: the editor's column (a potpourri of information about King and what he's up to); letters to the editor (with replies from Spruce); classified ads (mostly advertising limited-edition books for resale); reviews of upcoming King books, videotapes, and material; ads selling publications from the horror genre (small-press books, chapbooks, etc.); and King trivia (crossword puzzles, trivia lists). In addition, you'll frequently find interviews with other writers in the genre, reprinted articles about King that have appeared in newspapers, articles by the readers, and book reviews by authors other than King.

Future Plans

With the January 1989 issue, Christopher Spruce became the editor-publisher as Stephanie Leonard pursued other interests and became a founding editor. Spruce didn't change the formula, though. A poll of readers showed that they are getting exactly what they want: an emphasis on King, what's coming out and when, articles and reviews on King and, to a lesser degree, on other practitioners in the genre.

One change, however, was made. Based on feedback from the readers, Spruce has occasionally published short fiction from readers, an ideal way to showcase new talent.

There are no elaborate plans to expand the subscription base because, as Spruce explains:

> With a publication like this, there's a point of diminishing returns. It's all mail circulation and time-consuming to put it out. I'm fairly comfortable with the circulation where it is now [in the low thousands]. It's manageable and I'd like to keep it that way.

Ordering Information

A 6-issue subscription is $12.00 ($14.40 foreign, in U.S. funds); 12 issues, $20.00

A Halloween portrait: *Castle Rock* editor–publisher Christopher Spruce (in background) and former *Castle Rock* editor–publisher Stephanie Leonard (in foreground).

($25.00 foreign). Send a check or money order to Castle Rock, P.O. Box 8060, Bangor, Maine 04401.

Back issues are also available. Enclose a self-addressed, stamped envelope for more information.

Horrorfest
A Stephen King Convention

"Everyone had a fantastic time," concluded convention chairman Ken Morgan, who helmed the first Horrorfest convention, held May 12–14, 1989, in Estes Park, Colorado, at the Stanley—the hotel that inspired the fictional Overlook hotel in King's second novel, *The Shining*.

"It was a convention for Stephen King fans," explained Ken Morgan, who owns and operates a successful travel agency in Riverdale, Illinois.

Prefatory Matters

It began September 1986 when Morgan's wife gave him a copy of King's novel, *The Shining*. Hooked with that book, Morgan began collecting the other King books. His wife, noting his great interest, gave him a subscription to *Castle Rock* for Christmas.

Meanwhile, Morgan began recommending King's books to friends, some of whom refused to read the novels. Wondering if this was a typical reaction, Morgan decided, after reading *Castle Rock*, that he wasn't alone in his interest. Then he had a notion: Wouldn't it be fun to get some King fans together for a convention?

The original plan, explained Morgan, was to have an informal get-together, but inquiries from seasoned con attendees made him realize that in order to get people to attend, there'd have to be conventional programming. Morgan then attended science fiction conventions to find out what to do right—and what to avoid.

Opening Day and Beyond

The convention opened on May 12, 1989, and had 325 attendees—an impressive attendance for a first-time convention.

The convention officially started with the opening of the dealer's room, where a dozen merchants sold rare King books, collectibles, magazine subscriptions to small presses in the field, and memberships in horror-related fan organizations.

Later that night, a "get-acquainted" buffet-style dinner—boasting an impressive assortment of food—was hosted. Unfortunately, "the buffet was nothing close to what was promised," said Morgan. Afterward, a drawing was held for books, autographed by the guests of honor, followed by an address by Robert Hellis, a former employee of the Stanley, who gave a talk on the hotel and its haunted history—a talk he's given to numerous tour groups.

At midnight, authors began reading from their works, and horror movies were shown until dawn.

Snowbound

On Saturday and Sunday—as the rain turned into snow—convention programming included numerous panels, a King film festival, author readings, and the highlight of the convention: the first benefit auction for the Horror Writers of America, a fledgling organization for writers of dark fantasy. Material auctioned off included original manuscripts, copies of autographed novels, and memorabilia like a kite used in a promotion for a short story by Harlan Ellison—it went for $100.

Epilogue

Despite the cold weather that plagued Horrorfest 1989, the attendees took comfort in the knowledge that everyone suffered together, which provided the theme for Horrorfest 1990: Misery loves company.

To be held on May 11–13, 1990, at the Holiday Inn Hotel and Convention Center in Denver, Colorado, Horrorfest '90 promises to be a real treat for King fans and fans of the horror genre.

Although Horrorfest '89 was promoted as a Stephen King convention, subsequent cons will also emphasize the horror genre in general—an alternative to the World Fantasy Con, the annual gathering of horror aficionados that, lately, has become a gathering place for pros in the field.

Con chairman Ken Morgan has already firmed up the transportation and lodging arrangements, as well as the convention programming.

- Pre-registration is $15 through October 1, 1989; $20 through March 1, 1990; and $25 thereafter. (Registration at the door is $25.)
  Supporting memberships are also available at $10 ($15 outside the U.S.). Supporting members receive the *Horrorfest Press*, a newsletter published twice a year (September and March), and the con program book.
- Lodging at the Holiday Inn is $45 a night (up to four persons).
- Discounted airfare is available through Morgan with Continental Airlines.
- Discounted car rental is available through Morgan with Alamo Rent-a-car.

Guests of honor include Prudy Taylor Board (horror novelist), Edward

Bryant (science fiction author), James van Hise and Jessie Horsting (publisher/ editor of *Midnight Graffiti*), Vincent Jö-Nés (artist guest-of-honor), Thomas Schellenberger (fan guest-of-honor), and Dan Simmons (novelist).

Stephen King will also be invited, says Morgan, who noted that he was also invited on numerous occasions to the first Horrorfest but did not attend.

The programming will include the traditional Friday night buffet dinner (with drawings for various door-prizes), midnight readings, dawn-to-dusk films, dealer's room, benefit auction, and various panels. Because of the increased space available to the con committee, the con will also have an art show and a con suite, an amphitheatre for films, and hospitality suites.

Horrorfest 1991

Tentative plans are to hold the third Horrorfest on May 17–19, 1991, at the same site of the 1990 con: the Holiday Inn in Denver, Colorado. Bob Eggelton, an artist whose work has graced numerous horror novels, is the Guest-of-Honor.

For Information

Send a SASE to: Horrorfest '90, Attn: Ken Morgan, P.O. Box 277652, Riverdale, Illinois 60627-7652.

BOOK PUBLISHING

"My Say"
by Stephen King

Publishers Weekly, *the trade publication for the book industry, has an opinion page, "My Say," in which matters of interest to the trade are addressed.*

In this piece, Stephen King responds to a "My Say" column by Ron Busch that was published in the November 15, 1985, issue.

It's wonderful that Ron Busch has had some time to think about the problems in paperback publishing. . . . He has pinpointed the problem, but has missed the clearest cause.

Why aren't people waiting around for the paperback? I offer my own experience as an answer. During the first 24 years of my life I bought only one hardcover book—William Manchester's *Death of a President*—to give as a gift. Although I was (and am) a book-junkie, the idea of *buying* hardcovers never crossed my mind. I used to look into the windows of bookstores with the idle curiosity of, let us say, a construction worker looking at the necklaces in the display windows of Tiffany's. I grew up in lower middle-class circumstances, married early, became a father early. My first job as a breadwinner was pumping gas and some time after, I became a schoolteacher with a yearly income of $6,400. The hardcovers in our house always went back to the library in two weeks. What books we bought were paperbacks. I was not the exception but the rule. My good wife and I, along with those in our age group, *were* the paperback market in its golden age of sales. We were Baby Boomers, members of a generation with the widest reading ability and the greatest income expectation in history.

I started buying hardcovers after Doubleday sold the paperback rights of my first novel, *Carrie*, to New American Library for $400,000. All of a sudden I could afford to buy hardcovers. Maybe I beat some of my fellow Baby Boomers by a couple of years, and maybe I'm making more dough than most of them now, but

Scott Haskell, Photo courtesy of the *Bangor Daily News*

Stephen King signs *Danse Macabre* and Tabitha King signs *Small World* in a Bangor bookstore.

my experience still parallels theirs. We came of age in an economy depressed by war, a glutted job market, and financial recession. We, the media's Flower Children of '72, became the media's Yuppies of '84—making not just a living wage but a relaxing one.

What have we done with our discretionary income? Among other things, we have become bookbuyers. And what Ron Busch doesn't mention is this: we stopped waiting for the reprint because we could afford to buy at the source. I can trace that crucial market transition in my own career. Although Busch mentions me as one of today's bestselling authors who started in paperbacks, that is not the case; Doubleday was my original publisher. I don't think I got radically better between *The Stand* (which topped out at #12 hardcover and at #1 in paperback) and *The Dead Zone* (which was #1 on both lists); I think that many of the readers in my age-group had, like myself, finally reached a financial point in their lives when they no longer *had* to wait for the paperback.

Busch points to the fairly recent practice of discounting hardcovers as one of the reasons why paperback sales have lagged, and he's right, but he fails to put it in context. You can't discount an item unless it sells. If you try it, you take a beating. Discounting could not happen until volume sales made it possible. So my idea is simply this: paperback sales have not slumped because paperbacks finally broke the $3.95 threshold; similar fears about the $2.95 threshold proved unfounded. They slumped because paperbacks have become steadily less necessary to those in the mood to buy. Ironically, paperback prices have probably been pushed up for the same reasons that hardcover prices escalated so rapidly in the '60s and '70s: when your volume is off, you gotta raise your unit price and hope for a hit.

What can paperback publishers do? The obvious answer is not in-book advertising or independent production (which, in the movie business, has led not to the encouragement of creativity but to a repetitive series of sexy teenpix, slasher films, and neo-war movies) but a mind change. This is very traumatic for book people; they think well, but are innovative as a last resort.

Part of the problem is simply self-image. Since 1945 or so, paperback publishers have seen themselves simultaneously as the only game in town and the junkyard dogs of the book business. Now, suddenly, neither is true. That there is still an audience for paperbacks can be shown by a curious negative—the dog that *didn't* bark, as Holmes might have said. When John Saul and V.C. Andrews— both extremely popular writers of paperback originals—were published in hardcover, the results were disappointing, yet the sales of these writers in softcovers have been and continue to be phenomenal.

Sales potential exists now. Realization of that potential depends upon the willingness of paperback publishers to develop their own stable of reliable, salable writers (and this, as Busch indicates, depends to a large degree on the willingness of houses who sell both hard and soft to separate their trade and to drum into the heads of all concerned an 11th commandment: Thou Shalt Not Covet Thy Neighbor's Scribbler) and to widen their commitment to sell books not already pre-sold, either by the name of the writer or by their own megabuck investments.

Paperback publishers need to go back to the beginning and start looking not just for bucks but for good writers; to form a supportive bond with these writers. In the past, paperback publishers have been reapers. Now they must begin to plant and cultivate as well.

My Pretty Pony, the sixth book in the Artists and Writers Series published by the Library Fellows of the Whitney Museum of American Art, is a gift fit for a king. Limited to 280 copies, the book will most likely be out of print soon after publication, which isn't surprising. What did surprise King fans, however, was the price: $2,200. The most expensive King book ever to be published, *My Pretty Pony* was priced "in line with what the other books [in the series] cost," said series editor May Castleberry.

Explains Castleberry, the project began when artist Barbara Kruger, a King reader, suggested Stephen King as an author. May Castleberry then wrote to King, describing the series and the technical aspects of the project.

Three months passed with no word from King. Then Castleberry received a forty-page story of over nine thousand words written especially for this project. *My Pretty Pony* is, said Barbara Kruger in *Artnews,* "about a family in upstate New York, about a relationship between a child, his grandfather, and his horse."

The Artist

Barbara Kruger is a graphic commercial designer who lives in New York City. Her work has been "shown widely at museum and exhibitions places including the Whitney Museum of American Art, New York; *Documenta,* Kassel, West Germany; the Museum of Modern Art, New York; and the Venice Biennale, Italy," according to the brochure for *My Pretty Pony.*

In addition to doing the graphic design, Kruger rendered nine color lithographs.

Symbolic Collaboration

Unlike books on which the artist and writer work closely together, *My Pretty Pony* was midwifed by Castleberry; Kruger and King never had direct contact. "Not only didn't I want to go up to Maine, I didn't even ask to get from King any instructions on how to handle the text," said Kruger in an interview with *Artnews:*

> Because it's so much a story about life and death and time, I really wanted to visualize the literalness of time passing, so I used a real digital clock embedded

Courtesy of the Public Relations Department, the Whitney Museum of Art, New York, NY.

The limited edition of *My Pretty Pony,* published by the Whitney Museum—$2,200. (Note the *functioning* clock on the cover.)

in a piece of stainless steel as the cover. It was important for me to design the book using my experience in graphic design. I had to visualize the text not only in pages but also in terms of how the book is organized: the size of the materials, the typeface, the spacing and leading, the colors, and the papers we used.

Technical Specifications

According to the brochure:

The book was designed by Barbara Kruger and produced by May Castleberry, Artists and Writers Series Editor at the Whitney Museum of American Art. Nine [color] lithographs have been proofed and printed on Rives paper by Maurice Sanchez and James Miller at Derriere L'Etoile Studios in New York. The text has been set by hand and printed by letterpress in twenty-four point Century Schoolbook at A. Colish in Mount Vernon, New York, under the supervision of Jerry Kelly. Sixteen pages, including the title and colophon in Helvetica Bold, have been printed by silkscreen by Pinwheel in New York. The book has been bound in leather, cloth, and metal at BookLab in Austin, Texas, under the supervision of Craig Jensen. The stainless steel cover, inset with a Big Time digital timepiece, has been manufactured by Herman Hirsch at Hi-Tech Stainless Steel Specialties in Dallas, Texas. Each book measures $13^{1}/_{2}$ by 21 inches.

Limited Edition

The edition is limited to 280 copies. Of the 150 copies for sale to the general public, fifty have been sold at a prepublication price of $1,800 per book, with the remaining copies offered at $2,200. One hundred copies were reserved for Whitney Library Fellows, the museum's private collection, and patrons of the museum. Thirty copies made up the "artists' edition," identical to the other copies; Kruger and King each received fifteen copies.

Trade Edition

Castleberry explained that the plan is for the museum to copublish a trade edition with Alfred A. Knopf. The museum, as the book packager, will supply printed and bound books ready for distribution to Knopf, which will handle sales to the book trade.

A facsimile of the Whitney Museum edition, the trade edition will be published in hardback in October 1989 and sell for $50. A sixty-eight page hardback, $9^{1}/_{4}$ by $13^{1}/_{2}$ inches, this edition will have a print run set by King at 15,000 copies. Kruger has contributed nine color lithographs and sixteen illustrations.

Lord John Press

A small press that specializes in limited-edition books and broadsides, Lord John Press recently celebrated its first decade with the publication of *Lord John Ten: A Celebration.* With original short stories, essays, poetry, photographs, and a play from twenty-seven contributors, the book is indeed a literary and artistic celebration. Its limited, signed edition (200 copies, $100) is an elegant book that is unquestionably a treasure.

One author declined to contribute because he had nothing of suitable length. Instead, he offered a rare novella that publisher Herb Yellin quickly agreed to publish. The author? Stephen King. The work? *Dolan's Cadillac,* a work of fiction that had previously appeared as a serialized story in early issues of *Castle Rock* in 1985.

Dolan's Cadillac

It wasn't quite that easy, though. Yellin had been waiting for years for the right King project. The publisher recalled that it was "seven or so years after I had met him in San Francisco, and he had promised that I was third on his list of small presses to do a book. I am patient and *Dolan's Cadillac* fits in more with the type of books we publish. It is a story of revenge, a theme that I understand and appreciate, so the 'fit' was good."

The book was published in two editions: a limited signed edition of 1,000 copies ($100), and a deluxe signed edition of 100 copies ($250), both of which went out of print rapidly.

"Letters from Hell"

When Yellin read King's essay about the letters he received from his fans, published as "'Ever Et Raw Meat?' and Other Weird Questions" in the *New York Times* in 1987, he wrote to King for permission to publish it as a broadside, and King agreed. Retitled "Letters from Hell," the broadside was published in an edition of 500 numbered copies, signed by King. It was printed by letterpress in three colors on heavyweight Arches paper, twenty by twenty-five inches.

Yellin expects that, unlike *Dolan's Cadillac,* the broadside will be in print until fall 1989. (I strongly urge you to get a copy. The only King broadside published, it's a work of art.)

A Look Back

Lord John Press was founded in 1977 and is the one-man operation of Herb Yellin in Northridge, California. Despite its size, the publishing house has approximately seventy titles to its credit. Its list of authors is impressive, a virtual "who's who" in contemporary American fiction. (Among its authors are former President Gerald Ford, John Barth, Donald Barthelme, Ray Bradbury, Raymond Carver, and Ken Kesey.) Each book or broadside is published in a limited edition—rarely exceeding a few hundred copies—and then sold through mail order and specialty book dealers around the world. As you would expect, each book is a unique marriage of text and art, design and binding; each broadside, an elegant piece of design and printing, usually with specially commissioned art.

The Appeal of the Limited Edition

At a time when a new King novel is published in a print run of over a million copies in hardback and, later, reprinted as a paperback with a run of three million copies, why buy a limited edition?

As Howard Wornom, a recent customer of Lord John Press, explains:

> I never knew that people cared enough to do them *right*. I love books—I love the way that they're crafted, I love the way the pages turn, I love it when there's good paper stock in it, if the publisher does something interesting, intriguing or imaginative. I think the imagination and the love and care someone puts into *making* the book are just as important as the care that goes into writing the book.

A Look Ahead

An ambitious anthology, edited by Yellin, will be published in 1990. *Jagged-Cut Image* will include contributions from Clive Barker, Joyce Carol Oates, Stephen King, Peter Straub, Ray Bradbury, Ramsey Campbell, Whitley Streiber, and Dennis Etchison. "The arrangements are far from complete but this is an exciting project just to contemplate," says Yellin in a publisher's note in the 1987–88 catalogue.

Ordering Information

Catalogues are free. Write to Lord John Press, 19073 Los Alimos Street, Northridge, California 91326.

Philtrum Press
King's Book Publishing Company

The most interesting fact about Philtrum Press is its publisher, Stephen King. Philtrum Press is where he goes to publish whatever he wants. There commercial considerations are not a predominant concern, as they are with his trade publishers.

The backlist is short: *The Plant* (three pamphlets, irregularly published as Christmas greetings, a novel in progress), the first edition of *The Eyes of the Dragon* (a limited-edition book), and a novel by Don Robertson, *The Ideal, Genuine Man,* subsequently distributed by Putnam. (Of these, only the Robertson novel is currently in print.)

There is no frontlist. The truth is, one never knows what King will publish, or when. You may write to get on the mailing list, but the best way to find out what will be published is to subscribe to *Castle Rock*.

Here's what has been published:

The Plant

Unlike most of us who glut the mail with Christmas cards, King prefers, instead, to send something more personalized: like a limited-edition pamphlet of a novel in progress, *The Plant*. Like "Jerusalem's Lot," a short story in epistolary form, *The Plant* is told through the use of letters and diaries. It has been published infrequently in an edition of 226 copies (200 numbered, 26 lettered) and, says Harlan Ellison, is King in rare form: ". . . those of us who have been privileged to read the first couple of sections of *The Plant* . . . perceive a talent of uncommon dimensions."

The Plant is the story of an unpublished horror writer, Carlos Detweiler, who submits his novel, *True Tales of Demon Infestations,* to an editor at Zenith Books, John Kenton. Upon receiving the novel, Kenton is horrified to see lifelike photographs of rituals and human sacrifice. He promptly sends these to the police who search in vain for Detweiler. The latter sends Kenton a letter stating that a plant will be sent.

Because of its limited distribution—to King's friends only—installments of *The Plant* are expensive: $1,500 to $2,000 each.

The tale is far from completed, and no word has yet surfaced on publication in another edition. Notwithstanding, as all major King work has been made available in trade hardback or paperback editions, *The Plant* very likely will see print as a separate book, as part of a collection, or as a small-press book (a limited-edition book or, perhaps, a chapbook).

The Eyes of the Dragon

Three years before Viking published the trade edition of this novel with illustrations by David Palladini, Philtrum Press published it as a lavish limited edition with illustrations by Kenny Ray Linkous.

In an essay in *Castle Rock*—and available nowhere else—King talked at length about the story behind the publication of this book by his own press. It's a fascinating story, and if you want to read it in full, you can get the back issues from *Castle Rock* (June 1985, July 1985).

When the novel was completed, King realized it would be years before it could be published. In addition, it, unlike most of his books, was not horror; it was a fairy tale for children of all ages. Rather than let the completed book go unpublished for several years, King opted to publish it himself.

King enlisted the aid of Michael Alpert, a close friend and book designer. With a little serendipity, Alpert met an unpublished artist, Kenny Ray Linkous, who rendered the pen-and-ink illustrations. The plan, explained King, was to publish 1,250 copies—sell 1,000 copies so that he could afford to give away 250 copies to people on his Christmas greeting list. It was, at best, a breakeven proposition. Through a carefully administered lottery, all copies were sold. Now, five years later, the book is an expensive collector's item: the copies distributed to those on his Christmas greeting list command $1,500–$2,000 each; the ones sold through the lottery garner $750 each.

A beautifully designed book encased in a specially designed slipcase, this oversized volume was printed with handset type on imported handmade paper with numerous custom illustrations.

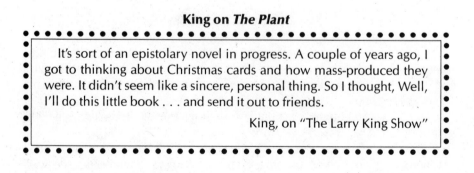

King on *The Plant*

It's sort of an epistolary novel in progress. A couple of years ago, I got to thinking about Christmas cards and how mass-produced they were. It didn't seem like a sincere, personal thing. So I thought, Well, I'll do this little book . . . and send it out to friends.

King, on "The Larry King Show"

The Ideal, Genuine Man

The second book published by Philtrum Press, *The Ideal, Genuine Man* is a contemporary novel by Don Robertson, who is described in the flap copy as "one of America's least-known and most articulate novelists."

Don Robertson is an authentic American voice. He has been acknowledged by King—along with Richard Matheson and John D. MacDonald—as a major literary influence on his own writing style.

Published in a trade edition and a limited edition (out of print), at $25 and $50 respectively, the novel was printed by the Meriden–Stinehour Press of Lunenburg, Vermont, and designed by Michael Alpert—the same team that put together *The Eyes of the Dragon* three years earlier. The work currently is distributed by Putnam and in its third printing. The retail price is $25.

Looking Down the Road

Philtrum Press has announced no books for 1989, but with King one can never be sure. If a book project strikes his fancy, he can afford to indulge himself, to the delight of his fans.

The best source of information on future titles is *Castle Rock*, the official King newsletter.

Specialty Publishers

Their names are the stuff of dreams—and nightmares: Phantasia Press, Dark Harvest, Land of Enchantment, Scream Press, Hill House, and the classic Arkham House. Typically one-person operations, specialty presses specialize in handsome, collectible editions of fiction and nonfiction by name authors. The editions are sold primarily through an in-house mailing list or through specialty dealers. They are seldom available in bookstores—except specialty stores that deal exclusively with this kind of material.

The best way to order is to deal directly with the publisher, or with a specialty dealer that handles orders by mail. This overview covers what you need to know about what Scream Press publisher Jeff Conner calls the "wonderful, wacky world of small-press publishing."

Appeal of the Limited Edition

By far the biggest selling point is that the limited edition sports the autograph of the author and, depending on the book, the autograph of the artist. Since some authors do not promote their works through book signings in bookstores or elsewhere, a limited edition may be the only way to get an autograph. (Stephen King, for instance, rarely attends bookstore signings or conventions; likewise, Peter Straub is somewhat reclusive. Both authors, however, have authorized limited editions of their books, which bear their signatures.)

Moreover, the limited edition, compared with the trade edition, is usually much more attractive: typography, artwork, and design are enhanced by special interior stock, endpapers, reinforced bindings, and (sometimes) slipcases.

Dealing with Small Presses

Because small presses are not big businesses, dealing with them requires a little more effort on your part.

1. *Get onto mailing lists.* Many books are announced months before publication and sold out long before publication. In some cases, they may be available only through an unusual arrangement; for instance, Philtrum Press had a lottery to sell 1,000 copies of *The Eyes of the Dragon* by King. The alternative?

Wait for the book to be offered on the collectors' market, but be prepared to pay collector prices.

2. *Subscribe to trade publications.* Because time is of essence in ordering, find out what's being published, by whom, and when by subscribing to *Castle Rock* (if you're a Stephen King fan) or *Locus* (for the horror, science-fiction, and fantasy fields; for subscription information, write to Locus Publications, P.O. Box 13305, Oakland, California 94661).

3. *Order early.* A book surely to be in demand may be out of print within weeks of publication. (Recently, Donald Grant published an anthology of original horror fiction, *Prime Evil,* signed by its thirteen contributors, including Stephen King and Peter Straub. The most expensive book he has ever published, *Prime Evil* went for $200 and sold out within weeks. Now, copies are $450 and up.) If you can't type, print neatly; illegible orders are impossible to decipher and will only delay shipment of your order.

4. *Be patient.* A magazine in the field charitably described Scream Press's publication schedule as "elastic." Publisher Jeff Conner explains in his catalogues that if you don't want to wait, then order from a specialty dealer when the book is out. As for publication delays, Conner invokes Murphy's law: "And hey, man, *shit happens!*"

5. *When corresponding, enclose a self-addressed, stamped envelope.* Most small presses deal exclusively by mail. If you've got a question, enclose a self-addressed postcard or stamped envelope for a reply. It's a basic courtesy, one that any small publisher will appreciate.

6. *Buy regularly from a specialty dealer.* One-stop shops for books in the field, specialty booksellers deal with limited editions all the time. They know what's available, advertise them in their catalogues, and carefully pack them to arrive in the best condition possible. Many are collectors themselves and are very concerned—some say obsessed—about book condition. *Don't* wait to buy when you've got a special book you want—the same one that everyone else is trying to buy. Be a regular customer and you'll be treated with a little extra attention and care. (For a list of recommended specialty stores, see Appendix 6; for a more detailed listing, see the article on pp. 120–122.)

7. *Inspect the book when you get it.* Because many of these books are bought by collectors, the book goes out of the shipping container and into a plastic bag—hidden defects and all. During the printing and binding process, or during the shipping process, inadvertent damage is possible. (I've had two limited-edition books arrive in damaged condition—one a $120 book, the other a $200 book. And, yes, the specialty publishers are used to dealing with this; they keep extra copies on hand for such accidents. Send your book back, preferably by UPS, and they'll send a replacement copy.)

Specialty Publishers

ARKHAM HOUSE (Sauk City, Wisconsin 53583). Catalogues issued. One of the oldest small presses in the field, and one of the most prestigious, Arkham House was the first to specialize in horror fiction. It's safe to say that Arkham House inspired many of today's small presses, especially Donald M. Grant and Whispers Press. Established by the late August Derleth—writer, author, and poet—Arkham House prints its books in beautiful, uniform editions; the paper is Winnebago Eggshell and the boards are Holliston Black Novelex. Its first book was H.P. Lovecraft's *The Outsider and Others,* published in 1939. (I've seen a copy for sale in a bookseller's catalogue at $800.) Arkham House has published some of the finest practitioners in the genre, including Ray Bradbury; his first book, *Dark Carnival,* published in 1947, is now worth $400 and up.

DARK HARVEST (P.O. Box 941, Arlington Heights, Illinois 60006). Catalogues issued. A relative newcomer to the field, Dark Harvest was established in 1983 by Paul Mikol and Scott Stadalsky. Twenty published books make up its list. Dark Harvest has published Stephen King, Dean Koontz, Rick McCammon, Clive Barker, and other prominent authors in the field. Using its in-house mailing list of fifteen hundred to eighteen hundred names as the principal means of getting the word out on new titles, Dark Harvest sends notices of new titles for which advance orders are taken once the book is on hand and ready to go to press.

Its *Night Visions* series, now in its sixth volume, is a continuing showcase for new talent and established masters. Mikol explained the genesis of the series. Anthologies rarely feature more than one story by any author; Mikol thought, why not have *more* than one story in the book?

Of special interest to King fans: *Night Visions 5,* edited by Douglas E. Winter, featured three new stories by Stephen King, three stories by Dan Simmons, and one long story by George R.R. Martin. (Volume 6 has just been published, with a long introductory essay by Dean R. Koontz.)

DONALD M. GRANT, PUBLISHER, INC. (P.O. Box 187, Hampton Falls, New Hampshire 03844). Catalogues issued. Established by Donald M. Grant, this highly regarded small press has published more King books than any other small press. With over a hundred books published since its inception in 1945, the house is a standard by which other small presses compare themselves.

The publisher takes advance orders when the book is on hand and ready to go to print. In cases of delays, it will send you a letter notifying you of the nature of the delay.

King titles published include: *Christine, The Dark Tower II: The Drawing of the Three, The Dark Tower: The Gunslinger,* and *The Talisman* (a magnificent two-volume, slipcased edition—the most elegant King limited published).

Prime Evil, a recent title edited by Douglas E. Winter, is an original anthology of thirteen stories by heavy hitters in the field, including Stephen King, Peter Straub, Clive Barker, and Dennis Etchison. The limited edition, signed by all thirteen authors and book designer/artist Thomas Canty, was encased in a red felt-lined tray case. Limited to 1,000 copies, and published at $200 a copy, the book went out of print in weeks and has doubled in price on the collector's market.

HILL HOUSE PUBLISHERS (P.O. Box 1783, Grand Central Station, New York, New York 10163). Books are announced through flyers. Hill House is a new specialty publisher and was named after the Shirley Jackson novel. It has published a beautiful edition of Peter Straub's *Ghost Story* (400 copies, illustrated by Stephen Gervais, signed by both author and artist; $50).

A recent book, *Faerie Tale* by Raymond E. Feist, has cover art by Don Maitz, and interior illustrations by Lela Dowling. It was limited to 500 numbered copies, signed by the author and artists, and published in March 1988 at a price of $75.

LAND OF ENCHANTMENT (P.O. Box 5360, Plymouth, Michigan 48170). Infrequent mailings. Ambitious publisher Chris Zavisa puts out classy, imaginative books. Published books include two oversized art books (*A Look Back* by Berni Wrightson, the horror illustrator; and *Satan's Tears* by Alex Nino) and Stephen King's *Cycle of the Werewolf* in an oversized edition.

The house's most recent title, *Twilight Eyes* by Dean Koontz, has illustrations by Phil Parks and was published in three editions: a collector's edition (50 copies) at $250; a signature edition (200 copies) at $75; and a trade edition.

LORD JOHN PRESS (19073 Los Alimos Street, Northridge, California 91326). Catalogues issued. Founded in 1977, Lord John Press recently celebrated its tenth anniversary with an elegant book, *Lord John Ten,* which is a superb example of small-press publishing at its finest. Publisher of *Dolan's Cadillac* and the broadside "Letters from Hell," both by Stephen King, Lord John Press does exquisite editions of works by major American authors. (See herein, "Lord John Press," on pp. 109–110.)

PHANTASIA PRESS, INC. (5536 Crispin Way, West Bloomfield, Michigan 48033). Catalogues issued. Publisher Alex Berman specializes in science fiction and fantasy. In business for eleven years, Phantasia Press has an excellent reputation for its handsome editions and modest prices. The current catalogue lists books by many top names in the field, including Orson Scott Card, Spider Robinson, L. Sprague de Camp, David Brin, C. J. Cherryh (numerous titles), Alan Dean Foster, Harlan Ellison, Mike Resnick, and Philip Jose Farmer.

In Phantasia's *Stalking the Nightmare* by Harlan Ellison, a writer of whom King writes at length in *Danse Macabre,* Stephen King contributes a memorable introduction to the book. In its second printing, the trade edition is $16. (If you have any interest in Ellison's work, order *Medea: Harlan's World*, the most "extravagant Phantasia publication," as Berman puts it. In its second printing, this book is beautifully illustrated by Frank Kelly Freas.)

PHILTRUM PRESS (P.O. Box 1186, Bangor, Maine 04401). Unlike the other small presses in this overview, Philtrum Press publishes infrequently. But when it does, the results are worth it. Philtrum has published the limited edition of *The Eyes of the Dragon*, three pamphlets of a work in progress (*The Plant*), and a new novel by Don Robertson. The publisher? Stephen King. (See herein, "Philtrum Press," pp. 111–113.)

SCREAM PRESS (P.O. Box 481146, Los Angeles, California 90048). Catalogues issued. Publisher Jeff Conner, who specializes in horror fiction, has the most ambitious program devoted to the horror genre. Founded in 1982 with the publication of Dennis Etchison's first collection of short fiction, *The Dark Country*, Scream Press has earned a reputation for innovative publishing. The imaginative Conner has a background in the graphic arts and design. He has published Clive Barker's *Books of Blood*, Ramsey Campbell, Dennis Etchison, Michael McDowell, and has announced books by Anne Rice (*Interview with the Vampire* in a typographically preferred text), Clive Barker (*Books of Blood IV–VI*), and Richard Matheson (an eighty-six-story collection, *Collected Stories of Richard Matheson*). Many of the volumes are illustrated with the work of J. K. Potter, the photographer/artist whose work has received critical attention and acclaim.

Conner published what many believe is one of the most beautiful limited editions—certainly the most imaginative—of a Stephen King book. Two years in the making, Conner's edition of *Skeleton Crew* is a massive, oversized, visually imaginative coffee-table book with illustrations by J.K. Potter.

Note: Scream Press is often tardy, but the wait is worth it. (It does confirm your order by postcard and has recently added a computerized system to update subscribers on delays in shipping.)

STARMONT HOUSE (P.O. Box 851, Mercer Island, Washington 98040). Catalogues issued. Specializing in scholarly books about the fantasy and science-fiction field, Starmont House has published eight books about Stephen King; two additional titles are slated for 1989. (For more information, see "Starmont House" on pp. 123–125.)

UNDERWOOD-MILLER (708 Westover Drive, Lancaster, Pennsylvania 17601). Catalogues issued. A long-time small press that has published more than one hundred fifty hardcovers since 1975, including some of the most important books in the field, Underwood–Miller is highly regarded in the field. Books published include *The Collected Stories of Philip K. Dick* (a five-volume set, 2,100 pages, nearly a million words), *The Selected Stories of Robert Bloch* (three volumes, 100 short stories, 1,248 pages), and numerous titles by Robert Silverberg and, of course, Jack Vance (U–M is the première Vance publisher).

Publisher of one of the first collections of nonfiction about Stephen King, *Fear Itself,* U–M followed up with other books on King: *Kingdom of Fear, Reign of Fear, Bare Bones,* and *Feast of Fear.* In addition, the house packaged *Stephen King Goes to Hollywood,* written by Jeff Conner (Scream Press publisher) and published by New American Library.

A recent title is *Harlan Ellison's Watching,* a collection of Ellison's essays on film (536 pages, $29.95 trade edition, $60 limited edition, signed by the author). For Clive Barker fans there is *Shadows in Eden* by Steven Jones. This is the first nonfiction book about Barker and was written with his complete cooperation. *Shadows* is an ideal book for anyone who wants to know more about the man of whom Stephen King said, "I have seen the future of horror, and its name is Clive Barker." (*Shadows in Eden* will be published in a trade hardback edition at $29.95, and a slipcased, numbered, and signed edition of 500 copies at $75.00.)

WHISPERS PRESS (70 Highland Avenue, Binghamton, New York 13905). Infrequent catalogues. The book publishing arm of *Whispers,* the award-winning literary magazine devoted to the field, Whispers Press is an infrequent but quality publisher. *Whispers* and Whispers Press are the work of Stuart D. Schiff, a long-time fan, collector, anthologist, and publisher. Schiff has published Fritz Leiber (*Rime Isle* with Tim Kirk illustrations), Basil Smith, Robert Bloch, Isaac Asimov, and many others. Write him for a catalogue and for subscription rates to *Whispers.*

Specialty Dealers

For anyone interested in buying first editions, limited editions, or other collectibles by science-fiction, fantasy, or horror writers, there's only one place to go: the specialty bookseller. All the dealers below issue catalogues.

MICHAEL AUTREY (13624 Franklin Street, No. 5, Whittier, California 90602; telephone, 213/945-6719, evenings only). A specialist in Stephen King and Clive Barker material, Autrey maintains a sizable inventory of titles.

L.W. CURRY (Elizabethtown, New York 12932). A specialist in out-of-print science-fiction, fantasy, and horror books, L.W. Curry is the author of *Science Fiction and Fantasy Authors: A Bibliography of First Printings of Their Fiction and Nonfiction*.

DREAMHAVEN BOOKS AND ARTS (1300 Fourth Street, S.E., Minneapolis, Minnesota 55414; telephone, 612/379-8924). Proprietor Greg Ketter deals not only in new and used fantasy, science-fiction and horror books but also in comic material (books, portfolios, and specialty publications).

BARRY R. LEVIN SCIENCE FICTION AND FANTASY LITERATURE (726 Santa Monica Boulevard, Suite 201, Santa Monica, California 90401; telephone, 213/458-6111). The showroom is open from Monday to Friday, 10:00 A.M. to 3:00 P.M., closed Saturdays, and open Sundays by appointment only. Levin deals extensively by mail order. Catalogues and newsletters are issued.

Established in 1973, this company specializes in the most collectible editions and states available. Barry R. Levin is considered an expert in the field of rare science-fiction and fantasy books, and is the source for the *crème de la crème* in collectibles. The January 1989 catalogue offered, among other things, a holographic notebook belonging to Stephen King ($6,000), *My Pretty Pony* by Stephen King (Whitney Museum, $2,300), *The Shuttered House* by H.P. Lovecraft ($800), the lettered state of *The Dark Tower: The Gunslinger* ($2,300), and carvings by poet Clark Ashton Smith ($500–$6,000).

OVERLOOK CONNECTION (P.O. Box 526, Woodstock, Georgia 30188; telephone, 404/926-1762). Named after the fictional hotel in Stephen King's *The*

Shining, Overlook Connection is a new company. Proprietors David and Laurie Hinchberger sell new and used books in the horror field through their irregularly published catalogue, a tabloid. The company is distinguished by the personal endorsements of David Hinchberger, a fan and an avid reader, and his overly enthusiastic minireviews of forthcoming books (I'd prefer to see more straightforward reportage). If you want a taste of what's being published in the horror field, Overlook's informal, chatty, and highly personalized catalogue is a good place to start.

BUD PLANT, INC. (P.O. Box 1689, Grass Valley, California 95945). Proprietor Bud Plant handles limited editions in the fantasy, science-fiction, and horror fields and the comic-book field. Plant is an established dealer who has been selling to collectors for two decades. His catalogues are thorough: illustrated, properly descriptive, and with specific recommendations on what to buy and why.

VAGABOND BOOKS (2076 Westwood Boulevard, Los Angeles, California 90025; telephone, 213/475-2700). A good source for American first editions, current and out of print. (Vagabond has hosted numerous author signings and will send you an announcement. You may then send in an order and get an autographed, sometimes personalized, first edition.)

ROBERT AND PHYLLIS WEINBERG (15145 Oxford Drive, Oak Forest, Illinois 60452; telephone, 312/687-5765). A six-issue subscription to the Weinberg catalogue is $3. An excellent source for new material in the field, this company is the mail-order dealer of choice. The November 1988 catalogue offers a wide selection of material organized by category: *horror* (fiction and nonfiction, trade publishers and specialty publishers, semiprofessional magazines), *calendars, fantasy* (fiction and nonfiction, trade publishers and specialty publishers, semiprofessional magazines), *mystery* (fiction, semiprofessional magazines), *odds and ends* (cartoon collections, paperbacks, fiction, fan magazines, portfolios, booklets), and *science fiction* (fiction and nonfiction).

Weinberg does not list books in his catalogue until the books are in print. (I wish everyone did that.)

Ordering Tips

1. When ordering by mail, it's a good idea to write your name and address *on the letter* because the envelope may be discarded.

2. Provide your work and home phone numbers in case there is a question about your order.

3. Because many dealers prefer to ship by UPS, list your street address; UPS does *not* deliver to a post office box. (If a dealer sends you a package by UPS to your post office box, UPS will usually send you a postcard and ask you to call a

phone recorder and leave your street address. This may delay delivery and in some cases cause the package to be returned to the sender.)

4. Send only a check or money order. Never send cash in the mail. (Some dealers accept credit cards over the phone; ordering information can be found in their catalogues.)

5. In the event you want a one-of-a-kind book, list alternative titles in case your first choice is sold out.

6. If you have a special interest, let the dealer know. He may contact you when a special item comes in. If there are specific items you want, let him know. If he doesn't have an item, he may be able to get it for you.

7. Be a regular customer. Make sure the dealer knows who you are and what you collect, and he'll look out for you.

8. On correspondence requiring a response, enclose a self-addressed, stamped envelope as a matter of courtesy.

Starmont House

*I saw a need to publish reference books in the fantasy
and science-fiction field.*

Ted Dikty

Ted Dikty's Starmont House is a small press that specializes in short-run books in the fantasy and science-fiction field. It is located in Mercer Island, Washington, far from Publisher's Row in New York City, and Dikty wouldn't have it any other way.

At sixty-eight, Ted Dikty, a long-time fan and publisher, has learned through trial and error how to publish books successfully. The founder of Carcosa House and a partner in Shasta House—a leading small press in the field in the fifties—Dikty is a seasoned publisher whose current catalogue boasts an impressive eighty titles in print with seventy-five more listed as forthcoming in 1989. It's an ambitious publishing schedule, one that spells profits if his winning formula remains constant: low typesetting costs (use the author's computer diskette to set type), small print runs based on advance orders (one hundred fifty to seven hundred fifty copies), little inventory (reprint small quantities, based on demand), and inexpensive printing (a Xerographic book printing and binding process developed by the Xerox Corporation).

The only criticism, according to Dikty, is that some of the books—particularly the earlier ones—are difficult to read. Set in typewritten text, they lack the grace and readability of typeset text. Dikty explains, however, that he's now using a laserprinter with traditional fonts like Times Roman to improve the appearance of the books.

Because 80 percent of Starmont's sales is to libraries, and because Starmont books are not available in bookstores, the best way to get them is to get the catalogue and order directly from the publisher. Because of the small print runs, however, Dikty recommends ordering new titles as early as possible. "Our system of publication does not allow for large stocks of any title, and any particular title may go out of stock quickly. While we generally reprint titles for which there is a demand, nevertheless there may be a considerable delay before copies are again available."

The bestselling title? Douglas E. Winter's book on Stephen King, the sixteenth book in the Starmont Reader's Guide series. Published at $5.95 in trade paperback in 1982, the book sold 3,200 copies. Dikty explains that he could have sold more copies, but when Winter sold a revised and expanded version to New American Library, the Starmont House edition went out of print. (NAL's edition, *Stephen King: The Art of Darkness*, is currently available in a mass-market paperback for $4.95.)

Noting the increased attention King was getting in scholarly circles and the popularity of King with the science-fiction and fantasy community, Starmont embarked on an ambitious program to publish books *about* King. To date nine books on King have been published—eight still in print—and two more are slated for 1989.

Titles by Michael R. Collings

The Annotated Guide to Stephen King is a primary and secondary bibliography. Available in paperback for $9.95 and hardback for $19.95, this 176-page book was published in 1986. Until the publication of Douglas Winter's definitive bibliography (perhaps a 1989 or 1990 release from Donald M. Grant, Publisher), the Collings guide will serve admirably for scholars, researchers, serious fans, and students.

The Films of Stephen King is a critical examination of the films based on King's work with the emphasis on "the inevitable seesaw between author and filmmaker."

The Many Facets of Stephen King takes a look at King's books from a thematic perspective. Available in paperback for $9.95 and hardback for $17.95, this 190-page book discusses the King canon by writing phases.

The Shorter Works of Stephen King (cowritten with David Engebretson). In paperback ($9.95) and hardback ($17.95), and published in 1985, this 202-page book is "a comprehensive study of King's short fiction . . . including not only plot summary but critical approaches to each story, identifying themes, symbols, and relationships between the story and the rest of King's work."

Stephen King as Richard Bachman is the first book-length study about the five books published under King's pen name, Bachman. In paperback ($9.95) and hardback ($17.95), and published in 1985, this 168-page book is a good overview.

The Stephen King Phenomenon broadly views King as a publishing phenomenon. In paperback ($9.95) and hardback ($17.95), and published in 1987, this 144-page book, unlike Collings' other books on King for Starmont, does not have a tight focus. Instead, it takes a broader approach with essays on *It* (with comments from King), King on the bestseller chart, King and the critics, and collecting King; a synopsis of King's college newspaper column ("The Garbage Truck"); and comments on artists who have illustrated King.

Titles by Other Authors

Discovering Stephen King, edited by Darrell Schweitzer. In paperback ($9.95) and hardback (17.95), published in 1985, this 219-page book is a mixture of scholarly essays and general-interest articles about King, the same formula Underwood–Miller has used in three collections of King criticism. (The editor's own contribution, "Collecting Stephen King," is too general, and in places, misleading or inaccurate.)

The Unseen King by Tyson Blue. In paperback ($9.95) and hardback ($19.95). Published in March 1989, this volume—set in laserset type—is an overview of little-seen (not unseen) King material. The book looks at juvenilia, college material, uncollected short fiction, screenplays, miscellaneous nonfiction, and what King terms the "true" limited editions.

The book's drawing card is an informative chapter discussing *The Plant,* the irregularly published chapbooks that are, in fact, installments of a novel-length work in progress.

Unfortunately, the book in general suffers from Blue's awkward prose and, I'm sure, unintentionally humorous comparisons between Blue as a fledgling writer and King.

Forthcoming in 1989

As the twenty-fifth book in the Starmont studies in literary criticism, *The Moral Voyages of Stephen King* by Anthony Magistrale will be a paperback ($9.95) and a hardback ($19.95). The author also wrote *Landscape of Fear: Stephen King's American Gothic* (published by the Bowling Green University Popular Press). Divided into two parts, the book is an analysis of King's major literary themes and philosophical concerns: as the Starmont catalogue describes it, the first half examines "the shape evil takes in his work" and the second half "analyzes the development of the non-traditional family units in King's canon, motherhood as a source for love and salvation, and the role of the writer-artist in his fiction."

First in a series of casebooks, *"The Shining" Reader,* edited by Anthony Magistrale. In paperback at $9.95 and hardback at $19.95, this book focuses on the King novel and the Stanley Kubrick film. Fifteen essays thoroughly examine King's second novel.

For a current catalogue, write to: Starmont House, P.O. Box 851, Mercer Island, Washington 98040.

Forthcoming in 1990

A seventh book by Michael R. Collings, *Infinite Explorations: Art and Artifice in Stephen King's It, Misery, and The Tommyknockers,* and *In the Darkest Night: A Student's Guide to Stephen King* by Tim Murphy.

AUDIO PUBLISHING

```
┌─────────────────────────────────────────────┐
│                                               │
│            Recorded Books                     │
│   Unabridged Stephen King Audiotapes          │
│                                               │
└─────────────────────────────────────────────┘
```

Heard any good books lately?

Ad slogan

In a country where there are forty-two million car cassettes and eighty million portable cassette decks, Sandy Spencer of Recorded Books—"head cook and bottle washer," as he puts it—has carved out a niche for his line of recorded books, unabridged readings of fiction and nonfiction.

Every month forty thousand subscribers receive the Recorded Books catalogue, published approximately every six weeks. In each issue eight to ten new titles are offered for sale or rental. It's like a book club, says Spencer, except there is no negative option—a selection automatically sent to you if you fail to respond. But unlike book clubs, Recorded Books offers its selections on a rental basis.

Libraries account for half of the sales; individuals, the other half. The latter either buy the tapes or, more typically, rent the tapes for a thirty-day period and return them in the pre-addressed, stamped self-mailer. The system works like a charm: you call in the order on the firm's toll-free line, use your charge card to pay for the rental, and Recorded Books ships your selection immediately. If you're on the East Coast, expect to get your selection in two or three days; if on the West Coast, up to six days. The thirty-day rental period begins the day you *receive* the tape, not when it is mailed. When you're finished, simply mail it back.

Stephen King frequently found himself in a car with commuting time on his hands. He preferred driving to New York to flying there to see his publishers, and so he would play Recorded Books' unabridged audiocassette book tapes during the long drive from Bangor.

Later, when King wanted his own work professionally recorded in unabridged readings, Recorded Books was the logical choice. Recorded Books now has an impressive selection of King material: thirty cassettes totaling forty-

"The Author Talks: Stephen King"

"The Author Talks: Stephen King": A Recorded Books audio-cassette, 60 minutes. A profile of and interview with Stephen King, narrated by Frank Muller. $5.50.

This promotional tape begins with King nervously anticipating his reading of "Mrs. Todd's Shortcut" from *Skeleton Crew*. Frank Muller, a professional reader who has read all the King material for Recorded Books, is seated next to King in the studio. King confesses:

> I feel very small sitting next to the master here. This is tough. It's like the understudy: *Get in there and dance your balls off, boy. You ready? Get it over with.*

King reads the story, which is followed by Muller's reading. The remainder of the tape is a creative blend of commentary by King, readings by Muller, and flashbacks by Muller as narrator talking about King's life and writing career, punctuated with the occasional sound of someone banging away at a typewriter and the noisy clatter of a letter-quality printer.

five hours, read professionally by Frank Muller. When there was a discussion on recording *Misery*, King declared himself in a Recorded Books interview: "I've written a book and I hope Frank Muller will read it. He will do such a fantastic job that the blind will see, the lame will walk, and the deaf will hear."

The King material available includes all four novellas from *Different Seasons*, and all the material from *Skeleton Crew*, which contains some of King's best work, including "The Mist" and "The Reach."

Who listens to the tapes? Spencer explains that the average customer is approximately forty years old (between thirty-five and forty-five), affluent (earning $30,000 a year and up), and commutes approximately one hour a day.

Spencer admits that even in the eighties—when bookstores carry both the printed and the audio versions of major titles—there's still a negative perception about books on tape: "These are for blind people, aren't they?"

In a word, no. People have disposable income but not disposable time. The constructive use of dead time (commuting by car, or being on a commercial flight) and the portability and high fidelity of the cassette deck (the Walkman and its copies) are primary factors that have made audiocassettes an alternative source of education and entertainment.

Founded in 1979, Recorded Books now has over four hundred separate titles, all *unabridged*. (King joked that if the firm did *It*, it would have to ship it in a

The Author Talks: King on Reading Books Aloud

It's the total experience of a book to read it aloud. It's a much more intimate experience to listen to a novel aloud. Most people, I think, who listen to novels aloud are people who are novel junkies or book junkies, and they would read matchbook covers if they were stuck alone. [But if] you read a book to yourself, sometimes your eye will skip. The page has a shape, the page has a form of its own, and sometimes if you're reading dialogue that's really interesting to you, and then you get a little block—it may only be six lines long of description or narrative—your eye will register the paragraph and some of the stuff in that paragraph, and drop to the dialogue again. But when you listen, you are not allowed to do that, so that sometimes you can fall totally into [the story] . . . it's almost scary the way it can work.

What I write might change if I wrote strictly for the screen. Having directed a picture, if I ever wrote the screenplay for another movie that I knew I was going to direct, I'm sure that it would have some effect on how I wrote that screenplay. But if I were to write a screenplay for someone else or for just a theoretical audience—never mind who the director would be—I wouldn't change a thing. My idea about production problems or special effects or difficult shots is that's the director's problem. It only would change my style if that were me. And as far as the novels go, I never think about that at all.

book carton. Based on the industry rule of thumb—twenty-five pages of book text equals a one-hour cassette—it would take *forty-six* cassettes to record the book.) Recorded Books has experimented with sound effects, but Spencer said he abandoned the idea pretty quickly. Sound effects, he explained, were too distracting for commuters. "With a good author and good text, you don't need anything else," said Spencer.

Stephen King would agree. Although not fond of abridged recordings—the audio equivalent of the Reader's Digest Condensed Book series—King had authorized a two-cassette abridgment of *Thinner,* published by Listen for Pleasure. Sandy Spencer explained that an abridgment can only be "a sample" of the actual book, since less than twenty percent of the book can be recorded. According to a report in *Publishers Weekly,* King said that "these people do amazing things with books to bring them into line for two cassettes." Still, King's preference is to have unabridged recordings made. (His own readings of the *Dark Tower* books were done on four cassettes for volume one in the series, and eight cassettes for volume two.)

Spencer says there are no plans at Recorded Books to do more King record-

Current Offerings

Available for thirty-day rentals or for purchase, the following unabridged readings of King's fiction, read by Frank Muller, are available:

1. "The Mist" from *Skeleton Crew,* #85230, 3 cassettes, RT (running time) 4½ hours.
   Rental, $9.50
   Purchase, $19.95

2. "The Breathing Method" from *Different Seasons,* #84066, 2 cassettes, RT 3 hours.
   Rental, $7.50
   Purchase, $15.95

3. "Rita Hayworth & Shawshank Redemption" from *Different Seasons,* #84063, 3 cassettes, RT 4½ hours.
   Rental, $9.50
   Purchase, $19.95

4. *Skeleton Crew* (Book One), #85210, 6 cassettes, RT 9 hours, with these stories:
   "The Raft"
   "The Reaper's Image"
   "The Monkey"
   "Cain Rose Up"
   "The Jaunt"
   "Beachworld"
   "Survivor Type"
   "Morning Deliveries"
   "Big Wheels"
   "For Owen"
   "The Man Who Wouldn't Shake Hands"
   "Word Processor of the Gods"
   "The Reach"
   "Uncle Otto's Truck"
      Rental, $12.50
      Purchase, $37.95

5. *Skeleton Crew* (Book Two), #85220, 5 cassettes, RT 7½ hours, with these stories:
   "Mrs. Todd's Shortcut"
   "The Wedding Gig"
   "Nona"
   "Paranoid: A Chant"
   "Here There Be Tygers"
   "The Ballad of the Flexible Bullet"
   "Gramma"
      Rental, $11.50
      Purchase, $34.95

6. "The Body" from *Different Seasons,* #84064, 4 cassettes, RT 6 hours.
   Rental, $10.50
   Purchase, $26.95

7. "Apt Pupil" from *Different Seasons,* #84065, 5 cassettes, RT 7½ hours.
   Rental, $11.50
   Purchase, $34.95

8. "The Ballad of the Flexible Bullet" (available separately, or with *Skeleton Crew* [Book Two]), #85330, 2 cassettes, RT 3 hours.
   Rental, $7.50
   Purchase, $15.95

9. "The Author Talks: Stephen King," #87380, 1 cassette, RT 1 hour. Purchase only, $5.50.

ings, which is unfortunate. Frank Muller, who has read all the King material for Recorded Books, has a feel for the material. But King fans will find other selections available that should curb their disappointment.

One of the three writers who greatly influenced King, Don Robertson, has had two books recorded: *The Greatest Thing Since Sliced Bread* (six cassettes running eight hours) and its sequel, *The Sum & Total of Now* (six cassettes running nine hours).

Ray Bradbury's classic *Fahrenheit 451,* from which King had got the epigram for *Firestarter,* is on four cassettes running over five hours.

And *Dracula,* using the original text, is on twelve cassettes running eighteen hours.

And for those of you who want to hear from the Ghostmaster General himself, there's an exclusive interview with King as part of "The Author Talks" series (No. 87380, $5.50). In this one-hour tape (part interview, part audio sampler), King talks about his work, narrator Frank Muller gives an overview of King's career, and there are readings (audio samplers) from King's work by the author and by Muller. (Throughout this book, in sidebars labeled "The Author Talks: Stephen King," King's comments, slightly edited, are reprinted.)

For a current catalogue, write to Recorded Books (P.O. Box 409, Charlotte Hall, Maryland 20622).

"The Mist" on Audiocassette
A Sound Idea

"The Mist": A ZBS Foundation audiocassette. 1984. Ninety minutes on chrome tape recorded in real time. Directed by Bill Raymond. Story adaptation by M. Fulton. Assistance provided by Dennis Etchison. Musical score by Tim Clark. $12.50.

When Kirby McCauley decided to edit a second volume of horror stories, he quite naturally asked his friend and client Stephen King for a contribution. As McCauley tells it in the introduction to *Dark Forces,* King's story grew from an original length of twenty thousand words to forty thousand words, a short novel.

A powerful work, "The Mist" is one of King's most visual stories, rich in imagery, best visualized in the mind's eye: skull cinema. With headphones on, the story comes alive, slowly enveloping you in a world where the unbelievable becomes believable. (Anyone who has seen the grade-B monster flicks of the fifties will find this dramatization a blast from the past.)

If you haven't read the story, I'll not give away any surprises, except to say that the story is a powerful and satisfying read and is ideally suited for a radio dramatization.

The plot is simple: After a summer storm, a strange mist—not fog—rolls into a small Maine town. The citizens barricade themselves in a supermarket, and soon realize that along with the mist have come monsters. Then the nightmare begins.

Many audiotapes have been done of King's works, including King's unabridged recordings of his first two *Dark Tower* novels, and unabridged and abridged recordings by other readers. But "The Mist" is unique—the first dramatization, the only one done in 3-D sound, and the only one recorded in real time.

Publishers Weekly styled it a

> *frighteningly real and unreal 3-D production, which lets conversation among characters, special effects and eerie music—rather than endless narration—do the work of scaring us. Chockful of sounds you don't want to know from, this is easily the most successful of the 3-D sound productions mentioned here [in a roundup review of horror audiotapes].*

131

Illustration by Kevin Brockway for the ZBS edition of "The Mist."

Art by Kevin Brockway

An Adventure Cassette by ZBS Foundation (a not-for-profit arts organization), "The Mist" is recorded on chrome cassette using state-of-the-art digital recording equipment and utilizes the Kunstkopf binaural sound, a recording process using a special microphone that gives the illusion of three-dimensional sound—best experienced with headphones, which greatly enhance the effect. (I've listened to the tape both through an expensive pair of speakers and through an inexpensive pair of headphones; by far, the headphones provided the better listening experience.)

How to Order

Send a check or money order for $14.00 ($12.50 for "The Mist" and $1.50 for shipping) to ZBS Foundation, R.R. 1, Box 1201, Fort Edward, New York 12828. If you have a Mastercard or VISA, call anytime at 1-800-662-3345 to place an order.

I recommend, however, that you write first to request ZBS's colorful, art-rich catalogue. It also offers "Sticks" by Craig Strete, based on a short story by Karl Edward Wagner ($10), ethereal music by Tim Clark, and two dramatizations of the misadventures of Ruby, "a smart, tough and sexy detective (our favorite galactic gumshoe)."

The Author Talks: King on Fidelity to the Work

FRANK MULLER: Don't all these different versions of "The Mist" begin to distort the original work?

STEPHEN KING: No. Not a recording, not a computer game, not a movie. In fact, probably a bad recording would hurt me more than anything else because the recording seems a lot closer to the mind of the writer. There was a graduate student who came to interview James Cain, who wrote *The Postman Always Ring Twice* and *Double Indemnity* and *Mildred Pierce*, and he moaned to Cain about what the movies had done to his books, and Cain immediately turned around and indicated a shelf behind him in his study and said, "Didn't do a thing. They're all right up there, so far as I can see."

Thinner on Audiocassette

Thinner *by Stephen King writing as Richard Bachman. A Listen for Pleasure audiocassette. 1985. 2 ¹/₂ hours. Two cassettes, Dolby sound. Abridged for recording by Sue Dawson. Produced by Graham Goodwin. $14.95.*

Thinner, a short novel, is professionally read by Paul Sorvino, who starts out by mispronouncing "Bachman" as "*Baych*man." Notwithstanding, Sorvino gives the story a professional reading.

A reading should be transparent; the voice should neither add to nor detract from the work. Fortunately, Sorvino's voice complements the book as the story comes alive.

Thinner is the only Bachman book available on audiocassette and the first novel by King to be adapted to audiocassette. (NAL later published the first two books in the *Dark Tower* series in unabridged readings by King.)

Durkin●Hayes Publishing Ltd., the publisher, has a full-color catalogue showcasing a very good selection of fiction (mysteries, thrillers, science fiction, horror, classics, contemporary titles, children's favorites) and nonfiction (autobiography, biography, and general).

Of particular interest to King fans is the line of horror tapes. Titles include *Phantom of the Opera* by Gaston Leroux (two cassettes), *Dracula* and *Dr. Jekyll and Mr. Hyde* (two cassettes), material by Edgar Allan Poe, *Psycho,* and two books by Peter Straub (King collaborator on *The Talisman*): *If You Could See Me Now,* and *Floating Dragon.*

For More Information

For a free full-color catalogue, write to: Durkin●Hayes Publishing Ltd., One Columbia Drive, Niagara Falls, New York 14305.

Thinner audiocassette and other Durkin • Hayes audiocassettes.

Photo courtesy of Durkin • Hayes Publishing Ltd.

CRITICS

Michael R. Collings
An Interview

If you have any interest in Stephen King beyond reading the books and seeing the movies, you'll inevitably run across Michael R. Collings' six books on Stephen King: The Annotated Guide to Stephen King *(a bibliography),* The Many Facets of Stephen King, The Films of Stephen King, The Shorter Works of Stephen King, Stephen King as Richard Bachman, *and* The Stephen King Phenomenon. *The encounter, I assure you, will be a pleasant one.*

Q: What are your academic credentials?

COLLINGS: I am an associate professor of English Humanities Division at Pepperdine University. By the time you finish your book, I hope to be a professor of English. I double as the director of the Creative Writing Program in the Communication Division. I received my Ph.D. in Milton and the Renaissance from the University of California, Riverside, in 1977.

Q: How many books have you published?

COLLINGS: I have published twenty-six books and chapbooks including six books on Stephen King, *Brian W. Aldiss, Card Catalog: The Science Fiction and Fantasy of Orson Scott Card* (a bibliography), *Piers Anthony,* and *Reflections on the Fantastic* (as editor for this collection of essays). In addition, I have published two books and twelve chapbooks of poetry; over fifty articles in books, journals, etc.; over a hundred reviews, primarily of science fiction and fantasy, including reviews of many King works; and over a hundred poems.

Q: What are you currently working on?

COLLINGS: Books on Orson Scott Card, C. S. Lewis, and four science-fiction/horror novels currently under submission through an agent.

Q: What is your background in the science-fiction field?

COLLINGS: I have held memberships in the Science Fiction Research Association, the Science Fiction Poetry Association, and the International Association for the Fantastic in the Arts; and have participated in conferences and as officers in them over the years. I've reviewed for the *SFRA Book Review, Fantasy Review, Extrapolation,* and the *Annual Review of Science Fiction and Fantasy.*

Q: Your teaching credentials?

COLLINGS: I have taught science fiction and fantasy since 1981, usually in an omnibus course called "Myth, Fantasy, and Science Fiction."

Q: When did you first read a King book?

COLLINGS: One of my students, David Engebretson, urged me to read *The Dead Zone* after a discussion in a creative-writing class; I did—and everything else I could lay my hands on. (David later cowrote with me *The Shorter Works of Stephen King* while he was still an undergraduate student at Pepperdine.)

Q: How did you come to publish six books on King at Starmont House?

COLLINGS: In early 1985—just after I sent Ted Dikty and Roger Schlobin the typescript for my second Starmont book (*Brian W. Aldiss*)—Ted called to say that King had admitted to being Richard Bachman. Since Douglas Winter's volume on King for the Starmont Reader's Guides series had been sold to New American Library as *The Art of Darkness,* Ted did not have a King volume anymore. He asked me to do one on the Bachman books—and have it camera-ready within two months. I said yes.

A week later, he called again and asked me to consider doing a replacement volume for the Winter book—an overview of King's primary works. I said yes.

A few days after that, he called again and proposed a seven-volume series, including a collection of essays to be edited by Darrell Schweitzer and books by me on the Bachman novels, King's novels (*The Many Facets*), collected and uncollected short fiction (*The Shorter Works*), King's films (*The Films of Stephen King*), a bibliography (*The Annotated Guide to Stephen King*), a study of King's place in contemporary American society (*The Stephen King Phenomenon*), and a concordance. I turned the last volume over to Engebretson, and when he was not able to finish it, discussed the project with Ted. Since my preliminary work on a concordance to *Carrie*—including only proper names, place names, and important themes, etc.—suggested that a concordance to all of King's works would take several years to complete and at least a thousand-page book to publish, Dikty decided to discontinue that part of the project.

Q: The Starmont catalogue lists a Casebook series. What is the scope of the project and what's the current status?

COLLINGS: Ted and I discussed a Casebook series, with a volume devoted to critical essays on each of King's novels. I originally agreed to edit the series, but had to turn it back to Ted when school responsibilities increased the next year. I am not sure if he is still working on that or not.

Q: What dealings have you had with Stephen King?

COLLINGS: King was generous and open in all my dealings with him. I sent him an initial letter outlining the series and assuring him that, however critical individual sentences might be, the thrust of all of the books would be positive—I do not believe in wasting my time writing studies of people whose works I do not think have value.

Over the three years of the project, he responded several times to my questions, writing long, informative letters; his secretary was equally responsive and supplied me with copies of several key stories, reviews, etc. I could not have asked for any better relationship.

```
┌─────────────────────────────────────────────┐
│                                             │
│      Stephen King and the Critics           │
│       A Personal Perspective                │
│        by Michael R. Collings               │
│                                             │
└─────────────────────────────────────────────┘
```

I am not so much scholar or critic as facilitator.

Michael R. Collings

Most of my attitudes toward criticism, scholarship, fans, and King are implicit in my article in *The Stephen King Phenomenon* and in the introduction to *The Many Facets of Stephen King*. I firmly believe that King speaks for our times; he touches on elements of American culture that are keystones to understanding ourselves. He is enormously popular—and scholars hate that. He writes for a popular audience—and academicians hate that. He tells stories for the sake of stories— and theorists hate that. He assumes the pose of naive storyteller—and doctoral candidates hate that. On the other hand, he is being increasingly dissected by academics, many of whom seem more spurred by the "publish and perish" syn drome than by any real desire to understand the nature of horror—and fans hate that. But—kids read him.

I moderated a panel earlier this year with Ray Bradbury, who argued that the ultimate value of his fiction was that it made kids want to read. The kids start there and then move on to (perhaps) better things. At the least, this is true with King. I have led several Teenage Book Discussion Groups for the local library. Generally, the groups muster twenty or so students to discuss an assigned book. When I came to talk about *Firestarter* or *Christine,* there were more than sixty. And last fall, when I spoke at a special session of the group to which parents and teachers were invited (I was to suggest what I saw as important in King, and the parents and teachers were free to explain why they did *not* want their children reading King), there were over eighty present. None of the parents or teachers voiced any criticism. King is not for all children, of course; but he can help them into the world of imagination.

On the other hand, working with King has hampered my own career and the careers of others who have seriously tried to add to the body of knowledge. Some universities simply do not count any work of science fiction, fantasy, or horror as a legitimate publication when professors are up for promotion. In my own case, I was turned down for a merit increase (in spite of having over three hundred published works in the past ten years) for two reasons: first, the Starmont books were printed from camera-ready copy rather than typeset, and therefore were obviously hackwork to be dismissed (I never did get any substantive criticism of the q*uality* of my work); and second, it was felt that I was wasting my time in the field as a whole—I should be working on yet another scholarly reinterpretation of Milton, or something similar. I have had colleagues introduce literature courses by noting that in that class, the students would read literature, "not that Stephen King stuff." I have had colleagues tell my students that they should never come into a university professor's office carrying a Stephen King novel. I have had colleagues disparage my work without ever having read either my criticism or King's novels.

Still, the climate may be changing. My division chairmen in Humanities and Communication have both been more than supportive. Both divisions have organized specific courses on science fiction and fantasy, including courses that use King's books as base texts. Both chairmen encouraged me in my work. The Seaver College Reassigned Time Committee has given me released time from teaching assignments to work on the King books, on a science-fiction novel, and on projects on Orson Scott Card and C.S. Lewis.

So my experiences have encapsulated the ambiguity that surrounds King himself. Accepted and rejected—often fanatically, and with few sound reasons.

My own belief remains unaltered, however. I try to stand midway between the academics who are surrounded by their dusty tomes and who seem interested in literature-as-artifact [new criticism] rather than literature as a reflection of living experience, and the unthinking fan who knows what he likes but has no idea *why* he likes it. I try to suggest that contemporary literature can meet the standards of academia; and at the same time the standards of academia can help fan readers understand the books better. I try to make suggestions about things in King—and anyone else I work with—that I found exciting and stimulating, then urge my readers to *return to the work and find out for themselves* if what I say is true. I am not so much scholar or critic as facilitator. Nevertheless, I remain true to the need for scholarship, academics (in the best sense of the word), and clarity.

The problem with censorship is simply stated: Where do you draw the line? King, who saw firsthand the chilling effects of censorship while directing Maximum Overdrive *in Wilmington, North Carolina, is no stranger to censorship. His books are among the most censored in American schools.*

In a 1977 interview published in King's hometown newspaper, the Bangor Daily News, *King spoke out against censorship. "It's repulsive to the whole idea of education," he said, commenting on the Lisbon High School English department's banning by secret vote of Solzhenitsyn's short novel* One Day in the Life of Ivan Denisovitch. *King observed: "I can't believe the dishonor the English department is calling down on the school. And I expect Solzhenitsyn must be confused and upset about having his book banned in the United States of America."*

The problem with censorship is like that of the Hydra—it is only temporarily vanquished.

Claiming the rights of a million Maine residents were being threatened, Stephen King took to the airwaves and newspapers of his home state during May and June to help turn back a referendum on censorship.

The referendum was rejected by Maine voters by a whopping 72 to 28 percent margin in a primary election held June 10.

I'm against it [the referendum initiative]," King told a radio audience June 6, "because I don't know what it will do."

The referendum was put forth by the Maine Christian League which sought to ban the promotion and sale of pornographic material in Maine. Rev. Jasper (Jack) Wyman, chairman of the Civic League, said the referendum was necessary to establish a law which would protect children from exposure to pornography and to reduce the incidents of child abuse and rape. Wyman, who debated King on a radio talk show prior to the referendum vote on June 10, asserted that scientists had found a direct link between the use of pornography and the commission of sex crimes, particularly those against children.

The central issue in the debate was whether the government should have the right to determine what materials adults should be allowed to read or view. Wyman argued that obscenity was not a protected form of free speech under the Supreme Court's interpretation of the First Amendment, and the court had defined obscenity in its many rulings on the issue over the years. Opponents of the initiative, including King, argued that "obscenity" does not have a universally accepted definition when applied to various print and film materials; that something pornographic to Wyman might not be pornographic to thousands of other citizens. Further, opponents said similar laws had been used in other states to remove books from school and public library bookshelves which were considered works of literature by most, but found to be obscene by a few.

King, who has had his books banned from some school libraries, said he didn't know what the law might result in. "Jack," he told Wyman during the radio debate, "you can sit there and say you know what it [the law] will do, but you don't. No one does. And that's why I'm against it. I'm against what I don't know about."

While decrying a television ad run by those against the referendum [the spot depicted a man in a black leather jacket setting fire to several paperbacks, including *Grapes of Wrath* and *Valley of the Horses,* and suggesting that could happen under Wyman's so-called antiporn law], Stephen, nevertheless, allowed that such an exaggeration might someday be possible should the referendum be enacted into law. "I hate that ad," he told Wyman. "I mean, the guy in it looks like a Nazi. But, you know, once you start down that road [to censorship], it might not be that far off. . . ."

Wyman, himself, wasn't above using scare tactics in the campaign. The referendum proponents ran commercials citing alleged evidence connecting child sexual abuse and exposure to pornography by criminals. The slogan used by the Civic League was this highly inflammatory line: "Do it for the children."

Wyman, a former state representative and a veteran of a few nasty political skirmishes, insisted that the referendum's passage would not result in the banning of any works with literary value. He said claims by referendum opponents that a similar law in North Carolina had resulted in the banning of books such as *Little Red Riding Hood, Huckleberry Finn,* and the "R" volume of the *Encyclopedia Britannica* [it had a section on reproduction] were totally false. King, who spent the summer of 1985 in North Carolina where he directed the making of *Maximum Overdrive,* said he saw firsthand the chilling effect the North Carolina obscenity statute had on bookstores and magazine dealers:

> When their antiporn statute became the law of the land last July . . . between Tuesday evening and Wednesday morning, all the Playboys and Penthouses disappeared from the news racks in the little convenience store where I stopped for my morning paper and evening six-pack. They went so fast it was as if the Porn Fairy had visited in the middle of the night.

In another store in Wilmington, the X-rated section of tape rentals disappeared overnight. In some cases, R-rated tapes, such as Brian De Palma's *Body Double,* were removed from the shelves. "'I'm not taking any chances,'" King quotes one storeowner as saying. "'They'd love to shut us down.'"

"Pass a law like this and where does it stop?" King asked in a column printed in the June 1 edition of the *Maine Sunday Telegram*.

King wrote:

> I think the idea of making it a crime to sell obscene material is a bad one
> because it takes the responsibility of saying "no" out of the hands of citizens
> and puts it into those of the police and the courts. I think it's a bad idea because
> it's undemocratic, high-handed, and frighteningly diffuse.

As a side note, it was only a couple of months ago that a school board in a town near Vancouver, Washington, voted to remove King's *The Shining* from the shelves of its Junior High library. The board, accepting arguments from supporters of the ban, agreed that there was too much vulgar language in the book. One woman even claimed she took time to count the incidents of vulgarity; her total: 156. The banning of the book caused a great stir in the community and prompted editorials and letters-to-the-editor at a number of newspapers in the area. The comments of those opposed to the ban were not a whole lot different in tenor than those made by King during the recent censorship debate in Maine.

King freely admits that censorship scares him because it threatens his livelihood—"my reason for living," as he put it to Jack Wyman. But he also fervently believes in the First Amendment guarantees made by our Constitution and in the idea that people living in a free country ought to be free.

WRITING

Clive Barker on Stephen King, Horror, and E.C. Comics

It was a kingly endorsement, the kind that launches careers. It was, in this case, Stephen King's enthusiasm for and honest appreciation of Clive Barker, a British writer whose explicit brand of horror has found fans on both sides of the Atlantic.

King's paraphrase of Jon Landau's quote about Bruce Springsteen, "I have seen the future of horror, and it is named Clive Barker," has been splashed on the covers of Barker's books. "He is so good that I am almost literally tongue-tied. He makes the rest of us look like we've been asleep for the past ten years."

Interviewed twice on "The Larry King Show" (May 6, 1987, and October 11, 1988), Barker acknowledged King's positive influence on his own career and the horror genre itself, and on morality as depicted in the classic horror comic books, the E.C. line.

On Stephen King

Anyone who is interested in the horror genre has to have some interest in King's work. Steve has reshaped the genre in the sense that he's made it accessible to readers who would never otherwise pick up a horror book. It opened up a huge, new market to us all. And he's a superb and accessible storyteller.

On King's Endorsement of Him

Steve's recommendations helped immensely. What happened, I think, is that I ended up having an audience—a much larger audience than I thought I was going to get. Steve is extraordinary, and I think it helped break the ice. It helped people to take the initial risk to buy my books.

On Writing Horror

What the public actually wants is to be given something fresh, a new idea or a new angle. All too often what happens is that they are given semidigested ideas; they've been given the same old stuff over and over again.

On Morality and E.C. Comics

I'm a great admirer of [E.C. Comics]. The E.C. Comics are very moral. A lot of horror fiction is very moral. And that's one of the things that's often missed by the fundamentalists that come and rage at me on radio shows, and people who send me copies of the Bible with passages from Deuteronomy underlined, telling me to study it. It's an interesting thing to me that we're dealing all the time with people telling us what's good and bad; when push comes to shove, they don't have a clue.

Photograph courtesy of photographer Greg Preston, coordinated by Michael Autrey

Clive Barker

An Interview with Harlan Ellison

*If one writes, one is an egoist. It is an enormous act of egocentricity to write,
because what is inherent in that act is to say,* What I have to say is
important enough for the rest of the world to hear.

Harlan Ellison

If you want to know what Stephen King thinks of Harlan Ellison as an individual,
check out King's introduction to *Stalking the Nightmare,* a collection of short
fiction by Ellison. If you want to know what King thinks of Ellison as a writer,
check out the lengthy write-up in King's nonfiction survey of the horror field,
Danse Macabre.

Ellison was born in 1934 in Cleveland, and attended Ohio State University.
There a professor told him he had no writing talent, whereupon Ellison told him
off and left college to pursue a writing career. (For years, the story goes, Ellison
sent the professor a copy of everything he had published.)

Ellison's first short story, "Glowworm," was published in 1954 in a science-
fiction magazine. In 1958 Ellison published his first two books, *Web of the City*
and *The Deadly Streets.*

Ellison's break came when Dorothy Parker reviewed his sixth published
book, *Gentleman Junkie* (a collection of short stories), in *Esquire* in 1962. It was
his first major endorsement, recognition from the mainstream.

This year will mark the publication of Ellison's forty-fourth book, *Harlan
Ellison's Watching,* a collection of film criticism to be published by Underwood–
Miller in July 1989. Although most of his books are collections of short fiction, he
has also published numerous collections of essays, and graphic novels (graphic
adaptations), and edited the ground-breaking original anthology series, *Dangerous Visions; Again, Dangerous Visions;* and, to be published, *Last, Dangerous
Visions.*

Best known for his short stories and essays, Ellison has won the Edgar
Award (from the Mystery Writers of America), the Nebula Award (from the Science
Fiction Writers of America), the Writers Guild of America Award (for Most Out-

standing Script), and the Silver Pen Award, given by PEN, the international writers' union.

In 1987 an important retrospective collection of his work was published by
Nemo Press, *The Essential Ellison.* (If you have not read Ellison, this book is a
good place to start; it will lead you to his other work.)

Ellison, who was fifty-five in May 1989, lives in Sherman Oaks, California,
with his wife, Susan. His most recent book is *Angry Candy,* a collection of short
fiction published by Houghton Mifflin Company in 1988; the book is now in its
fourth printing. (New American Library will publish the paperback edition.)

The following interview took place by phone early one Sunday afternoon in
March 1989, interrupting an otherwise quiet day at the Ellison residence. George
Beahm and Howard Wornom conducted the interview, which was transcribed
and edited by Beahm.

> *King is one of the most accomplished storytellers
> the twentieth century has produced.*
>
> Harlan Ellison

Q: What are King's strong points as a writer?

ELLISON: My feeling about Stephen's work is that there usually is a reason for any
particular writer hitting a strong note with a wide audience. It is a sense of identification with the concerns and beliefs in general of that mass audience, which is
why Alfred Hitchcock had such an unqualified success at his career. He was able
to tap the universal fears that people experienced. Stephen does the same thing,
and that, of course, is for me his strong point.

Stephen King is neither Marcel Proust nor is he Salman Rushdie,[1] to take the
current icon. King is one of the most accomplished storytellers the twentieth
century has produced. As a consequence, his strengths are in the storytelling
area, and his weaknesses are in more specific areas. For instance, I can't think of
any King novels with the possible exception of maybe *It* or the two *Dark Tower*
books, that could not have been told just as well as a novella.[2] This is to me the
main flaw in Stephen's work. There is very little complexity in his ideas. They are

---

1. The author of a controversial novel, *The Satanic Verses,* which, according to the late Ayotollah
Khomeini, offended the Islamic religion and is a "crime" for which the Ayotollah decreed the death
sentence on Rushdie. Despite a public apology, the Ayotollah maintained his position and the author
remains in hiding.

2. A work of fiction between twenty thousand and forty thousand words.

all ideas that have been done ad infinitum in the fantasy and horror genres.

But that doesn't really matter because he is a synthesizer in that he takes the free-floating icon that each idea has become, societally speaking; the kinds of things that have a mythic quality in and of themselves, like the death of Marilyn Monroe, the assassination of John F. Kennedy, the flight of the *Hindenburg*, the sinking of the *Titanic*, James Dean, Jack the Ripper, or the "Charge of the Light Brigade." These are all things that have transcended their reality and have a weight and a freightload of implication that goes far beyond the event or the person.

Stephen deals almost exclusively in these. He takes an idea *like* a vampire in *'Salem's Lot;* he takes an idea *like* a rabid dog in *Cujo;* he takes an idea *like* the haunted car in *Christine*. And he managed—if not to breathe new life into them— at least to examine them from a position of cultural currency that most writers cannot.

I've talked about this at considerable length in my pieces about Stephen— how and why he came to be famous.[3] He came to be famous by a fluke, in the same way Ian Fleming came to be famous. It's just a fluke that John Kennedy said that his favorite reading matter was these spy books about James Bond and, boom, everybody's behind them. It's the same kind of iconography that attached to Theodore Roosevelt, saying that his favorite reading was westerns; and for thirty years in this country, westerns went through a very big vogue.

Stephen's moment was the moment in *Carrie* where Carrie has her period in the shower and is ridiculed by the girls. This was such a tapping into the basic cultural mythology. All of a sudden, everyone was talking about this brilliant, new writer. In fact, they were talking about *that* scene. Stephen has been very, very blessed in being able to maintain the motor on that vehicle.

Q: Is it getting tired?

ELLISON: I think it's foolish to think that anyone can sustain forever a literary career at the level that Stephen's has been at for so remarkably long. It simply doesn't happen. If you were to go back to 1940, and you were to look at the popular magazines of the day, or to look at the books, you'll find the names of people who are not even known today. They have vanished absolutely and utterly because they were totally in the American grain, in the popular idiom, and their work did not sufficiently transcend that popular appeal to keep on, even for a Sinclair Lewis, who is virtually unread today. F. Scott Fitzgerald, were it not for the periodic resuscitation by aficionados, would be unread today.

Q: Too topical, so closely identified with the time?

ELLISON: Exactly. When a writer is *that* closely identified with the time, the writing

---

3. Elsewhere in this book, see *"Harlan Ellison's Watching,"* which gives the complete story.

becomes out of date. Having been writing for thirty-five years myself, I look back at stuff that I've done and I see where a lot of it was influenced by the tenor of the times. And that stuff is less important or less liable to live on than the stuff that has a certain universality, like "'Repent Harlequin!' Said the Ticktockman"; "I Have No Mouth and I Must Scream"; or "Jeffty Is Five."

Q: His strengths?

ELLISON: His strengths, I think, are in managing to write about people in a way that all of us can identify. That's such an inadequate phrase. I don't mean "identify with." He has the minutiae, the little touches, down right. It gives his books a sense of verisimilitude that other writers working in the same vein don't have. Stephen's books seldom challenge your sense of willingness to believe. You go into a Stephen King book and he pulls you right in, and you say, Yes, I can go with this, and he takes you through the membrane into the unbelievable stuff very simply and very quickly because he has that strength of character that is the core of any good book.

It's that old quote by William Faulkner about the only thing worth writing about is the study of the human heart in conflict with itself.[4] Stephen does that very, very well indeed, and I think that is where his great strength lies.

Q: How about as a stylist—his technique and grammar?

ELLISON: It's very hard to comment on Stephen's "technique" because sometimes it is so simply and smoothly done that it's like Fred Astaire's dancing, which is a comparison I've made on Steve's technique before, which is eloquent and extraordinary because it is almost no technique at all.

Q: Because of its simplicity?

ELLISON: Because of its invisibility. It's an invisible technique, and that, I think, is his great strength. I think he occasionally departs from that, because he's being conned by a lot of critics who put him down, because his work is so accessible. They say, *He's a good storyteller, but he's not a great classic writer.* This is not Stephen himself, alone, undergoing this; we all suffer from this. We all occasionally begin to perceive that we have to be serious in tone, otherwise we're not going to be taken seriously. We all begin to lust for posterity, and we think that if we write like Washington Irving, then we may have a better chance at it. This falls into the hands of the poetasters, the stick-up-the-ass guys who write for the *New York Review of Books,* who would have you writing absolutely impenetrable-fucking stuff just because they think that stuff's the high tone. We cannot all write

4. William Faulkner's assessment of the purpose of writing fiction, given in his Nobel acceptance speech.

like Henry James, nor should we. And I think that Stephen occasionally departs from his own clarity of style to satisfy, however unconsciously, the brickbats of this kind of person. He can't be condemned for it because no one is above that.

Q: What are your personal favorites of his works?

ELLISON: I suppose my personal favorite is *Carrie,* which is not to say that he has not been better later, because I think *The Shining,* for instance, is a much better book. But *Carrie* is pure Stephen King. It is Stephen King before any self-consciousness, before any attention was paid. It's Stephen writing for himself.

Q: Do you think he's being edited well?

ELLISON: I don't think editors are giving Stephen the kind of editing he needs and deserves, because he's Stephen King—and you don't fuck with Stephen King. I mean, if Stephen King wants to use wrong grammar or make a mistake, it's still Stephen King.

The editors with whom I'm acquainted are not the kind of intellectual backboards off which one wishes to bounce the ball of one's work.

Q: Do you think Sturgeon's law—that 90 percent of everything is crap, that it's merely average—applies to the field of horror today?

ELLISON: I think it applies much more—about 98 percent. If you look at horror—I hate the word *horror* because it's such a limiting term—

Q: Like branding yourself by virtue of being a member of a writers' organization called the Horror Writers of America?

ELLISON: Absolutely. As a matter of fact, Horror Writers of America is a wonderful organization because Dean Koontz, Joe Lansdale, Rick McCammon, and a few other guys have worked hard to make it as good an organization as it is. I think one of the biggest drawbacks to its being taken legitimately is its name: the minute you say Horror Writers of America, you are laughed at.

The crippling thing about horror is that it's going to be driven into the ground by publishers who have no love for it, who have no vested interest in it, who are there for the moment. It's no different than when they were doing series novels about adventure heroes until people got sick of them; then they said fuck it, and they abandoned that genre. Then they did historical romances until they played out that vein.

Now they've got a hold of the horror thing because Stephen King is hot. Well, if one Stephen King is good, then five hundred Stephen Kings must be better, they figure.

Q: Like Gresham's law.[5]

ELLISON: Exactly. And you take a low-end publisher living off what the dregs of what the medium can provide, and they say, Well, okay, we're not going to make five million dollars off this; we'll make a hundred thousand. Even if it's bad material that will poison the well. But how can you blame them? And Stephen King, for better or worse, has popularized an entire genre. When he got hot, the rest of the hyenas said, Here's some fresh meat; let's eat. And that's what's happening today. So when you ask if Stephen's vogue is dissipating, I would imagine so, because there are now nine million Stephen King imitators of one sort or another. Imitators only in the sense that they are working in that area, people working in the genre like Dean Koontz, Clive Barker, or Joe Lansdale. Their names are legion. Some of them are very good, and some of them are not very good, but they are all out there.

When there was only Stephen, when he had access to the market, solely and entirely, he could have his own way. Now, ten years later, after the deluge, people are getting jaded. Now, even a book as good as Dan Simmons's *The Song of Kali,* which is for my money one of the best novels of this sort of dark vision that has come along in the last quarter century, for crissakes—even a book like that pretty quickly vanishes.

Q: Has it come out in paperback yet?

ELLISON: There you are. It came out in paperback four years ago. It has never been reissued. It's been out of print. And here's Dan Simmons now moving on to *Carrion Comfort* and becoming a very important writer, and nobody can obtain his principal masterwork.

The whole structure of publishing has altered so completely in the last twenty-five years that even the best writers are doomed to oblivion. All you can hope for is to become wealthy and popular, and Stephen has accomplished that. In that way, he may have bought himself a little posterity. On the other hand, people who have been as popular as Stephen in the past are gone and are not read at all.

Q: On the subject of literary imitation, working in the same vein, do you feel that Koontz is breaking through with his own kind of books—a view Berni Wrightson shares with some others—now that he has access to this marketplace? Koontz's sales are around forty million books, worldwide; King's are sixty million.

ELLISON: I don't know whether Dean is breaking through with his own kind of books or not. I read Dean's books and I read Stephen's books, and one says, Well, okay, I got a good read out of it. But with the exception of *Misery,* I haven't read a

---

5. Bad money drives out good money.

good Stephen King book that will live in my memory forever like *Carrie* does. In Dean's writing, I think Dean, after all these years, is finding himself.

Dean had his voice a long time ago, but it was a very commercial voice. Now, Dean is going through a watershed, and on the other side of that watershed, he's going to be writing in a very different way. And if there's any "imitation" of King, it is only that he is working in the field that has now been subsumed into the mainstream by the presence of Stephen King. Stephen's work is important because it was there first. But there were so many people who were there a long time before him. Stephen King would not exist were it not for H.P. Lovecraft, Fritz Leiber, Algernon Blackwood, and Richard Matheson.

But at some point along the literary line, you find nodes; and in those nodes are people who have totally assimilated everything that has gone before, and added their own little element to it, and *boom,* it characterizes the totality of that particular literary line, that genre at that moment. That is what Stephen did. So the people who come thereafter—until a completely new breakthrough person occurs—are called imitators. I think that is hideously unfair.

Q: Is Clive Barker that breakthrough person?

ELLISON: No.

Q: Who is?

ELLISON: I only have a few candidates. One of them is Steve Rasnic Tem. One of them is Dan Simmons. Another one is Patrick McGrath. I also think there are people in the field who are vastly underrated, like Fritz Leiber, who remains fresh and new, even though he's not writing a lot of contemporary fantasy.

Q: What's the secret of writing?

ELLISON: The great secret of writing is not becoming a writer, it's *staying* a writer, year after year after year, book after book after book, until, at the end of an extended period of time, you look at the range of a person's work, and it's like a mountain range. In some places it reaches a high peak, like *Carrie* or a *Misery,* and in other places it dips into a valley, and you have a *Christine.* But it's all part of the same mountain range.

I think that you find a remarkable talent every once in a while who changes the face of things with the writing. It happens very, very seldom. The rest of the time, it's just people earning a living.

Q: I was looking at your book of collaborative short fiction, *Partners in Wonder*[6] and it made me think: What do you think of the King/Straub collaboration, *The*

---

6. Long out of print, this book, originally published in 1971 by Walker and Company, is a collection of collaborative short fiction by Ellison in collaboration with other writers.

Talisman? Do you feel that the third voice King alluded to in his interviews is in fact better than their separate voices, that it was a successful collaboration?

ELLISON: How do *you* feel about *The Talisman?*

Q: I think it's bland and very cold. I think it reflects more Straub than King.

ELLISON: What about you, George?

Q: I have to tell you that it's the only book of King's that I've tried to read several times, but I just couldn't get into it.

ELLISON: That's my opinion, too. I've tried to read the damned thing a half-dozen times.

Q: What happened is that you take King's colloquialism and his ability to tell a story, and you combine Straub's prose, and instead of a unique literary collaboration, what you've got is a bland, third voice. In *Partners in Wonder*—in stories like your collaboration with Roger Zelazny—there's a lyrical quality to that story in which you can see how well the collaborative process works. But it's just not there in *The Talisman.*

ELLISON: Also, I think the whole idea of computers—and doing books long distance by computers—is bullshit. I think the word processor makes the writing automatically distant. Every writer should go back to a manual typewriter or a quill pen. I don't mean to sound like a Luddite, but I see a passionlessness that is taking over to match the nature of the industry. I see writers writing slovenly— more and faster—with less involvement.

Q: What do you think of King's short fiction?

ELLISON: I think sometimes it is very good. I liked "The Monkey."[7] And I love *The Plant,* a sensational story that's not finished yet.[8] . . . Stephen's sent me a story for *Last, Dangerous Visions* that needs to be rewritten. The problem is, when you say, I'm going to talk to Stephen about rewriting, I'm going to make suggestions, it sounds as if you are trying to blow your own horn: Well, here I am, the smart, clever fellow who is going to teach Stephen King how to write. Well, I don't mean any such thing as that. What I mean is that I was sent a short story, and I think there's a lot more in it than Stephen had time to develop. The story deserves better, the work deserves better, and Stephen's reputation deserves better.

---

7. Collected in *Skeleton Crew.*

8. Three installments have been published to date by King's press, Philtrum Press, and distributed to friends and business associates on his Christmas mailing list.

Q: Because you've mentioned *Misery* as being King's best novel of his recent work, I'd like to know your thoughts on the fan mentality and the obsessive nature of fans, which you've also seen firsthand.

ELLISON: It is beyond the telling to explain what it's like to anyone who has not been through it as intimately as Stephen or I or as a few other people have.

Q: So many King movies have gotten poor reviews, but *Stand by Me* was an exception. What was the perception of that film out there in Hollywood?

ELLISON: My perception out here was that people did not even realize it was a Stephen King story. How could it be a King story? There was nothing with teeth or fangs in it; it's just a gentle story about some kids. But you look at the Stephen King films that have been made since then, like *Pet Sematary;* the advance reports that I've heard are that it's ghastly, a bad movie. I haven't seen it, and I don't mean to be passing along gossip, but that's the industry word.

Q: What do you think of Tabitha King's work?

ELLISON: There's a quality of kindness in it that is missing from Stephen's work. There are a number of women writers I read specifically because there is a quality of humanity, a kindness in their work. Tabby's stuff is quite different from Stephen's, and in some ways is far more mature. *

Terror in Toontown
by Howard Wornom

The line between horror and humor is a very fine line indeed, a distinction Howard Wornom—a Disney fan, a King reader, and a student of animation history—makes clear. So where does a dark writer like King get his ideas? Well, there's a dark part of town in a place called Toontown.

Where do you get your ideas?

It is "the bane of the writer's existence," as Stephen King once said. Only the nonwriter asks a question like this; only lame reporters and brain-dead fans whose imaginations have long since dried up from watching too much TV and reading *National Enquirer*.

Harlan Ellison, a writer who has no time for fools, has a stock answer: Poughkeepsie. He sends a check to a service in Poughkeepsie every week, and every week he gets a list of ideas.

And the mindless, like some reporters, believe him.

Writers of the fantastic have had a hard time dealing with this question because there simply is no answer that anyone lacking creative faculties will understand. Ideas come from asking *What if . . .* They come from having an imagination factor that far too many people do not possess. It is, to some, a magical secret.

Stephen King has, on occasion, used Ellison's reply when the dreaded question has been asked. He has also claimed that he doesn't know where his ideas come from; they just come.

Don't believe him. Take a look through the bulk of King's fiction and you may discover certain similarities that will disclose the source of much of his creative inspiration. A secret until now, it can be authoritatively revealed that a wealth of ideas—specifically ideas and bizarre events leading to the demise of many of King's characters—have been supplied to Mr. King by a little-known idea factory hidden in the heart of Toontown.

Toontown is not just a place where cartoon mice frolic with cute little bunnies, and where Tinkerbell flits with pixies and frost-fairies. There are dark places in Toontown where even few 'toons dare go; and this, I venture, is where Stephen King finds his ideas.

There is an unearthly quality to his fiction that sometimes borders on the cartoon-like; a quality that harks back to the chase gags of the Roadrunner and Coyote cartoons from Warner Brothers, warping reality with insights into the unreal.

The important word is *gags*—funny situations in stories—because King's tales abound with gags that bounce off unreality the way boulders bounce off Wile E. Coyote. And the reasons why the surreal events in King's fiction succeed are the same reasons the old Warner cartoons are still treasured today: According to Steve Schneider in *That's All, Folks!* "In the Warner cartoons, mental maturity was coupled with a youthful ebullience which insisted that, come what may, anything goes."

And anything goes in the world of Stephen King.

The Shining is filled with sinister touches that could only have come from the cartoon realm. Take the topiary animals: menacing, unmoving, yet the reader knows without thinking that, when Jack's back is turned, the things are gonna come alive like Audrey II singing "Feed Me," licking chlorophyll off their chops, ready to pounce. . . .

It's no surprise that Jack thinks he's seeing things out of the corner of his eye. He is. The Overlook is on the border of a backward universe where reality is skewed and *redrum* spells *murder.* Life becomes a deadly cartoon.

Even more cartoonish are gags from the excised prologue to *The Shining,* "Before the Play." In Scene I, a congressman chokes at dinner like a steel ball bouncing in a wicked pinball game:

> The pet congressman had clawed and clutched at his throat, he had turned first red and then purple, he had actually begun to *stagger* among the assembled company in his death-throes, bouncing from table to table, his wildly swinging arms knocking over wine-glasses and vases full of freshly cut flowers, his eyes bulging hideously at the assembled revellers.

Cartoons and death. Nobody really dies in cartoons. Shotguns blow up at point-blank range, and Daffy walks away with his beak rearranged on the back of his head. What's there to worry about? No blood, no gray matter speckling the wallpaper. *Nope, nothing wrong here.*

That's not the case in *'Salem's Lot,* where King's novel first brings together the cartoon world and the real. When Eva Miller's husband Ralph (a cartoon name) buys it in a shredding machine, he dies and stays dead—one of the few people who stay dead in the Lot.

> . . . it was kind of funny in a way, if you could call any such horrible accident funny. . . . His foot slipped in a puddle of water and son of a bitch, right into the shredder before their very eyes. Needless to say, the possibility of a deal went right down the chute with Ralph Miller.

Take a look at King's other novels: *It* is about a killer klown; *Thinner* is about a deadly diet (Maria Ouspenskaya meets Karen Carpenter); and ray guns are powered by Duracells in *The Tommyknockers*—a combination of bad '50s science-fiction, clichés and stereotypical Rube Goldberg inventions. But perhaps King's most cartoon-like novel is his "'Happy Days' gone mad": *Christine* is a cartoon road trip through the tormented landscapes of teenage lust and hormonal angst. Arnie is a stereotypical cartoon loser behind the wheel, and Christine is an evil twin to Roger Rabbit's Benny the Cab—only somebody's been filling her tank with joy juice from Hell instead of regular, and boy is she *pissed*.

Christine herself is a cartoon: she roars down the road like a tiger on the prowl, her tires hugging the asphalt with steel-belted claws. Her victims, like the reform school dropout with the cartoon name of Moochie, stare transfixed as Christine's hell-raging eyes bear down on them, her two tons of terror plow into them with teeth of chrome and steel.

The '57 Fury was the coolest of the tailfin, bad-ass cars of the '50s, and King immortalized it with his rock and roll "cartune" of a populuxe Fury come to furious life. It proved what he once said at a lecture: "Rock and roll will keep you young forever."

Situation Horror and King*

What I write when I write horror stories a lot of times are not exactly novels at all; they are sort of like situation comedies except with a twist going the other way. I like to tell people the difference between humor and horror is that it stops being humor when it starts being you. You laugh your head off when some guy slips on a banana peel, unless you are the one who does it; you bite down on your tongue and the end of it comes out and lands on your lap, and you say, "Oh no, it isn't so funny." And some guy laughs at you and you want to go over and cock the bastard, right?

And so, a lot of what I've written is situation horror; that's what I think of it. For instance, you take a book like *The Shining*: I can easily see casting the parts of Jack and Wendy Torrance with Lucy and Desi Arnez: [in melodramatic voice with a Cuban accent] "Lucy, I'm home!" I mean, imagine those guys. You know that he sort of hates her guts, and in the right situation, you know, isolated and everything, something like that could happen. It's possible. . . .

*From King's "Banned Books and Other Concerns: The Virginia Beach Lecture," September 22, 1986.

The novels notwithstanding, it's King's shorter fiction that is arguably the most cartoon-like. It's here where King's American realism borders against a Duckburg of surreal terror.

Take a look at "Survivor Type," the riches to rags story of a pusher née backdoor surgeon. Washed up on a barren rock of an island, he resorts to self-cannibalization to answer the question: "How badly does the patient want to survive?"

Pretty badly. By the climax, the patient, Dr. Pine (as in *pine away*), is tripping down Madness Lane, cutting off his own meaty parts so he can survive. All the while, he's singing "You . . . deserve . . . a break today . . . sooo . . . get up and get away. . . ."

Finally, there's not much of him left, so he has a choice:

> hahaha.
> Who cares. this hand or that. good food good meat good God let's eat.

Then the punch line: "lady fingers they taste just like lady fingers."
Mmmm. Them's good eatin'.

Then there's Uncle Otto's Cresswell—a second cousin to Christine and a truck that liked to creep up on Otto when he wasn't looking. The thing was, the engine had exploded back in '53 and the truck stayed in a field for thirty years—on the spot where Uncle Otto's partner got squot like a pumpkin under the Cresswell's "tilted snout." It was purely an accident, Uncle Otto said . . .

Maybe it was really the years of guilt that did in Uncle Otto; then again, maybe it wasn't, because when his nephew found Otto's body in the shack across the field from the truck, hot Diamond Gem oil spurted out of Otto's mouth, and then Quentin "reached forward and opened Uncle Otto's mouth."

"What fell out was a Champion spark plug—one of the Maxi-Duty kind, nearly as big as a circus strongman's fist."

Judge Doom's verdict: death by Texas tea.

You know, King has this thing for fat women. Annie Wilkes. Gramma. And I don't mean fat; I mean *monstrous*.

> this woman is so goddam fucking big and old she looks like oh jesus christ
> print dress she must be six-six and *fat* my god she's fat as a hog can't smell her
> white long white hair her legs those redwood trees in that movie a tank she
> could be a tank she could kill me her voice is out of context like a kazoo jesus if
> i laugh i can't laugh can she be seventy god how does she walk and the cane
> her hands are bigger than my feet like a goddam tank she could go through
> oak for christ's sake

"The Blue Air Compressor" has got to be one of King's strangest stories. The obscenely huge Mrs. Leighton is a cartoon symbol for male sexual fears (I'm not making this up—read King's Freudian interpretations in the story), and her demise comes straight out of the Warner Bros. shorts where characters get blown up like enormous balloons, then float innocently away.

But this is King Kountry, and things here are a little . . . meatier:

> The compressor turned on with a whoosh and a chug. The hose flew
> out of Mrs. Leighton's mouth. Giggling and gibbering, Gerald stuffed it back in.
> Her feet drummed and thumped on the floor. The flesh of her cheek and
> diaphragm began to swell rhythmically. Her eyes bulged and became glass
> marbles. Her torso began to expand. . . . The compressor wheezed and rack-
> eted. Mrs. Leighton swelled like a beach ball. Her lungs became straining
> blowfish. . . . She seemed to explode all at once.

The closest that one of King's "characters" come to the cartoons has got to be the thing in "The Crate"—even King admits that it is "a monster of such ferocity that it is really a cartoon." Feeding, it makes "the sound a teakettle makes when it has reached a rolling boil. . . . no cheerful whistle this, but something like an ugly, hysterical shriek" that "thickened into a low, hoarse, growling sound."

It's still alive after 134 years, and it swallows the janitor into its crate, which impossibly holds both bodies without bursting. Then Charlie Gereson makes a joke about its true identity: "They'd think you just came off a helluva toot and were seeing Tasmanian devils instead of pink elephants."

Maybe that's why Charlie buys it "under the stairs with grotesque, cartoonish speed." . . .

Tasmanian devils can't take jokes.

Night Shift probably contains the most cartoon-like of King's stories—and those are mostly about things that come alive.

("Gray Matter" is an exception: it's a beer drinker's nightmare, a cartoon realization of the cliché "It'll turn your brains to mush." And that it does.)

King likes living cars. His "Trucks," made into the anticlassic *Maximum Overdrive*, are mean machines. What we have are possessed 18-wheelers, pick-ups, tractors—at the least—that have a taste for blood mixed in with their diesel oil . . . and they're hungry. . . .

There's no reason for it all, but we don't really need a reason. All we need to know is that somebody left open the back door of the Toontown garage, and these rigs slipped into the real world with no one looking.

"Battleground" is like the '30s Christmas cartoons where the kids (or the generic toymaker) go to bed and their toys come alive for their own holiday revels. But the toy soldiers here don't freeze in their tracks when people see them:

> The soldiers were wearing minuscule army fatigues, helmets, and field
> packs. Tiny carbines were slung across their shoulders. Two of them looked
> briefly across the room at Renshaw. Their eyes, no bigger than pencil points,
> glittered.

Five, ten, twelve, then all twenty. One of them was gesturing, ordering the others. . . . The others whirled and unslung their carbines. There were tiny, almost delicate popping sounds, and Renshaw felt suddenly as if he had been stung by bees.

It isn't a toy wonderland for the doomed Renshaw: these toys are here to bag a Christmas turkey.

If there is any single creature from King's early stories that can successfully round out our tour through Toontown's idea boneyard, it is probably "the mangler." We have here your basic Hadley Watson Model-6 Speed Ironer and Folder, an assembly line monster that tries to fold poor Mrs. Frawley like a flannel sheet ("They took her out in a basket"), and breathes and hisses steam "like a dragon." Imagine Thomas Disch's *The Brave Little Toaster* performed by Jack Nicholson and you'll get an idea of what's going on. By the time it rips itself from its base, it is a modern-day Maleficent, transforming itself into a living beast from hell:

It was trying to pull itself out of the concrete, like a dinosaur trying to escape a tar pit. And it wasn't precisely an ironer anymore. It was still changing, melting. The 550-volt cable fell, spitting blue fire. . . . For a moment, two fireballs glared at them like lambent eyes, eyes filled with a great and cold hunger.

The reader's final view of the mangler as it begins its terrible rampage is of ". . . something black and moving that bulked to a tremendous height above them both, something with glaring electric eyes the size of footballs, an open mouth with a moving canvas tongue."

But this, like most of King's work, ain't no Disney movie. There's no neat, sweet ending, and the mangler is last heard roaring goodbye, "hot and steaming," down the street in search of further prey, just like the next King novel will rampage across the bestseller lists.

Well, that was a lot of fun, kids, but it looks like it's time for our cartoon cavalcade to say goodbye to all our company.

The applause light must be on: the music is coming up, and I can hear the laugh track swelling: Come on, kids—sing along!

S — T — E . . .
P — H — E . . .
N — K — I — N — G . . .
That's all, folks.

"Where Do You Get Your Ideas?"

The question reveals more about what the interrogator doesn't know than about what the fiction writer does know. It's the question that makes a fiction writer go a little c-r-a-z-y. It's the question posed by an innocent who lacks the imagination to answer it himself.

It's the question Stephen King has been asked endless times. He has some stock answers. "I get mine in Utica," he wrote in "Letters from Hell," a broadside published by Lord John Press. In an interview with Keith Bellows in *Sourcebook*, he replied: "Well, there's a great little bookstore on 42nd Street in New York called Used Ideas. I go there when I run dry." And in "On *The Shining* and Other Perpetrations," an essay that appeared in a small-press magazine, *Whispers*, he responded: "I get them at 239 Center Street in Bangor, just around the corner from the Frati Brothers Pawnshop."

The truth—which can't be reduced to a flip answer—is that the question in many cases can't be answered. It is too general and presupposes that ideas are like six-packs of Coke, packaged and ready to consume, available at the local convenience store when you run low.

Any work of fiction begins as a single idea that, fueled by creativity, grows until the story is told. In King's case, asking himself "what if" about what he's seen in the real world sets his imagination free.

Given the basic idea—the one that fired King's imagination—can you guess the work of fiction?

1. King, a recent college graduate, is unable to find a teaching job and takes a job at a laundromat in Bangor for $60 a week. One of his coworkers is a woman who quotes Scripture and makes King wonder: What kind of children would she have?

2. In a discussion with his wife and a friend, the subject of vampires came up. What would happen if vampires came to rural America?

3. After reading "The Veldt," Ray Bradbury's famous short story about a futuristic playroom in a house where the children can dream and the playroom makes the dream come alive, King toys with the concept and comes up with

161

On where King gets his ideas: "I get them at 239 Center Street in Bangor, just around the corner from the Frati Brothers Pawnshop."

    the idea of a novel, set in an amusement park, about a boy with psychic abilities.

4. King is in Boulder, Colorado, where his car had lost its transmission. It's dusk and King, walking across a bridge, has a disquieting thought: What if a troll heard the sounds of his boots on the bridge and jumped out to attack him?

5. King begins work on a *roman à clef,* a novel about Patty Hearst called "The House on Value Street," but can't write it because he can't rid his head of a news story about a biological spill endangering Salt Lake City.

6. Bill Thompson—King's first book editor—phones King one night and suggests he write a book about "the whole horror phenomenon."

7. King, a student at the University of Maine at Orono, inherits a ream of oddly cut bright green paper. In his sophomore year in college he reads Robert Browning's poem "Childe Roland." Two years later, he "played with the idea of trying a long romantic novel embodying the feel...of the Browning poem."

8. King toys with the idea of writing a story about a car whose odometer runs backward. And when it reaches zero, it will fall apart.

9. King accepts an assignment to write a story in calendar format, twelve vignettes to be written in twelve days. But the story grows.

10. The King family is living at Long Lake at Bridgton, Maine. The day after a freak summer storm King is at the local grocery store and has an idea: "I thought it was wildly funny—what *The Alamo* would have been like if directed by Bert I. Gordon."

11. King is in college and starts writing a work of fiction tentatively titled "Verona Beach," "a story about a woman who is a failed actress and her young son, living in a deserted resort area on the Atlantic coast while she waited to die, and what it would be like."

12. King starts work on two novels that don't pan out—"Welcome to Clearwater" and "The Corner"—and then begins a third, "a small-town story about a child-killer." The image in King's mind: A teacher gives an exam to his students. A girl turns her test in, touches his hand briefly, and the teacher tells her to go home immediately because her house is on fire.

13. King takes his ailing motorcycle to a mechanic in Bridgton, Maine. A dog comes out of the barn and growls at King. The mechanic explains that the dog probably didn't like King's face, and adds that it's the first time the dog has done that.

14. King is the writer-in-residence at the University of Maine at Orono. Living in Orrington in a house flanked by a major truck route, daughter Naomi's cat Smucky is killed. What if he buried the cat without telling her—and what if it came back to life?

15. King, wanting to write a story his daughter Naomi will read, writes a children's fantasy "with teeth." It is originally titled *The Napkins* and is published in a limited edition by his own publishing company.

16. It began with a traditional nursery rhyme and explored King's notion of technology gone amuck.

Answers

1. *Carrie*
2. *'Salem's Lot*
3. *The Shining*
4. *It*
5. *The Stand*
6. *Danse Macabre*
7. *The Dark Tower: The Gunslinger*
8. *Christine*

9. *The Cycle of the Werewolf*
10. "The Mist"
11. *The Talisman*
12. *The Dead Zone*
13. *Cujo*
14. *Pet Sematary*
15. *The Eyes of the Dragon*
16. *The Tommyknockers*

Part Three

A Look at the Books

This section is a book-by-book look at King's published and unpublished works, arranged alphabetically. Principally an overview for the general reader, this section's approach is not scholarly or critical in nature; Douglas E. Winter in *Stephen King: The Art of Darkness* and the works of Michael R. Collings—all in print—offer detailed examinations from those perspectives. Likewise, this section does not discuss King's films; Collings, Conner, and Horsting have written book-length studies that thoroughly cover the material.

Depending on the book, there may be a brief synopsis, the story *behind* the story, sidebars, an interview, and an article. For all books, tie-in product information is provided—editions available, films, and audiotapes. (Please note: Prices and availability are subject to change without notice, so check at your local bookstore for updated information.)

The section appropriately concludes with an exclusive interview with Douglas E. Winter, author of *Stephen King: The Art of Darkness,* the definitive biography and critical study of King. Winter's insights shed new light on King who, says Winter, "best deserves the title of America's storyteller."

Photo courtesy of the *Bangor Daily News*

Stephen King banging away on his IBM Selectric in his home office in Bangor.

The Bachman Books

But the fact that Thinner *did 28,000 copies when Bachman was the author and* 280,000 *copies when* Steve King *became the author, might tell you something, huh?*

Stephen King, introduction to *The Bachman Books*

Like a jigsaw puzzle with one large piece missing, the big picture came clearly into focus when the final piece was put in place. *Thinner,* the fifth Bachman book, published as a major title by New American Library, blew King's cover in 1984. Richard Bachman was a pen name for Stephen King.

What's surprising is that the secret was kept under wraps for so long, by so many. At King's request, those who knew of the pen name were sworn to silence. It was an impressive coverup. *Rage,* the first Bachman book, was published in 1977. Eight years later King commented in a *Time* cover story:

> "It should have been in TIME's Milestones," King grumbles. "Died. Richard Bachman, of cancer of the pseudonym."

After the news exploded in the media, the fallout began. Did King write under any other pen names? Which of the Bachman books were in print? Was there any consideration given to reissuing them in an affordable edition?

As it turned out, King did write under another pen name, John Swithen, used for a crime story, "The Fifth Quarter," which originally appeared in *Cavalier* magazine, April 1972. But *no* other works bore a pseudonym, though rumors were rampant. Bachman books in print? Only *Thinner* was available, in hardback. But when it was obvious that the demand existed for the four earlier novels, NAL collected them in an omnibus edition—consisting of *Rage, The Long Walk, Roadwork,* and *The Running Man*—and published it in October 1985.

Because the Bachman story has been chronicled in exhaustive detail, I'll not repeat what has been said—in King's own introduction to the omnibus edition,

The Bachman Books, in Winter's *Stephen King: The Art of Darkness,* and in an essay by Stephen Brown (among the first to discover and publicize the Bachman discovery), which appeared in *Kingdom of Fear.* If you want the full story, I commend these works to your attention.

Two things, I think, are important as to the use of a pen name.

First, the Bachman books have a fictional voice different from King's: the darker, pessimistic strains, those that accompany the traditional trappings of horror—the kind on which King built his name recognition—are generally not heard. *The Long Walk, Roadwork,* and *The Running Man* are science fiction; *Misery,* originally intended as a Bachman book, is psychological horror; *Rage* is psychological suspense. *Thinner,* the most recent Bachman book, is closest to King's "typical" horror style—a merging of Bachman and King's voices. And *The Dark Half* is almost a collaboration by Bachman and King.

Second, the primary reason why these books (excluding *Misery*) weren't published under King's name reveals much about the inner workings of the book publishing world, which has undergone radical changes from what was historically a gentleman's hobby into a conglomerate-dominated industry. The main concern of King's publishers was that, if the Bachman books were not released under his pen name, the market would be glutted.

As his publishers found out—to their surprise and delight—the reading public couldn't get enough of King. *The Bachman Books* and *Thinner* did predictably well; those, in turn, gave the publishers the confidence to publish in 1986–1987 four novels by King.

History repeated itself. The novels each did phenomenally well, undeniably attesting to the power of the brand name and to the huge appetite of King fans.

Mythconceptions

New York book publishers operate by sacrosanct rules. But King broke the rules, and proved that in the end *a book sells itself,* a fact that frustrates marketing people who want to believe otherwise. (If a book is bad, *nothing* can help its sales; but if it's good, the word eventually gets out.)

In retrospect, here's what King's publishers discovered about him and the marketplace, its myths and realities:

Rule 1: A bestselling author shall publish only one novel a year.

If you have a favorite author—King or anyone else—you'll buy all his books, regardless of when they are published. You won't select between two titles by the same author; you'll simply buy both, and forego buying a book by another author, the one you would have bought if your favorite author had no new book out. (After *It* was published, three other novels were scheduled for publication within a fourteen-month period: *The Eyes of the Dragon, The Tommyknockers,* and *Misery.* To no one's surprise, the sales were excellent. King's fans have a king-sized addiction.)

King summarized the situation in "Why I Was Bachman," his introduction to *The Bachman Books:* "I didn't think I was overpublishing the market . . . but my publishers did."

Rule 2: Short-story collections don't sell.

As a general rule this is true, unless the author is like King, with a readership that craves his work, no matter the form. Consequently, three collections of King's shorter work have been published, with impressive sales figures: *Night Shift, Skeleton Crew,* and *Different Seasons.* (The fourth, slated to be published in 1990 by Viking, is a collection of novellas.)

Rule 3: For a book to sell, the author must promote it.

Promotional gimmicks are frequently used to stimulate artificially the sale of books. But King doesn't need to use them to sell his books. He generally doesn't attend book signings, go on author tours, or attend conventions. The availability of his books, prominently displayed, is sufficient.

Even for books of marginal interest to King's readers—like *Nightmares in the Sky,* composed mostly of photographs, with an essay by King—the brand name is sufficient to generate sales. According to David Streitfeld, writing in the *Washington Post Book World,* February 1989, Viking printed a quarter-million copies of the book and sold a hundred thousand. This, concluded Streitfeld, proved that King's name is not magic.

The truth is, if you can sell a hundred thousand copies of a book like *Nightmares in the Sky,* it proves the exact opposite: King's name *is* magic. A new King novel can sell a million copies in hardback and three million in paperback, and those numbers indicate a large audience of which a small percentage *will buy anything* with King's name on the cover. The sale of a hundred thousand hardbacks of a work like *Nightmares* is impressive by any yardstick of sales in this industry. (If the book did not have King's introductory essay, how many copies would have been sold? Or would the book have been published at all?)

Then there are the over two-dozen books about King. One of them, a collection of interviews with King, had sold over a hundred thousand copies in hardback at $16.95 by its publication date!

There's no doubt about it: King's fans are legion, and they will buy virtually any book with his name emblazoned on the cover.

Rule 4: A brand-name author should write in a specific field to avoid confusing the reader.

Because King has been primarily categorized as a horror writer, any work that doesn't fit the mold will create identity problems, or so everyone thought. As it turned out, King's readers, who read his work because they like his storytelling, were glad to have four new King novels to read. That the Bachman books were distinctly different from King's horror material didn't stop the fans from pushing *Thinner* and *The Bachman Books* onto the bestseller lists.

In the end, only two factors are important: the book, and what the customer thinks of it. If the writer has done his job right—writing an honest book, writing to please himself first, and hoping it'll please others—nothing else really matters.

Thinner

Although *Thinner,* with its distinctive King-like prose, finally blew King's cover, it was only a matter of time, for several reasons. The Bachman books were all published by New American Library. The books were dedicated to people King knew. "Bachman" had never granted any interviews or made any appearances to promote the book. And the copyrights, with the exception of the first one, were filed in the name of King's literary agent.

Moreover, unlike the other Bachman books, *Thinner* was promoted heavily at the American Booksellers Convention in Washington, D.C., in 1984, where advance reading copies were distributed free to the book trade. Unlike the first four Bachman books, published in small runs in paperback, *Thinner* was published as a major title in hardback.

Bachman Returns?

Did Richard Bachman really die of cancer of the pseudonym, as King put it, or does Bachman live? Douglas E. Winter, in his interview later in this book, remarked that King's forthcoming novel, *The Dark Half,* which he's read in manuscript form, is by Stephen King *and* Richard Bachman, which was confirmed by editor/publisher Christopher Spruce in *Castle Rock.* So we may see a unique collaboration—the distinctive, but separate, voices of King and Bachman.

Editions Available and Tie-in Product

The Bachman Books
• A trade paperback, NAL, $9.95
• A paperback, NAL, $5.95
• A movie tie-in edition of *The Running Man,* a paperback, NAL, $3.95

Thinner
• A paperback, NAL, $4.95
• An abridged audiocassette, "Thinner," from Durkin•Hayes Publishing Ltd., $14.95

Carrie

Mr. King is a schoolteacher who lives in Maine
with his wife and two children.

From dust jacket of 1984 Doubleday edition

A Look Back

It is 1972, two years after Stephen King graduated with a B.S. degree in English from the University of Maine at Orono. King is an English teacher at Hampden Academy in Hampden, Maine.

The salary is $6,400 a year, and the money never goes far enough. Living in a trailer in Hermon, Maine, a small town west of Bangor, King finds that the demands of teaching take a toll on his writing time. He teaches six periods a day and grades papers in the evenings and on weekends, like most teachers. The mental energy and the time required make it difficult to write, but King persists. A writer who wants to write will write, regardless of the circumstances.

King is two pages into a short story. He discards them. His wife, Tabitha, literally pulls them from the trashcan. King continues writing, thinking he can sell the tale to Nye Willden at *Cavalier,* the magazine that had previously bought short stories from him. But the short story becomes a novella—a story some twenty-five thousand words in length—and it's obvious that *Cavalier* will not buy it, nor will any other magazine. King then expands the story to novel length and submits it to Bill Thompson, an editor at Doubleday and Company.

The rest, as they say, is history. Doubleday paid the author an advance against royalties of $2,500 and published the book in 1974 as a trade hardback with a cover price of $5.95. New American Library bought the rights to publish it as a mass-market paperback, paying $400,000, split fifty-fifty between Doubleday and King. And the film version, released in 1976, was a critical and financial success.

Before *Carrie*

Despite what some think, Stephen King was not an overnight success. Although *Carrie* was King's first *published* novel at Doubleday, King had previously submit-

171

ted *Getting It On* (later published as *Rage*) to Doubleday editor Bill Thompson, who asked King to rewrite it. The book was eventually rejected, and in an article published years after the fact in *Kingdom of Fear,* Thompson recollected that ". . . it still wasn't magic time. The scripts weren't strong enough for the first novel breakout, and they went back. . . ."

Carrie was also preceded by the writing of "The Aftermath" (an unpublished novel-length manuscript, a science-fiction tale written when King was sixteen years old), *The Long Walk* (later published as a Richard Bachman book), "Sword in the Darkness" (an unpublished novel, approximately one hundred fifty thousand words), *The Running Man* (later published as a Bachman book), and numerous short stories, published in *Cavalier* magazine, *Startling Mystery Stories,* and in other publications.

Telekinesis, *n.* The movement of objects by scientifically unknown or inexplicable means, as by the exercise of mystical powers.[1]

School Is Hell

Contemporary cartoonist Matt Groenig has made his reputation with a series of books using hell as a recurring theme: *Love Is Hell, Work Is Hell,* and *Childhood Is Hell.* And as King makes clear in this book, school is hell.

High school, especially. King, who had taught at the high school and college levels, knows that world well. High school is a microcosm of the real world, in which society is stratified. You are either with the "in" crowd or part of the "out" crowd.

As Holden Caulfield in *Catcher in the Rye* tries desperately to become part of the world around him and it refuses him, so Carietta White longs to become part of the in crowd, but can't. Alienated at home by her mother, Margaret White, a fundamentalist Christian, and alienated at school by her peers, Carrie is finally befriended by Susan Snell, who takes pity on her. Snell asks her boyfriend Tommy, on whom Carrie has a crush, to take Carrie to the prom. He agrees . . . and at the prom, something terrible happens. Carrie, a wild talent, unleashes her powers as all hell breaks loose.

Comments

Fifteen years after its first publication by Doubleday, *Carrie* remains a satisfying read, a story well told. Currently in print as a hardback from Doubleday and a paperback from New American Library (NAL), *Carrie* is a timeless story of alienation, an evocative portrait of high school society (school is hell). It exhibits many

---

1. *The American Heritage Dictionary of the English Language* (Boston: Houghton Mifflin Company, 1979), p. 1323).

of the fictional trademarks that would mark subsequent King novels: a main character with a "wild talent" (a term coined by science-fiction/fantasy writer Jack Vance); a fundamental honesty in the prose, the kind of writing that makes you trust the writer; a colloquial English that mirrors the way real people talk; a real world intruded upon by an unreal element (telekinesis, in this case); the rite of passage (Carrie growing from adolescence into adulthood); and a downbeat ending (typical of American naturalist writers, whom King admires).

Editions Available and Tie-in Product

- A trade hardback, Doubleday, $16.95
- A paperback, NAL, $3.95
- The movie, *Carrie*, directed by Brian DePalma, released in 1976, available in videocassette

For More Information

- "On Becoming a Brand Name," an essay by Stephen King, available in *Fear Itself: The Horror Fiction of Stephen King*, tells of King as a struggling writer and his successes with his three early books, *Carrie*, *'Salem's Lot*, and *The Shining*.
- "A Girl Named Carrie," an article by Bill Thompson, available in *Kingdom of Fear*, recounts the story of the publication of *Carrie* from the editor's perspective.

Hampden Academy, in Hampden, Maine, where King taught high school.

Stephen King Musical Lays Eggs on Broadway
by Dan R. Scapperotti

As King and his readers have found out, a book is one thing, a film adaptation quite another. The author's inimitable voice is preserved best in print form, and can be easily translated to an unabridged reading. Beyond that, his voice is compromised by the constraints other media impose.

This is clearly exemplified in the unsuccessful attempt to bring King's first novel, Carrie, *to the stage. Pure King, the book is a powerful read and was translated effectively to the screen. But* Carrie *as theater simply didn't work. It was an ambitious, but ill-starred, effort. After a handful of performances, the show closed.*

In this review of the play, Dan Scapperotti reveals what happened and why the play failed.

Stephen King comes to Broadway. But his stay is short-lived. Producer Friedrich Kurz must be given credit for sheer nerve. Adapting King's horror novel *Carrie* to the stage would be difficult enough, but to enshroud it in a musical format is daring. And disastrous. The ill-fated play, which opened on May 12 in New York and closed a couple of days later, had a bumpy road. After being lambasted by London critics the play was imported and underwent severe rewrites. Even director Terry Hands, the artistic director of the prestigious Royal Shakespeare Company, distanced himself from the production and "wasn't talking" prior to its première.

The show was written by Lawrence D. Cohen, who scripted the movie version directed by Brian DePalma in 1976. The play opens promisingly enough with "In," an exuberant calisthenics number headlining rock and roll stalwart Darlene Love as Miss Gardner, the gym teacher, and the girls of her class. The number flows into the famous shower scene, here abetted by the song "Dream On." The class does a strip number before discreetly walking into shower stalls simulated by opaque scrims.

Up to this point *Carrie* showed some evidence of life, but then the girl goes home and we meet Mom. Betty Buckley, who had the role of the gym teacher (Miss Collins) in the film, plays Margaret White, Carrie's oppressively religious mother. The role is so downbeat that it managed to bring the show's impetus to a dead halt. Buckley, a theatrical talent with a strong voice, is saddled with a succes-

174

sion of depressing ballads. Though she tries desperately, Buckley fails to rise above the material, and the show goes down with her.

One of the major problems with the play is that it seemed stuck in limbo somewhere between *Grease* and *Macbeth*. After downbeat songs like "Open Your Heart" and "And Eve Was Weak," the action plunges into a drive-in setting that has the whole high school class rollicking to a rock number, "Don't Waste the Moon."

The title role is played by Linzi Hateley. Her Carrie is a dumpy, unattractive misfit without the pent-up sensuality of budding puberty displayed by Sissy Spacek in the film version. Hateley can belt out a song, but doesn't evoke [the] sympathy needed to round out her character. Charlotte D'Amboise is effective as Chris, Carrie's nemesis and the school's reigning bitch goddess.

Hopelessly miscast is Gene Anthony Ray, who starred in *Fame* and the TV series it spawned. As Billy, the John Travolta role, Ray looks more like a Rasta-farian biker than a suburban high school kid. Billy agrees to help Chris in her plot against Carrie at the prom. After a ridiculous scene in which the kids harvest their vat of pig's blood, Billy casually walks up to Carrie, the unsuspecting, newly crowned prom queen and dumps the blood on her head, precipitating the final, fatal confrontation.

The horror elements in the play have been trivialized, effectively taking the heart out of the story. Carrie's unique telekinetic ability is showcased in "I'm Not Alone," a hollow, slightly amusing number. Locked in her room, Carrie sere-nades a dancing ensemble of prom shoes, powder puff and brush animated by her powers. Even worse, the big prom scene is a bust. Where it needed a dazzling display of theatrical fireworks, instead it looks like a disco with flashing laser lights. Amid the light show Carrie stands among red streamers still dripping with pig's blood so thick it looks like strawberry jam. The final set piece, instead of being tragic, elicited laughs from the audience. Following the prom massacre, Carrie rises up onto a long flight of heavenly stairs. She is comforted by Mom singing "Carrie" as she stabs the girl to death.

With forgettable music, emasculated horror, and inept drama, the play's clos-ing (after five performances) was a foregone conclusion. But *Carrie's* fate isn't likely to dampen Broadway's interest in adapting tales of terror for the stage. With the unbridled success of *Phantom of the Opera*, producers will still be checking out horror properties that could mine gold on the Great White Way.

Christine

It was like "Happy Days" gone mad.

Stephen King on *Christine*, from Virginia Beach lecture

Hell hath no fury like a woman scorned.

She's a man killer. She's almost twenty-one, with terrific headlights, a sleek body, and lines built for speed.

She's a 1957 Plymouth Fury, with a custom job, red and white.

She's Christine, and if you cross her, you'll have to deal with her unending fury. . . .

Malevolent Machines

King has explored this theme in numerous stories, notably "The Mangler" (in which an industrial speed ironer uproots itself and stalks the countryside, looking for its victims), "Uncle Otto's Truck" (an old, dilapidated truck inches, year by year, toward its intended victim), and most obviously in "Trucks," a short story that was collected in *Night Shift* and that formed the basis for the King-directed movie *Maximum Overdrive.*

"Trucks" is the tale of a small band of people making their last stand in a truck stop, surrounded by malevolent machines: Mack trucks, trailer trucks, and an ominous bulldozer come alive to prey on man. King later enlarges on this theme in *The Tommyknockers*—technology gone amuck.

In "Trucks," two teenagers drive their Fury into a truck stop, but the car gets smashed by the trucks. "The kids' Fury was lying on its roof at the end of long, looping skid marks in the loose crushed rock of the parking lot. It had been battered into senseless junk," writes King.

A smashed Fury . . . but will it come *alive*?

Synopsis

As King tells us in the prologue:

> This is a story of a lover's triangle, I suppose you'd say—Arnie Cunningham, Leigh Cabot, and, of course, Christine. But I want you to understand that

Christine was there first. She was Arnie's first love . . . I think she was his only true love. So I call what happened a tragedy.

As the novel opens, Arnie Cunningham (a seventeen-year-old nerd) is out cruising with his best friend, Dennis Guilder. It is the end of summer, the last summer before their senior year. As they pass a dilapidated Plymouth Fury, Arnie shouts for his friend to stop the car.

The Fury is Roland D. LeBay's, an army veteran who bought it while on active duty, and who would later see his daughter choke to death in the car, and his wife die in it. Christine (as LeBay christened the car) is for sale and Arnie buys her for $250.

Dennis thinks it's a bad buy and prophetically suggests that Arnie rename it: " 'If you've got to name it, Arnie, why don't you name it Trouble?' "

Christine's in bad shape, so they get her to a local garage, Darnell's. Arnie takes the abuse of the owner, Will Darnell, who has little use for him. Arnie, who has never stood up to anyone in his life, accepts the abuse as his lot. Because Arnie loves Christine, no personal sacrifice is too great. The rent's $20 a week for a stall, but he's got no choice: his parents won't let him park it in front of their house.

That night Dennis has a nightmare. He sees Christine starting up by herself in Darnell's garage. Christine is without blemish—perfectly reconstructed. And then there is "the terrible scream of rubber kissing off concrete and Christine lunges out at me, her grille snarling like an open mouth full of chrome teeth. . . ."

The nightmare is prophetic: Christine is alive.

As Dennis gets more involved, especially with a cheerleader, he sees Arnie less frequently. But Arnie doesn't care because he's spending almost all his time at Darnell's, nursing Christine back to health.

Later, Dennis has a second nightmare. LeBay, dead, is behind the wheel as Christine rockets out of the garage and toward Dennis.

Then Leigh Cabot comes into Arnie's life—a real sweetheart, easily the prettiest girl in school. As she falls in love with Arnie, Christine is jealous. There is, after all, no fury like a woman scorned. . . .

Comment

Although the character of Arnie Cunningham seems to owe a debt to *Carrie*—the story of an alienated girl in high school—it is much closer to another Arnie, Arnie Kalowski, the protagonist of an unpublished King novel, "Sword in the Darkness." In *Christine*, the young male protagonist, named Arnie, is in high school and is making plans to go to college. Arnie buys a 1958 Plymouth Fury for $250, which is his ticket to ride. His relationship with Leigh Cabot is constructive, but his relationship with Christine is destructive.

In "Sword in the Darkness," the young male protagonist, Arnie, is in high school and making plans to attend college. He buys a '56 Ford for $50. His relationship with Janet Cross is constructive, but his obsessive relationship with the sexually alluring Kit Longtin is destructive.

Christine, like King's other mainstream horror novels (*The Dead Zone* and *Firestarter*), is a good example of King's ability to tell a story that, while lacking the power of his early novels published by Doubleday, will certainly hold your attention from start to finish. If King were not a brand name, *Christine* would probably have been published as a paperback original and have sold well in airports, drugstores, and at newsstands—a diverting read, but not much more. *Christine* is the kind of book that, because it's so accessible, appeals to readers who would otherwise not read horror fiction. (If they read *any* horror fiction, chances are they only read King.)

Christine is mainstream horror, the kind that King popularized, and the kind that has brought him a wide readership that cares only about a story well told.

Editions Available and Tie-in Product

- A trade hardback, Viking, $22.95
- A paperback, NAL, $4.95
- The movie, *Christine,* from Columbia Pictures, available on videocassette from RCA/Columbia Home Video

It was a witch hunt.

It was the seduction of the innocent, if you believe the paralogism of Dr. Frederic Wertham, who found many willing allies in his fight to keep comics from corrupting the minds of children.

It was the 1950s, the era of Joseph McCarthy.

It was the death knell of E.C. Comics (Educational Comics, later called Entertaining Comics), a line that featured titles like *The Haunt of Fear, The Vault of Horror,* and *Tales from the Crypt.*

Cartoonist/artist Art Spiegelman, writing in *Print* magazine (November/December '88) tells what happened next:

> Lurid crime and horror comics with titles like *Teen-Age Dope Slaves, Reform School Girl,* and *Tales from the Crypt* [an E.C. title] led to congressional investigations, public comic-book burnings, boycotts, and quickly, to a "voluntary" code of standards that took most of the *fun* out of the funny books.

Though grisly, E.C. Comics were very moral: in the end, the bad guy got it. Educational comics? Well, yes, in their own fashion. Entertaining comics? Absolutely.

The World of the Creepshow

In *Creepshow* Stephen King and George Romero pay homage to E.C. Comics. A collection of five stories, *Creepshow* was published as an oversized comic book (a graphic album, as it's commonly called in the field). The cover art by Jack Kamen, an E.C. artist, shows a boy in bed reading *Creepshow,* with two King posters (*The Shining* and *Carrie*) on the wall behind him, next to a Romero poster for *Dawn of the Dead.* The interior art is by Berni Wrightson, generally acknowledged in the comic-book field as the première artist of the macabre.

"Father's Day" is a typical E.C. revenge-type story in which Nathan Grantham, the family patriarch, decides that, even after he's dead, he wants his just desserts; he will have his cake and eat it too, even if it means serving up someone's head on a platter.

"The Lonesome Death of Jordy Verrill" is the tale of a country bumpkin who discovers a meteor on his property and takes it to the local college's Department

Bob DeLong, Photo courtesy of the *Bangor Daily News*

Stephen King stands in front of movie poster for his movie *Creepshow 2*.

of Meteors, where he unsuccessfully attempts to sell it. He inadvertently breaks it open, spilling "meteorcrap" on his hands. And then, as you'd expect, the story grows on you. . . .

"The Crate" is the kind of story into which Wrightson can really sink his teeth. A beast with a ravenous appetite has remained in a chained crate stenciled "Arctic Expedition, June 19, 1834." After Professor Northrup discovers just *what* is in the box, he realizes the beast within is the perfect way to get rid of his nagging wife. By a ruse he gets Billie to come over to the basement of the science building where she becomes the monster's next crate date.

"Something to Tide You Over" is a typical E.C. story, using the theme of

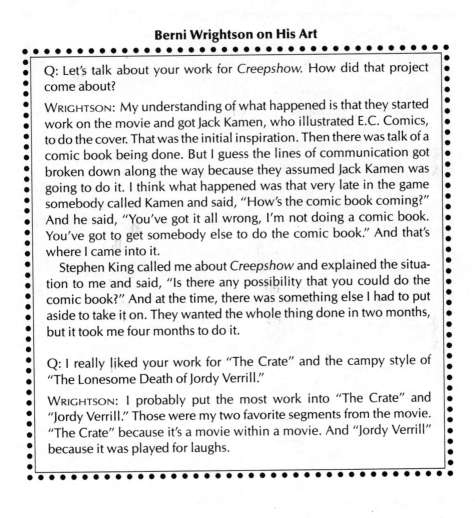

Berni Wrightson on His Art

Q: Let's talk about your work for *Creepshow*. How did that project come about?

WRIGHTSON: My understanding of what happened is that they started work on the movie and got Jack Kamen, who illustrated E.C. Comics, to do the cover. That was the initial inspiration. Then there was talk of a comic book being done. But I guess the lines of communication got broken down along the way because they assumed Jack Kamen was going to do it. I think what happened was that very late in the game somebody called Kamen and said, "How's the comic book coming?" And he said, "You've got it all wrong, I'm not doing a comic book. You've got to get somebody else to do the comic book." And that's where I came into it.

Stephen King called me about *Creepshow* and explained the situation to me and said, "Is there any possibility that you could do the comic book?" And at the time, there was something else I had to put aside to take it on. They wanted the whole thing done in two months, but it took me four months to do it.

Q: I really liked your work for "The Crate" and the campy style of "The Lonesome Death of Jordy Verrill."

WRIGHTSON: I probably put the most work into "The Crate" and "Jordy Verrill." Those were my two favorite segments from the movie. "The Crate" because it's a movie within a movie. And "Jordy Verrill" because it was played for laughs.

revenge. Harry Wentworth and Becky Vickers are in love, which sets well with them but not with Becky's husband, Richard, who finds out about the affair and buries both up to their necks on the beach during low tide. But the best-laid plans can be all washed up. . . .

"They're Creeping Up on You" is the last story in the book, using as its theme one of King's top ten fears: insects. It's the tale of Upson Pratt, a rich man who is bugged to death. . . .

Creepshow II

Like its predecessor, *Creepshow II* is a film anthology of three unrelated but interconnected King stories, adapted by George Romero. The stories are: "The Raft" (collected in *Skeleton Crew*), "Old Chief Wooden Head" (written especially for this movie), and "The Hitchhiker."

Unlike *Creepshow I*, *Creepshow II* did not have a tie-in comic-book edition, which is just as well. "The Raft" has its moments as a short story, but becomes comic-bookish on the screen. And neither "Old Chief Wooden Head" nor "The Hitchhiker" would benefit from a comic-book adaptation.

Comment

Both *Creepshow I* and *Creepshow II* are a tip of the hat from King and Romero to E.C. Comics, and nothing more. Moviegoers, accustomed to "hack and slash, cut and dice" horror movies would find these stories tame stuff by comparison. And King fans, having expected to see King's brand of horror translate well on the screen, found out again that Skull Cinema—the mind's eye—is still the best place to "see" his fiction come alive.

Edition Available and Tie-in Product

- A trade paperback, NAL, $6.95
- A movie, *Creepshow,* available on videocassette from Warner Brothers
- A movie, *Creepshow II,* available on videocassette from New World Video

Stephen King reads *Creepshow.*

Photo courtesy of the *Bangor Daily News*

Cujo

*No live organism can continue for long to exist sanely under conditions of
absolute reality; even larks and katydids are supposed, by some, to dream.*

Shirley Jackson, *The Haunting of Hill House*

Charity begins at home.

In the case of Joe Camber and his wife, Charity, there's not much charity. Joe,
who runs a garage on the outskirts of Castle Rock, Maine, terrorizes his wife and
their son Brett.

In another family in Castle Rock, there's not much charity, either. Vic Trenton watches his life disintegrate around him. On the work front, his small ad agency, ad worx (Portland, Maine), teeters on the brink of financial collapse because one of his major clients goes sour, and on the home front, he learns his wife is having an affair.

A relentlessly dark novel—the kind Richard Bachman might have penned if in a particularly morose mood—*Cujo* vividly shows the horrors of reality, and when the dog Cujo goes rabid, the realities of horror.

Synopsis

Set in Castle Rock, King's mythical small town in Maine, *Cujo* is principally the story of Joe Camber's two-hundred-pound Saint Bernard of the same name. The animal is not by nature a BAD DOG, but becomes one after being bitten on the nose by a bat.

For others in Castle Rock, life is similarly disorienting. Vic Trenton finds his business and his personal life falling apart. His wife Donna finds herself and her son Tad trapped in a broken-down Pinto that expires near Joe Camber's garage on the outskirts of town, with a rabid Cujo holding them at bay. And Steve Kemp—the local tennis pro who has had an affair with Donna—goes on a rampage, furious that Donna has finally rejected him.

Comment

When I saw *Easy Rider* the first time, I was stunned, like everyone else, at the casual killings of its two main characters, portrayed by Peter Fonda and Dennis Hopper. Movies just don't end this way, I thought. After *Easy Rider,* casual killing became so commonplace that it became a cliché—body count, both in movies and on TV, was the way to keep score.

Cujo prompted the same feeling. Tad's is a very natural, believable death, but you say to yourself: Books just don't end this way. Obviously, this is *not* a horror novel, certainly not the kind of horror you'd expect from King. If it was King's goal in this novel to portray the ugly reality of life, he succeeded. (It's so realistic that bad things happen to good people, and when you wonder why, you realize that life is like that.)

Cujo is unquestionably King's most pessimistic and, ultimately, realistic novel. At least one critic, Douglas E. Winter, writing in *The Art of Darkness,* feels that it's "one of King's best novels," but most agree with Harlan Ellison, who said in his film column, "Harlan Ellison's Watching," "Sometimes [King is] just okay, as in *Cujo* or *Christine*." My assessment is that Ellison is closer to the mark.

This book is grim reading, all the way. It's not the kind of book you would read for enjoyment. Its moral is simple: Life's a bitch and then you die.

Part of the problem King fans will have with this book is that they are used to horror fiction that, while obviously unreal, is truthful enough to *distract* them from the world and its ugly realities. But *Cujo* is not horror fiction, and it's not a fairy tale in which everything turns out happily ever after, despite its fairy-tale beginning, "Once upon a time. . . ."

What happens in *Cujo*—a dog becomes rabid and goes on the attack—could in fact happen, which is the real element of horror in this book.

I've read *Cujo* once, but can't imagine myself reading it a second time, because it's such a heavy dose of pessimism. But if you haven't read it, give it a try. You'll think, life can't be as bad as it is in this story. Or can it?

Edition Available and Tie-in Product

- Trade hardback, Viking, $22.95
- Paperback, NAL, $4.95
- The movie, *Cujo,* is available from Warner Home Video

Cycle of the Werewolf

When a new King novel sells a million copies in hardback and a year later three million in paperback, what's the point in publishing a new King book with a print run in trade hardback of only 7,500 copies?

Like Donald M. Grant's edition of *The Dark Tower: The Gunslinger,* which had a first printing of only 10,000 copies in trade hardback, Christopher Zavisa's Land of Enchantment edition of *Cycle of the Werewolf* had a small print run— 7,500 copies in trade hardback, most of which were sold to the science-fiction community. (Your local chain bookstore or independent bookstore never received copies to sell.) If you've never heard of fandom, here's an overview.

The World of Fans

It's a world that most people don't know about, but anyone who writes science fiction, fantasy, or horror knows it well. It's called fandom, and is composed of fans (*fan*atics, if you will), people who subscribe to the notion that fandom is either just a damned hobby or a way of life.

For many, it's a way of life. The fans correspond with one another, publish amateur publications (called fanzines), sponsor or attend conventions (so many that you could attend one a weekend for an entire year), and form local clubs where they socialize, comfortable in their knowledge that, by God, it's better to be a fan than be a mundane (fan slang for anyone who *isn't* a fan).

Locus and *S.F. Chronicle* are the two "newspapers" of the field, both providing in-depth information on what's going on in their world, with book reviews, articles, convention listings, and the like.

Many, but not all, of the professional writers in the field belong to the Science Fiction Writers of America. More recently, the Horror Writers of America was formed, and many who write what some call dark fantasy are members (yes, Stephen King is a member).

Then there are the awards. The membership of SFWA presents the Nebula Award, a beautiful Lucite cube with a spiraling Nebula galaxy inside. The fan community at large, gathering at its annual World Science Fiction Convention (held annually over Labor Day weekend), presents Hugo Awards, oversized silver rockets. And the membership of the World Fantasy Convention, which caters mostly to fantasy/horror enthusiasts, presents the Howard Award, a miniature bust of H.P. Lovecraft (a New Englander who published primarily in amateur

186

From *Cycle of the Werewolf* (opposite p. 32 in *Silver Bullet*).

Berni Wrightson on His Art

Q: Do people outside of the comics field know of your work?

WRIGHTSON: A lot of people outside the field think the only thing I've done was *Cycle of the Werewolf,* but I've done a lot more than that.

Q: How did it come about that you were selected to illustrate Zavisa's limited edition of *Cycle of the Werewolf?*

WRIGHTSON: Chris Zavisa put that whole thing together. It was his idea for a long time to do a project with Stephen King, with me as the illustrator. Chris wanted to do new material, a small project that he could handle as a [specialty] publisher. We were talking about it and Chris came up with the idea of doing a calendar. It'd almost have to be a werewolf story because the *only* thing *all* the months have in common is a full moon.

What I wanted to do would tie in with the dates of the calendar. Whatever year this was coming out we'd time it so that the events were happening on the same day as the calendar with the full moons. After we got this all worked out Chris approached King, who seemed excited by the whole idea. King started working on it as a calendar project. Each story was to be several paragraphs, a block of copy under the illustration, and under this, the calendar itself. As he was writing, King said the story began to grow on him, and he couldn't contain it to just a few paragraphs per month. Finally, it was becoming obvious that it was not going to be a calendar.

Q: Did you work closely with King on the art, or did you get a copy of the manuscript and work largely alone?

WRIGHTSON: King sent me the finished version and I just did the illustrations.

Q: What kind of feedback have you gotten from people that saw your work for the first time?

WRIGHTSON: After the book was published by NAL, I was at the grocery store and paid with a check. The clerk looked at the name on the check and asked, "Are you the guy that did [the art for] *Cycle of the Werewolf?*" I told him I was. Then he said, "I loved that. I bought two copies and I cut pictures out of the first copy to hang them up." I wonder which pictures he cut out.

publications and in *Weird Tales,* a pulp magazine that also published Robert E. Howard, who is best known for his Conan tales).

More than just readers, fans are publishers. While many are content to write letters to fellow fans, others contribute to fanzines, and yet others decide to go from being fan to pro and submit fiction to semiprofessional and professional markets.

Among the more ambitious fans are the specialty publishers, typically one-person operations, publishing fiction and nonfiction by some of the biggest names in the field. Unlike their counterparts on Publishers Row in New York, the specialty publishers offer modest advances against royalties, print small quantities, and sell primarily to those in the fantasy and science-fiction community. But they offer what the New York publisher can't: a close working relationship in which the author is part of the publishing process; a beautiful edition in which the typesetting, design, and binding enhance the text; and illustrations (both color and black and white) by leading fantasy artists.

It's the world of the limited edition, the craft of publishing beautiful books—slipcased, numbered, signed—and is worlds apart from the unimaginative trade editions that New York publishers *must* print because of economics.

Land of Enchantment

Christopher Zavisa is a specialty publisher. Unlike Donald M. Grant, Dark Harvest, and Scream Press, Land of Enchantment publishes infrequently, but when it does, it's a production to remember. Before publishing *Cycle of the Werewolf,* Zavisa's publishing credits included an oversized collection of Berni Wrightson artwork (*A Look Back*), a retrospective from Wrightson's early days to his work for *Frankenstein;* an art book on Filipino artist Alex Nino (*Satan's Tears*), profusely illustrated with full color plates; and, most recently, a sumptuous edition of Dean Koontz's *Twilight Eyes,* illustrated by Phil Parks.

Stephen King in the Land of Enchantment

How King came to publish *Cycle of the Werewolf* at Zavisa's specialty press is an interesting story, told at length in the introduction to *Silver Bullet* and also in a two-part article, "The Politics of Limited Editions," published in *Castle Rock* (June and July 1985).

As the story goes, it was October 1979 and King was attending the World Fantasy Convention, in Providence, Rhode Island. King was approached by Zavisa, who wanted to publish a calendar and market it through the chain bookstores, Waldenbooks and B. Dalton Bookseller. Berni Wrightson would render the illustrations, and King would write a dozen vignettes, approximately five hundred words each, one for each month.

Then the story grew. The initial concept was clever, certainly original, but incapable of containing the story, which required a larger canvas. King, who emphasizes telling the story above all else, found himself with a book on his hands.

0-9603828-2-8

Art by Berni Wrightson

Back cover design for the Land of Enchantment edition of *Cycle of the Werewolf.* (Variations of this drawing were done as originals laid in with the collector's edition.)

Publication History

The book was published in 1983 by Land of Enchantment in an oversized hard-back book, 8½ by 11 inches. The trade edition was limited to 7,500 copies. (Various states of a limited edition were published, signed and numbered, with the signatures of King and Wrightson, including a "collector's edition," in which was laid into the book an original drawing of a werewolf by Wrightson.)

In 1985 NAL published *Cycle of the Werewolf* as a trade paperback at $8.95. Later that year, however, a new edition was published under the title *Silver Bullet*, a tie-in to the movie of the same name. (*Silver Bullet* had, in addition to the complete contents of *Cycle of the Werewolf*, a new foreword by King, eight pages of photos from the movie, and King's screenplay.)

Synopsis

It's January and a blizzard assaults a small Maine town, Tarker's Mills. The flag-man for the GS&WM Railroad, Arnie Westrum, is playing cards with himself and hears a scratching sound on the door . . . then a pounding. The door splinters and the werewolf attacks. The cycle of the werewolf has begun.

Each month with each full moon, the killings continue . . . but Marty Cos-law, a crippled boy confined to the wheelchair, knows who the werewolf *really* is. Boy against werewolf—who wins?

Comments

Cycle of the Werewolf is a lightweight story that covers familiar King territory. It is set in a small Maine town, a typical King background. The characters, for the most part, are stereotyped; though they are fleshed out somewhat, the brevity of the story demands that characterization be sacrificed to story. And the identity of the werewolf is too predictable—who *else* could it have been?

It would have been interesting to see Zavisa, King, and Wrightson stick to the original, fascinating concept: a calendar with a story vignette. Still, the story's a fast read, and though not prime King material, it obviously wasn't meant to be. It's King having fun, playing with mood and atmosphere, and it's Wrightson doing what he does best: illustrating the horrific in grisly, beautiful detail.

Edition Available and Tie-in Product

- A trade paperback, NAL, *Silver Bullet* (incorporating *Cycle of the Werewolf*), $9.95
- The movie, *Silver Bullet*, a Paramount Picture, available on videotape from Paramount Home Video

Danse Macabre

It's my Final Statement on the clockwork of the horror tale.

Stephen King, introduction to *Danse Macabre*

Where do you get your ideas?

In the case of *Danse Macabre,* the idea came from King's editor at Double-day, Bill Thompson. As King tells in his "Forenote" to the book, Thompson called him and asked, " 'Why don't you do a book about the entire horror phenomenon as you see it? Books, movies, radio, TV, the whole thing.' "

As a writer who loves the genre, one who has read widely and deeply in the field, King is eminently qualified. In this book King takes a long, affectionate look at the field.

The book begins with the story on how he was hooked on horror, at age ten, at a theater in Stratford, Connecticut, where he saw *Earth vs. the Flying Saucers.* Look to your skies . . . look to your skies . . . and when they did, when the lights went up in the middle of the movie, the theater manager announced to the dis-believing audience that *Sputnik* had been launched, that the Russians had one up on us in the space race.

The rest of the book moves from that fateful moment to the early 1980s, and in the process you will learn much about the horror field and, especially, about King and his fiction.

For those of you who have yet to buy the book—because it's nonfiction, and your steady diet is King fiction—I have good news: King's colloquial prose, com-bined with his in-depth knowledge of the field, will hold your attention. If you are a newcomer to the horror field—its books, its movies, its dark practitioners, and most of all its colorful history—then you're in for a long walk through the dark woods with King as your guide, pointing out everything you need to know. If you fancy yourself an aficionado of horror, then this book will inspire you to reread some of your favorites. Like all good criticism, this book illuminates other works, revealing aspects perhaps you have overlooked.

The book is divided into ten chapters and two appendices: the first appen-dix, King's recommended viewing list of 100 movies (1950–80); the second, his

The Author Talks: King on the Loss of Innocence

I was in Stratford, Connecticut, watching *Earth vs. the Flying Saucers,* which is about aliens coming from space to the earth with these death rays and everything, and the movie stopped and the manager walked out and said, "I have to announce to you that the Russians have just launched a space satellite." And it was a Saturday matinee and we all just sat totally stunned. You know, a Saturday matinee audience, they're all loud and throwing stuff and everything, and everybody just shut up. We couldn't believe it. This was not the way things were supposed to work. We've *seen* all the movies. This *never* happened. *The bad guys were first!* I mean, it's like that Russian guy knocking out Rocky Balboa or killing him. *How could this be?* And that was really, I would say, the first incident in the ending of my childhood.

Your childhood doesn't die all at once. It sort of blights like a plant.

recommended reading list of 100 books (1950–80). It's not likely that, unless you have spent many hours haunting bookstores and theaters, you would have read all the books and seen all the movies. No matter. The lists are a good place to start, if you want to take an unaccompanied walk where dark things grow. (After reading *Danse Macabre,* the territory may still be new to you, but it won't be as forbidding.)

For those of you who haven't read King's nonfiction, this book is a good place to start. Though King has written over two dozen books, *Danse Macabre* is unique because it is his *only* collection of nonfiction, which is a shame. King has written well over one hundred pieces of nonfiction, from which a book could easily be assembled. (You might want to check with your library to see if it has Ursula K. LeGuin's now out-of-print collection of nonfiction, *From Elfland to Poughkeepsie,* edited by the late Susan Wood. If you have any interest in the fantasy field, that book is required reading, especially the essay from which the book takes its title.)

If you know someone who hasn't read King, give him two books, a kind of show-and-tell: *'Salem's Lot* will show him what King's fiction is all about, and *Danse Macabre* will *tell* him about, as King put it, "the clockwork of the horror tale."

A storm rages outside, but inside the ballroom we're dancing the night away. I feel a tap on my shoulder. I glance behind me, and it's Stephen King. He's cutting in because he wants the next dance with you. The lights are flickering. Now they're out. As I leave, I hear his final words to you: "May I have the pleasure?"

Edition Available

• A paperback, Berkley Books, $4.95

King on *Danse Macabre*

I wrote *Danse Macabre* for a friend of mine, Bill Thompson, who edited all my early books at Doubleday. He asked me: If I was sitting in a bar room with a friend and I could say everything that I thought about horror fiction, horror movies, and what it all means—because I'm asked [those] questions time and time again—would I be interested in doing a book like that?

Stephen King, on "The Larry King Show"

The Dark Tower

Above all else, I'm interested in good and evil, whether or not there are powers of good and powers of evil that exist outside ourselves.

Stephen King, in *Castle Rock*

In the special Stephen King issue of *Whispers* (August 1982)—a small-press literary magazine published by Stuart D. Schiff, who also runs Whispers Press—Schiff wrote:

> No, I am not a partner with Donald Grant although I would certainly like the opportunity to join up! Still, my never-ending praise for his publications might make it appear I have a financial interest in his press. The reality of the situation is that Don does great work and [as] such deserves praise. He has just produced what might possibly be the most important book ever from a specialty press. It is Stephen King's *The Dark Tower: The Gunslinger* (HC, $20; *signed* by author and artist, 500 copies, $60) as illustrated by Hugo-Award winner, Michael Whelan. The book is an epic tale, weird and unlike anything else King has written. The Whelan artwork is superb. The trade hardcover has "only" a 10,000 copy run. No sarcasm is intended by my quotation marks. King's hardcovers normally sell *many* times that number so the book may sell out quickly. Regarding the materials, Don has spared no expense. The paper is special, there are colored pictorial endpapers, five color plates, and the usual other expertise the field has come to expect from Grant. Do not miss this book.

The book, promoted only within the science-fiction and fantasy community, went quickly out of print. A year later, when Doubleday published *Pet Sematary* and listed *The Dark Tower* as a novel in a listing of other books by King, the phone calls and letters began. King fans who routinely await each King book with eager anticipation were surprised a King novel had been published that they neither had heard of nor had the opportunity to buy.

The firestorm began. King's readers besieged booksellers and King's trade publishers, and some even wrote to King trying to get a copy of the book. For the first time, here was a book-length work of fiction by King that you couldn't go into a bookstore and order.

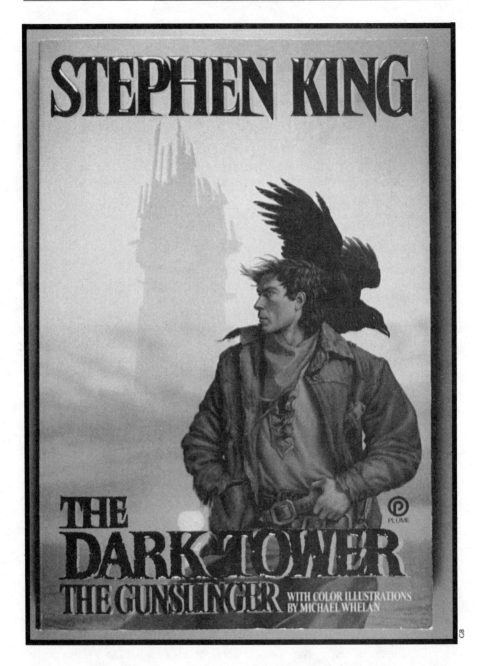

Cover to NAL's trade paperback edition of *The Dark Tower: The Gunslinger,* with artwork by Michael Whelan.

King, surprised at the interest, authorized Donald M. Grant to issue a second edition. As King explained in an essay, "The Politics of Limited Editions," a second run of 10,000 copies went quickly out of print. King commented: "This, I have discovered, was a little like pissing on a forest fire in an attempt to put it out."

Supply and Demand

From 1982 to fall 1988 the book remained out of print. People who wanted to read the stories haunted bookstores for the original issues of *Fantasy and Science Fiction*, wherein they had appeared, but even that proved difficult. Booksellers knew of the demand and priced copies accordingly. Meanwhile, the Grant books spiraled in value.

A Man Called Slade

Long before Roland the Gunslinger stalked the desolate world of *The Dark Tower*, Stephen King wrote about Jack Slade, the "roughest, toughest (queerest?) gunslinger in the American Southwest."

Serialized in *The Maine Campus* (June to August 1970), and available only in microfilmed copies, "Slade" recounts how gunslinger Jack Slade is hired by Miss Sandra Dawson to fight Sam Columbine, who is plotting to take over her ranch.

Slade, who wears twin .45s, smokes Mexican cigars, drinks "three zombies" in one standing, and shoots first and asks questions later, fights and shoots but doesn't romance his way through this parody of the western genre. When Sandra Dawson, a vixen with "heaving bosoms," throws herself at Slade and says, "Anything I can do to help you, Slade, *anything!*" Slade knows what to do. He remains true to his first, true love, Miss Polly Peachtree of Paduka, Illinois, who was killed when a "flaming Montgolfier balloon" crashed into the barn where she was milking cows. Growls Slade: "My mom told me about girls like you."

Does Slade dispatch varmint Sam Columbine (of the Rotten Vulture Ranch)? Does Slade save Sandra Dawson (of the Bar-T Ranch) from the depredations of Columbine? Most important, does Slade administer justice with his twin .45s? I won't say, except to tell you that Sandra Dawson has a big secret that, when revealed, explains everything.

Like any good western, the story ends with Jack Slade riding off into the sunset on his trusty steed, a black stallion, Stokley.

To make matters more difficult, King had no intentions of authorizing a trade edition. In "The Politics of Limited Editions," King cited three reasons for his reluctance. First, it wasn't "the common rural/suburban *milieu* of the archetypal Stephen King novel." Second, "I believed then and believe now that more general readers would feel both shocked and cheated by the book's lack of resolution—it is, after all, the first section of a much longer work." And, third, there was the question of overpublishing.

After the Stephen King firestorm, however, the first and third points were no longer relevant: King fans wanted his books and wanted the opportunity to judge for themselves. On the second point, "the lack of resolution," the problem was minimized by scheduling the publication of the second book within a half year of the first book.

In September 1988 the book was announced as the lead title in NAL's fall–winter catalogue for 1988–89. *The Dark Tower: The Gunslinger* was published in a trade edition at $10.95. Preceding the book, however, was the unabridged audio-tape reading by King: a boxed, four-cassette package at $29.95.

NAL and *The Dark Tower*

NAL made sure everyone knew just how special this book would be. In its catalogue, NAL explained:

> In 1982, the world's most popular novelist published a book that almost no one has been able to buy or read. *The Gunslinger,* the first stanza in a much longer work called *The Dark Tower,* had only 30,000 [Editor's Note: 20,000] hardcover copies printed in its special limited edition. King's devoted fans quickly pushed the prices of these hard-to-find books up to $1000 each. Finally, with the publication of *The Gunslinger* in trade paperback, his millions of loyal readers can rejoice!

The Dark Tower II: The Drawing of the Three

In 1987 Donald M. Grant published the second book in the series, *The Dark Tower II: The Drawing of the Three.* Issued in a limited edition and a trade edition, and illustrated by Phil Hale, the book went out of print in months. The limited edition (850 copies, numbered, and signed by King and Hale) was published at $100 and now commands up to $500 (or more) on the secondary market. The Grant trade edition, with a 30,000-copy print run, was published at $35 and now goes for $65–$125, with an average sale price of $85.

In March 1989 NAL released an unabridged, eight-cassette set of *The Dark Tower II,* read by Stephen King; the set sold for $34.95. Immediately following was the release of the book in trade paperback, with the Phil Hale illustrations (including a new cover by Hale), at $12.95.

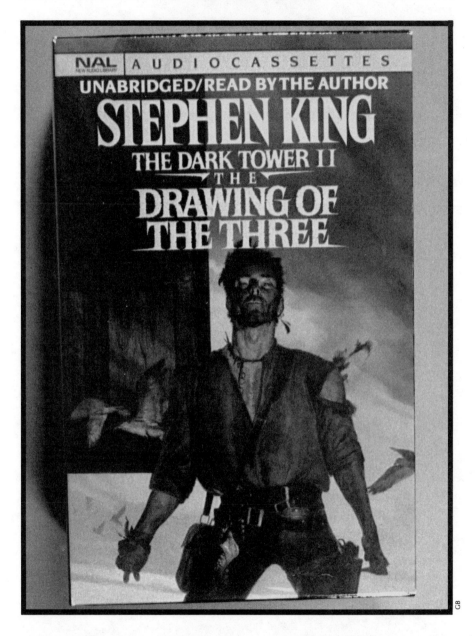

Cover to NAL's audiotape cassette set *The Dark Tower II: The Drawing of the Three*, with art by Phil Hale (commissioned especially for the NAL edition).

Unlike the stories in the first collection, published in *The Magazine of Fantasy and Science Fiction* from 1978 to 1981, the stories in the second book were more mature—not surprising, considering the time gap. *Publishers Weekly,* which panned the first *Dark Tower* book, damned the second with faint praise:

> Although these minor but revealing books (which King began while still in college) are full of . . . adolescent portentousness, this is livelier than the first. Roland enters three lives in the alternate world of New York City: junkie and drug runner Eddie Dean, schizophrenic heiress Odetta Holmes and serial killer Jack Mort. If King tells us too little about Roland, he gives us too much about these misfits who are variously healed or punished exactly as expected. Typically, King is much better at the minutiae and sensations of a specific physical world, and several such bravura sequences (from an attack by mutant lobsters to a gun store robbery) are standouts amid the characteristic headlong storytelling.

More *Dark Tower* Books to Come

In the "Afterword" to the second book, King said that he expects the series to continue:

> The third, *The Waste Lands,* details half of the quest of Roland, Eddie, and Susannah to reach the Tower; the fourth, *Wizards and Glass,* tells of an enchantment and a seduction but mostly of those things which befell Roland before his readers first met him upon the trail of the man in black.

When *The Waste Lands* gets written, the quest will continue. As King promised in his afterword to the first book:

> I do know this: at some point, at some magic time, there will be a purple evening (an evening made for romance!) when Roland will come to his dark tower, and approach it, winding his horn . . . and if I should ever get there, you'll be the first to know.

Editions Available and Tie-in Product

- *The Dark Tower: The Gunslinger,* trade paperback, NAL, $10.95
- *The Dark Tower: The Gunslinger,* paperback, NAL, $4.95
- *The Dark Tower: The Gunslinger,* four unabridged audiocassettes, NAL, $29.95
- *The Dark Tower II: The Drawing of the Three,* trade paperback, NAL, $12.95
- *The Dark Tower II: The Drawing of the Three,* eight unabridged audiocassettes, NAL, $34.95

The Dead Zone

In John Kennedy Toole's great comic novel *A Confederacy of Dunces,* Ignatius J. Reilly's worldview is dominated by the wheel of fortune:

> As a medievalist Ignatius believed in the *rota Fortunae,* or wheel of fortune, a central concept in *De Consolatione Philosophiae,* the philosophical work which had laid the foundation for medieval thought. Boethius, the late Roman who had written the *Consolatione* while unjustly imprisoned by the emperor, had said that a blind goddess spins us on a wheel, that our luck comes in cycles.

It's the same wheel of fortune that marks the life of Johnny Smith, who in *The Dead Zone* has a phenomenal run of luck at the carnival where he unerringly picks the right numbers, every time, and walks away with hundreds of dollars.

But the wheel spins . . . and Smith has an auto accident that puts him into a coma for almost five years, during which time the world has inevitably moved on.

When Smith regains consciousness, he has a strange power: by touching someone else's hand, he can see that person's life as a continuum: past, present, and future. And when he shakes the hand of Greg Stillson at a political rally, he sees the future . . . and it's a dark vision.

Smith must make a deliberate decision; he must act, or not act. Does the wheel of fortune dictate our lives (the philosophy of determinism), or do we have free will, a choice we can make that can alter the events in our lives?

Smith is an ordinary man gifted (or damned) with an extraordinary power. But with that power comes responsibility. He can use it for good or, by ignoring it, let evil run its course. It's a moral dilemma, one that Smith must resolve within himself.

Comment

The Dead Zone is one of King's best novels, principally because it's a step away from the traditional trappings of horror—werewolves, ghosts, vampires, and hauntings—that, in the minds of many, mark King's fiction.

The premise for Smith's ability—an auto accident that, somehow, triggers paranormal powers—is derived from the notion that, despite what we think, we know very little about how the human mind works.

There was once a news story (and, no, I can't remember where it appeared) of a woman who had sustained head injuries and while undergoing surgery "relived" a specific childhood incident in detail, with all her senses, as a result of a scapel that momentarily touched part of her brain.

It is Smith's "gift" that, as the novel progresses, becomes increasingly important, as Smith's world shifts from a personal perspective to a much larger perspective, one in which he can exercise his free will and change the course of history.

Editions Available

- A trade hardback, Viking, $22.95
- A paperback, NAL, $4.95

Different Seasons

In his afterword to *Different Seasons*, Stephen King explains the dilemmas of being typecast as a horror writer. *Carrie*, as King points out, is about a girl with the power of telekinesis; *'Salem's Lot* is about a small town in Maine overrun by vampires; and *The Shining* is about a resort hotel in Colorado with an evil history.

The logical deduction would be that King's next book would be a horror novel.

But what if things had turned out differently? What if King had taken the other route?

The following, obviously fictitious, interview was conducted by Rusty Wornom at the King's winter residence in Bangor, Maine. King, dressed in L.L. Bean clothes, sat next to a Vermont Castings woodstove, with a six-pack of Coors beer, Silver Bullets.[1]

King, the prominent Maine regionalist, talks about the genesis of his first collection of novellas, *A Change of Season*, and his desire to publish, for the first time, straight horror novels.

"It's a problem," admits King. "But my publishers got a little nervous when I told them that I wanted to write a straight horror novel."

On the desk were two manuscripts: *Second Coming* (242 pages), a novel about vampires in a small Maine town, and "Blaze" (173 pages), a literary homage to Steinbeck's *Of Mice and Men*.

"After my editor read both books, he wanted to publish 'Blaze.' The book's got a real Bachman flavor to it, and I almost published it under that pen name. I thought my editor would want to publish *Second Coming*, but as he pointed out to me, horror doesn't sell."

"What are you working on next?" I asked.

"I've got a novel called 'Sword in the Darkness.' It's a long book—485 manuscript pages, about 150,000 words. Like *Carrie*, it's mostly about high school hell, but it's set against the backdrop of a race riot in a medium-sized town in Maine."

"After that?" I asked.

"I've been wanting to write a straight horror novel, but the publishers were

---

1. Ethrane Wimbey, "Stephen King: A Change of Season," in *Maine's Regional Writers.* (Newport News, Virginia: GB Publishing: 1982), p. 65.

concerned about how to market it. So I asked them if they would be interested in a collection of novellas—mainstream stuff, but with elements of horror. Then, after that, I can write about things that go bump in the night."

"What's in *A Change of Season?*" I asked.

"The four stories have all been published before. The *New Yorker* published 'The Body,' the *Saturday Evening Post* published 'The Breathing Method,' *Prison Digest* published 'Rita Hayworth,' and Ed Ferman—my man!—at *F&SF* took 'Apt Pupil' and ran with it. 'The Body' has been optioned by Reiner for a movie; 'Apt Pupil' is also under option. I liked the stories and wanted to collect them in one book. So, for me, it's a change of season. It's my way of saying that I *do* write horror. I think my readers will understand."

"Why the shift into horror?" I asked.

"I've always written horror, but after the first few books, the publishers were concerned that it might create confusion in the marketplace. There was some discussion about using my pen name, Richard Bachman, for the straight horror stuff, but as you know, Robert Weinberg blew the whistle, and the publishers figured I should use my own name."

"Any ideas on what your first horror novel will be?" I asked.

"I've been kicking around an idea about a large publishing house in New York that's haunted by ghosts—authors who died, waiting for royalties, who have come back to haunt the publisher, an E.C.–type story—but I dunno. It may be a little too far out."

"You mean the ghosts?"

"No. The publisher," replied King, as he reached for another Silver Bullet.

Different Seasons

As King astutely points out in his afterword to *Different Seasons,* there's no real market for novellas, works of fiction that are too long to be short stories but too short to be novels. Magazine editors won't buy them, and unless you are a name author, the chance of getting a collection published is small indeed.

King readers, expecting his unusual brand of horror, come into this book with false expectations. Instead, what's served up is mainstream fiction with elements of horror: "Rita Hayworth and Shawshank Redemption," "Apt Pupil," "The Body," and "The Breathing Method."

All the stories are well told—I believe King cannot tell a dull story—but two stand out: "Apt Pupil," the kind of mainstream horror that puts a deep hook in you, and "The Body," adapted by Robert Reiner as *Stand by Me* for the screen.

Different Seasons also points out King's versatility as a writer, a fact frequently overlooked by reviewers. Unlike other writers, King's range of literary output is impressive: short stories, novellas, novels, nonfiction, screenplays, and poetry. The story dictates the form.

"Apt Pupil"

I die with a joyful heart in the awareness of the immeasurable deeds and achievements of our soldiers at the front, and the contribution, unique in history, of our youth, which bears my name.[2]

There are two kinds of horror stories: the kind you know could never happen, and the kind that could. As Clive Barker said on the "Larry King Show," memorable horror fiction "does a bunch of things simultaneously: it arouses the imagination, it disturbs, and it also scares."

"Apt Pupil" succeeds brilliantly on all three counts because the tale is uncomfortably close to reality—it could happen.

"Apt Pupil" is the story of a sick symbiosis between a thirteen-year-old "all-American kid" named Todd Bowden and a former death-camp commandant, Mr. Dussander, who had hopes of living out his life in anonymity in suburban Los Angeles under the name of Arthur Denker.

But Bowden, who discovers that his own "GREAT INTEREST" is an obsession for the grisly details of the Holocaust, blackmails Dussander into telling him about the "gooshy stuff." Dussander does . . . but the price is high, and both Bowden and Dussander must pay.

Comment

There is no need for aliens to invade as in *The Invasion of the Body Snatchers* to make monsters out of men. "Apt Pupil" makes the chilling point that monsters are among us, but that we can't readily recognize them because they appear perfectly normal. By the time we do, it's too late.

Because the horror originates from inside Todd Bowden, just as it's reawakened in Dussander, it hits home: There's a little of Todd Bowden in all of us.

Stand by Me

When *Stand by Me,* produced by Robert Reiner, was released in summer 1986, the movie was *not* promoted as a Stephen King movie. Only those who had read "The Body" in *Different Seasons,* or those who watched the end credits roll, would have noticed. The movie, the sleeper of the season, was a critical and financial success. The reason *Stand by Me* succeeded whereas most other King movies have failed? It was a faithful adaptation that successfully translated the prose on the screen. Simply put, *Stand by Me* is pure Stephen King, and proved that King *could* translate effectively to the screen.

---

2. Adolf Hitler, in his final Political Testament (April 29, 1945).

"The Body"

Intensely autobiographical, "The Body" is set in King's mythical Castle Rock, Maine. It is a coming-of-age yarn, the kind that either succeeds brilliantly or fails miserably. In King's case, it's a resounding success, a powerful work of fiction that draws on King's recollections of what it was like to grow up as a twelve-year-old boy in 1960.

Principally the story of Gordie Lachance, a mirror image of King as a young writer, the plot is straightforward. Gordie and his three friends set off on a trip to view the body of a boy who had been hit by a train. They journey from childhood to the first stage in adulthood and learn about life and, more important, themselves.

As adults, we grow up and forget what it is like to be a child, but in "The Body" King takes us back with him and shows us, in achingly real detail, what it's like to be young again.

Editions Available and Tie-in Product

- A trade hardback, Viking, $22.95
- A paperback, NAL, $4.95
- A movie, *Stand by Me* (an adaptation of "The Body"), from Columbia Pictures, available on videocassette
- "Apt Pupil" on audiocassette, an unabridged reading (Recorded Books), on five cassettes, $34.95
- "The Body" on audiocassette, an unabridged reading (Recorded Books), on four cassettes, $26.95
- "The Breathing Method" on audiocassette, an unabridged reading (Recorded Books), on two cassettes, $15.95
- "Rita Hayworth & Shawshank Redemption" on audiocassette, an unabridged reading (Recorded Books), on three cassettes, $19.95

For More Information

The afterword by King to *Skeleton Crew* gives the background of each story.

Dear Walden People[1]
by Stephen King

To give advance information to its chain stores, Waldenbooks had published an informal newsletter distributed only to its stores and to publishers who subscribe to the newsletter. My speculation is that the piece that follows was written by King because Different Seasons *is not the typical King book—it's a collection of novellas minus the kind of horror usually associated with King—and store managers and customers might have been a little confused without it.*

I've been asked if *Different Seasons,* my book of four short novels, means that I've reached the end of my interest in such uplifting and mentally edifying subjects as ghouls, ghosts, vampires, and unspeakable things lurking in the closets of little kids. After all, these questioners point out, three of the four novellas deal with nonhorror themes—prison escape, little boys whose curiosity is perhaps too big for their own good, more little boys on an unlikely—but all too possible—quest. My response is to point out that the *fourth* story in *Different Seasons* (which my youngest son, Owen, persists in calling *Different Sneezes*) is pretty gruesome. It concerns a doctor, a rather peculiar men's club, and an unwed mother who is extremely determined to give birth to her baby.

No, I've always been one of the Halloween people, and I guess I always will be. I've got a vampire bat and a rattlesnake on my desk—both mercifully stuffed—you get the idea. Yet I don't think anyone can write just one sort of fiction *all* the time. Herman Wouk, author of such grim and sweeping epics as *The Winds of War* and *The Caine Mutiny,* has also written a hilarious novel of childhood, *The City Boy*. Gregory McDonald, known for those two unlikely detectives Fletch and Flynn, has written an amusing novel about a lonely-hearts columnist on a city newspaper (*Love Among the Mashed Potatoes*). Travis McGee fans might be surprised to learn that John D. MacDonald has written a good deal of science fiction, including two damn fine science-fiction novels (*Wine of the Dreamers, Ballroom of the Skies*). And Evan Hunter (a.k.a. Ed McBain), who is often associated with the gritty world of urban crime courtesy of the 87th Precinct, has written at least one western (*The Chisolms*) and a science fiction novel (*Find the Feathered Serpent*).

Writers of grue sometimes also go straight. Richard Matheson, who has created vampires aplenty in *I Am Legend* (filmed as *The Omega Man,* with Charlton

1. Reprinted with permission from *Book Notes* (August 1983), a Waldenbooks' publication.

Heston) and is the author of innumerable classic short stories (*Duel,* for instance, which became the classic Steven Spielberg film of the same name) in the horror field, has published a war novel (*The Beardless Warriors*). Roald Dahl, first known for the grimly ironic stories in *Kiss Kiss* and *Someone Like You,* is now as well known for his whimsical stories for children.

The point is, when you live in your imagination a lot of the time, it may take you anywhere—anywhere at all. The four stories in *Different Seasons* were written for love, not money, usually in between other writing projects. They have a pleasant, open-air feel, I think—even at the grimmest moments (I haven't been able to get away from horror entirely, even here—there's a scene in one of the stories where a fellow tosses a cat into the oven and bakes it—*you're warned*) there's something about them, I hope, that says the writer was having a good time, hanging loose, worrying not about the storyteller but only the tale.

I had some fun with 'em, and that's usually a pretty good sign that the reader will have some fun too. I hope so, anyway. That's enough for now, I guess, so let me close with just a cordial word of warning: remember that when you turn out the light this evening and climb into your bed, *anything* could be under it—anything at all.

The Eyes of the Dragon

Once upon a time. . . .

Those are magic words, promising a trip to a place that doesn't exist except in the world of imagination.

Stephen King begins *The Eyes of the Dragon* in a similar fashion, so close that you could easily drop those words in the first sentence: "Once [upon a time], in a kingdom called Delain, there was a King with two sons."

Written primarily to please his daughter Naomi (to whom the book is dedicated, along with Peter Straub's son, Ben), *The Eyes of the Dragon* is both a children's book and an adult novel; it is, in fact, an adult fairy tale.

Like *Winnie the Pooh, The Hobbit, The Wind in the Willows,* and other classic books written for an audience of one (the author's son or daughter), *The Eyes of the Dragon* is Stephen King reaching out through his fiction to please his daughter. In an article in the February 1987 issue of *Castle Rock,* King explained that daughter Naomi paid him the ultimate writer's compliment: "[t]he only thing wrong with it was that she didn't want it to end. That, my friends, is a writer's favorite song. . . ."

The Eyes of the Dragon is written from the heart, and King shows us the heart of good fiction: an engaging tale that can be read by a child with adult sensibilities or an adult who acknowledges the child within himself and can see the world with a sense of wonder, an imaginative sixth sense that keeps him young at heart.

Philtrum Press

In a long essay, "The Politics of Limiteds," King explains the primary reasons for self-publishing *The Eyes of the Dragon.* When the book was finished, because King's publishing schedule was full through 1988, a trade edition was not a viable option. And unlike King's other novels, *The Eyes of the Dragon* was "a story which seemed to me primarily a children's tale."

Self-publishing also enabled King to fulfill many obligations: to himself as a writer who feels that publication is the final step in the writing of a book; to his daughter Naomi, who would see the book dedicated (in part) to her, and who could then put a copy on her shelf; to the two hundred fifty friends on the Kings' Christmas list who would get the book instead of *The Plant* that year; and to his fans in the fantasy community, the ones who eagerly subscribe to each limited-edition King book, guaranteeing a sold-out edition before publication.

Because *The Eyes of the Dragon* was published by King's own Philtrum Press, it, more than any other King book, reflects the author in every stage of publication. As publisher, King enlisted the aid of two principal people to help him put the project together: a long-time friend, Michael Alpert, the designer for *The Plant;* and through Alpert, Kenneth Linkous, a then unknown artist who went to Alpert's frame shop in Bangor with the intention of having a piece of fantasy art matted and framed for presentation to King, in the hopes that he might be considered for a future book project.

The printing was handled by Stinehour Press (Lunenburg, Vermont), the company that printed *The Plant* and would later print Philtrum Press's second book, Don Robertson's *The Ideal, Genuine Man* (a 1978 title).

King's sister-in-law, Stephanie Leonard (then King's secretary and editor/publisher of the King newsletter, *Castle Rock*), acted as the executive secretary for Philtrum Press; in addition to writing the ad copy that ran in small-circulation magazines, she undoubtedly assisted in innumerable other ways.

Michael Alpert: Book Designer

In a long essay in the August 1985 issue of *Castle Rock,* Alpert explained how he, working closely with King, arrived at the basic design of the book:

> We decided that the finished book would be quite large in format, printed from metal type on fine acid-free paper, illustrated with black-and-white line drawings, bound attractively in a sturdy binding, and housed in a matching protective slipcase. This was the general basis from which I began to work on the details of my design.

More than just a designer, Alpert has a thorough background in printing and is also a poet; his poetic sensibilities helped shape the book:

> From my point of view, a book is very definitely a *private theater,* and the presentation of a book's content is very much like the presentation of a play through creative stage-design. Just as the dimming of lights in a theater lets an audience know that they are about to be invited into a world of fantasy, so the design of a book can give visual and psychological space between the content of the book and the rest of the universe. The primary work of a book-designer is to make sure that nothing interferes with a reader's immersion into the text.

Reading is a very private experience—a personal relationship between the book and the reader, with the author as the bridge. If the writer does his job, the reader willingly suspends his disbelief and is immersed into the text, as put by Alpert. The reader is transported from the real world and "falls" into the book.

The Eyes of the Dragon: The NAL paperback edition (in the foreground) and the title page to the Philtrum Press edition (in the background). Note: On the right side is the slipcase.

Kenneth Linkous: Illustrator

An artist who has an affinity with King's work, Linkous rendered the pen-and-ink illustrations for *The Eyes of the Dragon*. The artwork, in the tradition of illustrated books (almost a lost art today), was an integral part of the book's design. The work included illustrations for the title page and the chapter headings; and spaced throughout were quarter-page and full-page illustrations.

The illustrations look like etchings, especially on the heavy paper stock selected by Alpert for the book, stock which intentionally had the texture and feel of linen napkins (*The Napkins* was the original title of this book).

The illustrations are marvelous and, to my mind, evoke the essence of the book much better than the David Palladini illustrations used for the Viking trade edition and the NAL paperback.

The Lottery

King's popularity guaranteed that the book would sell out its first and only Philtrum Press printing. The only pressing question was how to distribute the edition equitably. In the end, a lottery was held and a thousand names were drawn. Stephanie Leonard then sent out a letter requesting payment of $127 ($120 for the book, $7 for postage).

Those lucky enough to have bought the book were in for a real treat. The finished book, reflecting King's vision from conception to delivery, is pure art: a delightful story, wonderful illustrations, a beautiful edition.

The limited edition weighs almost five pounds, measures approximately $8^1/4$ by $13^1/4$ inches, is protected by a matching slipcase, and reflects uncompromising production values in typesetting, design, illustration, printing, and binding.

Since its original publication in 1984, the limited edition has, predictably, become an expensive collector's item, enhanced by the fact that this edition was published by King's own press. If you can find a copy, the price is likely to be a princely $750. But for the majority of owners, the book is a kingly treasure, not for sale at any price.

Viking Press Edition

The Eyes of the Dragon was published in hardback by Viking in 1987. The text remained essentially the same, despite some minor changes and a few additions, including a scene that amplified the nature of friendship between Peter (the first-born son of the king) and his best friend, Ben.

The major change was in art. A new artist was commissioned to render new illustrations. It's a matter of personal taste, but I prefer King's original choice for illustrator, Kenneth Linkous. David Palladini, a professional artist, seems not to have an affinity with fantasy illustration. (Imagine what the book would have been like if the art had been rendered by a fantasy artist like Alicia Austin or Tim Kirk, both well known in the science-fiction and fantasy field for their evocative work.)

The dust jacket, I might add, was imaginatively designed. In addition to the bold colors, the impressed printing suggests the texture of a dragon's scale—a nice touch.

For whatever reasons, the first edition did not credit Philtrum Press with having published a limited edition, an oversight corrected in later editions at King's request.

Comment

On the title page, the book is called "a story by Stephen King," suggesting that it's more a fable than anything else. Approximately a hundred thousand words, the story is somewhat of a surprise for King fans who think that he can write only horror, a popular misconception prevalent also among mainstream reviewers who don't, or won't, read King carefully. In an introduction to King's *Night Shift*, the late John D. MacDonald observed that King, having shown his ability to write

Marc Blanchette, Photo courtesy of the *Bangor Daily News*

Stephen King and Kenny Ray Linkous hold up artwork to *The Eyes of the Dragon.*

horror and humor, "can write in any area." Translation: King's a writer, first, and he's apt to write about anything that interests him; so don't fall into the trap of stereotyping him as a horror writer, because you'll only trap yourself.

Synopsis

Dear reader, you probably think I'm about to give you a detailed synopsis, but I'm not. After all, it would give away the story, wouldn't it?

But this I'll tell you. It's a tale about a dragon and the king who killed it; a young and beautiful queen who has two sons, Peter and Thomas, one of whom becomes the man who would be king; and an evil magician—old as the hills—named Flagg, who harbors terrible secrets.

My advice to you: buy the book and take the trip to Delain. When you're finished, you'll probably agree with me that a sequel is definitely in order.

Editions Available

- A trade hardback, Viking, $18.95
- A paperback, NAL, $4.50

Firestarter

"Get away," she hissed. "Take your monster and get away."

Norma Manders to Andy McGee about his daughter Charlie, the firestarter

It's one of those mysteries that make you scratch your head and wonder *why they did that.*

I refer, of course, to the abysmal artwork on the cover of *Firestarter,* both on the hardback edition (which is par for the course) and, surprisingly, on the paperback cover. The purpose of cover artwork is to catch your attention and move you to pick up the book. In King's case, it may be that his name alone on the cover—printed in bold, oversized letters, with the book title underneath—would have been sufficient. But there is no excuse for slapping mediocre art on the cover when better work was available—for instance, Michael Whelan's wraparound color cover for the Phantasia Press edition of *Firestarter.*

Once you get past the cover, however, *Firestarter* is a solid little story based on a fascinating premise: The superpowers have operations designed to locate and test "wild talents," possibly for military use.

Telekinesis (moving objects by the power of the mind), telepathy (reading minds), pyrokinesis (mind-induced spontaneous combustion)—all are presumed to be more fiction than fact, as King asserts in his afterword to the paperback edition; however, there is evidence that points to the contrary, especially pyrokinesis.

Firestarter is the story of an eight-year-old girl, a pyrotic, the only child of Andy and Vicky McGee, both of whom participated in a government-sponsored experiment in college, in which they were administered a hallucinogen called Lot Six.

As it turns out, Lot Six is an experimental drug that has far-reaching effects. Andy McGee has the power to dominate others mentally (depending on their I.Q.); wife Vicky becomes telekinetic, able to move objects with her mind. In both Andy and Vicky, the powers are weak and therefore limited. However, in the case of their daughter Charlene (nicknamed Charlie), the power was present as an infant, and as she grows, the power grows.

Artwork courtesy of Michael Whelan

© 1980, "Firestarter," cover to the Phantasia Press edition of *Firestarter.*

On Whelan's Painting for *Firestarter*

Perhaps Whelan's single most acclaimed work has been his stunning painting for a limited edition of *Firestarter* by Stephen King. Many critics of fantasy art consider it the finest piece of illustration yet done for King's work.

The Penguin Encyclopedia of Horror and the Supernatural (1986)

It is only through Charlie's will power *not* to use her wild talent that it is kept under control. As other children have been toilet-trained at an early age, Charlie was fire-trained. She knows that nothing good can result from doing the BAD THING, and that her parents made it very clear that she is not to use her power.

But as she grows older, the power grows stronger in her. Aware of that, a government agency known simply as the Shop has mobilized a small army of seven hundred men to find, capture, and test her, in an effort to harness her power, perhaps for military use.

Like Carrie, Charlie has an almost inconceivable power; it exists, and it has enormous destructive potential. But in the case of Charlie, it's held in check— until her father bids her use it.

The real horror in the novel, however, is not eight-year-old Charlie McGee, who is cursed with an ability she never wanted, who uses her power with great reluctance because of her upbringing, but who *must* use it to protect herself and her father from harm. The real horror, King suggests, is the excessive power of government—even in a democratic society. (Civil servant, said Robert A. Heinlein, means civil *master*.)

Total freedom is total responsibility, but in the case of the government, is it in fact responsible and accountable to the people? Or are there things we don't know about? King suggests that the government can do any damned thing it pleases, with an army of civil servants to do its bidding. That kind of power inevitably breeds moral corruption, and an environment in which evil is perpetrated usually in the name of national security.

Firestarter is, on one level, "just a novel, a made-up tale with which I hope you, reader, have passed a pleasant evening or two," says King in his afterword. On another, more serious, level it is a thought-provoking look at what King perceives to be the dark side of democracy—a world shrouded in shadow but nonetheless real, wherein government agencies have absolute power; a world of tyrant and toady—and their victims.

What If . . .

Imagine what would have happened if, as a result of the hallucinogen given to Charlie's parents, Charlie had been born insane. Now *there's* a real horror story.

Editions Available and Tie-in Product

- A trade hardback, Viking, $22.95
- A paperback, $4.50 (with an afterword not in the hardback edition)
- A movie, from Universal Pictures, available in videotape from MCA Home Video

Michael Whelan
A Premier King Illustrator

Art directors usually in charge of "packaging" bestselling authors like Stephen King don't see me as the kind of person to do those covers.

Michael Whelan

If ever there were the perfect artist to illustrate Stephen King, that artist is surely Michael Whelan. If you won't take my word for it, observe his cover on the Phantasia Press edition of *Firestarter.* See what I mean?

Or look long at the color plate opposite page 208 in NAL's trade paperback edition of *The Dark Tower: The Gunslinger.* You can't miss it—it's the one with the Gunslinger at the edge of the beach, looking out over the ocean, with the sun setting . . . and the Dark Tower in the background . . . hazy . . . real . . . and unreal. See what I mean?

But, you protest, Whelan's a science-fiction and fantasy artist! He doesn't do horror, does he?

Yes, he does, and when he does, he knows exactly what he's doing, what effect he wants to achieve, and how best to achieve it in a painting. As the principal artist in the Donald A. Wolheim (DAW) anthology series, The Year's Best Horror Stories, Whelan has consistently demonstrated his affinity with illustrating horror. The cover to number fourteen, with a hobgoblin in a child's closet, could be the illustration to King's "The Boogeyman." Then there's the cover he's titled "The Doll," used for number eleven in the series: a round-faced doll with one eye gouged out hangs at the end of a hangman's noose . . . and two children, a boy and a girl, are in shadow behind the doll. These two children are bad seeds, their eyes shining with an unholy light.

To Whelan, horror illustration is not visual explicitness—it's more subtle, more suggestive, and ultimately more powerful. Explains Whelan, "You have to make a distinction between horror and *grand guignol.* Some artists can't seem to dissociate horror from blood-and-guts illustration. I think horror is the *anticipation* of violence."

In the Beginning

Whelan remembers how it all started. He saw a promotional flyer for a comic-book convention (the 1974 San Diego Con) on the bulletin board at the school he attended, the Art Center College of Design in Los Angeles. "I looked at it and a voice spoke in me and said, 'It is time to get out of school and get serious.'"

Whelan tore the flyer off the wall and went home to gather artwork for the art show at the convention. Recalls Whelan, "Nothing was priced over fifteen dollars." But everything sold and Whelan was encouraged to exhibit at the World Con, the annual convention for science-fiction fans. Once again, Whelan's art sold out, and Whelan knew he had found a permanent home.

A Working Professional

Encouraged by the reception in the science-fiction community, Whelan submitted color slides to Donald A. Wolheim, publisher of DAW Books in New York. "The rest, as they say, was history," says Whelan.

Since that time Whelan has rendered over three hundred paintings for DAW Books and Ballantine/Del Rey and other publishers, won nine Hugo Awards for the Best Professional Artist in the field, garnered three Howard Awards, published two art books (*Wonderworks* by the Donning Company and *Works of Wonder* by Del Rey, both in print), and earned a well-deserved reputation as one of the most popular, top-paid artists in the field. After nearly fifteen years as a working professional, Whelan can look back at the credits and admit that he has a good track record.

Although Whelan would like to do more horror illustration, the opportunities are scarce: timing, stereotyping, and the art budget are the big problems.

Timing: Because he schedules his work a year in advance, he can't accept last-minute assignments, which often means turning down projects he would love to do if he had the time. (Asked to do the second *Dark Tower* book, Whelan declined because it would have meant reneging on earlier commitments. Similarly, he turned down the fiftieth-anniversary editions of Tolkien's books—*The Hobbit* and the trilogy, a dream assignment for Whelan—because of previous commitments he wouldn't break.)

Recalls Whelan when offered the *Dark Tower* and the Tolkien assignments, "Both nearly drove me crazy because I tried every way I could to work them into my schedule, but it was impossible."

Another point: Whelan, regarded as a professional's professional, always comes through. Once, when he broke his hand after a karate session, he had the doctor put his hand in a cast *holding a paintbrush* so he could finish his current assignment, according to interviewer Dale Johnson, who conducted a long interview with Whelan for *American Fantasy*.

Artwork courtesy of Michael Whelan

"The Doll," cover to one of the *Year's Best Horror* anthologies.

Stereotyping: Whelan has done so much nonhorror material that he is not the artist that comes immediately to mind when one thinks of horror illustration. Whelan admits, "I'm a science-fiction and fantasy artist," but adds that his definition *includes* horror. Still, because he loves doing horror, he makes the time to do The Year's Best Horror Stories series for DAW, even though it pays less.

Art budget: Because Whelan is one of the most popular artists in the field, and because his covers sell books, he gets top dollar for his work. But because most horror books do not sell as well as the books Whelan typically illustrates, the art budget just can't justify Whelan's usual fee, so Whelan has, on occasion, made concessions. For a series of seven H.P. Lovecraft books, Whelan rendered two oversized paintings, so that multiple covers could be created.

In an interview with *American Fantasy,* Whelan summarized the difficulties:

> . . . [W]hen Del Rey was publishing the H.P. Lovecraft books . . . they only had a budget for two covers, and they're wondering whom they could hire to do [them]. Alan Dean Foster, bless his soul, suggested to Lester [Del Rey] that they try me. Judy said, "Michael Whelan does horror?" and I'd been doing The Year's Best Horror series for what, eight years up to that point? It's so absurd, but they were so used to using me only in the limited capacity of certain fantasy and science fiction books that it hadn't even crossed their minds.

When Donald M. Grant contracted to publish Stephen King's *The Dark Tower: The Gunslinger,* the contract was written so that the artist would be "mutually acceptable" to both the publisher and the author. Grant and King agreed that Michael Whelan would be a good choice. Recalls Grant, "We both thought that Michael was at the top of the game," and King "certainly liked Michael's work, so we were in accord there."

In an ad for the book, publisher Grant admits that it is "unlike anything bestselling author Stephen King has ever written; indeed, it is unlike anything anyone has ever written. And it is a volume that begs for illustrations!"

For the book, published in 1982, Whelan rendered five full-color paintings, color endleaves, chapter-head illustrations, and end-piece illustrations. In 1988 NAL published the trade edition and Whelan rendered a new painting—a romantic portrait of the Gunslinger with Zoltan, a talking crow, perched on his shoulder; in the background, the sun is setting and the dark tower looms.

The finished work for *The Dark Tower* pleased Whelan, but if he had his choice, he would redraw some of it. After all, he says, it has been years since it was published. He now sees ways to improve it.

Stephen King's reaction to Whelan's work? "King was very pleased," said publisher Donald M. Grant.

After that assignment, Whelan found himself on King's personal Christmas greeting list and, over the years, received the installments of *The Plant,* as well as the Philtrum Press edition of *The Eyes of the Dragon.*

Dream Assignments

When asked what he thought of the cover paintings on King's books, Whelan is charitable and admits that in many cases the art just doesn't do the book justice. (Compare the two covers to *Firestarter* and you'll see what he means. The Steven Stroud cover, used for the hardback and paperback editions, lacks the sense of wonder that is present in Whelan's cover for the Phantasia Press edition.)

Whelan would have welcomed the opportunity to do any King cover, or a cover to a Clive Barker book, but he especially would have liked to do the covers to *Firestarter,* *'Salem's Lot,* and *The Shining.*

Currently on the shelf, waiting to be read: *It* by Stephen King.

Current Projects

Michael Whelan, now thirty-eight, is at a turning point in his career. After working sixty to eighty hours a week for nearly fifteen years, he's slowing down . . . a bit. The demands of producing a painting a month—measuring two by three feet for a front cover, three by four feet for a wraparound cover—keep him busy, but he's balancing the workload with his personal life (wife Audrey, daughter Alexa, and newborn son Adrian).

And for the first time he's doing work for himself. "I call it my self-commissioned work," he says. The work is a series of oversized paintings, four by four feet and up, and is "intensely allegorical and metaphysical." The series may be hung at a gallery in two years, but there's no hurry because there's no deadline.

Future Projects

Whelan's published covers read like a "who's who" in the science-fiction and fantasy field: Robert A. Heinlein (*The Cat That Walked Through Walls* and *Friday*), Isaac Asimov (the Foundation series), Arthur C. Clarke (*2010: Odyssey Two*), Anne McCaffrey (the Pern series), C.J. Cherryh, and Michael Moorcock (the Elric of Melnibone series), to name a few.

Whelan is currently working on a cover to Ray Bradbury's classic *The Martian Chronicles.* After that, he'll be working on a cover to a posthumous collection of letters, *Grumbles from the Grave* by Robert A. Heinlein (a 1989 Del Rey hardback). Other work includes a painting for a new Anne McCaffrey novel and a painting for Joan Vinge's *Snow Queen,* which was originally issued with a cover by Leo and Diane Dillon, whose work Whelan much admires. "It'll be a hard act to follow," he admits.

Joe Bob Briggs!

He's a Texas humorist, a nationally syndicated columnist, a TV personality, and most of all a no-holds-barred drive-in movie critic. He writes "some of the funniest, most perceptive film and social criticism that you will ever read," says Big Steve King (as Joe Bob dubs him) in his introduction to Joe Bob's collection of movie reviews, *Joe Bob Goes to the Drive-In*.

The movies Joe Bob reviews are not the usual bullstuff; the titles tell all: *Blood Feast, Curse of the Cannibal Confederates, Surf Nazis Must Die*, and *Make Them Die Slowly*. In other words, there will likely be a good bit of blood, sex, violence—none, I hasten to add, gratuitous!

These movies don't make it to the seven-in-one theater beehives where you suck overpriced sugar water, munch warmed-up popcorn (not freshly popped here!), and stare at a postage-stamp-size screen. If you want to see these little gems, you head for a drive-in. As Joe Bob frequently reminds us, there's only one way to watch a movie: "Under the stars like God intended, in the privacy of my personal automobile."

Sitting under the stars in his big Detroit chrome mountain, Joe Bob has seen his share of King flicks, and in the review to follow, excerpted from *Joe Bob Goes to the Drive-In*, he tells what he likes about King's *Firestarter*.

King, the guest of honor at the Third Annual World Drive-In Movie Festival and Custom Car Rally in Dallas, and one of only two recipients of the Joe Bob Briggs Lifetime Achievement Award, is clearly Joe Bob's kind of writer: an American original.

A Review of *Firestarter*

Big Steve King has a new flick out called *Firestarter*. (This is only Steve's second movie in two months and the fourth or fifth one in the last year. What's wrong, big guy, you send the typewriter out for repairs?) What we got here is a little girl who when she gets mad she can stare at your shirt and turn your body into Bananas Foster.

It's the same little girl from *E.T.*, the indoor-bullstuff flick that gave monsters from outer space a bad name, and the way you know she's about to turn somebody into a Roman candle is she stares real hard and her hair flies out sideways like a birddog that's backed into an electric fence. The CIA is trying to catch the little girl so they can strap her on a B-52 and nuke Russia.

David Keith is her daddy, and she and him are running around accidentally setting people's shoes on fire because the CIA killed the little girl's mommy and stuffed her in the ironing closet so she wouldn't talk about the LSD experiment that turned em all into psychic cherry bombs. David Keith was so p.o.ed about that that he made two G-men into blind zombies just by scrunching his hands up through his hair and staring at em like they just totaled his Camaro. That little stunt got em in so much trouble that they had to go hide out at Art Carney's house.

Then the CIA tries to kidnap the little girl, only when they get there she goes out on the front porch and lasers about sixteen government agents and turns

Photo courtesy of the *Bangor Daily News*

Meeting in front of King's home in Bangor, prior to a May 9, 1984, world première of *Firestarter,* from left to right: Dino De Laurentiis (producer), Drew Barrymore (who plays Charlie McGee in the movie), John Supranovich (Northeast COMBAT Executive Director), and King.

their cars into Tinker-Toy sets and makes Art Carney's farm look like Miami Beach after the frat boys from Georgia got through with it.

Anyhow, the CIA holds the two of em prisoner so they can study the little girl and watch her turn wood chips into Boy Scout campfires and make cinder-block walls into a gravel parking lot, and George C. Scott acts like he's the janitor so he can get the little girl to be his friend and do whatever it is that Martin Sheen wants her to do. Martin Sheen is the boss of the CIA, and one time he says to George C. Scott, "You know, if she ever figures this out, you're gonna know what a steak feels like inside a microwave oven."

But he's wrong. It's better than that. By the final scene we got enough quick-fried FBI agents for a fire-juggling act on *Star Search*. These guys look like somebody just poured lighter fluid on Richard Pryor.

Hot stuff. Forty-five dead bodies, a new 1984 record. Nine motor vehicle explosions, including a copter. One gallon blood. No breasts. (The only choices were the little girl and Louise Fletcher, so, hey, what can I say?) One beast (George C. Scott as a cigar-store Indian). Extra points for the exploding-golf-cart scene. Great kung fu scene (Big George kills a guy with a single chop on the nose). Exploding heads. Drive-In Academy Award nominations for Drew Barrymore, the little girl, and Mark Lester, the director who never lets the plot get in the way of the special effects.

Three and a half stars for the body count alone.

Joe Bob says check it out.

Harlan Ellison's Watching

I. In Which We Scuffle Through the Embers

If tomorrow's early edition of *The New York Times* bore the headline STEPHEN KING NAMED AS DE LOREAN DRUG CONNECTION, it would not by one increment lessen the number of Stephen King books sold this week. Goose the total, more likely.

If Tom Brokaw's lead on the NBC news tonight is, "The King of Chiller Writers, Stephen King, was found late this afternoon in the show window of Saks Fifth Avenue, biting the heads off parochial school children and pouring hot lead down the necks," it would not for an instant slow the rush of film producers to put under option his every published word. Hasten the pace, more likely.

If your cousin Roger from Los Angeles, who works for a food catering service that supplies meals to film companies working on location, called to pass along the latest hot bit of in-group showbiz gossip, and he confided, "You know Steve King, that weirdo who writes the scary novels? Well, get this: he worked with Errol Flynn as a secret agent for the Nazis during World War II!" it would not drop the latest King tome one notch on the *Publishers Weekly* bestseller listings. Pop it to the top of the chart, more likely.

Stephen King is a phenomenon *sui generis*. I've been told he is fast approaching (if he hasn't already reached it) the point of being the bestselling American author of all time. In a recent survey taken by some outfit or other—and I've looked long and hard for the item but can't find it so you'll have to trust me on this—it was estimated that two out of every five people observed reading a paperback in air terminals or bus stations or suchlike agorae were snout-deep in a King foma.

There has never been anything like King in the genre of the fantastic. Whether you call what he writes "horror stories" or "dark fantasy" or "imaginative thrillers," Steve King is the undisputed, hands-down, nonpareil, free-form champ, three falls out of three.

This is a Good Thing.

Not only because King is a better writer than the usual gag of bestseller epigones who gorge the highest reaches of the lists—the Judith Krantzes, Sidney Sheldons, Erich Segals and V.C. Andrewses of this functionally illiterate world—or because he is, within the parameters of his incurably puckish nature, a "serious" writer, or because he is truly and in the face of a monumental success that would warp the rest of us, a good guy. It is because he is as honest a popular writer as we've been privileged to experience in many a year. He writes a good stick. He never cheats the buyer of a King book. You may or may not feel he brought off a particular job when you get to page last, but you *never* feel you've been had. He does the one job no writer may ignore at peril of tar and feathers, he *delivers.*

Sometimes what he delivers is as good as a writer can get in his chosen milieu, as in *Carrie* and *The Shining* and *The Dead Zone* and *The Dark Tower.* Sometimes he's just okay, as in *Cujo* or *Christine.* And once in a while, as in the *Night Shift* and *Different Seasons* collections, he sings way above his range. (And those of us who have been privileged to read the first couple of sections of "The Plant," King's work-in-progress privately printed as annual holiday greeting cards, perceive a talent of uncommon dimensions.)

So why is it that films made from Stephen King's stories turn out, for the most part, to be movies that look as if they'd been chiseled out of Silly Putty by escapees from the Home For the Terminally Inept?

This question, surely one of the burning topics of our troubled cosmos, presents itself anew upon viewing *Firestarter* (Universal), Dino De Laurentiis's latest credential in his struggle to prove to the world that he has all the artistic sensitivity of a piano bench. Based on Steve King's 1980 novel, and a good solid novel it was, this motion picture is (forgive me) a burnt-out case. We're talking scorched earth. Smokey the Bear would need a sedative. Jesus wept. You get the idea.

The plotline is a minor key-change on the basic fantasy concept King used in *Carrie.* Young female with esper abilities as a pyrotic. (Because the people who make these films think human speech is not our natural tongue, they always gussie up simple locutions so their prolixity will sound "scientific." Pyrotic was not good enough for the beanbags who made this film, so they keep referring to the firestarter as "a possessor of pyrokinetic abilities." In the Kingdom of the Beanbags, a honeydipper is a "Defecatory Residue Repository Removal Supervisor for On-Site Effectation.")

The conflict is created by the merciless hunt for the firestarter—eight-year-old Charlene "Charlie" McGee, played by Drew Barrymore of *E.T.* fame—that is carried out by a wholly improbable government agency alternately known as the Department of Scientific Intelligence and "The Shop." Charlie and her daddy, who also has esper abilities, though his seem to shift and alter as the plot demands, are on the run. The Shop has killed Charlie's mommy, for no particularly clear reason, and they want Charlie for their own nefarious purposes, none of which are logically codified; but we can tell from how oily these three-piece suiters are, that Jack Armstrong would never approve of their program. Charlie and her daddy run, The Shop gnashes its teeth and finally sends George C. Scott as a comic-book hit man after them; and they capture the pair; and they run some special effects tests; and Charlie gets loose; and a lot of people go up in flames; and daddy and the hit man and the head of The Shop all get smoked; and Charlie hitchhikes back to the kindly rustic couple who thought it was cute when she looked at the butter and made it melt.

The screenplay by Stanley Mann, who did not disgrace himself with screen adaptations of *The Collector* and *Eye of the Needle,* here practices a craft that can best be described as creative typing. Or, more in keeping with technology, what he has wrought now explains to me the previously nonsensical phrase "word processing." As practiced by Mr. Mann, this is the processing of words in the Cuisinart School of Homogeneity.

The direction is lugubrious. As windy and psychotic as Mann's scenario may be, it is rendered even more tenebrous by the ponderous, lumbering, pachydermal artlessness of one Mark L. Lester (not the kid-grown-up of *Oliver!*). Mr. Lester's fame, the *curriculum vita,* that secured for him this directorial sinecure, rests upon a quagmire base of *Truck Stop Women, Bobbie Jo and the Outlaw* (starring Lynda Carter and Marjoe Gortner, the most fun couple to come along since Tracy and Hepburn, Gable and Lombard, Cheech and Chong), *Stunts* and the awesome *Roller Boogie.* The breath do catch, don't it!

Like the worst of the television hacks, who tell you everything three times—Look, she's going to open the coffin! / She's opening the coffin now! / Good lord, she opened the coffin!—Lester and Mann reflect their master's contempt for the intelligence of filmgoers by endless sophomoric explanations of things we know, not the least being a tedious rundown on what esp is supposed to be.

The acting is shameful. From the cynical use of "name stars" in cameo roles that they might as well have phoned in, to the weary posturing of the leads, this is a drama coach's nightmare. Louise Fletcher sleepwalks through her scenes like something Papa Doc might have resurrected from a Haitian graveyard; Martin Sheen, whose thinnest performances in the past have been marvels of intelligence and passion, has all the range of a Barry Manilow ballad; David Keith with his constantly bleeding nose is merely ridiculous; and Drew Barrymore, in just two years, has become a puffy, petulant, self-conscious "actor," devoid of the ingenuousness that so endeared her in *E.T.*

And what in the world has happened to George C. Scott's previously flawless intuition about which scripts to do? It was bad enough that he consented to appear as the lead in Paul Schrader's loathsome *Hardcore*; but for him willingly to assay the role of John Rainbird, the ponytailed Amerind government assassin, and to perform the part of what must surely be the most detestable character since Joyboy's mother in *The Loved One,* Divine in *Pink Flamingos* or Jabba the Hut, with a verve that borders on teeth-gnashing, is beyond comprehension. It has been a while since I read the novel, but it is not my recollection that the parallel role in the text possessed the McMartin Pre-School child molester mien Scott presents. It is a jangling, counter-productive, unsavory element that is, hideously, difficult to sweep from memory. That it is in some squeamish-making way memorable, is not to Scott's credit. It is the corruption of his talent.

Dino De Laurentiis is the Irwin Allen of his generation, coarse, lacking sub-tlety, making films of vulgar pretentiousness that personify the most venal atti-tudes of the industry. He ballyhoos the fact that he has won two Oscars, but hardly anyone realizes they were for Fellini's *La Strada* and *Nights of Cabiria* in 1954 and 1957—and let's not fool ourselves, even if the publicity flaks do: those are *Fellini* films, not De Laurentiis films—long before he became the cottage industry responsible for *Death Wish,* the remakes of *King Kong* and *The Hurricane,* the travesty known as *Flash Gordon, Amityville II* and *Amityville 3-D, Conan the Barbarian* and the embarrassing *King of the Gypsies.*

But Dino De Laurentiis is precisely the sort of intellect most strongly drawn to the works of Stephen King. He is not a lone blade of grass in the desert. He is merely the most visible growth on the King horizon. Steve King has had nine films made from his words, and there is a formulaic reason why all but one or two of those films have been dross.

II. In Which We Discover Why the Children Don't Look Like Their Parents

Pinter works, though he shouldn't; and I'll be damned if I can discern why; he just does. Bradbury and Hemingway don't; and I think I can figure out why they don't, which is a clue to why Stephen King doesn't either. Xenogenesis seems to be the question this time around, and if you'll go to your Unabridged and look it up, I'll wait right here for you and tell you all about it when you get back.

Times passes. Leaves flying free from a calendar. The seasons change. The reader returns from the Unabridged.

Now that we understand the meaning of the word Xenogenesis, let us con-sider why it *is* that King's books—as seemingly hot for metamorphosis as any stuff ever written by anyone—usually wind up as deranged as Idi Amin and as cruel as January in Chicago and as unsatisfying as sex with the pantyhose still on: why it *is* that the children, hideous and crippled offspring, do not resemble their parents.

First, I can just imagine your surprise when I point out that this thing King has been around in the literary consciousness a mere ten years. It was just exactly an eyeblink decade ago that the schoolteacher from Maine wrote:

> Nobody was really surprised when it happened, not really, not at the subconscious level where savage things grow. . . . Showers turning off one by one, girls stepping out, removing the pastel bathing caps, toweling, spraying deodorant, checking the clock over the door. Bras were hooked, underpants stepped into. . . . Calls and catcalls rebounded with all the snap and flicker of billiard balls after a hard break. . . . Carrie turned off the shower. It died in a drip and a gurgle. . . . It wasn't until she stepped out that they all saw the blood running down her leg.

Second, I'll bet none of you realized what a fluke it was that King took off so abruptly. Well, here's the odd and unpredictable explanation, conveyed because I happened to be there when it happened. (Who else would tell you this stuff, gang?)

Doubleday had purchased *Carrie* for a small advance. It was, in the corporate cosmos, just another mid-list title, a spooky story to be marketed without much foofaraw among the first novels, the "learn to love your brown rice and get svelte things in 30 minutes" offerings, the books one finds in the knockoff catalogues nine months later at $1.49 plus a free shopping bag. But King's editor read that opening sequence in which the telekinetic, Carrie White, gets her first menstrual experience before the eyes of a covey of teenage shrikes, and more than the lightbulb in the locker room exploded. Xeroxes of the manuscript were run off; they were disseminated widely in-house; women editors passed them on to female secretaries, who took them home and gave them to their friends. That first scene bit hard. It was the essence of the secret of Stephen King's phenomenal success: the everyday experience raised to the mythic level by the application of fantasy to a potent cultural trope. It was Jungian archetype goosed with ten million volts of emotional power. It was the commonly-shared horrible memory of half the population, reinterpreted. It was the flash of recognition, the miracle of that rare instant in which readers dulled by years of reading artful lies felt their skin stretched tight by an encounter with artful truth.

Stephen King, in one apocryphal image, had taken control of his destiny.

I'm not even sure Steve, for all his self-knowledge, has an unvarnished perception of how close he came to remaining a schoolteacher who writes paperback originals as a hobby and to supplement the family income in his spare time when he's not too fagged out from extracurricular duties at the high school.

But just as Ian Fleming became an "overnight success" when John F. Kennedy idly mentioned that the James Bond books—which had been around for years—were his secret passion; just as *Dune* took off in paperback years after its many rejections by publishers and its disappointing sale in hardcover, when Frank Herbert came to be called "the father of Earth Day" and the novel was included in *The Whole Earth Catalog*; just as Joseph Heller, Joseph Heller's agent, Joseph Heller's publisher and the Eastern Literary Establishment that had trashed *Catch-22* when it was first published, began trumpeting Heller's genius when *another* literary agent (not Heller's), named Candida Donadio, ran around New York jamming the book under people's noses, telling them it was a new American classic; in just that inexplicable, unpredictable, magic way, Doubleday's in-house interest spread. To *Publishers Weekly,* to the desk of Bennett Cerf, to the attention of first readers for the film studios on the Coast, to the sales force mandated to sell that season's line, to the bookstore buyers, and into the cocktail-party chatter of the word-of-mouth crowd. The word spread: this *Carrie* novel is hot.

And the readers were rewarded. It *was* hot: because King had tapped into the collective unconscious with Carrie White's ordeal. The basic premise was an easy one to swallow, and once down, all that followed was characterization. That is the secret of Stephen King's success in just ten years, and it is the reason why, in

my view, movies based on King novels never resemble the perfectly decent novels that inspired them.

In films written by Harold Pinter as screenplay, or in films based on Pinter
plays, it is not uncommon for two people to be sitting squarely in the center of a
two-shot speaking as follows:

> CORA: (Cockney accent) Would'ja like a nice piece of fried bread for
> breakfast, Bert?
> BERT: (abstracted grunting) Yup. Fried bread'd be nice.
> CORA: Yes . . . fried bread *is* nice, in't it?
> BERT: Yuh. I like fried bread.
> CORA: Well, then, there 'tis. Nice fried bread.
> BERT: It's nice fried bread.
> CORA: (pleased) Is it nice, then?
> BERT: Yuh. Fried bread's nice.

Unless you have heard me do my absolutely hilarious Pinter parody, or have
seen every Pinter play and film out of unconstrained admiration for the man's
work—as have I—then the foregoing copy cannot possibly read well; nor should
it, by all the laws of dramaturgy, *play* well on-screen. But it does. I cannot decipher
the code; but the cadences work like a dray horse, pulling the plot and character
development, the ever-tightening tension and emotional conflict, toward the goal
of mesmerizing involvement that is Pinter's hallmark.

We have in this use of revivified language a sort of superimposed verbal
continuum at once alien to our ear and hypnotically inviting. To say more, is to
say less. It *does* work.

But if we use the special written languages of Bradbury and Hemingway as
examples, we see that such "special speaking" does *not* travel well. It bruises too
easily.

Perhaps it is because of the reverence lavished on the material by the sce-
narists, who are made achingly aware of the fact that they are dealing with *literature,* that blinds them as they build in the flaws we perceive when the film is
thrown up on the screen. Perhaps it is because real people in the real world don't
usually speak in a kind of poetic scansion. Perhaps it is because we love the
primary materials so much that *no* amount of adherence to source can satisfy us.
But I don't think any of those hypotheses, singly or as a group, pink the core
reason why neither Bradbury's nor Hemingway's arresting fictions ever became
memorable films. When Rock Hudson or Rod Steiger or Oskar Werner mouth
Bradburyisms such as:

> "Cora. Wouldn't it be nice to take a Sunday walk the way we used to do,
> with your silk parasol and your long dress swishing along, and sit on those
> wire-legged chairs at the soda parlor and smell the drugstore the way they

used to smell? Why don't drugstores smell that way anymore? And order two sarsaparillas for us, Cora, and then ride out in our 1910 Ford to Hannahan's Pier for a box supper and listen to the brass band. How about it? . . . If you could make a wish and take a ride on those oak-lined country roads like they had before cars started rushing, would you *do* it?"

or Gregory Peck or Ava Gardner carry on this sort of conversation from Hemingway:

> "Where did we stay in Paris?"
> "At the Crillon. You know that."
> "Why do I know that?"
> "That's where we always stayed."
> "No. Not always."
> "There and at the Pavillion Henri-Quatre in St. Germain. You said you loved it there."
> "Love is a dunghill. And I'm the cock that gets on it to crow."
> "If you have to go away, is it absolutely necessary to kill off everything you leave behind? I mean do you have to take away everything? Do you have to kill your horse, and your wife and burn your saddle and your armor?"

what we get is the auditory equivalent of spinach. The actors invariably convey a sense of embarrassment, the dialogue marches from their mouths like Prussian dragoons following Feldmarschall von Blücher's charge at Ligny, and we as audience either wince or giggle at the pomposity of what sounds like posturing.

This "special speaking" is one of the richest elements in Bradbury and Hemingway. It reads as inspired transliteration of the commonplace. But when spoken aloud, by performers whose chief aim is to convey a sense of verisimilitude, it becomes parody. (And that Bradbury and Hemingway have been parodied endlessly, by both high and low talents, only adds to their preeminence. They are *sui generis* for all the gibes.)

The links between King and Bradbury and Hemingway in this respect seem to me to be the explanation why their work does not for good films make. That which links them is this:

Like Harold Pinter and Ernest Hemingway, Ray Bradbury and Stephen King are profoundly allegorical writers.

The four of them *seem* to be mimetic writers, but they aren't! They *seem* to be writing simply, uncomplicatedly, but they aren't! As with the dancing of Fred Astaire—which seems so loose and effortless and easy that even the most lump-footed of us ought to be able to duplicate the moves—until we try it and fall on our faces—what these writers do is make the creation of High Art seem replicable.

The bare bones of their plots . . .

A sinister manservant manipulates the life of his employer to the point where their roles are reversed.

An ex-prizefighter is tracked down and killed by hired guns for an offense which is never codified.

A "fireman," whose job it is to burn books because they are seditious, becomes secretly enamored of the joys of reading.

A young girl with the latent telekinetic ability to start fires comes to maturity and lets loose her power vengefully.

. . . bare bones that have underlain a hundred different stories that differ from these only in the most minimally variant ways. The plots count for little. The stories are not wildly inventive. The sequence of events is not skull-cracking. It is the *style* in which they are written that gives them wing. They are memorable not because of the thin storylines, but because the manner in which they have been written is so compelling that we are drawn into the fictional universe and once there we are bound subjects of the master creator.

Each of these examples draws deeply from the well of myth and archetype. The collective unconscious calls to us and we go willingly where Hemingway and Bradbury and Pinter . . . and King . . . beckon us to follow.

Stephen King's books work as well as they do, because he is writing more of shadow than of substance. He drills into the flow of cerebro-spinal fluid with the dialectical function of a modern American mythos, dealing with archetypal images from the pre-conscious or conscious that presage crises in our culture even as they become realities.

Like George Lucas, Stephen King has read Campbell's *The Masks of God,* and he knows the power of myth. He knows what makes us tremble. He knows about moonlight reflecting off the fangs. It isn't his plots that press against our chest, it is the impact of his allegory.

But those who bought for film translation *'Salem's Lot, Cujo, Christine, Children of the Corn,* and *Firestarter* cannot read. For them, the "special speaking" of King's nightmares, the element that sets King's work so far above the general run of chiller fiction, is merely white noise. It is the first thing dropped when work begins on the script, when the scenarist "takes a meeting" to discuss what the producer or the studio wants delivered. What is left is the bare bones plot, the least part of what King has to offer. (Apart from the name *Stephen King,* which is what draws us to the theater.)

And when the script is in work, the scenarist discovers that there isn't enough at hand to make either a coherent or an artful motion picture. So blood is added. Knives are added. Fangs are added. Special effects grotesqueries are added. But the characters have been dumbed-up, the tone has been lost; the mythic undercurrents have been dammed and the dialectical function has been rendered inoperative. What is left for us is bare bones; blood and cliché.

It is difficult to get Steve King to comment on such artsy-fartsy considerations. Like many other extraordinary successful artists, he is consciously fearful of the spite and envy his preeminence engenders in critics, other writers, a fickle audience that just sits knitting with Mme. Defarge, waiting for the artist to show the tiniest edge of hubris. Suggest, as I did, to Steve King that *Cujo* is a gawdawful lump of indigestible grue, and he will respond, "I like it. It's just a movie that stands there and keeps punching."

How is the critic, angry at the crippling of each new King novel when it crutches onto the screen, to combat such remarks? By protecting himself in this way—and it is not for the critic to say whether King truly believes these things he says in defense of the butchers who serve up the bloody remnants that were once creditable novels—he unmans all rushes to his defense. Yet without such mounting of the barricades in his support, how can the situation be altered?

Take for instance *Children of the Corn* (New World Pictures). Here is a minor fable of frightfulness, a mere thirty pages in King's 1978 collection *Night Shift*; a one-punch short story whose weight rests on that most difficult of all themes to handle, little kids in mortal jeopardy. Barely enough there for a short film, much less a feature-length attempt.

How good is this recent adaptation of a King story? *Los Angeles* magazine began its review of *Firestarter* like so: "This latest in a seemingly endless chain of films made from Stephen King novels isn't the worst of the bunch. *Children of the Corn* wins that title hands down." That's how bad it is.

Within the first 3½ minutes (by stopwatch) we see four people agonizingly die from poison, one man gets his throat cut with a butcher knife, one man gets his hand taken off with a meat slicer, a death by pruning hook, a death by sickle, a death by tanning knife . . . at least nine on-camera slaughters, maybe eleven (the intercuts are fastfastfast), and one woman murdered over the telephone, which we don't see, but hear. Stomach go whooops.

Utterly humorless, as ineptly directed as a film school freshman's class project, acted with all the panache of a grope in the backseat of a VW, *Children of the Corn* features the same kind of "dream sequences" proffered as shtick by Landis in *An American Werewolf in London,* De Palma in *Carrie* and *Dressed to Kill,* and by even less talented of the directorial coterie aptly labeled (by Alain Resnais) "the wise guy smart alecks." These and-then-I-woke-up-and-it-had-all-been-a-bad-dream inserts, which in no way advance the plot of the film, are a new dodge by which Fritz Kiersch, *Corn's* director, and his contemporaries—bloodletters with view-finders—slip in gratuitous scenes of horror and explicit SFX-enhanced carnage. This has become a trope when adapting King's novels to the screen, a filmic device abhorrent in the extreme not only because it is an abattoir substitute for the artful use of terror, but because it panders to the lowest, vilest tastes of an already debased audience.

It is a bit of cinematic shorthand developed by De Palma specifically for *Carrie* that now occurs with stultifying regularity in virtually *all* of the later movies made from King's books.

I submit this bogus technique is further evidence that, flensed of characterization and allegory, what the makers of these morbid exploitation films are left with does not suffice to create anything resembling the parent novel, however fudged for visual translation. And so fangs are added, eviscerations are added, sprayed blood is added; subtlety is excised, respect for the audience is excised, all restraint vanishes in an hysterical rush to make the empty and boring seem scintillant.

Children of the Corn is merely the latest validation of the theory; or as *Cinefantastique* said in its September 1984 issue: "King's mass-market fiction has inspired some momentous cinematic dreck, but *Children of the Corn* is a new low even by schlock standards."

Of the nine films that originated with Stephen King's writings, only three (in my view, of course, but now almost uniformly buttressed by audience and media judgments) have any resemblance in quality or content—not necessarily both in the same film—to the parent: *Carrie, The Shining* and *The Dead Zone.*

The first, because De Palma had not yet run totally amuck and the allegorical undertones were somewhat preserved by outstanding performances by Sissy Spacek and Piper Laurie.

The second, because it is the vision of Kubrick, always an intriguing way of seeing, even though it is no more King's *The Shining* than Orson Welles's *The Trial* was Kafka's dream.

The third, because David Cronenberg as director is the only one of the field hands in this genre who seems artistically motivated; and because Christopher Walken as the protagonist is one of the quirkiest, most fascinating actors working today, and his portrayal of Johnny Smith is, simply put, mesmerizing.

But of *Cujo's* mindlessness, *Christine's* cheap tricks, *Firestarter's* crudeness, *'Salem's Lot's* television ridiculousness, *Children of the Corn's* bestial tawdriness and even Steve's own *Creepshow* with its intentional comic book shallowness, nothing much positive can be said. It is the perversion of a solid body of work that serious readers of King, as well as serious movie lovers, must look upon with profound sadness.

We have had come among us in the person of Stephen King a writer of limitless gifts. Perhaps because Stephen himself has taken an attitude of permissiveness toward those who pay him for the right to adopt his offspring, we are left with the choices of enjoying the written work for itself, and the necessity of ignoring everything on film . . . or of hoping that one day, in a better life, someone with more than a drooling lust for the exploitation dollar attendant on Stephen King's name will perceive the potential cinematic riches passim these special fantasies. There *must* be an honest man or woman out there who understands that King's books are about more than fangs and blood.

All it takes is an awareness of allegory, subtext, the parameters of the human condition . . . and reasonable family resemblance.

It

Wouldn't it be great to bring on all the monsters one last time?
Bring them all on—Dracula, Frankenstein, Jaws, The Werewolf,
The Crawling Eye, Rodan, It Came from Outer Space, *and call it* It.

Stephen King, in *Time*

At 1,138 pages, *It* is King's longest novel and, according to King's note at the end of the book, took four years to write.

Like other King novels, *It* was heavily promoted. The book was released in September 1986. Book-of-the-Month Club featured it as a main selection. To make sure it went over big, the publisher went all out: a first printing of eight hundred thousand copies; a publicity, advertising, and promotion budget of $400,000; major advertising in the book trade and in major U.S. markets, backed by radio advertising and national publicity. In short, there was no way you wouldn't know *It* was on its way.

King on *It*

This novel percolated for about three years. The idea just sort of pogoed into my mind. I was walking over a wooden bridge and it was almost dark. I was wearing a pair of boots, and I could hear my footsteps, and I flashed on this story, "Billy Goats Gruff," with the troll under the bridge ("Who's that trip-trapping over this bridge?"). And I thought, Okay, that's what I want to write about. I want to write about a real troll under a real bridge. So two or three years went by, and finally I sat down to write it. About four years and sixteen hundred pages later, it was done.

Stephen King, on "The Larry King Show"

The standpipe on Thomas Hill, Bangor, used in *It*.

In the bookstores, *It* was heralded by advance-order easels, full-color posters, window streamers, ceiling signs, and a button that read, "*It* is coming."

It finally came.

Weighing in at nearly four pounds, *It* was an instant bestseller, dominating the charts, like other King novels. But then, predictably, the critics sharpened their knives and began carving. *It* is too long. The book has over a thousand pages.

Despite its intimidating length—three hundred pages longer than *The Stand*—the book has its advocates and its critics. Two of the most prominent King critics, Douglas E. Winter and Michael Collings, praised it. Winter, writing in *Art of Darkness,* said: "Although it is certainly premature to talk of a *magnum opus* for a writer of King's age, no better description of *It* is available." And in a front-page review Collings wrote, "*It* literally transcends itself, to stand as the most powerful novel King has written."

In a vein similar to that of the opening paragraph of *Danse Macabre, It* begins with the notion that "the terror" might end in another twenty-eight years. The novel then unfolds slowly, building up to a climactic confrontation between It and its nemeses.

The Author Talks: King on *It* and Childhood

FRANK MILLER: I read somewhere that your father abandoned your family when you were just a kid. That must make your kids very special.

STEPHEN KING: Yeah. I just finished writing sixteen hundred pages of prose about that. I just finished a novel called *It* and my editor is working through the final draft now. I worked on this book for five years. I don't think it will ever be on Recorded Books because you'd have to send it in a carton to people.

I made a New Year's resolution: Never write anything bigger than your own head. *It* isn't really about It or monsters or anything. It's about childhood, and it's about my ideas that you reexperience your own childhood and are finally able to put it away and become an adult with no regrets by raising your children. I could be wrong, but it's just an idea that I have.

Because of its complexity, the plot cannot be summarized easily, nor should it. King has stated that this book sums up his thoughts on childhood (and rites of passage) and monsters. He neatly combines the two by depicting a group of Losers (six men and one woman) that meet It as children, only to return as adults to fight *It* and an ageless monster simply called It, that assumes whatever form it chooses.

It is an ambitious novel, certainly a summing up for King, and paves the way for books like *Misery* (a psychological suspense story), *The Eyes of the Dragon* (essentially a children's story), *The Tommyknockers* (a 1950s science-fiction novel), and *The Dark Tower II: The Drawing of the Three* (the second installment of a series of perhaps six or seven).

Is *It* good? Yes. Is *It* too long? Perhaps. (Almost certainly, say others.) Is *It* worth reading? Yes.

Editions Available

- A trade hardback, Viking, $22.95
- A paperback, NAL, $5.95

ID by Charles McGrath

The weight alone (3 lbs. 7¹/₂ oz.) would seem the right heft for a doorstop and the wrong one for a best seller. But [Stephen] King has become a brand name himself, and his publishers ordered a supernatural first printing of 800,000 copies—and then demanded five additional printings, for a current total of 1,025,000 copies.

Stefan Kanfer in *Time*

If ever a King novel invited parody, *It* did. One of King's longest novels—over eleven hundred pages—the book was perceived as either the best thing he had written, or the worst.

Douglas E. Winter called it King's "magnum opus," and Michael R. Collings, who read the manuscript, concluded:

> Although it has its share of crudities and harsh language, overt violence, stylistic infelicities (including repetitions of particular phrases that may simply be inevitable in a novel approaching half a million words), and some stereotyping of characters, at the end, *It* literally transcends itself, to stand as the most powerful novel King has written.

But others, notably Don Herron, felt that the King wore no clothes, and said so. In *Reign of Fear,* the third collection of King criticism, editor Herron concludes that *It* was "two tons of crap in a five-ton crate." (King, in a *Penthouse* interview, offered his own tongue-in-cheek assessment: "I thought it would be a good one to go out with. Called *It.* I should call it *Shit.*")

Later, in a letter to Michael R. Collings, subsequently published in the July 1986 *Castle Rock,* King commented:

> I'm pleased that you liked the book so well. Actually, I like it pretty well myself, but when I saw that ludicrous stack of manuscript pages, I immediately fell into a defensive crouch. I think the days when any novel as long as this gets much of a critical reading are gone. I suspect part of my defensiveness comes from the expectation of poor reviews, partly from my own feeling that the book really is too long.

No matter what you think of the novel, a parody was inevitable, and Charles McGrath wrote "ID" which appeared in the *New Yorker* in its December 29, 1986, issue.

The terror, which has already lasted fifteen weeks and which may never end, for all I know, began with the men and the chainsaws.

The men

The chainsaws

Every twelve months or so they came to the verdant glens and leafy forests outside the small mill town of Weesquapeckett, in central Maine. Sometimes they came a little sooner, sometimes a little later . . . but always they came.

(The men. The chainsaws.)

They came early in the morning usually, when the dew was still on the fields and the mist was rising from the Weesquapeckett River, which flowed right through town, and by nightfall they were gone, carrying away with them, on long rumbling trucks, hundreds of thousands of feet, millions of feet, of prime Maine timber. Pine and spruce, maple and birch, oak and ash—it didn't matter as long as it was wood.

But this time it was different. The men came, big men, some of them missing fingers and toes, and they stayed for days on end. Everywhere you went you could hear the awful *brrrpppbrrrpppbrrrppp* of their saws, and the air was filled with a raw, resinous smell, an earthy, sweet smell, a fateful and ineluctable smell. It was the smell of sap—the smell of trees cut down before their time.

The men levelled the pinewoods behind the Weesquapeckett Elementary School, they took down the ancient elms in front of the Congregational Church, they clear-cut the Gillespies' apple orchard, they lopped off the pink dogwood that old Pete Darby had planted on his wedding day, fifty-five years before. And one morning a small boy in faded Fruit of the Loom pajamas woke to see one of the chainsaw men standing by *his* tree—the one from which Dad, the boy's dad, had hung a neat old Goodyear tire as a swing. The boy in the Fruit of the Looms was Chuckie Douglas. He was six. The year before he had been five, and in another year he would be seven. After that he might be eight.

"H-h-h-h-hey, w-w-w-what are you d-d-d-d-d-d-d-doing?" Chuckie stuttered. He stuttered a lot, and when he wasn't stuttering he was suffering from tonsillitis and adenoids and asthma. He was the sort of boy whose dialogue you might reproduce typographically by just closing your eyes and holding down a few keys on your I.B.M. Selectric.

The man lifted up his protective goggles and squinted at the boy. Then he grinned, in a way that was both leering and goofy—an expression that, had he been older, Chuckie might have recognized from dust jackets and American Express commercials—and he said, "Paper, sonny. Got to have more paper." He put his goggles back down, yanked once, twice on the starter cord of his chainsaw—it was a big black-and-yellow McCulloch, still smoking in the early-morning stillness—and

BRRRRRRRRRRRPPP

A thought is working its way up through Chuckie's brain, like groundwater seeping into a basement where the Black & Decker sump pump is on the blink. It is not a very clear thought, just a trickle—something you might not even notice until the Du Pont Antron carpeting in your rec room was half soaked. Chuckie's thought has to do with the chainsaw men and those movies that come to the Weesquapeckett Twin-Vu, out on Route 1—those movies about the kids who can start fires by crossing their eyes or who talk to their cars or have pet gerbils with rabies or who always know where to find dead stuff. Every time the chainsaw men come, it seems to Chuckie, one of those movies is sure to follow—not right away maybe, probably not for months, but sooner or later—and Chuckie wonders if there is any connection. He ponders this for a while and then decides: Naaaah. The thought goes away, and it's as if that sump pump had suddenly kicked back on again—*rrrrwhhheeeeeeeeee*—and was beginning to suck all that basement water out. But weeks later, if you went down the cellar steps and sniffed carefully, you might still smell a hint of mildew, of dampness, of *moisture*. Your basement wouldn't be *flooded*, or anything like that, and you could still watch TV down there, or listen to records, but it wouldn't be completely dry, either, and someday you might have trouble selling your house.

When the men had finally gone this time, there was not a tree to be found anywhere in Weesquapeckett, and the surrounding countryside was so flat and clear that you could look all the way to the Atlantic Ocean, a hundred miles away. But except for Chuckie no one seemed to notice. That autumn the townfolk went out just the same and raked their yards, stirring up clouds of thick, heavy dust that lingered for days. In Miss Hanson's third-grade class at Weesquapeckett Elementary—which would be Chuckie's class in just three years—the children wrote their autumn compositions just as they always had, correctly using, in order, the words "chlorophyll," "foliage," and "russet," and at recess they jumped cheerfully into imaginary leaf piles, never once complaining about their sprained knees and broken ankles.

Early in October something else happened. One rainy night a man named Lew Dickinson was driving in a panel truck from the Harrisonburg, Virginia, branch of the R.R. Donnelley & Sons printing company up to Bangor, Maine, where he was supposed to drop off fifty cartons of he didn't know what—whatever goddam best-seller they'd loaded him up with now. He was making pretty good time, listening to an old Everly Brothers tune on the radio and tapping the beat on the steering wheel, when he came over the Weesquapeckett Bridge—a solid-iron trestle bridge built in 1924 by the Portland Iron Works and dedicated by Calvin Coolidge himself, a bridge that had withstood decades of heavy logging traffic—and his truck *dropped right through the roadway* and into the Weesquapeckett River below. It bobbed there for a minute, then tipped and sank, and who knows where it finally came to rest. All that could be seen the next morning was an enormous hole in the asphalt, a terrible wreckage of ironwork underneath, and, floating on the icy waters a mile or so downstream, some sodden cardboard flaps and a few sheets of paper printed in Garamond No. 3.

A couple of weeks later, on Halloween night, part of the main floor fell through at the Weesquapeckett Public Library, sending the entire section of books shelved under "Authors Ka-Ki" crashing into the basement, where Bob Wilson, the night janitor, was sneaking a smoke. He was crushed almost instantly— turned to *mush*, really—but not before his hideous scream had awakened the entire town. The police determined later that the shelving and floor beams beneath had been subjected to what they called "almost supernatural stress." They also found out that Lew Dickinson and Bob Wilson had both failed ninth-grade English: neither one was much of a reader.

Something was wrong with Dad. For weeks now he had been coming home with something big and heavy in his Samsonite briefcase—something he didn't want Chuckie or anyone else to know about—and he complained all the time about how much his right arm hurt. No one was supposed to know this, but that arm was now at least three feet longer than the left. When Dad thought he was alone and allowed himself to relax, the arm would come shooting out from his sleeve and dangle almost to the floor. The right cuff off Dad's Arrow drip-dry barely reached to his elbow.

There was something else, too. Instead of drinking Miller Lite in front of the TV, the way he usually did, and making fun of that Louis Rukeyser on "Wall Street Week," Dad now went up to his room right after supper every night, lugging that same monstrously heavy briefcase. He would yawn and stretch (his left arm) and pretend to be tired, but Chuckie was pretty sure he didn't sleep in there. The bedroom light stayed on for hours—Chuckie could see it shining from underneath the door, casting a sickly, guillotine-shaped glow on the hall carpet—and when Dad came down in the morning, his right hand thrust deep in his pocket, his eyes would be black and burning, filled with horrible intelligence, horrible *awareness*, and if you asked him to pass the Parkay margarine or the Welch's grape jelly he would pretend not to hear. Once, though, he forgot, and when Mom asked for the Domino sugar he let his right hand, attached to that horrible elastic limb of his, reach across the table. But he *misjudged the distance*. There was a thumping, splatting sound, the sound a car makes running over a dead animal on the road, and Chuckie's cereal bowl, still half full, went

OOOOOOOOOOOooooooooooo

whooshing through the air, while, drop by drop, his milk leaked down, cold and white and lifeless, upon the uncaring linoleum.

Far, far from Maine, on the Atlantic, the Italian liner L'Avventura was a day out of Fort Lauderdale, on the second leg of a trip from New York to Kingston and back, when the mate, Guido Correlli, noticed that she was listing badly to port and taking in water through the third-class portholes. He rang the purser on the ship's phone and yelled, *"Marrone,* our ballast, she's shifting! Look at the *manifesto.* The cargo in Fort Lauderdale, we have taken on too much—too much *petrolio,* or *something!"*

"Manifest shows nothing, Signore," the purser reported. *"Niente.* We take on nothing in Lauderdale, except—*un momento*—here it is. *Si,* just a couple of members of the Book-of-the-Month Club. . . ."

At that very instant, Chuckie Douglas, who had been asleep in his room in Weesquapeckett, awoke with a start. He had been dreaming a dream so awful he couldn't even remember what it was, but what was even worse was that now, even though he was wide awake, he seemed to have a bright-orange life jacket on over his pajamas.

Mom is going through Dad's briefcase. From somewhere she hears a voice calling *Stop, stop! You're violating his civil rights!* but she refuses to listen, she keeps searching. She locates what she is looking for, and there is only one way to describe the sensation she experiences in her head as she settles down with what she has found. It is as if she had turned on the refrigerator light in the deepest, darkest, coldest part of her mind—the place where leftovers are kept. It is not very bright, this little bulb. It wouldn't work as a Kodak flash attachment. It's not even as strong as the overhead dome light in a Chevy Camaro. But it does the job. On the wire racks there, down in that part of herself where she never looks, Mom sees things not meant to be seen: half-filled jars of gooey brown stuff, Saran Wrapped hunks of moldy, cheeselike crud, square Tupperware containers of some whitish-gray guck. Yecccch! Mom can't believe it. How did this stuff get *here,* inside her *mind?* She quickly slams the door and the light goes out. But she knows she'll be back. She tilts her head back and shivers, a wave of revulsion surging through her, a wave so powerful it makes her smile. She just might not get around to fixing dinner tonight.

Now they are both up there all the time.

Mom and Dad

In bed

Chuckie tries to ignore them. He washes his own clothes in Woolite in the kitchen sink and he eats Chef Boy-Ar-Dee straight from the can. But he can't entirely keep his mind off that upstairs bedroom and what's going on up there, there on the bed with the Laura Ashley sheets and matching pillowcases and dust ruffles. Sometimes, if he listens carefully, he can hear his parents whispering in there, reciting multisyllable words in a language he has never heard before:

"batrachian," "chitinous," "ichor." And there are other sounds, too: pants and groans and cries of pain and surprise. What are they *doing* in there?

"M-m-m-m-m-m-mom? D-d-d-d-d-d-d-dad?"

The entire house seems to be holding its breath, everything is going black, until Chuckie remembers something. He opens his mouth and begins to exhale, inhale. Then he pushes open the bedroom door and forces himself to look. They are both lying on the bed (*Mom, Dad*), his mother on the right side, his father on the left, their heads almost touching. Something heavy is pressing on Dad's chest, flattening him back against the mattress, causing him to heave with exertion. His face is red and sweaty, his eyeballs are bulging and feverishly flitting from left to right. Mom is leaning over him, rapidly moving her lips and tearing with her fingers at the thing on top of Dad—the heavy thing, shining and brownish in the light from the bedside table—and the thing seems to fly apart now into hundreds, thousands of fluttering white pieces.

Suddenly Chuckie understands. They will want him to do this, too, some-day. They will *make* him. They will force him to do it for hours and hours until he says he likes it. The thing is a book, and Mom and Dad are

Oh my God

they are reading.

The book dedication is to "Stephanie and Jim Leonard, who know why. Boy, do they." I won't speculate on Jim Leonard's experiences with rabid King fans, but I can tell you that Stephanie Leonard, for many years King's secretary and the editor/publisher of Castle Rock, *knows firsthand what it's like to deal with the fans—the good, the bad, and the ugly.*

Just before the *Time* cover story on King hit the stands in October 1986, "somebody hit the custom-made wrought-iron fence that helps protect his family's privacy." So reported Bob Haskell in a feature article, "The Price of Fame," from King's hometown newspaper, the *Bangor Daily News.* As Haskell explained:

> The Kings woke up one morning a couple of weeks ago . . . to discover that the wings of his bats on each side of the main gate had been clipped off, and that the three heads of the mythological metal griffin atop one of the corner posts also had disappeared. . . . Most people are satisfied with an autograph. Steve King, as far as I know, has scrawled his name on everything from his books to paper napkins that has been thrust at him.
>
> Other people, who are a little more daring, ask to have their pictures taken with celebrities. And Steve King has patiently stood beside men and women and boys and girls while waiting for the Instamatic to flash because that also goes with the territory.
>
> Then there are those who are not content unless their piece of the celebrity is a bit of cloth torn from his shirt, or a shoe, or the wings of the bat from his private fence which is also a historical landmark.

Happily, the purloined goods were returned, and craftsmen restored the pieces, but it drove the point home to King: fame is a double-edged sword for the celebrity. For no matter what he does, or how much he believes he's a private citizen, a few fans of his have taken a permanent walk on the wild side.

The Horrors of Success

Like moths drawn to an open flame, overzealous fans converge on the bright light in their otherwise mostly empty lives. Drawn into a fictional world that is more

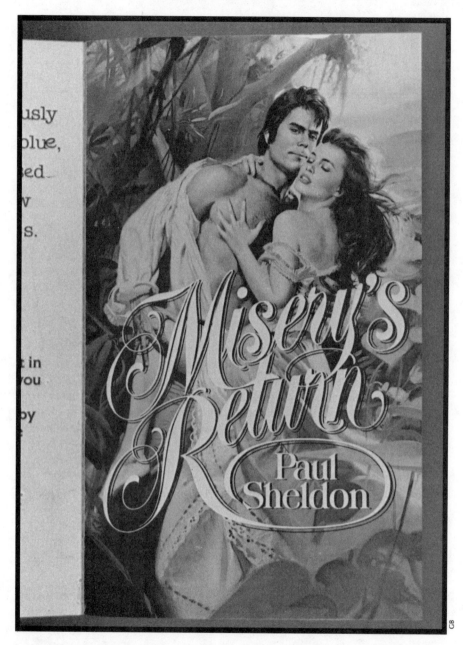

Interior double-cover to the paperback edition of *Misery,* published by NAL. (This is the fake cover, *Misery's Return* by Paul Sheldon, the protagonist of *Misery*.)

real to them than the real world, they take up permanent residence in never-neverland, wherein the writer becomes a kind of God who has made order in his own universe. King knows the phenomenon well. As he put it in an interview with Michael Kilgore for the *Tampa Tribune:*

> The occupational hazard of the successful writer in America is that once you begin to be successful, then you have to avoid being gobbled up. America has developed this sort of cannibalistic cult of celebrity, where first you set the guy up, and then you eat him.

It began early in his career. After *Carrie* and *'Salem's Lot* were published, King was awaiting the release of his third novel, *The Shining,* and shared his concerns about being a bestselling author. In a 1977 interview with King for *Writer's Digest,* Mel Allen reported:

> One of the newest pressures is the demand from reporters, schools, clubs, service organizations and the like for interviews and appearances. These have risen as fast as his climb to the top of the bestseller lists.
>
> King is starting to say no for the first time. But he feels torn. "On the one hand I want to accommodate people; on the other I need the time for myself. Yet every time I say no, I hear them thinking, 'That stuck-up bigshot writer. . . .'"

Welcome to My Nightmare

A King insider shared with me some anecdotes that showed what it's like to live under the microscope.

King is in Wilmington, North Carolina, having dinner with family and friends at a restaurant. Surprisingly, nobody approaches him for an autograph. As King leaves, he sees a long line of fans waiting outside, waiting for an autograph. . . . King is at a bookstore, signing books. The line of customers with King books in hand stretches down *both* sides of the mall, blocking store entrances and angering store managers. After an extended period of signing, it becomes physically impossible to sign another book. Rather than go out the front way, past the long line of fans who have waited patiently, King asks to be let out through the back door. For whatever reasons, he is not allowed to do so. He walks out the store, into the mall, where long lines of disappointed fans wait with books in hand.

Synopsis of *Misery*

Misery loves company.

Annie Wilkes, an ex-nurse, lives alone in Sidewinder, Colorado, in a farmhouse with two cows, six hens, and a sow named Misery, named after her favorite character, Misery Chastain. Her unwilling companion is Paul Sheldon, who has made his fortune by writing bodice-rippers.

It's a "marriage" made in hell.

Sheldon, ecstatic after killing off Misery Chastain in what he hopes is his last Misery novel, *Misery's Child,* heads west in his 1974 Camaro. He's also buoyed by the fact that he's just finished a book he *wanted* to write, *Fast Cars*; it will bring him the critical attention he deserves. Fortified with too much Dom Perignon, Sheldon is driving through Colorado and gets caught in a snowstorm. He goes off

Stephen King's Number-One Fan
A *Real* Horror Story*

So anyway, this book is about fans, particularly about number-one fans. I've been thinking about number-one fans for a long time because I get a lot of mail, and a lot of it is signed "Your number-one fan." And when I was doing a "Tomorrow" show at Rockefeller Plaza in New York seven or eight years ago, you come down and at 30 Rockefeller the most important thing to know when you're done is where your car is, because there are these autograph people that wait for you. And in some cases, they are just autograph collectors; in other cases, their eyes are sort of empty and they are sort of weird. They don't know why they want that autograph; they just know that you are somebody who is on TV. You are projected through the air, which makes you somebody who is not really real, but sort of a celebrity or something. And then there are other people whose eyes are not only sort of empty but they look sort of like haunted houses that say not only is nobody home, the place is haunted. And this guy was one of those. He was this sort of thin, willowy guy, clutching at me, saying, "Will you sign this? Will you sign this?" And he had a piece of paper, and I signed it, and I go for the limousine. And he's got the Polaroid and he says: "Can I get my picture taken with you? Can I get my picture taken with you?" And I said, "Yeah, real quick," and he gives the camera to somebody, and he gets the Polaroid and while it's developing he says, "Will you sign it? Will you sign it?" And I said "Yeah," and he's got this special pen. You know he's been there before because it's almost impossible to write on a Polaroid—everything beads up. And I sign it: "Best Wishes to Mark Chapman from Stephen King." It was the guy who killed John Lennon. And in the course of our discussion, he described himself as . . . *my number-one fan.*

*From King's Virginia Beach lecture, September 22, 1986.

the road . . . and into the world of Annie Wilkes, a psychotic who "nurses" him back to health. She is, of course, Sheldon's "number-one fan."

Unfortunately, Wilkes discovers that her favorite character, Misery Chastain, is killed in *Misery's Child.* (If she had bought the hardback, she would have known, but she's one of those persons who *are waiting for the paperback.*) But she's got Paul Sheldon, and she hooks him on pain killers, and he brings Misery back to life in *Misery's Return,* written especially for Annie Wilkes—a limited edition of one copy, a unique collectible.

As Sheldon feverishly fights his own pain and a psychological battle with his nurse-captor, he writes his way through *Misery's Return,* using a manual typewriter that throws letters. Sheldon realizes at the end that it's either himself or Wilkes. But Wilkes has weapons Sheldon hadn't counted on, and Sheldon has a few surprises, too. Anyone for barbecue?

Publishing Notes

Jacket copy is mostly hyperbole to snare readers. But what are we to make of this flap copy: "[King] owes his fans a love letter. *Misery* is it"? Surely the copywriter was engaging in thinly veiled sarcasm or irony. *Misery,* if anything, is hate mail.

The cover art by Bob Giusti suggests the novel without giving it away. Sheldon, a prisoner of the wheelchair, is in the bleak world of Annie Wilkes, whose dark shadow covers him . . . and whose hands wield an ax; outside it is bleak winter, with a blood-red barn providing the only color. In a bloody scrawl across the cover is the word *Misery.*

The cover to the paperback edition is even more restrictive. The wide-angle perspective used for the hardback becomes a tightly focused closeup of Paul Sheldon, who is in shadow from the silhouette of Annie Wilkes, ax in hand.

Comments

In his foreword to *Night Shift,* King remarks the horrors you don't believe in and those you do:

> When you read horror, you don't really believe what you read. You don't believe in vampires, werewolves, trucks that suddenly start up and drive themselves. The horrors that we all do believe in are of the sort that Dostoyevsky and Albee and MacDonald write about. . . .

With make-believe horror, it's all a joke. All that is required, as Samuel Taylor Coleridge put it, is the willing suspension of disbelief. On the other hand, real horror strikes deep, like the visceral shock of seeing a deep cut that exposes white bone.

Misery is real horror. You are left with the impression that, yes, it could happen. Ask yourself, What if took the obsessive nature of those number-one fans went just one step further? The answer, as King suggests in *Misery,* is something you don't want to experience.

Thomas Tessier, in *Reign of Fear,* correctly states that real horror is subversive in nature. It gets under the skin. Douglas E. Winter, a most perceptive critic in the field, affirms the same in a long interview ("The Dark Dreamer") herein, at the end of Part 3. In *Faces of Fear* (a collection of interviews conducted by Douglas E. Winter), King expresses the same in his wonted colloquial manner, commenting on "Apt Pupil" (a novella in *Different Seasons*):

> The "Apt Pupil" story . . . is just dreadful. My publishers called and protested. They were very disturbed by the piece. Extremely disturbed. It was too *real.* If the same story had been set in outer space, it would have been okay, because then you would have had that comforting layer of "Well, this is just make-believe, so we can dismiss it."
>
> And I thought to myself, "Gee, I've done it again. I've written something that has really gotten under someone's skin." And I do like that. I like the feeling that I reached between somebody's legs like that.

Misery is also a brilliant portrait of the obsessive nature of writing, inexplicable to nonwriters. King deliberately allows an occasional glimpse into that dark area.

Misery will get under your skin. It is subversive horror, and shows that the real world and the make-believe world of the fiction writer are close indeed, and that, paradoxically, truth can be stranger than fiction . . . sometimes.

Editions Available

- A trade hardback, Viking, $18.95
- A large-print edition in hardback, G.K. Hall & Co., $20.95
- A paperback, NAL, $4.95

Night Shift

If you enjoy reading short fiction, chances are good that you don't go to the bookstore and look for a collection by your favorite author. Chances are, you'll pick up a magazine because that's where short fiction is being published. Likewise, if you write fiction and hope to make a living at it, here's a piece of shopworn advice: Write novels. Write short stories on the side, when you can *afford* to, but think big and write novels. As one wit observed: "Americans prefer fat books and thin women."

It's a marketing problem. Publishers know that, generally, short-story collections don't sell, which is why they prefer to publish novels. But if you've got a following, then the publisher *might* issue a collection of fiction. Case in point: Stephen King, who preceded the publication of this collection with three novels.

Night Shift comprises twenty short stories, eleven of which were originally published from 1970 to 1975 in *Cavalier* magazine, for which King got paid $250–$300 each, according to editor Nye Willden. (This collection also has stories that were published in better-paying markets: *Gallery, Cosmopolitan,* and *Penthouse.*)

If you've read King's novels but have, for whatever reasons, not read his collections, give *Night Shift* a try. I think you'll like it. The late John D. MacDonald, who wrote the introduction to the book, obviously did. At the end of the short introduction, MacDonald said, "If you have read this whole thing, I hope you have plenty of time. You could have been reading the stories."

But before you get to the stories, there's a lengthy foreword by King, an extended discussion on writing, why he writes horror, and the purpose of horror fiction. If you read it carefully, it'll tell you more about King as a writer than volumes of scholarly books about King, dissecting every aspect of his storytelling craft. But as King points out, it all boils down to this: storytelling. "[I]f the story does hold you, all else can be forgiven."

And that, my friends, is the secret of King's success: He's a consummate storyteller, and he knows that's his primary responsibility to the reader.

The stories in *Night Shift* are an eclectic collection. "Graveyard Shift," frankly, is not for the squeamish. "I Am the Doorway," a science-fiction/horror story, inspired the cover design for the paperback edition. The E.C.–type story "The Ledge" will put you on the edge. And "The Children of the Corn" was adapted for a movie that, by consensus, holds the dubious honor of being the worst film adaptation of King's fiction. And there's much, more more.

Again, if you have read King's novels but not his short fiction, try this collection, then read *Skeleton Crew,* then *Different Seasons.* You will see that rarest of writers: a writer who is developing his craft, a writer who realizes that, in the end, as King reminds us in his epigram to *Different Seasons,* "It is the tale, not he who tells it."

Editions Available and Tie-in Product

- A trade hardback, Doubleday & Company, $17.95
- A paperback, NAL, $4.95
- A hardback, in an omnibus edition (Stephen King), with *The Shining, 'Salem's Lot,* and *Carrie*; out of print, but I've seen copies in independent bookstores for $13.00 and up
- A set of audiotapes, unabridged readings, from Warner Audio Publishing, repackaged for Waldentapes; out of print, but available in some smaller bookstores: "Jerusalem's Lot," "I Am the Doorway," "Night Shift," "I Know What You Need," "The Last Rung on the Ladder," "The Boogeyman," "Graveyard Shift," "One for the Road," and "The Man Who Loved Flowers"
- *Children of the Corn,* New World Pictures, available on videocassette from Embassy Home Entertainment
- *Cat's Eye,* MGM/United Artists, available on videocassette from Key Video. (A film anthology, *Cat's Eye* has two segments based on material from *Night Shift:* "Quitters, Inc." and "The Ledge")

An Editor's Reminiscence
by Nye Willden

It was 1972 and a young writer named Stephen King was still a year away from signing a contract for his first novel, Carrie. *Living in a nondescript trailer in Hermon, Maine, King was writing and selling short stories to Nye Willden, the fiction editor for* Cavalier *magazine who, among others, discovered the late cartoon genius Vaughn Bodé.*

King fondly recalls Willden, calling him "a good angel" in a long essay, "On Becoming a Brand Name," in Fear Itself.

In this short reminiscence, Willden recalls his encounters with King, who even at that early stage in his career showed an impressive talent.

Most of the stories published in Cavalier *were collected in King's first short-story collection,* Night Shift.

"Graveyard Shift" was King's first story published by us and "I Am the Doorway" was the second. As an editor for a men's magazine which dealt primarily in sexually or erotically oriented fiction, Stephen's story was an exception and had it been written by someone less talented it probably wouldn't have made it. But to be honest, I was very impressed, sensing that there was something very out of the ordinary about this writing. I was so excited that I called our "free lance" fiction editor, Mr. DeWalt, on the phone (he read a lot of the slush material for us and still does) and read him the story. He had the same feeling that I did that here was a major talent in the making. I was not at all surprised by Stephen's subsequent success and still am not, although the scope of it is a bit mind-boggling.

We never did much editing of his work. I recall one time we didn't like the ending of a story, or there was something that had to be eliminated because it didn't fit somehow and I called him and he asked that he be allowed to make the change, which he did.

Cavalier pays on publication but on occasion Stephen would call and ask if we could pay in advance and we always did. He was having a difficult time financially.

Stephen was always a very friendly, easygoing, grateful and accommodating young man who came down to New York fairly frequently, and he'd come to my office. We got to know each other fairly well and had lunch occasionally. He was a big, warm teddy bear with a very boyish, impish grin and absolutely serious and dedicated to his writing. From the very beginning he struck me as someone with a purpose and he was never deterred from that. My last direct contact with Stephen was when he called me here in Florida about seven years ago and asked me if I knew of some out-of-the-way place where he and Tabitha and the kids could go just to get away. I called Sanibel Island on the west coast of Florida and found them a house to rent for a week. The island was, at that time, very private and somewhat sparsely populated and they had a wonderful time walking the beach and looking for shells (it's called the shell capital of the world because there are literally millions of shells on the beaches). He came back through Miami and came up to see me . . . still the same friendly guy. Fiction editor Maurice DeWalt was invited to one of his editor's parties; I think it was for *The Dead Zone* and was at the Tavern on the Green. DeWalt had never met Stephen and reports that he was gracious and funny and expressed how grateful he was to me and Doug Allen, the publisher, for our kindness to him in the early days.

We did pay him a bit more than our usual rate after his first few stories because we knew he was special. I think that was about $250 or maybe even $300 a story.

About "Cat from Hell," I came across this marvelous photo of a cat's face (from UPI, I believe) and half of it was black and the other half white. And it looked very intriguing. I thought up the idea of a short story content to be based just on the photo. Then I thought how much more interesting it would be if Stephen would write just a short beginning to the story to kick off the contest and writers would then expand on it. So, I sent the photo off to Stephen and he wrote back shortly after, enclosing a complete short story titled "The Cat from Hell." "I can't write part of a story," he explained. "That would be like having half a baby. So, take part of the story for your contest and then perhaps you'd like to publish my story in its entirety later on as a comparison with your contest winners, or do whatever you wish with it," he wrote. That is exactly what happened. We published the winning story, which was very good, and then the next month we published "The Cat from Hell" in its entirety. By this time, as you know, Stephen was world famous, but was still the same gentle, nice, kind man he had been for seven years . . . and although I have lost touch with him I'm sure he'd respond immediately if I wrote him. I think his lack of egomania is what still makes his books so wonderfully believable for his public. I find it a bit amusing . . . no . . . charming that he still expresses gratitude to Dugent for giving him his chance at publication. My attitude is one of gratitude for having the opportunity to have rubbed shoulders with genius—and there's sure as hell no argument that that is what he possesses in his genre—and to have had my name included in some of his forewords and acknowledgments. We've never tried to exploit our association with Stephen and never would (the mentions have all come from him) and we signed over all rights to his stories immediately upon his request. But it's great to pick up a book by or about him and see my name mentioned. It was, and is, a pleasure to know him, not just because of his fame but because he is a genuinely nice human being.

Gary Hart Is Strange
and So Is This Movie About Cornflake Kids
by Joe Bob Briggs

One of the most powerful stories in Night Shift *is "Children of the Corn." Unfortunately, what most people remember about this story is that they saw the abysmal film adaptation.*

Though King's work has suffered badly at the hands of inept filmmakers, "Children of the Corn" is by consensus the worst adaptation to date. More's the pity, since it could have been a dramatic, shocking short film.

In this movie review Joe Bob Briggs, the king of drive-in critics, concludes that it's "a decent drive-in flick" despite "too much plot getting in the way of the movie."

Last week I drove out the Grapevine Highway to take Wanda Bodine to see this flick called *Children of the Corn*, about these kids in Nebraska that like to carve up their parents and make gasahol, but then Wanda made some remark about how cute Gary Hart is and I'm sorry but I had to stop the Toronado in the middle of I-35 North and tell her that the drive-in was a family place, and if she started mentioning members of Congress again I was gonna have to do a little elective neurosurgery, if you know what I mean and I think you do.

But while I'm thinking about it, let's get this out of the way right now. How many people are sick of Gary Hart? Could we have a show of hands, please? I thought so.

Nice hair, though, Gary.

Before I tell you about the giant groundhog mushroom cloud in *Children of the Corn,* I need to get down to the nitty here. A lot of you turkeys are reading this column for the first time this week, and you're probly thinking, Who is this guy? What is this? Why am I reading this? Where can I get a good massage?

There's a few things you need to know.

Numero uno: I review DRIVE-IN movies. For you people in San Francisco, that means OUTDOORS. In Communist Russia, you can't do this. Drive-ins are illegal in Communist Russia. But we are privileged to watch movies the way God intended us to see em, in the personal privacy of our own automobiles. I don't want to have to say this again. Understand?

Numero two-o: If you like indoor bullstuff like *E.T.,* please go get in your Toyota and fold your body into a balloon animal and drive to the mall.

Numero three-o: Maybe you're like my friend Chubb Fricke, who played two weeks on the PBA tour in 1948 and never has quit talking about it ever since. Chubb is what's known as an old fat guy. Old fat guys are easily offended. Old fat guys shouldn't read this column. All of the old fat guys should turn directly to the fishing report so they can go down to the Legion Hall and tell somebody about all the crappie that's biting on Lake Tawakoni.

Numero four-o: Or maybe you're a member of the National Organization of Bimbos. The National Organization of Bimbos says I don't respect women. The National Organization of Bimbos says I "endorse violence against women." I've said it before but I'm gonna say it right here again: I am violently opposed to rape, brutalization, beheadings, disembowelings, arms and legs hacked off with chainsaws, hypodermics through the eyeball, power drills through the stomach, those scenes in the movies where the monster squeezes girls until their eyes pop out and they explode, butcher knives across the knees, and spears through the ear, unless it's necessary to the plot.

Okay, now that we've weeded out all the wimps and been canceled in seventeen cities, I feel much better about myself.

Let's talk Big Steve King. Steve's a pretty scary guy. Wanda Bodine went under the seat three times on this one. Better than *Cujo,* not quite *Dead Zone,* but what the hey? Steve delivers, right?

Children of the Corn starts off one day when the Babtist church in Gatlin, Nebraska, is letting out and everbody is headed over to the coffee shop to eat something greasy and disgusting like meat loaf. Only once they try the coffee they start grabbing their throats like somebody just forced em to watch a Bob Hope special, and then they start making noises like a major Maytag appliance starting to break down, and then their kids come in the restaurant and start mowing them down with meat cleavers and sickles and pickaxes. One guy gets held down while they stick his hand in the automatic roast beef slicer. It's okay, though, because nobody was ordering.

Now it's three years later, and this little kid is running through the cornfields with a suitcase, trying to make it to the highway, but a man with a butcher knife in his holster turns the kid into shishkebab meat and then puts him out on the road so some tourists will run him down like a potato pancake.

Then this movie starts to get grisly.

I don't want to go into all the plot here, because it's boring, but basically what we got is a bunch of little brats that killed all the grownups in town and now they make gasohol all day and murder tourists and worship this kid named Isaac who has a Buster Brown haircut and stands about two foot six and looks like Charlie Brown with a piece of goat meat lodged in his throat. There's also a kid named Malachai who looks like Alfalfa with his hair grown out like a hippie, and Malachai likes to kill little dogs and old-coot gas-station owners. I call em the Cornflake Kids.

Anyhow, these two tourists come along and figure out something's wrong when the streets of the town are deserted and rotten cornstalks are sticking out everywhere. This doctor and his blonde girlfriend go walking through all these buildings full of cornstalks and after about fifteen minutes they say, "There's something strange about this town." The Rhodes scholar who says this gets hung up on a cornstalk cross so they can sacrifice her to He Who Walks Behind the Rows. But first they have to wait for Amos. Amos is the nineteen-year-old wimp who likes to carve on his chest with a farm implement and drain his blood into a cup so everybody can drink it. Amos wants to "go to Him" by strapping himself up there on a cross while the Cornflake Kids crowd around him and do a Vienna Boys Choir number. Amos and the blonde bimbo are gonna "go to Him" together, because the bimbo's husband is hiding out in the atomic-bomb shelter with a couple little kids who have been hiding out from Isaac and playing Monopoly for the last three years.

A little too much plot getting in the way of the movie, but a decent drive-in flick anyhow. Ten dead bodies. One dead dog. No breasts. One motor vehicle chase. About two pints blood. Heads do not roll. Hands roll. Excellent groundhog-mushroom-cloud monster. Great scene where Peter Horton, the tourist with an IQ of 24, gets strangled by a demon cornstalk. Drive-In Academy Award nominations for Courtney Gains as the hippie Alfalfa, John Franklin as Charlie Brown, Fritz Kiersch, the guy who made this sucker, and Big Steve, who made it all possible. Three and a half stars.

Pet Sematary

Suffer the little children to come unto me.

Mark 10:14

It was a cold, clear day in December 1988 as I pulled my rented car into the parking lot of a convenience store in Orrington, Maine. I asked one of the locals for directions to the pet cemetery, and after he obliged, he said, "There's nothing left up there, you know."

I knew that but wanted to see for myself. I pulled back onto Route 15, a north-south road flanked by the Penobscot River.

I followed the directions and pulled up onto a bumpy dirt road. On my left I passed two apple trees with withered fruit. Atop the hill sat a red-brick farmhouse. I drove up, parked the car, and got out. Concerned that someone might still be living there, I stood outside the car, waiting to be approached. Nobody came. I headed into the woods, walking in a wide circle.

No trace remained of the "pet sematary," as King called it. But my guess was, it was beyond the makeshift wall of stone deep in the woods.

I took a few pictures, got back into the car, and headed down the dirt road, stopping where it met Route 15. A young girl who lived across the street stopped me before I could turn the car onto the street.

"Anything I can help you with?" she asked.

"I just wanted to see the original pet cemetery," I replied. "I'm doing some research on a book about Stephen King."

She pointed to a two-story white house on the east side of Route 15. "That's where he used to live when he was here," she said. The house flanked the truck route.

"I know there's nothing left of the pet cemetery, but my guess is that it was beyond the pile of rocks in the woods to the right of the house."

"That's where it was." She paused, then added, "A couple of years ago, it was vandalized. They took the gravestone markers. Nothing's left."

"The house looked empty. I hoped nobody minded," I said.

"There's a woman who lives in the house. I was going up to see her."

"Please convey to her my apologies for my intrusion."

She said she would, and headed up the road.

The *real* pet cemetery in Orrington, Maine.

I almost pulled onto the road, but around the corner came an eighteen-wheeler, a dinosaur of a truck lumbering down the twisting country road. It roared by, buffeting the car as it passed.

As I headed back to Bangor, I was amazed at the number of large vehicles on Route 15. It's a dangerous road, inviting accidents and inevitably taking a toll on the local cat and dog population.

Pet Sematary

Pet Sematary was published by Doubleday because of a contractual dispute. As Charlton and Mark explain in *The Writer's Home Companion,* because of tax purposes King elected to take a fixed amount ($50,000 a year) from Doubleday; but when the balance owed was over $3 million, payout on that would have covered sixty years. Because of a potential IRS problem, Doubleday wanted " 'due consideration' " to terminate the agreement and accepted *Pet Sematary,* which had a first printing of a half-million copies.

Pet Sematary is a disturbing novel, the kind of subversive, realistic horror that exemplifies great horror fiction. If, as King has said, horror fiction is a rehearsal for death, then this novel is a danse macabre. It's the story of Dr. Louis

Rich Hewitt, Photo courtesy of the *Bangor Daily News*

The *Pet Sematary* movie set in Ellsworth, Maine.

Creed who, like his fellow practitioners, sometimes cheats death by prolonging life; but ultimately death wins. It is the story of a man who forgets that he can't play God, that despite the miracles of science and the life-support systems that can prolong life, at best, he can only postpone the inevitable for a very short time.

But what if he could return the dead to life? Should man cross the reach? *Pet Sematary* answers that question.

The original idea for the novel came from "The Monkey's Paw," a short story by an Englishman, W.W. Jacobs. In it a man is granted three wishes. With his first wish, he asks for a sum of money. He gets it, but the price is high: it's blood money, given to him as a result of his son's death. With the second wish, he asks for his son to come back from the dead. As he hears an ominous sound at the front door, he frantically makes his inevitable third wish.

The remaining inspiration for the story came from real life: the pet cemetery near the house, and the death of a family cat, a victim of the truck route in front of the house. What next? What if, instead of a cat, one's own child had been killed?

Synopsis

Dr. Louis Creed takes a new position as the head of the college infirmary at the University of Maine. He moves his family from Chicago to a small town in Maine, where he buys a house alongside a major truck route.

One day his daughter's cat, Winston Churchill (Church), is killed, a victim of one of the many trucks that traverse the route.

Behind the house is the pet cemetery, and beyond it the "real cemetery," an ancient burial ground of the Micmac Indians, which is where he buries Church.

Then Church returns, but not the Church they knew and loved. Church is changed.

The real horror begins afterward, when Creed decides to play God, not once, but twice, tampering with the natural progression of life from birth to death, for which there's hell to pay.

Film Adaptation

As *USA Today* reported in its April 25, 1989, issue, *Pet Sematary* "scared away the competition and set a box-office record over the weekend: It grossed $12 million, the biggest opener ever for a movie released in the first half of the year."

In the "Show" section of the paper for that day, a review of the film appeared, headlined "Stephen King's Gravely Flawed *Pet Sematary.*" The reviewer, Matt Roush, liked the novel but not the adaptation:

The home King rented in Orrington, Maine, where he wrote *Pet Sematary.* (The actual site of the cemetery is behind the house, in the woods, next to a large farmhouse on a hill.)

His [King's] script is an awkward jumble of flashbacks and stock shocks further hamstrung by generally tepid acting. It reduces his 1983 bestseller—a daringly dark fable about death, grief and resurrection, with nary a hint of redemption—into a standard horror flick.

At this writing, the reviews have just started appearing. However, if the *USA Today* review is any indication, King fans who were hoping this film would be a faithful adaptation may be disappointed.

Editions Available and Tie-in Product

- A trade hardback, Doubleday, $19.95
- A paperback, NAL, $4.95
- The movie, *Pet Sematary*

A Real Pet Cemetery

Pets that are buried here have received an awful lot of love, and somebody cared enough about them to give them a final resting place.

Cherie Blood, Resident Manager
Garden of the Pine Pet Memorial, Virginia Beach, Virginia

The loss of a pet can be emotionally devastating, and a pet burial is no laughing matter. Says Cherie Blood: "I don't think a pet cemetery—and I would like to be quoted on this—should be taken lightly, emotionally. I don't think that anybody should make fun of anything that somebody has loved. To that person, they loved it. I just think that folks should never criticize the way anybody else feels."

Blood, who lives on the grounds at the Pet Memorial, is an animal lover. She has many nearby friends: squirrels, a resident opossum, an occasional deer, rabbits, and numerous birds.

The Memorial was founded in 1957 by Jesse and Kathrine Mercer, animal lovers who had set aside twenty acres for the purpose of providing a final resting place for pets. Since 1957, Blood says, some six thousand pets have been buried on the premises. (Blood estimates that there is enough room on the premises to accommodate the demand for plots for the next half century.)

Dogs outnumber cats on the premises by three to one. But other animals are present also: ferrets, guinea pigs, and birds; and occasionally the more exotic: a lion (from the local zoo), some K-9 dogs from the police department, a deer, and a goat.

In addition, there are "cremains" for fifteen people, including the Mercers. Explains Blood, "More and more, people are requesting that, when its their time to go, they be buried with their pet. It's in their will. We have quite a few."

Costs

The cost for a pet burial varies, depending on the size of the pet and whether or not a bronze marker is requested. For a small pet (twenty pounds or smaller), the cost is $240 for the basic package, which includes the viewing, the burial in a three-by-six-foot plot, and a standard white marker. For a medium-size pet (thirty to forty-five pounds), the cost is $270. And for a large pet, like a Doberman, the cost is $320.

The costs vary primarily because of the varying sizes of the pine coffin, each lined with taffeta.

The plot is marked with a flat white marker (one brick wide, two bricks long) bearing the pet owner's last name. The marker is positioned at the foot of the grave. (A bronze marker will cost an extra $130, but they last forever. The marker is engraved with the pet's name, the dates of birth and death, and a favorite sentiment.)

Other pet cemeteries may have tombstones, but at this one all the markers are flat. Explains Blood: "It's a bear when you try to mow around those suckers, especially when you've got this many of them."

Blood says that there are five to ten services a week. They try to schedule no more than two a day, one at 11:00 A.M. and the other at 2:00 P.M. A viewing and service normally take about forty-five minutes.

Logistics

In most cases, the deceased pet is picked up by the Pet Memorial as soon as possible because "pets are not embalmed." This is especially important in the summertime if the deceased is a dog. Says Blood: "I don't mean to be gross, but in the summertime if you go to work and come home eight hours later, and the dog passed away an hour after you left home, the dog has been exposed to heat and maggots [for seven hours]. In the summertime, maggots will infest a pet within an hour, and once that happens, we have no way of fixing that."

But that is the exception. More typically, pets look quite natural in death. "When they are viewed, they do look better than people because pets have fur that can be fluffed up. Pets look very natural; they look as if they're just asleep."

To prepare the pet, the Memorial closes its eyes, puts in its tongue, and forms its legs in a nice, comfortable-looking pose. Many owners place a memento in the coffin. Dog owners typically put in a picture of themselves with their pet, dog chewies, dog bones, favorite toys, the dog leash or collar, a favorite bowl, or a

Pat Flagg, Photo courtesy of the *Bangor Daily News*

"As seen from the rear of one of the homes, a shell is being built around the cape to convert it into an old Victorian house."

favorite blanket. (In some cases, when a healthy pet has died and an older pet is sick, the older pet is put to sleep, and the two are buried together.)

Heaven Can Wait

Emotional attachment to the pet makes this a particularly devastating time for the owners. Some ask if the pet will be in heaven when it's their time to go. Blood handles it delicately and appeals to the Bible, which says that because pets don't have souls, they cannot go to heaven. Some owners, however, are adamant. They have told Blood that if their favorite pet isn't waiting for them in heaven, they don't want to go there; heaven can wait.

Young children especially find the loss of a pet crushing. "If you have a twelve-year-old child and the pet is fourteen, that child grew up with that pet. To that youngster, the loss is devastating. We have to handle it very carefully when a child views a pet," says Blood.

In fact, the emotional attachment to a pet may even transcend familial love, according to Blood: "I hear many people tell me that they have grieved more over pet loss than they actually have over some family members that they've lost. For someone who doesn't understand that, it may sound damned strange. But if you haven't seen Aunt Bessie in thirty years, it's kind of hard to get all torn up when she doesn't make it through."

After the Service

After the pet is buried, the pet is not forgotten. Owners visit on special days like pet birthdays. And on major holidays, the cemetery looks like an outdoor flower shop. "The cemetery looks pretty. Pet owners go all out for the holidays," says Blood.

But sometimes the frequent visits are not enough. For those who can't handle the loss, a support group was formed. Members meet at the Memorial and share a common bond: pet bereavement. Unless you've been there, you don't know what it's like. Blood explains: "People who have never loved or shared their love with a pet don't realize how emotional it is to lose a pet that they've lived with for a long period of time, regardless of whether it was a cat, bird, dog, or fish. It's devastating to people. This is not something that should be taken lightly. To them, that pet was their baby."

I asked Blood if there was anything that pet lovers should keep in mind when the time came to give their pet a final resting place.

She replied: "I tell people that if we take all the goodness, the loyalty, the devotion, the sincerity that the pets share with us and we learn from that, we go on to help other animals during our lifetime. Then the pet that is buried is never truly dead but, instead, lives on through every test that we'll ever have in our lives. That is probably the final tribute that you can give."

The Author Talks: King on Being Typecast

I never think of myself as anything but a writer. I just sit down and write stories. I can remember after having published *Carrie* and having turned in two manuscripts to my editor, and him saying, "I would really like to do *'Salem's Lot,"* which is a vampire book. But he looked so glum about it, and I said, "Why do you look that way, Bill?" He said, "Because if we publish it you're going to get typed as a horror writer." And my immediate response was, "Let them call me what they want to call me. I mean, names are names, and that's fine. It doesn't bother me."

'Salem's Lot

Dracula.

Like its namesake, the novel is ageless. The tale, almost a century after its original publication, still irresistibly attracts.

In print in numerous editions, *Dracula* remains the classic vampire tale, its power undiminished—a stark contrast to the numerous comical treatments of the vampire in fiction and film.

Cut to Richard Matheson's *I Am Legend.*

Interviewed by Douglas E. Winter in *The Art of Darkness,* King explained that after reading *I Am Legend* (a novel in which vampires haunt suburban Los Angeles), he realized he could write about horror on his own terms: "I had read Poe and I had read a lot of Gothic novelists, and even with Lovecraft I felt as though I were in Europe somewhere. I knew instinctively that I was trying to find a way to get home, to where I belonged."

King Comes Home

King transported the vampire legend from Europe to Maine and gave it a new life by treating it seriously. He counterbalanced the unreality of the vampire myth with the down-home reality of a small town in Maine. How the characters react is the basic story.

In *'Salem's Lot,* King knew exactly what he was doing, and it shows. The novel is a brilliant achievement. Other writers in the field probably wished they had written it.

'Salem's Lot has remained, according to Douglas E. Winter in *The Art of Darkness,* "over the years, King's personal favorite; and . . . the single most influential of his books upon other writers of horror fiction."

It's easy to see why. In *'Salem's Lot,* his second published book, King creates a richly imaginative fictional world with a texture unmatched in his later novels, except *The Shining,* his third book. The writing crackles with a nervous energy found only in *Carrie, The Shining,* and, to some extent, *The Stand.* Then there's the lyrical prose, the seductive quality of good writing, and from one who has said his style is the literary equivalent of a Big Mac and fries. The text has a hypnotic, dreamlike quality that evokes the mood of Shirley Jackson's *The Haunting of Hill House.*

Synopsis

After a quarter century, writer Ben Mears returns to 'Salem's Lot, where as a boy of seven he spent happier days. Crossing the Falmouth town line, Mears sees "two boys walking a road parallel to the expressway with fishing rods settled on their shoulders like carbines." It's the kind of idyllic scene of Small Town, USA, that Norman Rockwell would have memorialized with a few brush strokes.

Mears motors into town and is drawn to the Marsten residence, an old house that is a conduit of evil. "It had waited for him," King writes, and we know it will draw others because the Martsen house draws evil.

Languorously, the small town comes alive and we meet its residents: Jack and Hal Griffen, two young boys whose father owns a dairy farm; Irwin Purinton, the milkman; Eva Miller, who runs the only boardinghouse in town, where Ben Mears takes a room and where Eva's old lover, Weasel Craig, dreams of days long gone; Sandy McDougall, a seventeen-year-old stuck in a trailer in the middle of nowhere, married to a mechanic, and raising a newborn child instead of pursuing her dreams of being a model; Bonnie Sawyer (Miss Cumberland County of 1973), a hot little number whose illicit affair with Corey Bryant livens their otherwise drab lives; Dud Rogers, the hunchbacked custodian of the town dump, whose fantasies are populated by Ruthie Crockett, a young girl who taunts and jeers him; Mabel Werts, the town gossip, a grossly fat woman whose tools of the trade are a high-powered pair of Japanese binoculars and the telephone, the lines of which

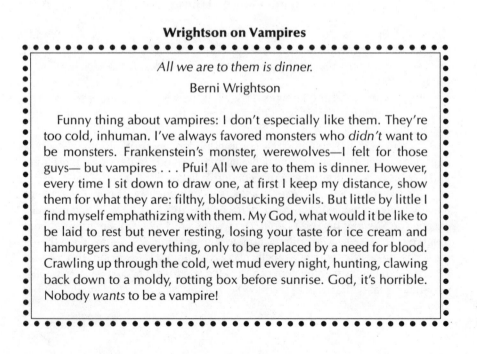

Wrightson on Vampires

All we are to them is dinner.

Berni Wrightson

Funny thing about vampires: I don't especially like them. They're too cold, inhuman. I've always favored monsters who *didn't* want to be monsters. Frankenstein's monster, werewolves—I felt for those guys— but vampires . . . Pfui! All we are to them is dinner. However, every time I sit down to draw one, at first I keep my distance, show them for what they are: filthy, bloodsucking devils. But little by little I find myself emphathizing with them. My God, what would it be like to be laid to rest but never resting, losing your taste for ice cream and hamburgers and everything, only to be replaced by a need for blood. Crawling up through the cold, wet mud every night, hunting, clawing back down to a moldy, rotting box before sunrise. God, it's horrible. Nobody *wants* to be a vampire!

buzz with her illicit trade; and other characters, each with his own secrets, in a town that holds dark secrets.

The town is now ready, ripe for the arrival of Richard Throckett Straker, a tall, bald outsider and the emissary of Barlow, a vampire. Straker buys the Marsten residence and a retail establishment, and awaits the arrival of Barlow.

Then everything goes to hell . . . literally.

Comment

In a 1969 installment of "The Garbage Truck," a column King wrote for the campus newspaper at the University of Maine at Orono, King wrote, "There are strange things in the world." He then described specific incidents that supported his argument, including one that foreshadowed *'Salem's Lot*:

> In the early 1800s a whole sect of Shakers, a rather strange, religious persuasion at best, disappeared from their village (Jeremiah's Lot) in Vermont. The town remains uninhabited to this day.

Later, in *Night Shift* (published as a hardback by Doubleday in 1978), King uses the epistolary form in "Jerusalem's Lot" to unfold a tale about "a small, deserted village" by the same name. The yarn tantalizes but does not satisfy.

Not so with *'Salem's Lot*. Here King tells the complete story, whose power has not diminished over the years. *'Salem's Lot* is a rare fusion of the real and the unreal, with such richness of detail that a sequel is obviously in order—one of the few King novels that warrant such consideration. Unfortunately, no sequel is planned, according to King, which is a pity because *'Salem's Lot* is King in rare form. Like other great horror novels, *'Salem's Lot* is a fictional world that warrants a second visit . . . but not at night.

Editions Available and Tie-in Product

- A trade hardback, Doubleday, $19.95
- A paperback, NAL, $4.50
- A made-for-television movie, *'Salem's Lot*, that ran 220 minutes; available in a condensed version on videocassette from Warner Brothers, with a running time of 112 minutes
- A movie, *A Return to 'Salem's Lot*, "based on characters created by Stephen King." A Larco Production, available on videocassette from Warner Brothers
- An audiocassette of "Jerusalem's Lot" from *Night Shift*, read by Colin Fox; produced by Warner Audio Publishing and available from Waldentapes
- A short story, "One for the Road," collected in *Night Shift*

The Shining

Interviewed in February 1977 by Literary Guild, Stephen King talked about the inspiration for *The Shining*:

> I wanted to spend a year away from Maine so that my next novel would have a different sort of background. While we were living there we heard about this terrific old mountain resort hotel and decided to give it a try. But when we arrived they were just getting ready to close for the season, and we found ourselves the only guests in the place—with all those long, empty corridors. . . .

Stanley Hotel

According to a brochure for its guests, the Stanley is an "old mountain resort hotel," as King called it, located in Estes Park, Colorado. A luxury resort hotel, its guests have been "Molly Brown, John Philip Sousa, and Theodore Roosevelt, to name but a few. (In recent times, author Stephen King stayed for some time at the Hotel, drawing on its turn-of-the-century ambience. . . .)"

Originally conceived as a play, and written after *Carrie* and *'Salem's Lot*, *The Shining* is King's ghost story, set in the Overlook Hotel in Colorado. The hotel has a heritage of dark doings and festers with evil, and is now biding its time, waiting for Jack Torrance.

Synopsis

Torrance is a desperate man in a desperate situation. After being fired from his last job, with the lingering shadow of alcoholism over him, Torrance retreats to Colorado where, through the influence of an uncle, he secures a position as the winter caretaker for the Overlook Hotel.

What Torrance doesn't know is that the place has a checkered past, a fact he discovers after uncovering a scrapbook in the basement. Among the hotel's dark secrets: Delbert Grady, the 1970–71 winter caretaker, went crazy, killing his two daughters, his wife, and then himself.

Determined to put the past behind him, Torrance plans to use his free time to write a five-act play, *The Little School*. But his wife fears for their future, and his son Danny shares her fears, except that he *knows* there's reason for his fears.

268

Danny has a gift—the shining—whereby he catches glimpses of the future. Just as his father was predestined to come to this hotel, so Danny is fated with precognition. It works this way: Danny's imaginary friend Tony reveals the future to him in dreams. In one Danny sees the word "Redrum" (*murder* spelled backward) but doesn't know what it means. Danny also sees his father hunting him down in the hotel, with a roque mallet in hand, smashing the walls as he exhorts his son to take his medicine!

Danny's only ally is the hotel cook, Dick Hallorann, who, like Danny, has the shining. When Danny shares his fears with Hallorann, the cook tells him that nothing in the hotel can hurt him, if he'll ignore it and look the other way. Then Hallorann leaves, informing Danny that if there's an emergency, he'll come running. Hallorann then leaves for Florida.

But Danny *knows* that nothing good can come out of this place because evil begets evil. In Jack Torrance's case, the hotel slowly, insidiously, takes control of him, and turns him into the monster he had hoped would remain hidden deep within him. Then the horror begins.

The Author Talks: King on *The Shining* and Raising Children

Sometimes you confess. You always hide what you're confessing to. That's one of the reasons why you make up the story. When I wrote *The Shining*, for instance, the protagonist of *The Shining* is a man who has broken his son's arms, who has a history of child beating, who is beaten himself. And as a young father with two children, I was horrified by my occasional feelings of real antagonism toward my children. Won't you ever stop? Won't you ever go to bed? And time has given me the idea that probably there are a lot of young fathers and young mothers both who feel very angry, who have angry feelings toward their children. But as somebody who had been raised with the idea that father knows best, and Ward Cleaver on "Leave It to Beaver," and all this stuff, I was really sort of sickened by my own feelings when I would think to myself, Oh, if he doesn't shut up, if he doesn't shut up. . . . So when I wrote this book I wrote a lot of that down and tried to get it out of my system, but it was also a confession. Yes, there are times when I felt very angry toward my children and have even felt as though I could hurt them. Well, my kids are older now. Naomi is fifteen and Joey is thirteen and Owen is eight, and they're all super kids, and I don't think I've laid a hand on one of my kids in probably seven years, but there was a time. . . .

Comment

The Shining is King's breakthrough book, displaying King's strengths as a horror writer: vivid imagery, powerful storytelling, sympathetic characters (including one with a tragic flaw), an evocative setting, and the essential intrusion of evil. Structured like a Greek tragedy, *The Shining* is tightly written, moving quickly through its scenes at a brisk pace, as the evil becomes more pervasive and Jack Torrance descends slowly into a personal hell.

    The Shining was King's third published novel but his first hardcover best-seller—the first of many to come. Despite others working in the genre, King was already being billed by his publisher as "the undisputed master of the modern horror story," a title to which he then took exception. Later there would be no dispute.

Editions Available and Tie-in Product

- A trade hardback, Doubleday, $19.95
- A paperback, NAL, $4.95
- The movie, *The Shining*, directed by Stanley Kubrick, available on video-cassette from Warner Home Video
- For more information, see King's essay "On *The Shining* and Other Perpetrations," and the prologue to the novel, "Before the Play," both published in *Whispers* magazine (August 1982).

Skeleton Crew

If you can't write poetry, you'll write short stories. If you can't write short stories, you'll write novellas. And if you can't write novellas, you'll write novels. (I guess the next step would be a trilogy, a tetralogy, or, God help us, a never-ending story like Hubbard's *Mission Earth.*) The idea's not original with me—it might have been Faulkner—but it's a writing law of inverse proportions: the shorter the work, the more difficult it is to write.

Here's its corollary: most writers of fiction feel most comfortable at specific lengths. Ray Bradbury, for instance, has built his reputation on short stories. Harlan Ellison, of course, is best known for his short fiction.

But occasionally there's the mercurial writer for whom the work dictates the length: poetry, short stories, novellas, short novels, and full-length novels. It's a gift that gives a writer tremendous versatility. Stephen King is one such writer.

Like *Night Shift, Skeleton Crew* is an eclectic collection, the work of a maturing writer.

Skeleton Crew is composed of work from diverse sources: anthologies that only the science-fiction or horror enthusiast would probably have seen *(Dark Forces, Shadows, Terrors,* and *New Terrors),* specialty publications *(Twilight Zone, Ellery Queen's Mystery Magazine, Startling Mystery Stories, Weird Book,* and *Fantasy and Science Fiction),* and mainstream magazines *(Redbook, Gallery, Yankee,* and *Playboy).* The range of publications affirms what Ray Bradbury discovered with his horror stories in the forties and fifties: a good story can sell virtually anywhere.

This collection has two "bookends" by King. Up front is a chatty, informal introduction, the kind of one-on-one that Harlan Ellison popularized in his numerous collections of short stories. And in the back "Notes" tells the story behind the story—interesting reading, especially for writers and those who ask, "Where do you get your ideas?"

In between are two poems, a short novel, and nineteen short stories of various lengths. As you'd expect, the subject matter varies considerably, ranging from "Survivor Type," which sold to Grant's *Terrors* anthology, to "The Reach," originally published in *Yankee* magazine as "Do the Dead Sing?" As others (particularly Winter and Collings) have dwelt at length on each story in this collection, I want briefly to discuss three works that, I think, are must reads: "The Mist," "Milkman #2," and "The Reach."

"The Mist"

In his introduction to *Dark Forces*, anthologist Kirby McCauley, who had previously edited *Frights*, relates the genesis of the book. An English publisher suggested McCauley put together an anthology of original horror fiction for him. It struck McCauley as a good idea—a kind of horror/fantasy equivalent of Ellison's ground-breaking trilogy, *Dangerous Visions* (of which two have seen publication)—and McCauley proceeded to contact potential contributors.

King, of course, was one. At the time, it seemed that no anthology in the field could be considered complete unless it had a King offering.

King's contribution was a short novel, "The Mist," a story that grew from twenty thousand words to forty thousand words. As you'd expect, "The Mist" was properly placed up front as the first story.

I could say many things about "The Mist." I could elaborate on why it's one of my favorite King stories, why it's such an imaginative story and why Berni Wrightson—who discussed the idea with me—thinks it would be a terrific little illustrated book with his inimitable work. But I won't.

The plot: In a small town in Maine, the day after a freak summer storm, a strange mist comes from nowhere. David Drayton, in the company of his son Billy and neighbor Brenton Norton, goes to the grocery store to get some supplies. While there the shoppers watch the mist roll in, and become trapped in the store. Then the horror begins.

It's the kind of story that King can tell well, a perfect example of how King constructs a story. At the phobic pressure point the line between reality and unreality blurs . . . mists over . . . as the town's inhabitants must adjust to life in a

Skeleton Crew: The Limited Edition

Scream Press is a maverick small press that published the limited edition of *Skeleton Crew,* one of the most beautiful and imaginatively designed limited-edition King books ever published. It weighs over five pounds and measures approximately eight by twelve inches. Illustrated by J.K. Potter, slipcased, numbered, and signed by both King and Potter, the edition of one thousand copies originally sold for $75; now it sells for $300–$350 on the secondary market. (A zippered, leatherbound edition was also published; these copies go for $1,250–$1,500.)

brave, new world. *How they react* is what King explores in this short work; the characters and their conflicts come sharply into focus against a backdrop of a mist that hides the spawns of hell.

A reviewer once said of King's work: "The first sentence starts a reader's internal movie projector humming." It's the difference between "seeing" it in your mind and seeing it on the screen. It's the reason why "The Mist" would probably suffer from a film adaptation. Fortunately, "The Mist" works wonderfully as a work of fiction, as an unabridged reading on audiocassette, and as a radio dramatization.

"Big Wheels: A Tale of the Laundry Game (Milkman #2)"

"Milkman #2" is a wonky story that, to me, shows how fiction can move, slowly, from the real world into the unreal world; from a world of normalcy to a bizarre world in which irrationality becomes the norm.

In a small Maine town Rocky and his friend Leo—their spirits bolstered by a case of I.C. beer—set off on a mission: to get a state inspection sticker for Rocky's 1957 Chrysler. As Leo correctly observes, "Nobody in his right mind is gonna inspect this—I told you that." Four hours before midnight, they find "Bob's Gas & Service," owned by Leo's high school friend Bob Driscoll.

Driscoll reluctantly gives the car a sticker, and as Rocky and Leo drive off, the car lurches off into an unreal world.

"The Reach"

An award-winning tale—it won a World Fantasy Award in 1981 for short fiction— "The Reach" is the last entry in *Skeleton Crew.* It is the story of Stella Flanders, at the end of her life, who sets off on a journey across the Reach, the stretch of land between Goat Island (where she has spent all her days) and the mainland.

There is so much I could tell you about this elegiac story, but all I'll say is this:

Nebel

A limited edition of "The Mist" was published in 1986 in Germany. A beautifully produced book, limited to 500 numbered copies, copies imported into the U.S. were seized by U.S. Customs because of copyright infringement; consequently, of the original print run, fewer than fifty copies are in existence.

Last summer when my father died unexpectedly, I reread this story . . . and it put a hard lump in my throat. This is what you need to know: The reach is wide and the dead do sing.

Editions Available and Tie-in Product

- A paperback, NAL, $4.95
- In *Creepshow II,* one segment, "The Raft"
- On an episode for "The Twilight Zone" (TV show), "Gramma"
- On 3-D audiocassette, "The Mist," from ZBS Foundation and Simon & Schuster Audioworks. Also in an unabridged reading, Recorded Books, three cassettes, $19.95
- On audiocassette, unabridged readings, Recorded Books, *Skeleton Crew: Book One,* six cassettes, $37.95, consisting of:
    "The Man Who Wouldn't Shake Hands"
    "Word Processor of the Gods"
    "Morning Delivery: Milkman #1" [story title, "Morning Deliveries (Milkman #1)"]
    "Big Wheels: Milkman #2" [story title, "Big Wheels: A Tale of the Laundry Game (Milkman #2)"]
    "For Owen" (a poem)
    "Survivor Type"
    "The Jaunt"
    "Beachworld"
    "The Raft"
    "The Reaper's Image"
    "The Monkey"
    "Cain Rose Up"
    "The Reach"
    "Uncle Otto's Truck"
- On audiocassette, unabridged readings, Recorded Books, *Skeleton Crew: Book Two,* five cassettes, $34.95, consisting of:
    "The Ballad of the Flexible Bullet"
    "Nona"
    "Paranoid—A Chant" (poem)
    "Here There Be Tygers"
    "Mrs. Todd's Shortcut"
    "The Wedding Gig"
    "Gramma"

- On audiocassettes, unabridged readings, *Stories from Skeleton Crew* from Warner Audio Publishing and also from Waldentapes (both out of print); six cassettes, $34.95:

  "The Monkey"
  "Mrs. Todd's Shortcut"
  "The Reaper's Image"
  "Gramma"

- On audiocassette, "The Author Talks: Stephen King," an interview/profile of King, with readings by King and Frank Muller; one tape, $5.50

The Author Talks: King on Skull Cinema

In fact, this one story in *Skeleton Crew* has been optioned and dropped three times, and that's "The Mist," because the special effects for a movie would be extremely challenging. They are easily manufacturered in your mind, which is one of the unique things about either reading or, in particular, listening to that particular story unroll. The special effects that your mind makes are perfect.

The Stand

Just the flu.

From "Night Surf," in *Night Shift*

A scene from *Amadeus* doubtless struck a responsive chord in Stephen King. Mozart (played by Tom Hulce) has just finished conducting a performance of his latest work and is awaiting a sign of approval from Emperor Joseph II (a musical dilettante, played by Jeffrey Jones). Instead, the emperor damns the work with faint praise. Unable to identify what disturbs him about the work, the emperor asks his court-appointed musical advisers (to a man, obsequious) for their observations. One quickly volunteers that Mozart's work is too long, that it has too many notes. The other sycophants nod in agreement.

Mozart, dumfounded, tells the emperor that the work has *exactly* the required number of notes—no more, no less. The emperor persists—Mozart should cut the work. Exasperated, Mozart finally asks: Specifically, *which* notes should be cut?

The emperor has no answer.

As rewriting is the author's responsibility, editing a book is the publisher's duty, and it falls upon the in-house editor to work hand in hand with the writer to make the book as good as it can be. Unfortunately, other considerations—marketing, for one—sometimes dictate how the book is to be published, regardless of editorial considerations.

As King explained in his 1986 public lecture in Virginia Beach, Virginia, *The Stand* fell victim to marketing considerations. King said that four hundred pages were cut, but that he would restore them in a revised edition.

Revised Edition

If King meant manuscript pages—not book pages—the revised edition would add seventy-five thousand words to the existing edition. Put otherwise, King had deleted from the original book *wordage equivalent to a novel.*

According to a Doubleday spokesman, the revised edition is scheduled for publication in 1990 as a trade hardback. In the April 1989 issue of *Castle Rock*, editor/publisher Christopher Spruce provided an update:

> Doubleday has the manuscript for the unexpurgated *Stand* in hand. King figures the extended version of the book may run another 500 pages depending on what type size and page size the publisher comes up with for the book. A limited edition of 500 copies is now planned. Both the limited edition and the trade edition will feature pen-and-inks by Berni Wrightson, says King.

Novel's Popularity

Despite its formidable length, over eight hundred pages, the novel is a favorite among King readers, especially teenagers. (A *Castle Rock* poll showed that its subscribers overwhelmingly voted *The Stand* as their favorite King novel. In another poll, taken by a San Francisco–based talk-show hostess, *The Stand* was the all-time favorite of the listeners.)

Literary Epic

To King, story is the dominant element in fiction, and everything else, especially the literary form, is scaffolding for it. In this case, the story demanded a large canvas, so the epic was the literary form.

Anyone who has read J.R.R. Tolkien's epic fantasy, *The Lord of the Rings* (commonly referred to as LotR), can see its influence on *The Stand*. Tolkien's tale, set in a mythical Middle Earth, is about the courageous stand of Frodo Baggins, who must leave behind everything he cherishes and travel to Mordor, the land of the enemy, where he must destroy his ring, a talisman of terrible power. Capture of the ring by the enemy could mean the enslavement of all the people of Middle Earth.

The Stand is a contemporary epic fantasy set in a world devastated by a super-flu, an AIDS-like virus for which there is no defense, except a natural immunity. Only a handful of people survive the exposure—99.4 percent of those exposed will die. Just the flu. . . .

The novel does not begin at its logical starting point—a biological experiment gone awry at a top-secret laboratory in California. Instead, you are introduced to a car plowing into Bill Hapscomb's gas pumps at a Texaco station near Arnette, Texas. The driver has the super-flu and tries to escape, but he's too late. The fatal bug claims him soon after Hapscomb and his buddies pull him from the car, which stinks of death.

Then the plague spreads . . . and the few survivors have dreams that draw them either to the Dark Man, Randall Flagg, who beckons them to Las Vegas, or to Mother Abagail, who beckons them to Boulder, Colorado.

Berni Wrightson on His Art for *The Stand*

Q: In several interviews over the years, Stephen King has alluded to your illustrations for the revised edition of *The Stand*. What art did you render for the book?

WRIGHTSON: I did twelve pen-and-ink interior illustrations. The deal was done with Stephen, who commissioned and paid for them, and not with the publisher.

Q: When you illustrated *The Stand,* did you work from the revised version or the original version?

WRIGHTSON: I worked from both. There are two or three drawings that, if you haven't read the excised stuff, you wouldn't know what it's from. I think something like two hundred fifty pages of manuscript was cut out of the original manuscript. In the revised version, there's material involving the Trashcan Man that is really going to change your mind about how you are going to feel about him. And bits and pieces, here and there, that clarify things or add another dimension to it. And some material involving a new character that is just some of the creepiest stuff you've *ever* read.

Q: You've mentioned before that the original illustrations are being done as sixteen-by-twenty inch pen-and-ink pieces. Are there any plans to do a portfolio of your work from *The Stand*?

WRIGHTSON: I've been approached by several people who have seen the work that they'd like to do a portfolio or prints, but I told them, "Let's not even talk about it until the work is published. It's unfinished business." I've been paid for the pieces but they haven't been used yet. Until the book is published, I don't want to discuss it.

[At press time, it appears that Doubleday will be publishing both the limited edition of 500 copies and the trade edition, both of which will have the Wrightson illustrations. (Check the King newsletter, *Castle Rock,* for updates.)]

Comment

Richly complex and satisfying, *The Stand* is a magnificently sustained tale, moving from science fiction to fantasy, from a technological world of order to a world of disorder, one in which a Bhopal-like disaster assumes catastrophic dimensions.

It is a parable of our times. We have engineered toys and gadgets we don't understand, and technological terrors we may not be able to control.

Editions Available

- A trade hardback, Doubleday, $19.95 (in 1990, the unexpurgated edition, $30.00)
- A paperback, NAL, $5.95
- For an interesting preview of *The Stand,* read "Night Surf," a short story published in *Cavalier* magazine in August 1984 and collected in *Night Shift*

The Talisman

I never could understand how two men can write a book together;
to me that's like three people getting together to have a baby.

Evelyn Waugh, in *The Writer's Quotation Book*

Annie Wilkes points out to author Paul Sheldon in *Misery* that "a writer is God to the people in the story. . . ."

It's true. A writer controls his fictional universe, creating it and populating it with imaginary people, who like real people live or die as the circumstances dictate. For this reason it's rare when writers collaborate because, frankly, it's a literary experiment with nothing but risks. The result will be either a resounding success or an unmitigated failure, rarely something in between. Thus a literary collaboration, especially one of novel length, is an act of courage or sheer foolhardiness. One thing is certain, though. A collaboration considered successful will combine the best of all possible worlds: the best of each writer with none of the drawbacks of either.

In a world where books are treated as product, literary experimentation is discouraged, and publishers look backward instead of forward, I think it's always a delight to see someone walk the literary tightrope. That it's done at all provokes wonder.

An act of courage? Sheer idiocy? *You* decide. Either way, it's a sign that the writer is willing to stretch himself, take a chance.

In 1971 Harlan Ellison—a writer who doesn't like to repeat himself—published *Partners in Wonder,* a collection of fourteen short stories written by him with other writers. It's a fascinating book, one in which the fictional voice changed as Ellison's voice merged with those of the other writers.

As Ellison correctly observed in his introduction to the book, "The reward of *successful* collaboration is a thing that cannot be produced by either of the parties working alone." In other words, don't collaborate on a book that you can write yourself. Why bother?

Surely the silliest cover ever with King as the subject, from the defunct magazine *Twilight Zone*.

From the onset, *The Talisman* was a target of opportunity for virtually everyone: mainstream critics (who complained that its status as a bestseller on publication meant that it couldn't be good), mainstream King fans (who carped that they wanted only King—and who the hell is Peter Straub?), and reviewers (who gleefully jerked the starter cords on their chainsaws and decided it was time to get to work—Brappa–rappa–BRAPPA–BRAAAAPPPP!).

After discounting the Stephen King sycophants—*everything* King writes is just simply wonderful, doncha think?—and the natural animosity of mainstream critics, you're left with the only ones who matter: those who bought the book and what they think.

These people are divided into two camps: those who read the story and loved it, and those who, for whatever reasons, couldn't read it.

Try as I did on several occasions, I just couldn't get into the story. Having read (and reread) virtually all the King novels and a number of Straub's novels, I find that *The Talisman* remains an oddity on my King bookshelf: the unread book. (I might add that I felt the same way, initially, about Tolkien's trilogy, *Lord of the Rings*. On the third try, I got into the story and it swept me away. When I finished, I was sorry that the story had ended.)

I'll try again, of course, but what's interesting to me is that I'm not alone. I've talked to other people who read widely and deeply in and out of this field, people who have read all of King and all of Straub, and they either loved *The Talisman* or couldn't get into the story.

It happens. So read the book and tell me what *you* think.

Meanwhile, here's what I think. On one hand, there's King's riveting narrative that keeps you turning the pages until you look up with bloodshot eyes and see that it's long after midnight; you're physically and mentally exhausted, but it was worth it. On the other hand, there's Straub's solid, mortised prose that unfolds slowly, a contemplative prose that reminds you of Henry James. And when the two prose styles were combined in *The Talisman*, the result was a third voice that is neither King nor Straub—a creative synthesis of the two, which can't be separated. (It's a fool's game to try and figure out who wrote what because both writers are so good that they can imitate themselves, parody their own work, or evoke the style of each other.)

Those who expected another *Christine* or *Pet Sematary*—the two novels that preceded the publication of *The Talisman*—were inevitably disappointed. (I'm sure the Straub fans felt similarly surprised.)

In the end, both King and Straub were satisfied with the result. Certainly the publishers were happy, because the book predictably hit the bestseller lists. And millions of readers bought the book, most of whom probably read and enjoyed the story.

So where does that leave me? Well, at some point down the road, I'll take the first step and read *The Talisman*. After all, it's got an interesting premise—it's a quest novel, a bounce off Mark Twain's *Tom Sawyer,* considered to be *the* American novel—and I'm looking forward to walking with Jack Sawyer (who *must* find the Talisman in order to save his dying mother), who moves through our world and the world of the Twinners (a parallel universe populated with people who live in our world).

Editions Available

- A trade hardback, Viking and G.P. Putnam's Sons, $18.95
- A paperback, Berkley, $5.50

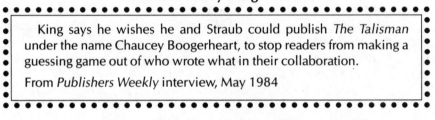

Who Is Chaucey Boogerheart?

King says he wishes he and Straub could publish *The Talisman* under the name Chaucey Boogerheart, to stop readers from making a guessing game out of who wrote what in their collaboration.

From *Publishers Weekly* interview, May 1984

A Coupl'a Authors Sittin' Around Talkin'
by William Goldstein

It's a chummy photograph by Andrew Unangst, published on the back jacket flap of The Talisman: *A bearded King, his arm around Peter Straub, and Straub, his arm around King, hamming it up for the camera. Both gentlemen are grinning broadly.*

Their mutual friendship and respect laid the groundwork for The Talisman.

In this piece, Goldstein tells how the book was conceived, a fascinating story in its own right.

They met in England in 1976 or 1977, at Brown's Hotel in London. Each had read the other's books, and they had corresponded a bit. "We had a drink or two and got along well enough that we thought we could sit down and have a meal," Stephen King remembers. "So we went along to Crouch End, Peter's house, my wife and I."

He stops to pinpoint the date. "I do remember this. You can find out. When we came back, Stephanie, my sister-in-law, who was staying at our little house in Fleet, came out and said, 'You'll never guess what happened! Bing Crosby died.'"

Feeding the straight line, King adds, "And now Marvin Gaye is dead." Peter Straub jumps on it: "Yeah, we ought to get together more often, Steve. We could undermine the recording industry."

It is one day after April Fool's Day, one day after Gaye's been shot, and King and Straub are back together again, this time for jacket photographs at the New York studio of Andrew Unangst, on Park Avenue South. The two bestselling authors have written a novel together, and it is for this novel, *The Talisman* ($18.95), that they are taking jacket photographs. The book, to be published in November by Viking in a 500,000-copy first printing, is not a horror novel (and not "what we expected to do," King and Straub agree), but don't be disappointed: it is an imaginative tour de force, "new territory for both of us," the authors believe; and "a stronger novel as a work of art than I expected to write in collaboration with anybody else," King declares, "including Peter or any writer."

The Talisman tells the story of Jack Sawyer, a twelve-year-old boy who must cross the United States in search of . . . well, let's just say the Talisman and its magic properties. But there's more—another world, in fact: a Middle-Ages–like place called the Territories, which is a mirror reality of our real world, an "America without guilt, or without fear," according to Straub, populated by "twinners," who are counterparts of characters in the modern narrative. In getting to the Talisman, Jack (and some friends along the way) travels in both worlds, "flipping" back and forth between them, meeting up with a lot of adventures, learning a lot about good and evil, trust and love.

Writing a book together was King's idea. "Steve proposed to me," Straub says. "That was in 1978, very late at night, in the house I had in London. I think he just said, 'Why don't we collaborate on a book sometime?' And I said, 'Great.' We'd had about a million beers," Straub laughs, King echoing, "Yeah." "I remember the coffee table was filled with beer bottles," Straub continues.

"And I wasn't responsible, either," King adds, "because I had the flu or something, remember? It was real bad. Yeah, it was one of those things you just say, and then you think to yourself, well, it's a good idea, we'll probably never do it. But it's the way people feel when they get married. . . ." "Yeah," Straub jokes, "the 'Let's-Give-It-a-Whirl' approach."

Work wouldn't begin until years later because each writer had contracts to fulfill. Straub's two books would take him four years, he estimated. And King, also for contractual reasons, thought four years was the soonest possible time. (Though Straub worked only on *The Talisman* while writing with King, King had other commitments to complete simultaneously. As he says, "I got into a jam. My mother used to say when I was a kid, if I was a girl I'd always be pregnant.")

That made it 1982. "So," Straub explains, "we only made a *date*, which gave us a lot of time to think about it and kind of dream up what we might do." King "yeah"s in. The two seem the perfect collaborators: they finish each other's sentences, agree with everything the other says, adding details, "yeah"s and punctuating laughter like Motown backup singers. Their stories mesh and their voices become one.

Sitting together on a couch, they look startling different, Straub clean-shaven in navy blazer, khakis, white shirt, tie and black loafers, King in a white tuxedo shirt and jeans, bearded (though he tells the photographer to get a last good picture of it because it's coming off that night), wearing brown suede shoes rubbed raw in spots at the toe.

Straub recalls that *The Talisman* "really got on wheels" during the author's several drives from King's house in Center Lovell, Me., to Portland, 64 miles away, during one Thanksgiving. "We spent a lot of time in this car ['Talking,' interjects King] talking about the idea," Straub says. "We needed the time, and during those drives we basically came up with the Territories, and with the fact that when you travel in the Territories, you also travel in this world."

It was the to-ing and fro-ing between themselves, both say, that made *The Talisman* possible. "Either one of us could have written a book," jokes Straub as King leans further back into the couch to make his statement: "If somebody had held a gun to one of my children's heads, and said, 'Write *The Talisman* by yourself,' I could have written *a Talisman*, but it wouldn't have been the same thing."

King and Straub wrote an outline for *The Talisman*, dividing up the writing assignments between them. The summer before they actually started writing, Straub suggested to King that they each buy a word processor to facilitate the collaboration. King agreed, though he doesn't like working on a word processor: "It makes me feel like that man in the James Bond movie [*Thunderball*], where he's caught in the exercise machine. I get into it and can't get out. It just scrolls up and up and up and I feel like those words are all under glass."

(King types his manuscripts on an IBM Selectric, has a secretary type it over into the system ["Idle hands do the devil's work, and she loves the machinery, anyway"], and then he rewrites on terminal; this is how he revised *Christine* and *Pet Sematary*, in part to make the rewriting quicker so he could work on *The Talisman*.)

King's Wang and Straub's IBM were hooked up by telephone, and each would send the other his material upon completion. After a year of writing, King says, "we suddenly realized we were working on a book—mostly thanks to me—that was approximately 9,000 pages long." Straub interjects: "That's right. If we pursued our outline doggedly, neither one of us would still be alive. But we would have a huge pile of pages, almost unreadable. In the original outline, we put that boy [Jack] through too many harrowing trials. Too many to read. But the outline is a very exciting book; the original conception seems more feverish and violent."

"*Much* more violent," King amends. "Not that there still isn't quite a lot of gore and grue. . . ." We try to figure out which version *PW* had seen: the toned-down version, or an earlier attempt? King exclaims: "The key question is: 'Was there a cat that came out through a Coke dispenser [in one scene]?'" No. "Well, we trimmed everything back a bit," Straub confesses. Both feel, as King expresses, that "there's a lot of love in the book."

Originally, the book "was gonna be a 'Go-Get-It-and-Bring-It-Back,'" says King. "Finally, we just decided it was gonna be a 'Go-Get-It.' Because it was just out of control. And I was the major reason it was out of control. To begin with, I was truckin' along and Peter was truckin' along and we were doing great and 'Isn't this fantastic?'" Then there took place "The Thanksgiving Putsch," in 1982, at the Long Wharf Marriott in Boston, a hotel next to the Aquarium ("an important source of imagery," says Straub). "We had to do something else. . . .

"Steve was more aware of this than I and, struck by inspiration, said, 'Look, let's just cut off the last half of this outline. That way . . .'" Straub summarizes the plot. "That solved a lot of the interior aches both of us had."

Weaving together their writing styles was never a problem for either of the authors. "At the beginning," says Straub, "we almost unconsciously tried to imitate the other's style." But that ended after about 100 pages. King, of course, concurs. "After 150 pages or so, it became a collaborative style. And I've never written that way before, and I'll probably never write that way again, unless Peter and I go back to the Territories." (There are no plans to do so, the authors say.) "Or decide we want to go to St. Louis or something," he adds, laughing aloud. "I wouldn't dare," he swears.

"I'll tell you something, though, I really felt that some locks came off my mind from writing this together ['Oh, yeah']. I felt sort of safe for the first time in five or seven years in a creative way because I felt that Peter was my safety net, and if I ran out, there would be somebody there to say, 'Do this,' or 'Why don't you try that?' When we did the outline," he continues, "it was like, it was like a couple of those Craftmaster paint-by-numbers, not for anybody else, but for themselves." But that assemblyline affair was transformed into a creation. "Part of you is your collaborator," King says. ("Uh-uh," Straub nods.) "Or it was in this case."

The novel is more a fantasy (in the tradition of the *Wizard of Oz* and *Alice in Wonderland*, to both of which there are allusions in *The Talisman*) than either Straub or King has written before. The concept of the hero was important to the pair, and they read several books about "The Hero," i.e., the epic hero, the meaning of hero, stages of heroic development, the Christ figure and apotheosis ("which," says King, "is something Jack never goes through, thank God").

With this in mind, King says, they began writing. "Anytime you create a story," he begins critically, "there's always talk about how serious writers, which Peter and I are supposedly not, are serious because of their grasp of an entire spectrum of literary concerns. When in fact, if you have a story that is a good story, and then if you determine you will play fair according to the rules of human nature as you understand them and the way the world works at every turn, then by necessity you will write a fairly serious piece of work that accurately reflects human concerns and human mores and ways.

"So I don't think that either one of us knew much beyond the fact that we wanted to write a story that had a strong hero, who was also a sort of picaresque hero, not a Tom Sawyer or Huckleberry Finn clone, but to at least play with the ideas of the travelling person, the travelling hero. . . ."

"Who is changed by his travels," Straub chimes in. ("Travellin' Jack" is one of the protagonist's nicknames.)

"Jack's Mississippi is the Interstate Highway," King says, only partly joking. "I guess what we came out with was something along the lines of the words we've used: sunny, cheerful, in places it's funny, in places it's sad. It plays a little bit," he explains, "in an impish way, with these Leslie Fiedler ['Yeah'] conclusions about dark and light in America, 'Come back to the raft, Huck honey,' the homosexual thing it plays with all that, but it doesn't even hope to do it that well. When you talk about concerns, maybe you," he trails off, turning to Straub, "maybe you want to address that."

Straub turns away from the subject. "No, no, I never feel at ease talking about my concerns because they seem to me to be the least part of a book, mainly because they are the concerns of the book, and not necessarily my concerns." King bellows out, "Yeah, that's it!" The two laugh loudly and seem satisfied to have settled the issue between themselves.

Did writing the book together help them individually as writers? Neither really comments, instead taking the chance to extol the virtues of his partner. "I'm sure that Steve understood the characters with more depth than I did." King disagrees: "That's not true at all; I'd say that Peter brings a depth of style I can't muster, a more mature sense of character; a feeling of urbanity I could never have brought."

"Oh, Steve," Straub jokes, "I thought you brought that." King continues, "I can't think of any weaknesses that I overcame, except that, as I say, it's like stepping into a third person, and that was interesting. But as far as shortcomings, flaws, that sort of thing, I'm not gonna say anything. Because there will be enough other people who'll say those things." They laugh together as King imitates someone saying, "'This is a big lumbering white buffalo.' And I'm waiting for some critic to take a huge Weatherby 395 rifle to its hump. . . ."

"And blast away," says Straub, breaking them both up again.

The Tommyknockers

My own philosophy has always been that I don't care how the gadgets work;
I care how the people work.

Stephen King from WB 145

In the Persian Gulf: On July 3, 1988, at 10:47 A.M. (local time) the USS *Vincennes*—a sophisticated $1.2 billion state-of-the-art cruiser—monitored the departure of a plane that took off from the Bandar Abbas Airport. At 10:54 A.M. the *Vincennes* fired two missiles at the aircraft, destroying it in midflight. Unfortunately, it was a tragic error. The computer had mistakenly identified a commercial airline jet (177 feet in length) with an F-14 (62 feet). The result: 290 civilians dead.

In the film *Maximum Overdrive* (based on King's short story "Trucks") earth passes through the tail of a comet . . . and inexplicable things happen: ordinary kitchen objects come alive, electronic machines tell off its customers, and large trucks corner human prey in a diner. Technology has gone amuck; men are at the mercy of the machines they created. The film is a technology terror tale that is more fantasy than science fiction. And it's a cautionary tale for our times, one that attempts to make sense of our world and the way it works—and the ways it doesn't. Put differently, when Pandora's box was opened, technological terrors emerged, over which we have little control. Among its terrors, the ultimate weapons of destruction, gadgets capable of megadeath, of destroying all life on this planet: nuclear weapons.

Have we become slaves to technology? What control do we really have over these gadgets? What happens when the technology runs rampant?

The message was hammered home in the science-fiction movies of the 1950s, the first decade after the Bomb: Aliens come to earth and inform us that they are a dying race, that their inability to control their technology has led to the destruction of their world. In *The Tommyknockers,* King suggests that we may be the next to go, unwitting victims of the technological toys we have created and don't fully understand.

288

As King does not in the film explain the scientific rationale for the comet's effect on inanimate objects, he does not in his novel explain any of the Rube Goldberg–like gadgets that are jury-rigged by the inhabitants of Haven, Maine, under the influence of an ancient race that perhaps crash-landed on earth fifty million years ago. Nor does King care. What he does care about, though, is what happens to the people. And that, of course, is the story of *The Tommyknockers*.

Strange Doings in Haven, Maine

The novel opens with Roberta Anderson looking for wood on a logging road behind her farmhouse in Haven, Maine. Anderson, a thirty-seven-year-old writer of westerns, stumbles over three inches of metal protruding from the ground. When she touches it, it emits a faint vibration. Puzzling. What she doesn't know is that it's the tip of a spaceship buried there for fifty million years.

We're not informed how the ship got there, or why it was there in the first place; this is not science fiction per se. It is, instead, science fiction with a healthy dose of King's unique blend of fantasy and horror.

All we know is that the ship is a technological boogeyman, exerting an evil influence over Haven's inhabitants, who are all in the process of "becoming."

Roberta Anderson is affected first and, like the others to follow, initially physiologically, then psychologically. In Anderson's case, she loses teeth and weight, and has irregular, heavy periods—symptoms not unlike those of radiation poisoning. As Anderson is assimilated into the collective consciousness of the Tommyknockers, she is able to tinker with gadgets, inventing the scientifically impossible: a house that runs entirely on D-cell batteries; a manual typewriter controlled by mental telepathy—up to five miles away—whether she's awake or not, allowing her to write a novel in four weeks flat; and a modification on her Tomcat minitractor that is marked "Up." Levitation? Whatever it is, the Tomcat now operates noiselessly.

Roberta Anderson's former lover, a poet named Jim Gardner, senses that she is in danger and heads toward Maine. Gardner, unlike Anderson and the others in the town, is immune to the effects of the Tommyknockers, the creatures from a timeless race that built the ship.

Like Roberta, others in the town are in the process of becoming; many are creating technological toys without realizing the consequences. Becka Paulson, whose husband Joe has been cheating on her, jury-rigs the television set so that, when her husband turns it on, it electrocutes him. Nancy Voss, who works at the post office with Joe Paulson, invents a machine to sort mail by itself. Hilly Brown, using a magic kit, modifies it with electronic parts from Radio Shack to create a gadget that makes his brother disappear . . . to Altair-4, a planet light-years from earth. Mabel Noyes invents a gadget that polishes silver; when used, it zaps her into a twilight zone in a fraction of a second.

The gadgets are created by people who have no earthly idea what they are doing, or what the consequences of using them will be—the moral dilemma of our time, suggests King.

As the town's inhabitants are welded together in a mind meld—a collective consciousness—and the Tommyknockers isolate the town from the rest of the world, the evil becomes more pervasive, and Jim Gardner is the town's only hope for salvation. He's immune to the effects of the Tommyknockers, but what can one man do against the invasion of those bodysnatchers?

Editions Available

- A trade hardback, G.P. Putnam, $19.95
- A paperback, NAL, $5.95

Stephen King: An Interview with Waldenbooks[1]

WB: Would you call *The Tommyknockers* science fiction, as opposed to horror? Do you even think of yourself as a horror writer these days?

KING: A guy asked me that after *The Shining* came out. Doubleday actually sent me out to seven cities to promote that book. I ate a lot of chicken and stuff like that. The guy started off a question by saying, "As a horror novelist, do you think that . . ." And then paused and said, "Do you mind me calling you a horror novelist?" I said, "Call me whatever you want. Just make sure that the people know my new book is in the stores." The fact is, I don't categorize what I do.

WB: But *The Tommyknockers* does lean more toward science fiction than your previous novels, doesn't it?

KING: It's science fiction of a type. But the people who write science fiction are going to look down their noses at it and say, "This is crap, because it doesn't say how anything works." There's a suggestion that the spaceship in *The Tommyknockers* is propelled by mental power. There are also suggestions made that there are physiological and psychological changes going on with these people called "the becoming." But it's never explained how those things happen. It's not a book like *The Legacy of Heorot* by Larry Niven, Jerry Pournelle and Steven Barnes, which is about colonists in a faraway world. That book's a really good read and a fast read and a good monster story. But I would say that *The Tommyknockers* is science fiction of a different type.

---

1. Reprinted with permission from *WB* #145, a Waldenbooks' Newsweekly.

WB: Is it science fiction the way *The Invasion of the Body Snatchers* is science fiction?

KING: The science-fiction people like to categorize what they do. They even talk about it in the sense of hard science fiction, like Larry Niven does, and soft science fiction, like *The Invasion of the Body Snatchers*. My own philosophy has always been that I don't care how the gadgets work; I care how the people work.

WB: Was it a conscious decision to move away from the horror genre, as you did with *The Eyes of the Dragon?*

KING: No. It just happened. With *The Eyes of the Dragon*, it was a little bit different because I did want to reach my daughter with that book. I knew she didn't like horror and gushy things. But in the end, I did her the courtesy of writing the book for myself—which is the only way good books get written. That sounds conceited and egotistical as hell but it's only the truth. Writers write books that they can't find in libraries. With *The Eyes of the Dragon*, I made a conscious decision that it was going to be a book that would be cast more in the mold of the stuff that my daughter likes. She likes books about the horse clans and about wizards and magic. So I went for that—but on my terms. I also did *The Tommyknockers* on my terms. If *The Tommyknockers* comes close to anything, it comes close to being a kind of bounce on *Forbidden Planet*, which was, in itself, a bounce on Shakespeare's *The Tempest.*

WB: Do you believe in spaceships, UFOs and aliens?

KING: That's a real Mike Wallace question. I'd say that if it were a question brought before an English jury, I would opt for the verdict "not proven," which we don't have in America. I rather suspect that any interested people from worlds where there is interstellar life—worlds where there might be races capable of coming to other star systems and exploring—would probably be worlds where the impulse would be to observe rather than conquer. It would be more like safaris to Africa with cameras instead of guns. And any interest that they had in us might well have evaporated anyway, because we've gone so far down the road to self-destruction that we're literally drowning in our own shit. The real joke, when you look back on all those movies from the '50s where the flying saucer people say, "We are the last of a dying race," is that we're going to be the ones saying that to some other poor dupes.

WB: *The Tommyknockers* deals with the threat of nuclear war, among other things. Is that a subject that concerns you a lot?

KING: Sure. It concerns me a lot and that's what the book tries to say—and not in any preachy way. I never wrote a book to espouse a principle or a theme. I never did anything but write to entertain myself. But what usually happens is that halfway through a book, there comes a time when you say to yourself, "Wait a minute! *That's* what I'm writing about." In the case of *The Tommyknockers*, what I was writing about were gadgets. I had to write this book to realize that all of these things—the Minute Man, the Skyhawk, the Polaris submarine—are nothing but gadgets. If we kill ourselves, that's what we're going to do it with: a lot of Disneyworld gadgets of the sort that kids build with chemistry sets.

WB: You say in the preface to *The Tommyknockers* that it was "not so much written as gutted out." What does that mean?

KING: That it went on and on. It was a hard one to write, just to keep track of all those people in the story and to make the story cohere. When I finished the first draft, it looked like the Bataan Death March, with lots of cross-outs and stuff. I locked myself in the bathroom and I laughed hysterically and cried and then laughed again. I never did that with a book. I finally finished the rewrites and the whole process took about five years before I was happy with the book.

WB: So *The Tommyknockers* was written, or begun, before *Misery*?

KING: Oh, yes. It goes back a long way, because I had first tried to write the book when I was a senior in college. I was just not able to deal with the characters then— particularly the character of Jim Gardner. I didn't have enough understanding of his sort of self-destructive personality. I knew that such self-destructive people were out there. But I didn't know why. In those days if somebody was maladjusted, as far as I was concerned, it was because they were homosexual. That's the only reason I could think of. The idea that you could be self-destructive because you loathed yourself wasn't there for me then.

WB: Is Jim Gardner another of your characters who [are] "beautiful losers," as they've been called?

KING: I have written a lot about outsiders, people who don't fit in very well with the system. Jim Gardner does bear some resemblance to Jack Torrance from *The Shining*, except that I think Jack is a better man. In the same situation, Jack Torrance would have blown the whistle one hell-of-a-lot quicker than Jim Gardner does, because Jack actually has his shit together; it was the hotel that bent him back and forth until he broke.

WB: *The Tommyknockers* is scary, but it's also funny in parts. Do you use humor to break the tension—or because you're a funny guy?

KING: The humor just comes out. I guess it's a pacing device. I do know that in good horror movies, you have to give people something to laugh at—or else they'll find something to laugh at that you didn't want them to laugh at. Mostly, I'll be writing and visualizing something and I'll see something funny. There's a scene in *The Tommyknockers* where Jim Gardner gets drunk at a party and is terribly obnoxious. I cringed because he was so embarrassing. Yet at the same time, when he chases that guy with the umbrella and it pops open, I found that extremely funny.

WB: *The Tommyknockers* follows *Misery,* which got very favorable reviews. Why do you think the critics liked *Misery* so much?

KING: Because they didn't see it as a horror novel. They saw it as something that could really happen. Famous people can fall into the clutches of their most psychotic fan. You can have the fatal juxtaposition of somebody like that guy Mark Chapman and John Lennon.

WB: Do you care what the reviewers write about your books?

KING: Yes, I do. I read the reviews very carefully. If all the reviewers are saying the same thing that I did right, they're right. But if they're all saying I did something wrong, I probably did it wrong and I want to learn and do it better next time. There was a time when the idea of criticism was to make the writer a better writer, as well as to perform a consumer service for the reader. I think criticism should still fulfill that, although it does that less and less. What happens more often is that you'll get reviews like I did for *Different Seasons.* The reviews were pretty good for that book. But almost every review would single out one of the four stories and say, "This story isn't as good as the others." But they always picked a different story to say that about. So finally, I just disregarded them all and said to myself, "They're all pretty good stories."

WB: Do you watch the bestseller lists or do you just assume that your books will hit the number-one spot?

KING: I don't assume anything. I don't know why people read my stuff, but I'm glad that they do. I like to entertain people, but beyond that, I don't really watch the bestseller lists.

Elaine Koster at NAL called me last summer and said, "Congratulations."

I was on vacation down in western Maine with my wife and I said, "Thank you very much. What are you congratulating me for?"

She said, "Don't you know?"

I said, "No. What?"

And she said, "The paperback edition of *It* has been number one for two weeks."

I said, "That's wonderful," and tried to think of something else to say and couldn't. I was glad, but that was it.

WB: So you didn't mind when *Presumed Innocent,* a first novel, knocked *Misery* out of the number-one spot last summer?

KING: Oh, no. That was great. I do remember thinking about it, though. I happened to be reading that book at the time and I remember saying to somebody, "Oh, no! I bought this guy's book and the son-of-a-bitch just knocked me off the number-one spot!" But I was really only kidding. It's great to see somebody come on the list who has never been on there before. You always see the same tired, tacky old names on there—including mine—week after week after week. As a writer who was just breaking in, I used to get rejection slips and I used to comfort myself by saying, "Well, sooner or later, these guys Michener and Uris have to kick it one of these days."

WB: Is that why you've been so generous in your endorsements of such lesser-known writers as Clive Barker?

KING: Clive is real good and people should know that. I get real excited by books that are good. I felt that way about the last few Jonathan Kellerman books. I thought, "My God, this guy is great."

WB: Is it true that *'Salem's Lot* is your favorite of your books?

KING: It's my favorite of the stories. I think *The Dead Zone* is the best-plotted of all the books.

WB: I read someplace that you were thinking of writing a sequel to *'Salem's Lot*. True?

KING: Not anymore. Too much time has gone by.

WB: Will you ever do another collaboration with Peter Straub, like *The Talisman*?

KING: I think I will do it again in a couple of years. But it will be something a good deal shorter, something completely different.

WB: Will *The Tommyknockers* be a movie?

KING: I think it would make a great movie, but as to whether or not somebody will buy it, I don't know.

WB: So you aren't involved in producing or directing your own movies these days?

KING: Not at all, at the moment. The movie version of *The Running Man* is about to come out this fall and I don't know any more about it than you do.

WB: Are you still an avid baseball fan? Some of us were hoping you'd buy the Yankees from George Steinbrenner—or at least write a baseball novel.

KING: Bite your tongue—I hate the Yankees! I'm a Red Sox fan. And yes, I've thought about writing a baseball novel a lot. In fact, I have an idea, but I'm not going to tell you what it is. It's been kicking around for a while and I might sit down and try to write it some day.

WB: What is your next book?

KING: I don't have a "next book." *The Tommyknockers* was the clearance sale. I'm working on some stuff but I'm not really working very hard. I'm not anxious to publish anything right now. My God, people have got to be sick of me. I did four or five books in one year. *The Tommyknockers* is my last shot for a while. I'm taking off.

WB: Is there any career—other than writing or moviemaking—that you'd like to pursue?

KING: Yes. I'd like to play rock and roll. I play an adequate rhythm guitar but I'm not very versatile. So I guess I'll stay with writing. I kind of like it.

Jack Walas, Photo courtesy of the Public Information Office at the University of Maine at Orono

King delivers commencement address (1987).

The Stephen King Collection
Deposits at the University of Maine at Orono

It began with a conversation in the summer of 1974 between Stephen King and Eric Flower, the Special Collections librarian at the Fogler Library at the University of Maine at Orono (UMO). When King visited the Special Collections, Flower discussed the possibility of his depositing *Carrie* in the collection.

In November 1975 Flower wrote to King, who then lived in Bridgton, Maine, and asked if King had collected "all the pieces, i.e., your original typescript, the galleys and proofs, etc." King gathered the book in its various forms and deposited it in the Special Collections at the Fogler Library at UMO. Since that time King has deposited the bulk of his manuscripts in the Special Collections, and additions are expected.

For any scholar, student, researcher, or writer working on a King project—especially his early work—the Special Collections is an invaluable resource. Here is a list of what has been deposited:

1. Box 718, Papers, *Carrie*:
   a. typescript manuscript
   b. second draft
   c. third draft
   d. final galley
   e. foundry proof

2. Box 1005, Papers, *The Stand*
   a. original typescript
   b. second draft
   c. final galley
   d. foundry proof

3. Box 1006, Papers, *Night Shift*
   a. original typescript
   b. a second copy of the manuscript
   c. final galley
   d. foundry proof

4. Box 1007, Papers, *The Dead Zone*
    a. original manuscript
    b. photocopy of typescript

5. Box 1008, Papers, *The Shining*
    a. original manuscript
    b. final galley
    c. foundry proof
    d. typescript entitled "The Shine"

6. Box 1009, Papers, *Jerusalem's Lot*
    a. original manuscript
    b. correction pages

7. Box 1010, Papers, original typescripts
    a. 4 pages, "Your Kind of Place" (an unpublished essay)
    b. 4 pages, "Culch" (an unpublished essay)
    c. 22 pages, "The Ledge" (a short story collected in *Night Shift*)
    d. 8 pages, "The Boogeyman" (a short story collected in *Night Shift*)
    e. 44 pages, "The Monkey" (a short story collected in *Skeleton Crew*)

Tabitha and Stephen King hold hands during ceremony (1987).

Eric S. Flower (head of Special Collections at the Fogler Library, at the University of Maine at Orono) reviews correspondence files of his letters, and King's replies, in regard to the deposits of King manuscripts.

  f. 8 pages, "Time in a Glass That Ran" (an unpublished short story originally titled "The Last of Her")
  g. 23 pages, "And Sometimes They Come Back" (a short story collected in *Night Shift*)
  h. 2 pages, "Paranoid/A Chant" (a poem published in *Skeleton Crew*)
  i. 76 pages, "The Aftermath" (an unpublished novel-length manuscript written when King was sixteen years old)
  j. 173 pages, "Blaze" (an unpublished mainstream novel)
  k. 485 pages, "Sword in the Darkness" (an unpublished mainstream novel)
  l. 242 pages, *Second Coming* (the first version of *'Salem's Lot*)

8. Box 1011, Papers, correspondence [letters from fans, press material, personal correspondence from friends]

9. Box 1012, Papers, *Firestarter* (additional deposits anticipated)
   a. foundry proof

10. Box 1013, Papers, *Cujo*
    a. typescript manuscript
    b. galley

11. Box 1014, Papers, *Pet Sematary*
    a. typescript manuscript
    b. galley

12. Box 1015, Papers, *Christine*
    a. typescript manuscript

13. Box 1016, Papers, *Skeleton Crew*
    a. photocopy of typescript

14. Box 1017, Papers, *The Talisman*
    a. photocopy of typescript

King Deposits Sought for Special Collections

Eric S. Flower, the head of the Special Collections Department, is seeking deposits for the Stephen King collection. The depository for King's manuscripts, with published and unpublished material currently on hand, the department wants to increase its holdings to include books, magazines, promotional material, pamphlets, audiotapes, videotapes, and any other material by or about Stephen King.

Because of space restrictions and the possibility of duplication, *do not* send anything until after Mr. Flower has agreed to accept the material.

Write to:

Eric S. Flower
Head, Special Collections
Raymond H. Fogler Library
University of Maine
Orono, Maine 04469

The Unpublished Work

*I probably have four novels in the trunk that just happen to be DOA
[dead on arrival]. They're not good books. My definition of how you know
when a book's a bad book is that even when you're drunk
you can't read it and say, "This is a good book."*

Stephen King, on "The Larry King Show"

An unpublished novel is a literary curiosity. But when the work in question is by a popular writer like King, curiosity can become an obsession for die-hard fans, scholars, and collectors.

Over the years, in various books about King, there have been numerous references but few details about King's unpublished work. In *The Art of Darkness*, for instance, Douglas E. Winter notes that *Carrie* was preceded by two thousand pages of unpublished work, but no further details are provided.

King's unpublished work, mostly novels, comprises completed works, which include "The Aftermath," "Blaze," and "Sword in the Darkness" (also called "Babylon Here"), and incomplete works, which include "The Corner," "The Milkman," "Welcome to Clearwater," and "The Cannibals."

Also, in various interviews King has said that he plans a sequel to *'Salem's Lot,* and even gives a preview of it in *The Art of Darkness.* But his most recent statement, on "The Larry King Show" in 1986, puts that idea to rest: "I think the time has gone past. There was a long time when I really wanted to do that, and now so much time has gone by that the answer is probably no, and it's probably just as well."

Special Collections

In the Special Collections Department of the Fogler Library at the University of Maine at Orono, King deposited in 1980 three unpublished novels, all in original typescript: "The Aftermath" (seventy-six single-spaced pages), a short novel about postatomic America, written when King was sixteen years old; "Blaze" (173 double-spaced pages), a suspense melodrama; and "Sword in the Darkness," also referred to as "Babylon Here" (485 double-spaced pages), a long novel that has

301

been reported to be about a race riot but that in fact spends over 80 percent of its wordage examining the horrors of high school hell.

In interviews, King has referred to "Blaze" and "Sword in the Darkness" as bad books, unsuccessful efforts. King has made no reference to "The Aftermath," which by word count is a short novel. More important, it is King's first novel, written at age sixteen; this short novel was a dry run for the more ambitious works to come.

Over the period of a week I read those three unpublished novels. Though King considers the longer works to be dead on arrival, I feel that he is too harsh. These are not bad books. As early works in first drafts with only minor corrections, they are not publishable, nor should the question be raised. But they are important historically, showing us what they have in common, and something of the writing apprenticeship of a young Stephen King.

Because "Aftermath" is properly juvenilia, and both "Blaze" and "Sword in the Darkness" are, by King's admission, trunk novels (implying unpublishable status), it is unlikely that these will see print in any form. I have therefore refrained from providing a detailed synopsis because, after all, they are King's stories, not mine.

The three works are compulsively readable and exhibit many of the qualities associated with King's fiction: strong narrative, carefully drawn characters, the use of brand names, the use of colloquial English, and (as with his other early works, notably the Bachman books) a pervasive pessimism.

Despite the inevitable flaws (some minor, some major) in these stories, one fact stands out: King is a born storyteller. If you can't tell a story, nothing else matters. Technical flaws are correctable, but not the inability to tell a story. These works clearly demonstrate that King always had a talent for writing.

Let's look, then, at this trio and we'll see a foreshadowing of King's later, more ambitious works.

1. "The Aftermath"

Overview

Written by King at age sixteen, "The Aftermath" exists as an original typescript, seventy-six pages, single-spaced. There are between forty-five thousand and fifty thousand words. Very little editing has been done. A note by King indicates a retype to come, which may not have been done. Written at the same time that he began *Getting It On* (later retitled *Rage,* published in 1977 as a Bachman book), "The Aftermath" is important because it is King's first attempt at a full-length manuscript, a short novel.

Photo courtesy of the *Bangor Daily News*

Stephen King's yearbook picture from high school.

The work comprises three parts: Part I, three chapters; Part II, twelve chapters; and Part III, one chapter.

Introductory Comments

Written in the third person, "The Aftermath" explores the question that the protagonist, a teenage survivor type named Larry Talman, almost answers at the end of the story: "Are the evils of government any worse than the evils of anarchy?"

King writes about life in America after the bomb is detonated. Armageddon was August 14, 1967. Talman, who is eighteen, finds that everything's gone to hell in a handbasket. The thin veneer of civilization has been stripped away and people are intent only on surviving as best they can.

At this point the story begins.

Synopsis

Larry Talman, in the company of ex–Sun Corps soldier Ian Vannerman, infiltrates the Sun Corps, a paramilitary organization that represents law and order in a postapocalyptic world. The goal: to destroy the Sun Corps.

Displaying an ability for math, Talman is given early access to DRAC, a behemoth computer, and meets Reina Durrell, whom he met earlier in his travels. She now programs DRAC.

Talman's mission is to destroy DRAC, and he and Vannerman work out a plan to do so.

At the last minute, Talman, in love with Durrell, tries to reason with her, convince her that the Sun Corps is inherently evil, but he fails. He then carries out his mission and detonates a small explosive device that destroys DRAC, and kills Durrell—something Talman had foreseen.

As Talman escapes, heading to a helicopter with Vannerman at the controls, Talman confronts and kills a Lovecraftian monster, a Denebian sent to earth to prepare the way for an alien invasion. The Sun Corps, as it turns out, was a front for the Denebians.

Talman escapes with Vannerman in a helicopter. Leaving Tennessee, they head toward Chicago. But Talman has a change of heart and asks to be set down. Talman gets out of the helicopter and continues on his own way.

Strengths

- Storytelling. The story moves quickly with a narrative drive typical of King. In the first page, King establishes the setting, introduces the main character, and injects drama by introducing an immediate conflict that gets the story off to a brisk start. Seduced by the storytelling, I couldn't put the book down, even knowing how the story would end.

- Striking imagery. King's novels are very much movies of the mind. King's cinematic technique is heightened by the use of vivid images. (On the second page, King refers to the "flatly-cracking deer-rifles" of the looters. It's an accurate, truthful description and brings the story alive through memorable details.)
- Room for expansion. In many instances King could have fleshed out the detail, introducing subplots that show life in the aftermath. But the novel's brevity (less than fifty thousand words) precluded deviation. The details are present and lend depth to an otherwise relentless narrative that will inevitably pit man against computer.

Weaknesses

- Minor characters. Throughout the book minor characters are introduced briefly, then quickly taken off-stage. If the characters have no reason to exist, they should remain off-stage. If they are introduced, it should be to advance the story, introduce a subplot, or flesh out the background.
- The love interest between Reina and Talman is unconvincing.
- The final confrontation becomes unintentionally comical as a Lovecraftian monster is introduced at the last minute.
- The numerous espers (mind readers) in Sun Corps make it unlikely that Talman and Vannerman could go as far as they did. Certainly one, or both, would have been found out. (No explanation is given of the espers' failure to detect even their own.)
- The basic question remains largely unanswered: "Are the evils of government any worse than the evils of anarchy?" The question is quickly dispatched in Part III, which consists of one chapter.

Major Themes

"The Aftermath" shows that even at an early age, King began exploring themes that would become King staples: technology out of control, plagues, the destruction of contemporary society, "wild talents" (as King styles ordinary people with extraordinary mental capabilities), rite of passage, and, typical of the Bachman books, a downbeat ending.

Summary

"The Aftermath" is, as Douglas E. Winter says, a remarkably mature first effort. Although much is derivative, there's much to admire. King, at sixteen, clearly showed an ability to tell a story. Any editor who read this and knew the author's age would be understandably impressed.

His rejection letter might have read something like this:

From the Editor's Desk

Dear Mr. King:

Thanks for sending "The Aftermath." I enjoyed reading it very much, but I must confess it's not quite up to our standards. (The part about the Denebian monster is straight out of H.P. Lovecraft.) Still, it's a good first try, and I hope you'll try us again.

Sincerely,
THE EDITORS

2. "Blaze"

Overview

At the time *Carrie* was submitted to Doubleday, King was working on two novels: the first, "Blaze," was completed on February 15, 1973; the second, "Second Coming," would later be extensively rewritten as *'Salem's Lot* and subsequently published as King's second novel.

After *Carrie* was purchased, King discussed with his editor at Doubleday, Bill Thompson, what would be submitted next. He showed him two books—"Blaze" and "Second Coming." King tells the story in the afterword to *Different Seasons*.

"Blaze," explains King, "was a melodrama about a huge, almost retarded criminal who kidnaps a baby, planning to ransom it back to the child's rich parents . . . and then falls in love with the child instead."

As King says in the afterword, Thompson decided that "Second Coming" was the stronger of the two, an assessment shared by King, and "Blaze" went back into his trunk.

"Blaze" has 173 double-spaced pages, some fifty thousand words, and twenty chapters. A partial rewrite exists, 106 double-spaced pages. From the notes scribbled in the margins of the first draft, someone other than King had read the work and made editorial suggestions (perhaps Thompson?).

The book's dedication reads: "This book is for my mother, Ruth Pillsbury King." (Later that year, 1973, his mother succumbed to cancer. She lived long enough to see her son sell his first novel, but not long enough to see it published.)

Introductory Comments

In his afterword to *Different Seasons,* King says that "Blaze" is a "literary imitation" of John Steinbeck's 1937 novel *Of Mice and Men.*

In Steinbeck's short work, titled from a phrase in Robert Burns's "To a Mouse," Lennie (a simple-minded giant) and George (his mentor and protector) are farm workers who one day hope to live off the fat of the land. But things do go awry, and George does what he has to do to "save" Lennie from himself.

"Blaze" is a bounce off *Of Mice and Men*, with a twist: the main character, Blaze (Claiborne Blaisdell, Jr.), is a mildly retarded man who, through his associations with George Rockley (a two-time punk), is seduced into the world of crime.

In the rewrite, George Rockley is changed to Arch presumably because of the inevitable comparison to the Steinbeck character of the same name.

Written in the third person, and incorporating five flashbacks that illuminate Blaze's youth, the novel is an otherwise straightforward unfolding of the plan by Blaze and his ghostly mentor George to kidnap a baby and hold it for ransom.

Synopsis

Blaze, with the "help" of George Rockley, plans to kidnap the infant son of a prominent businessman. Blaze abducts the child and as best he can cares for it until the ransom drop is made.

Blaze leaves numerous clues behind and his trail is picked up by the authorities, who close in on him and corner him in a cave. Fleeing on foot with the baby, to which he has become emotionally attached, Blaze makes an unsuccessful attempt to cross a frozen river. He is shot and killed, and the infant is returned to the parents.

Strengths

- The story is well told, moving quickly, developing logically out of Blaze's relationship with his partner in crime, George Rockley.
- Using flashbacks as a literary device to flesh out the character of Blaze, King effectively generates sympathy for Blaze, who like Carrie is more a victim of circumstance than an inherently evil person.

Blaze's early childhood was, from the beginning, marred with bad fortune and personal tragedy. The product of a broken home, Blaze is a sympathetic character whose attempts to find friendship inevitably end in tragedy.

Weaknesses

- The ending is predictable. The question is never "will he get away?" but how long can he stay out of the reach of authorities.
- The real-life difficulties of caring for a newborn child make it unlikely that Blaze could have taken care of the child as he did in this story, especially in cases where the baby was left unattended for long periods.

Summary

"Blaze" is, as you'd expect, an entertaining read. King's storytelling is so strong that you temporarily forgive lapses in logic and points that stretch credulity.

Like Carrie, Blaze is a tragic figure, a person desperately trying to join society, and failing. And like Carrie, Blaze commits evil acts but is himself not inherently evil. Blaze, in the end, is a victim of society.

Although King thought enough of the tale to give it to Bill Thompson as a possibility for publication, I can see why Thompson opted instead for "Second Coming," later reworked as 'Salem's Lot. Still, it's not a bad book, but it doesn't strike me as being publishable either, because of its major flaws.

3. "Sword in the Darkness"

Overview

The longest unpublished King work, "Sword in the Darkness" exists as an original typescript, 485 pages, double-spaced. The approximate wordage is one hundred fifty thousand. The novel was finished on April 30, 1970, in Orono, Maine. Also referred to as "Babylon Here" in other critical studies on King, this novel was briefly discussed in King's article "On Becoming a Brand Name":

> Book #2 was a 500-page novel about a race riot in a major (but fictional) American city. At the time—I was twenty—it didn't strike me as either particularly presumptuous or particularly comic that a fellow who had grown up in a Maine town of 900 souls should take a city of millions for his setting, or that this same fellow, who graduated from high school in a class of just over 100, should focus much of the action on a high school with a multiracial student body of 4,000-plus.

King also wrote, in the same article, that the book went to a dozen publishers and eventually found its way back to King. His assessment: "The race riot novel really isn't that good. . . . Book #2 is only a badly busted flush."

Synopsis

Arnie Kalowski is a lad with a future. Planning on attending MIT, Kalowski suddenly finds the fabric of his life torn apart. His sister, Miriam, is pregnant and commits suicide; his mother suffers a brain tumor and dies suddenly. His father, in the wake of the double death, becomes increasingly preoccupied.

Kalowski, who in many ways resembles Arnie Cunningham, the high school senior in *Christine*, tries to make sense of his life. He unsuccessfully initiates a relationship with Janet Cross, but is eventually drawn to Kit Longtin, a sexy, saucy blonde who, like Steinbeck's Cathy Ames in *East of Eden*, uses sex to manipulate men.

Meanwhile, the town learns of the coming of Marcus Slade, who sits in a hotel in San Francisco and thinks of his trip to the sleepy town of Harding, which he will visit in June.

The town officals fear that the coming of Slade, a black activist lawyer, will touch off a race riot.

Knowing Slade will come, a local street gang plans to seize the opportunity and loot the city during the rioting, which the gang will in fact help initiate.

Slade arrives and, after a provoked incident at the high school where he is speaking, the riot kicks off . . . and the town burns.

Comment

When I first read that this novel had made the rounds and had been rejected a dozen times, I was curious. Why? Having read the novel, I can see why. It's really not about a race riot at all. In fact, the rioting doesn't even begin until page 400—of a 485-page book. Mostly the novel explores high school life, from which it draws its strength.

Moreover, the riot scenes, as King realized, just aren't convincing. Without a thorough grounding in how city officials work together to execute contingency plans in riot conditions, King's riot scenes tend to be painted with a broad brush and are therefore unconvincing.

What's left is the story of Arnie Kalowski, one that could have been developed and, in fact, was strong enough to carry the novel.

In many ways, it's King's continued exploration of life in high school, a companion book to *Carrie* and *Christine*, but with no horror element. The characters in this story are believable, flawed people:

- Henry Coolidge, the principal of Harding High School, who is sexually obsessed with his blonde niece, Kit Longtin, who attends the high school.
- Kit Longtin, who attempts to blackmail Coolidge to get what she wants: a ticket out of town.
- Arnie Kalowski, who tries desperately to initiate a loving relationship with Janet Cross but, instead, finds Kit Longtin irresistible.
- Meg DeClancy, a student who tries to seduce one of her teachers, John Edgar, and after failing, cries rape, hoping to discredit Edgar permanently.
- Bill Danning, who gets his secretary Miriam Kalowski pregnant and who, when confronted with her declaration of love, coldly tells her that he doesn't love her, whereupon she leaves and commits suicide.

"Sword in the Darkness" is not, as King suggests, a bad novel. It's a failed novel—but one that can teach a writer much about the craft of writing.

A fascinating read, this unpublished work is the most sexually explicit one King has ever written, perhaps a small marvel in light of its date of composition: 1970.

Summary Comments

In a way it's unfortunate that these three works may never see print. The only place to read them—if you have the time and the patience—is at the University of Maine at Orono, in the Special Collections Department of the Fogler Library.

Just as some people were delighted when they discovered that King had written five novels under the Bachman pen name, I was surprised and elated when I learned that these tales—mentioned but never discussed in other books about King—were available to the public.

My initial question before reading these early works was, Did they show promise? I was pleased to find out that not only did they show promise, but all were stories well told—an innate skill that King first displayed at age sixteen.

The Dark Dreamer
An Interview with Douglas E. Winter

As *The Stephen King Companion* draws to a close, it seems only fitting that Douglas E. Winter should have the last word. Critic, anthologist, editor, writer, and spokesman for the horror field, Winter is the author of the acclaimed critical appreciation of King, *The Art of Darkness*.

An attorney by day and a writer by night, Winter is currently working on *The Stephen King Bibliography* (to be published by Donald M. Grant.) He has also edited a horror anthology, *Prime Evil*, with contributions from major writers in the horror field, including King, Peter Straub, Clive Barker, and Whitley Strieber.

The interview was conducted by George Beahm and Howard Wornom at the Winter's residence in Alexandria, Virginia.

Q: Where would horror be today if King were not writing in the field? What would have happened?

WINTER: Horror fiction was growing before Stephen King. There were several bestselling novels and films that were produced before Steve appeared on the scene—remember Ira Levin and Bill Blatty. There were a number of people writing horror fiction in that time period, and that number was growing. It wasn't until very late in the 1970s that horror really became a generic marketing category. An ever-increasing number of horror novels were being published, but it was not until Steve penetrated the hardcover bestseller lists that all publishers began to perceive of horror as a separate marketing category.

Q: But obviously Steve was there at the right place at the right time.

WINTER: There is an element of that, but if you look and parallel other writers who were working during the same time period—Peter Straub, for example—Straub was writing his early horror novels *not* in reaction to Stephen King. Peter Straub was in Ireland and England and didn't know that Stephen King existed until *after* King published two horror novels. Charlie Grant was writing horror fiction during that time period. A number of other people were writing horror fiction during that time period before Stephen King emerged as a "phenomenon." What Steve did was to bring the message home to the publishing world, and in certain repects to the film world, that his kind of fiction could be immensely popular.

Q: In the reviews of *The Art of Darkness* the only major point of criticism I've read is that there's nothing very critical about King.

WINTER: What I think you mean by that is not much that's negative, which wasn't the point of the book. The book explains in the foreword what it's supposed to be about. And it says that it's intended as both a reader's guide and a literary appreciation. My view was that I was being given the opportunity to present a large reading public—including a lot of people who are not fans of the genre—with not only a discussion of the books of Stephen King, but also a context and something about horror fiction in general. It was not my purpose to engage in a kind of positive-negative, pros and cons approach, but rather to produce a book that championed Steve's work, and leave that kind of judgmental criticism to others.

Q: What kind of reaction have you gotten from people who've read your book on King?

WINTER: It's all been good. I got a ton of letters when the book first came out. I would always get these letters from school kids, from teachers, from librarians, from federal prisoners—all telling me how much they enjoyed the book. Most of the letters would have a postscript: how can I find a copy of *The Dark Tower*? I really did receive some nice feedback from the book. There's obviously a tremendous number of Stephen King fans out there, and I think this was the sort of thing that they were waiting for, that was perfect for them, because it more or less organized the fiction and I think also served as a real companion, and I hope illuminated the books a great deal. That was the intent of it, to say: here's not only some fiction that you're reading for enjoyment, but there are messages, there are themes, there are subtexts here that are important. To me, that's always been key: to consider what fiction is about and how it affects me and my thinking. I always hate it when people discount Steve as being just an entertainer, because he's not. The same thing's true about other major writers of horror fiction. And here was my opportunity in this book to make clear some very significant things that were going on.

Q: Do you feel the negative comments about his work come from people who don't read his work, or don't read it carefully, or perhaps it's a knee-jerk reaction to the fact that it's popular and therefore must not be good?

WINTER: I think popularity is always a negative factor, but let's face it: a tremendous amount of extremely popular fiction is awful. So it comes with the turf. On the other hand, everyone has his point of view. I tend to think, from what I've read of the negative criticism of Steve's work, that most of it is based on his popularity and the fact that he's a personality now, as well as a writer, and not on an understanding of either his fiction or horror fiction. On the other hand, there are some negative critiques that I've seen that are entirely fair and honorable, that you shouldn't ascribe to ill motivations but to someone's critical or aesthetic perspec-

Douglas E. Winter in his home office; behind him is his five-foot shelf of his published books, plus a poster of *The House by the Cemetery,* directed by Italian director Lucio Fulci (1989).

tive being a little bit different. And sometimes I find myself agreeing with those people.

Q: Was King directly involved in *The Art of Darkness?*

WINTER: No. He read it when it was first done, and then he gave me the dirty pictures back. Actually, he was terrific in terms of sitting for a number of interviews. And he and Stephanie Leonard helped me out in tracking some things down, both biographical and bibliographical. But otherwise it was my book, and I think that it shows. I attempted to use the interview material to illuminate my observations about his work, except in those few, rare cases where the book was really tied into Steve to a great deal, like *Pet Sematary,* for example, where he gave me the only interview he's ever going to give on that book. As a result, the book is able to integrate my critical views and his personal views.

Q: Unlike all the other books about King, your book is the exception because you know King personally and professionally, and there *are* many personal insights.

WINTER: And I think that's very important. That is my major difficulty with academic criticism. I know Michael Collings and I like him a great deal, but I recall reading his review of *Faces of Fear* in which he said: This is all very interesting, but ultimately we must consider books as texts, and it's the text that's important. And that's the academic's view. Whatever's within the four corners of the book is what is important to an academic. I'm a writer first, a critic second, and what's important to me as a writer is not only what I put on the page. For example, there are so many things about King's life that inform what he's written, and so many things about life as he sees it that he's attempting to inform by his fiction, that you can't view his books within their four corners. I think it's impossible to do that without really skewing what the book is about.

The only way I could have written *Art of Darkness* was in the way it's written. It's an effort to put everything in a context, to give you that big picture of what is beyond each book, what went into the book, why the book was created in the first place, what's underlying the book, what it's after. To do otherwise is to say: here's the text, and now because I've read a lot of other texts, I'm going to tell you how it fits in with other texts. There's nothing wrong with that, but as a writer—and I think most writers I know join me in this view—it's an approach that is kind of peculiar. It does not express things about the book that the writer wanted expressed. It expresses things that the academic, in looking at the book, wants to express.

Q: New criticism has its advocates. . . . It's interesting that Collings has more recently come around to the notion, especially with King, that the book is more than simply an artifact; it's a reflection of an individual at a certain time in his life, a notion that Harlan Ellison reinforces in his essays.

WINTER: I think that's absolutely true. . . . My other concern with King criticism, and this isn't addressed to Michael, is the degree to which it is narrow-minded in the sense that it's a criticism of King and nothing else. And this is another question of context. That's why I attempted to put, in the beginning of *The Art of Darkness*, Steve's fiction in the context of all horror fiction because clearly it is. Steve's been reading horror fiction since he was little. His early efforts were at replicating horror fiction written by others, and he's been significantly influenced by those writers. And that's also part of the context, wholly apart from the biographical. You have to be able to understand Steve in the context of other writers, as well as understand other writers in the context of Steve. A lot of people whom I've seen writing about King . . . he's the only writer of contemporary horror fiction that they've read. The only Peter Straub that they may have read is whatever Peter contributed to *The Talisman*, and that's a ludicrously tunnel-like approach.

Q: I'm sure you have some strong feelings that a lot of the criticism, in addition to not being informed, suffers from a fan-boy mentality, the fan criticism in which everything King writes is wonderful, and there's no critical objectivity. Typically, this kind of "critic" has not read widely or deeply, in or out of the genre; he has read only Stephen King.

WINTER: That's absolutely true, and you see it not only with Stephen King but also with Clive Barker, another good example.

Q: In *Art of Darkness*, you've mentioned three unpublished works by King: "The Aftermath," "Blaze," and "Sword in the Darkness." Have you read these works?

WINTER: I've read "The Aftermath." It's great fun.

Q: You also mentioned "The Cannibals." Was this novel ever completed?

WINTER: I don't think so. Years ago Steve showed me this weird file card that he had for it. I think he was just writing it as sort of a goof while they were filming *Creepshow,* and that afterward he read J.G. Ballard's *Highrise,* which uses a similar idea. Maybe that's the reason he gave it up.

Q: Did it explore the theme of cannibalism?

WINTER: Yeah. On the other unpublished stuff: "The Aftermath" he wrote when he was sixteen; that was sort of a sizable novel. And "Sword in the Darkness" was highly influenced by John Farris; it was kind of a Harrison High type of novel. And *Blaze* is just this weird book that was kind of Bachmanish, which is one way of describing it.

Q: The current issue of *Castle Rock* (February 1989) indicates that King is out of retirement—

WINTER: I don't think he was ever in retirement. I think that was a misunderstanding by some people about what he said.

Q: It seemed to me that he was just taking a break. . . . A story broke in *S.F. Chronicle* from an anonymous source who provided titles to the upcoming King books that were not identified by title in the front-page story in *Castle Rock.*

WINTER: I didn't see the story, so I don't know what they said the titles were. There's *The Dark Half,* and to my knowledge there's an untitled novella collection. He's recently completed a novel called *Needful Things.*

Q: The story broke in a number of publications, so there's a lot of confusion on just what precisely is going to be published beyond the bare bones provided in the King newsletter. . . . King has spoken about the fact that he's planned a sequel to *'Salem's Lot,* and later he's said that he's not planning a sequel, that it's been too long, and he won't write it. Do you think he'll write the book?

WINTER: It's hard to say. He's told me both, yes and no. I think Tabby King had the best idea of all. She told me that she wanted to write the sequel, and in fact she said that it would be great if a bunch of people were authorized to write sequels.

Q: A shared world?[1]

WINTER: No. They would write their own sequels. There would be like five authorized sequels to *'Salem's Lot.* I'd write one. I know Charlie Grant would. I bet David Morrell would. People who were influenced strongly by *'Salem's Lot* can sort of concoct their own sequels and see what happens. If they didn't communicate with each other, it would be interesting to see what kind of books they would produce.

Q: I wanted to ask about Stephen King's "Night Flier."[2] In talking to King, did he look at that as a sequel to *'Salem's Lot.* A lot of people think it is.

WINTER: I think he seems it in part as a sequel to *'Salem's Lot,* but also it follows up on *The Dead Zone:* Richard Dees, the sleazoid reporter of "The Night Flier," is a character from *The Dead Zone*.

Q: Do you know of the circumstances regarding the release of the videotape, *Return to 'Salem's Lot*?

WINTER: No, but I suspect that what happened was that there was something in the original contract for the production of the television miniseries that allowed use of the title or somehow allowed it to be spun off. I haven't seen the video, actually. From what I've heard, I don't want to.

Q: Have you had an opportunity to read *The Dark Half*? I ask because he's said it's a "riff on the Frankenstein theme," after saying, after *It,* that he had said everything he wanted to about monsters in that book. I feel that no matter what he writes, he'll always go back to horror because that's where his heart is.

WINTER: I think you may be right, but I don't think you're right about *The Dark Half.* It's a very short novel, a tough book. There is an aspect to the book that's pure Jim Thompson . . . it's a tough, lean book. It's extremely violent; it *is* a riff on the Frankenstein theme, but not in the way you think.

Q: I see you're being very cautious and not revealing all.

WINTER: I'd prefer you find out for yourself. I don't like previewing books for people because I just love to experience books so much. . . . There are some things about the book that I love tremendously. This was another book that just

---

1. In a shared-world book, a common setting is used, populated with characters by different writers. If *'Salem's Lot* were done like this, you might see Douglas Winter, Peter Straub, David Morrell, Clive Barker, and others writing stories using King's characters, setting, and background from *'Salem's Lot,* with perhaps new characters introduced by these authors.

2. The lead story for Winter's anthology, *Prime Evil,* published by NAL in hardback (1988) and paperback (1989).

leaped out at me. I don't know if it's still going to be published by Stephen King and Richard Bachman, but that's the way that it's written in manuscript . . . as a collaboration.

Q: Going back to *The Art of Darkness,* did NAL consider the book to be a success in terms of sales?

WINTER: Yeah. It was a very successful hardcover. It was very gratifying. It also depends on what you mean by "successful." We're not talking about King-like success here; we're talking relative to other hardcover books. I think the first royalty statement showed 20,000 copies sold in hardcover. And for a book today, that's quite good because a lot of novels are being published in runs of 10,000.

Q: But booksellers don't know where to put it in their stores.

WINTER: That's a *big* problem.

Q: Chuck Miller, who with Tim Underwood has put together a number of books about King, said that the sale of their King books in bookstores was handicapped by the improper placement of their titles. Was this a problem with your book?

WINTER: I had a bit more success with mine because it says *Stephen King: The Art of Darkness,* and it is a literary biography of sorts, whereas a collection of essays—like the Underwood–Miller books—where do you put them? Bookstores had trouble enough trying to figure out where to put *Prime Evil.* Where do you find anthologies in bookstores today? They're usually back in the classics, and in fact I found *Prime Evil,* in a lot of stores, sitting back there among the classics because that's where they put their collections of short stories. It's going to be interesting to see what they do with the paperback.

Q: We were talking earlier about Tabitha King. Do you feel she's more of a Maine writer than King?

WINTER: Tabitha King . . . there is an aspect of her work in which she is a very strong regional writer, and I say that in a complimentary sense. We're talking about Faulkner, O'Connor, or a Steinbeck. There is regional power in her books. In other words, part of the power of her fiction is its setting, its people. It is a peculiar kind of people who live within that peculiar kind of setting. Now, on the other hand, I don't think that limits her powers, as it does some regional writers. I think that she's also very capable of communicating the peculiarities of that region to outsiders like me. I've read, for example, some other Maine writers who make the society so alien that essentially it *becomes* an alien society, and you don't feel that you understand that much about it.

Q: Tabitha King's most recent novel has gotten excellent reviews. I think she's tried very hard to downplay the fact that she's married to Stephen King. She wants her books to be judged on their own merits, but I think that even that can be difficult for a lot of reviewers.

WINTER: Oh, sure, it's got to be. And particularly for the kind of reviewers we mentioned earlier whose number one awareness is that Stephen King is very popular and makes a lot of money at what he does. And that can't help but throw a shadow over her work, which is unfortunate.

Q: Isn't Hilary Ross your editor at NAL?

WINTER: Yes.

Q: You mentioned earlier about editors and their involvement in editing books. Was Ross active in both *The Art of Darkness* and *Prime Evil*?

WINTER: It depends on what you mean by "active." Less so, I think, in *The Art of Darkness* than in *Prime Evil*. She was, of course, one of the inspirational forces on *Prime Evil*. The way that book came about was very interesting. I was being interviewed by the *Washington Post* in 1986, perhaps, or 1985, on the appearance of the paperback of *The Art of Darkness* and *Faces of Fear*. They were, as usual, curious about the fact that I was a Washington lawyer as well as a writer. And one of the questions they asked me was what was I going to do next. And I said, "One of the things I'd like to do is try to put together a state-of-the-art collection of horror fiction for the close of the 1980s." A couple of weeks later, I was up in the offices of New American Library in a meeting with Hilary, and she whipped out the interview from the *Washington Post* because their clipping people and publicity people, of course, had had it. And it was underlined with all the references to *The Art of Darkness,* and then she said, "You know, I was reading this and I saw this thing about what you'd like to do. Are you really interested in doing that?" I said, "Well, of course. I wouldn't have said it if I wasn't." She said, "Well, you know, we've been seeing a couple of horror anthologies lately that have been submitted to us for potential paperback sale, or whatever, and we'd been thinking that this would be an area that we might like to get into. But nothing that we've received has been particularly good." And she asked me about several of the books. And she said, "Particularly in light of this article, if there's anyone who would seem to be the ideal person to edit a book, a quality horror anthology, a hardcover, it would be you." And I said, "Well, I think you're right." So I walked down the street to my agent's office with a big grin on my face, and we made them a proposal. And thus was born *Prime Evil*.

Appendices

As someone who has diligently tried to track King's prodigious output for the last fifteen years, I can tell you that it's a formidable task. I imagine Douglas E. Winter would agree. (Winter's bibliography of King material in *The Art of Darkness* is being expanded for publication as a separate book, *The Stephen King Bibliography,* and is due from Donald M. Grant, Publisher, possibly in 1990.)

Because this book is primarily for King's general reader—the one who, typically, has not had access to anything beyond the trade hardback and paperback releases—I have provided detailed information on what precisely is available and where to order.

For anyone with more than a casual interest in King, the following six appendices should be an invaluable reference, a good place to start if you want more information. (The information is current as of July 1, 1989.)

Appendix 1, "Books in Print," lists every King book currently in print, and by publisher. (Information is also provided on forthcoming titles.)

Appendix 2, "Books About King," contains a minireview of each book. To date, all the books on King have been scholarly in nature; however, the most accessible general guide is Douglas E. Winter's *Art of Darkness,* written in cooperation with King. Beyond that, you may want to try *Bare Bones* (a collection of interviews with King) and some of the Underwood–Miller collections of essays about King and his work. (The Starmont House books, while excellent, are scholarly in nature; serious fans, students, scholars, researchers, and teachers will find them invaluable.)

Appendix 3, "Filmography and Videography," drawn primarily from secondary sources, lists each King film, original videotape productions, and the general-release videotapes of the movies.

Appendix 4, "Audiocassettes," provides detailed information on the dramatizations, abridged and unabridged readings, and taped interviews.

Appendix 5, "Book Collectibles," provides detailed information on the current market values of the first editions and limited editions of King's books published in the U.S. Exhaustively researched by Barry R. Levin—the leading rare-book dealer in the fantasy and science-fiction field—this guide conveys the data in standard bibliographic form.

Appendix 6, "Resources," lists places where you can get the various King material reviewed and discussed throughout this book, with buying tips.

Appendix 1
Books in Print

Because of King's continuing popularity, virtually the entire canon of King's work is available in hardback and paperback. If your bookstore does not have a title, it will be glad to special-order the book for you. (It normally takes two to six weeks, and prepayment may be necessary.)

The list below, current as of July 1, 1989, gives the publisher, edition, and retail price. (Prices and availability are subject to change without notice.) A trade paperback is an oversized, quality paperback (approximately 5½ by 8½ inches, or 6 by 9 inches). A paperback is a mass-market edition, usually printed on low-grade pulp paper (approximately 4¼ by 7 inches).

If a book is out of print (O.P., meaning unavailable from the publisher), it is so noted; however, because copies may still be available locally, the title is listed.

1. *The Bachman Books* (an omnibus collection of the first four Bachman novels)
    a. New American Library (hereafter, NAL), hardback, $19.95, O.P.
    b. NAL, trade paperback, $9.95
    c. NAL/Signet, paperback, $5.95
   Note: A movie tie-in edition of *The Running Man,* a NAL paperback, is available for $3.95.

2. *Carrie*
    a. Doubleday, hardback, $16.95
    b. NAL, paperback, $3.95

3. *Christine*
    a. Viking Press, hardback, $22.95
    b. NAL/Signet, paperback, $4.95

4. *Creepshow*
   NAL, trade paperback, $6.95

5. *Cujo*
    a. Viking Press, hardback, $22.95
    b. NAL, paperback, $4.95

6. *Cycle of the Werewolf*
   a. NAL, trade paperback, $8.95
   b. NAL, trade paperback, as *Silver Bullet*, $9.95

7. *Danse Macabre*
   Berkley, paperback, $4.95

8. *The Dark Tower: The Gunslinger*
   a. NAL, trade paperback, $10.95
   b. NAL, paperback, $4.95

9. *The Dark Tower II: The Drawing of the Three*
   a. NAL, trade paperback, $12.95
   b. NAL, paperback (scheduled for 1990)

10. *The Dead Zone*
    a. Viking, hardback, $22.95
    b. NAL, paperback, $4.95

11. *Different Seasons*
    a. Viking, hardback, $22.95
    b. NAL, paperback, $4.95

12. *The Eyes of the Dragon*
    a. Viking, hardback, $18.95
    b. NAL, paperback, $4.50
    c. G.K. Hall & Co., hardback, large-print edition, $21.95

13. *Firestarter*
    a. Viking, hardback, $22.95
    b. NAL, paperback, $4.50

14. *It*
    a. Viking, hardback, $22.95
    b. NAL, paperback, $5.95

15. *Misery*
    a. Viking, hardback, $18.95
    b. NAL, paperback, $4.95
    c. G.K. Hall & Co., hardback, large-print edition, $20.95

16. *Night Shift*
    a. Doubleday, hardback, $17.95
    b. NAL, paperback, $4.95

17. *Pet Sematary*
    a. Doubleday, hardback, $19.95
    b. NAL, paperback, $4.95
    c. G.K. Hall & Co., trade paperback, large-print edition, $9.95, O.P.

18. *'Salem's Lot*
    a. Doubleday, hardback, $19.95
    b. NAL, paperback, $4.50

19. *The Shining*
    a. Doubleday, hardback, $19.95
    b. NAL, paperback, $4.95

20. *Skeleton Crew*
    a. Putnam, hardback, $18.95 (out of stock, nearing O.P.)
    b. NAL, paperback, $4.95

21. *The Stand*
    a. Doubleday, hardback (first edition), $19.95
    b. Doubleday, hardback, second edition, to be published in May 1990 (tentatively priced at $30.00)
    c. NAL, paperback, $5.95 (first edition)

22. *Stephen King* (omnibus collection of four Doubleday novels)
    William Heinemann, Inc., current price not known; out of print, but still available in some bookstores. (Note: Using the Heinemann sheets, Peerage Books published this omnibus collection in a boxed set with *Isaac Asimov* and *Robert Ludlum*; the set had a suggested retail price of $75. Bound in simulated leather [or perhaps bonded leather], *Stephen King* has a ribbed spine, gilt edges, and printed marbled endpapers.)

23. *The Talisman*
    a. Viking and G.P. Putnam's Sons, hardback, $18.95
    b. Berkley, paperback, $5.50

24. *Thinner*
    a. NAL, hardback, $12.95, O.P.
    b. NAL, paperback, $4.95

25. *The Tommyknockers*
    a. G.P. Putnam's Sons, hardback, $19.95
    b. NAL, paperback, $5.95

1989

- *My Pretty Pony* (Whitney Museum), $2,200

- *My Pretty Pony* (Alfred A. Knopf trade edition copublished with Whitney Museum), hardback, $50

    In spring 1989, the Whitney Museum published a limited edition of *My Pretty Pony.* The book sold for $2,200. Alfred A. Knopf will be copublishing the trade edition in October of 1989, with a retail price of $50. The print run of the Knopf edition will be set at 15,000 copies, a restriction imposed by the author. Book specifications: 68 pages, hardback, $9^{1}/_{4}$ by $13^{1}/_{2}$ inches; 9 lithographs and 16 illustrations. (There is no word on whether subsequent printings will be authorized by King.)

- *Dolan's Cadillac* (Lord John Press)

    Already out of print, *Dolan's Cadillac* (64 pages), published by Lord John Press, is a story that was serialized in early issues of *Castle Rock.* (If this were to appear in print again, in book form, it would most likely be in a collection, like *Skeleton Crew.*)

- *The Dark Half* (Viking), hardback, $21.95

    From the copy in Viking's book catalog (September–December 1989), here's what the publisher tells us about the book:

    The sparrows are flying again. With this odd announcement recalling a childhood trauma, Thad Beaumont wakes to the nightmare of George Stark. Thad is a writer, and for 12 years he secretly published novels under the name of "George Stark" because he was no longer able to write under his own name. He even invented a slightly sinister author bio to satisfy his many fans of Stark's violent bestsellers. But Thad is a healthier man now, the happy father of infant twins, and starting to write under his own name again. He no longer needs George Stark, and in fact he has a good reason to lay Stark to rest. So, with nationwide publicity, a bit of guilt, and a good deal of relief, the pseudonym is retired.

    In the small town of Castle Rock, Maine, where Thad and Liz keep a summer home, Sheriff Alan Pangborn ponders the brutal murder of Homer Gamache. The bloody fingerprints of the perpetrator are all over Homer's pickup truck . . . and they match Thad Beaumont's exactly. Armed with hard evidence, Sheriff Pangborn pays the Beaumonts a visit. Suddenly, he too is thrust into a dream so bizarre that neither criminal science nor his own sharp mind can make sense of it.

    At the center of the nightmare is the devastating figure of George Stark, Thad Beaumont's dark half—impossibly alive and relentlessly on the loose—a killing machine that destroys everyone on the path that leads to the man who created him. As Stark approaches, as Thad and Liz contend with the escalating horror and implacable threat of his existence and Thad reaches inside his own mind to mount a defense, Stephen King's growing legion of fans will find themselves squirming in the master's heart-stopping, blood-curdling grip—and loving every minute of it.

Stephen King lives in Bangor, Maine. His pseudonym, Richard Bachman, is still at large.

Perhaps Bachman did not, as King put it, die of cancer of the pseudonym. Perhaps like Lou Ford—of whom King writes about in his introduction to *The Killer Inside Me* by Jim Thompson—Bachman (or at least his spirit) lives again in George Stark:

> He is the boogeyman of an entire civilization, a man who kills and kills and kills, and whose motives, which seemed so persuasive and rational at the time, blow away like smoke when the killing is done, leaving him—or us, if he happens to be the sort who kills himself and leaves the mess behind with no explanation—with no sound but a cold psychotic wind blowing between his ears.

1990

• *The Stand* (revised edition)
The second edition of *The Stand* will be published by Doubleday in May 1990 in hardback at $30.00. At this writing plans are being made for a signed, limited edition of 500 copies. It will have the 12 pen-and-ink illustrations by Berni Wrightson. Christopher Spruce reports in the April 1989 issue of *Castle Rock:*

> Doubleday has the manuscript for the unexpurgated *Stand* in hand. SK figures the extended version of the book may run another 500 pages depending on what type size and page size the publisher comes up with for the book. . . .

Though there has been no recent word on what precisely will be contained in the expanded version, Douglas E. Winter wrote in *Stephen King: The Art of Darkness* that the revised edition would include:

> [A]mong other things, a prologue and epilogue; a long interlude involving the Trashcan Man's travels across the country, in which he meets "the Kid," a reincarnation of Charles Starkweather; and Stephen King's "future shock" version of capital punishment.

• In the fall, the second book in the four-book deal will be published. Reports say it will consist of two novellas, "Secret Word, Secret Garden," and "Sun Dog," but there has been no official confirmation of title or contents.

1991

In the fall, the third book in the four-book deal will be published. Reports say the novel will be titled *Needful Things,* but there has been no official confirmation of the title.

1992

In the fall, the fourth of the four-book deal will be published. Reports say the novel will be titled *Dolores Claiborne,* but there has been no official confirmation of the title.

Other Books

In an interview with Janet Beaulieu that was published in the March 1989 issue of *Castle Rock,* King "estimates the next volume [in the *Dark Tower* series] is probably two or three years in the future." In an afterword to the second *Dark Tower* book, King stated that the title of the third book will be *The Waste Lands*; and that the fourth will be titled *Wizard and Glass.*

Book-of-the-Month

BOMC is offering what they call the "Stephen King Library." Currently, eighteen books by King are available. Members should write to BOMC for current prices. (Note: *The Dark Half* and the three subsequent books will be offered by BOMC, which will bring the total to 22 titles.)

Appendix 2
Books About King

An author who appeals to cultists, mainstream readers, and academicians, King is the subject of numerous books, both authorized and unauthorized, and is likely to be the subject of many more to come.

This checklist provides basic information on what is available and what has been announced. If a specific edition is out of print, it is so noted (O.P.).

1. *The Annotated Guide to Stephen King: A Primary and Secondary Bibliography of the Works of America's Premier Horror Writer* by Michael R. Collings. (A detailed bibliography current to 1986. An update is not being planned at this time, according to the editor and the publisher.) Starmont Reference Guide, No. 8. Starmont House, 1986.
   a. hardback, $19.95
   b. trade paperback, $9.95

2. *Bare Bones*, edited by Tim Underwood and Chuck Miller. (A collection of interviews culled from approximately two dozen sources, from well-known periodicals like *Playboy* to specialized publications.)
   a. limited edition of 1,252 copies, Underwood–Miller, 1988, $75, O.P.
   b. hardback, McGraw–Hill Book Company, 1988, $16.95
   c. trade paperback, Warner Books, 1989, $8.95

3. *Discovering Stephen King*, edited by Darrell Schweitzer. (A collection of essays about King.) Starmont Studies in Literary Criticism, No. 8. Starmont House, 1985.
   a. hardback, $17.95
   b. trade paperback, $9.95

4. *Enterprise Incidents Presents Stephen King* by James Van Hise. (Magazine size, 8½ by 11 inches, saddle-stitched, an informal discussion of King's novels and short fiction, a mingling of personal responses and criticism. Heavily illustrated by various artists.) New Media, 1984, O.P.

5. *Fear Itself: The Horror Fiction of Stephen King*, edited by Tim Underwood and Chuck Miller. (The first collection of essays about King, this book was the first of three collections of essays that Underwood–Miller published.)

    a. limited edition of 225 numbered copies, signed by the contributors (including Stephen King), O.P.
    b. trade hardback, Underwood–Miller, $13.95, O.P., 1982
    c. trade paperback, NAL, $7.95, O.P.
    d. paperback, NAL, $4.50

6. *The Films of Stephen King* by Michael R. Collings. (A study devoted to films made from King's movies. No photographs or illustrations.) Starmont Studies in Literary Criticism, No. 12. Starmont House, 1986.
    a. hardback, $17.95
    b. trade paperback, $9.95

7. *The Gothic World of Stephen King: Landscape of Nightmares*, edited by Gary Hoppenstand and Ray B. Browne. (A collection of scholarly articles about King's works.) Bowling Green State University Popular Press, 1987.
    a. hardback, $25.95
    b. trade paperback, $12.95

8. *Kingdom of Fear*, edited by Tim Underwood and Chuck Miller. (A second collection of articles about King from Underwood–Miller.)
    a. limited edition, 500 numbered copies, signed by 13 contributors (but *not* by Stephen King), Underwood–Miller, $50, O.P., 1986
    b. trade hardback, Underwood–Miller, $25, O.P., 1986
    c. trade paperback, NAL, $7.95
    d. paperback, NAL, $3.95

9. *Landscape of Fear: Stephen King's American Gothic* by Tony Magistrale. (A scholarly examination of King's work.) Bowling Green State University Popular Press, 1988.
    a. hardback, $25.95
    b. trade paperback, $12.95

10. *The Many Facets of Stephen King* by Michael R. Collings. (A thematic treatment of King's shorter works.) Starmont Studies in Literary Criticism, No. 11. Starmont House, 1986.
    a. hardback, $17.95
    b. trade paperback, $9.95

11. *Reign of Fear*, edited by Don Herron. (The third collection of essays about King, this book is currently available only as a limited edition from Underwood–Miller. Though an ISBN was given for a trade hardback edition from U–M, no such book currently exists.) Underwood–Miller, 1988.
    Limited edition of 500 numbered copies, signed by 17 contributors, $75 (though the book is *about* King, it is not signed by him).

12. *The Shorter Works of Stephen King* by Michael R. Collings and David Engebretson. (A look at the short fiction of King by collection; each work has a synopsis and a critical analysis.) Starmont Studies in Literary Criticism, No. 9. Starmont House, 1985.
    a. hardback, $17.95
    b. trade paperback, $9.95

13. *Stephen King* by Douglas E. Winter (series editor, Roger C. Schlobin). (The first reader's guide on King that, expanded and revised, would subsequently be published by NAL in three editions.) Starmont Reader's Guide, No. 16. Starmont House, 1982, $5.95, O.P.

14. *Stephen King: The Art of Darkness* by Douglas E. Winter. (The best reader's guide to Stephen King that, according to the author, is "an intermingling of biography, literary analysis, and unabashed enthusiasm. . . .") NAL.
    a. hardback, 1984, $14.95, O.P.
    b. trade paperback (expanded and revised), 1986, $7.95
    c. paperback (with the same text as the trade paperback edition, according to Winter), 1986, $4.95

15. *Stephen King as Richard Bachman* by Michael R. Collings. (An in-depth look at King's use of the Bachman pen name, and critical appreciations of the Bachman books.) Starmont Studies in Literary Criticism, No. 10. Starmont House, 1985.
    a. hardback, $17.95
    b. trade paperback, $9.95

16. *Stephen King at the Movies* by Jessie Horsting. (In magazine format, 8½ by 11, square-bound like *Creepshow,* this book was a Starlog Press publication, distributed by NAL. A profusely illustrated overview of the movies made from King's books.) A Starlog/Signet Special, 1986, $9.95, O.P.

17. *Stephen King: The First Decade, CARRIE to PET SEMATARY* by Joseph Reino. (A study of some of King's novels.) A volume in Twayne's United States Author Series. Twayne Publishers (a division of G.K. Hall & Co.). 1988. Hardback, $17.95

18. *Stephen King Goes to Hollywood* by Jeff Conner, produced by Tim Underwood and Chuck Miller, packaged for NAL. (A look at King's movies, important for a behind-the-scenes look at how the movies were produced, and insights on the art of the deal in Hollywood. Author Conner is the publisher of Scream Press, a maverick specialty press that published, among other books, a limited edition of *Skeleton Crew*). NAL, 1987.
    a. hardback, $19.50
    b. trade paperback, $9.95

19. *The Stephen King Phenomenon* by Michael R. Collings. (A look at King as a publishing phenomenon.) Starmont Series in Literary Criticism, No. 14. Starmont House, 1987.
    a. hardback, $17.95
    b. trade paperback, $9.95

20. *Teacher's Manual: Novels of Stephen King* by Edward J. Zagorski. (A small pamphlet, about 4 by 7 inches, printed on newsprint with a glossy cover, this 46-page, saddle-stitched publication is available from the Education Department of NAL. It is organized in four major sections: an introduction, providing an overview of the horror genre and King's place in the genre; a note on educational applications; a look at six King novels; and a look at the short fiction in *Night Shift*.) NAL, 1981. No cover price.

21. *The Unseen King* by Tyson Blue, from Starmont House. (A study of the little seen work of King: juvenilia, college material, limited-edition books, etc.)
    a. hardback, $19.95
    b. trade paperback, $9.95

1989: Forthcoming

1. *Feast of Fear: Conversations with Stephen King.* (A second collection of interviews, this companion book to *Bare Bones* collected forty-seven interviews.) Underwood–Miller.
    a. limited edition of 500 numbered copies, 319 pages, $75

2. *The Moral Voyages of Stephen King* by Anthony Magistrale. (Scheduled for publication in 1989, this book focuses on King's critical literary themes and philosophical concerns.) Starmont Studies in Literary Criticism, No. 25. Starmont House, 1989.
    a. hardback, $19.95
    b. trade paperback, $9.95

3. *"The Shining" Reader,* edited by Anthony Magistrale. (To be published in 1989, this will collect 15 essays focusing on King's third novel, considered a classic *genus loci* story.) Starmont Studies in Literary Criticism, No. 30.
    a. hardback, $19.95
    b. trade paperback, $9.95

1990

Note: These books do not have firm publication dates. The best way to keep informed on their release is to subscribe to *Castle Rock,* or contact the publisher.

1. *Infinite Explorations: Art and Artifice in Stephen King's It, Misery, and the Tommyknockers* [working title] by Michael R. Collings. A scholarly examination of King's more recent novels. Possibly "early 1990," according to the publisher. Tentatively priced at $11.95 in trade paperback, and $21.95 in hardback.

2. *In the Darkest Night: A Student's Guide to Stephen King* by Tim Murphy (Starmont House). A bibliography. Possibly "early 1990," according to the publisher. Tentatively priced at $11.95 in trade paperback, and $21.95 in hardback.

3. *The Shape Under the Sheet: The Complete Stephen King Encyclopedia* by Stephen Spignesi. Pierian Press. To be published in 1990, this encyclopedia will be 8½ by 11 inches, hardback, 400–500 pages, at $35–$50. (A limited edition, signed and numbered by the author and other contributors, will be published by the Overlook Connection, a mail-order bookseller.) Illustrated with 25 pen-and-ink drawings by Katherine Flickinger and over 40 photographs (mostly movie stills and dust-jacket photographs by James Leonard), the book is principally a reference work with an annotated concordance of people, places, and things (10,000-plus entries), and an alphabetical, cross-referenced listing of all the characters in King's fiction. The book will also have many essays, articles, and interviews.

4. *The Stephen King Bibliography* by Douglas E. Winter. Donald M. Grant, Publisher, Inc. No publication date has been set, but the author feels it may be 1990. A revised and expanded version of the bibliography published in *Stephen King: The Art of Darkness,* this bibliography promises to be the definitive guide to every work published *by* King and *about* King.

5. *The Stephen King Quiz Book* by Stephen Spignesi. To be published in August 1990 by New American Library as a paperback.

Appendix 3
Filmography and Videography

There are currently three books available on King's movies: *The Films of Stephen King* by Michael R. Collings (Starmont House, 1986), *Stephen King at the Movies* by Jessie Horsting (Starlot/Signet Special, O.P., 1986), and *Stephen King Goes to Hollywood* by Jeff Conner (NAL, 1987). For detailed information on the stories behind the movies, movie stills (color and black-and-white), credits, etc., please consult those books.

Unfortunately, there are differences in the credits for the films and video-cassettes, depending on which book you read. This appendix, then, should be considered only as a guide and not as a definitive reference, for it was necessarily compiled principally from these and other secondary sources.

As we have noted, King, a cinematic writer, has not translated well to the screen. Although King considers the movies separate and distinct from the books on which they are based, comparisons are inevitable. Some works have trans-lated very well—notably *Carrie, The Dead Zone,* "Gramma" (from *Skeleton Crew*), and a novella from *Different Seasons* ("The Body," titled *Stand by Me* for the film version)—but most of the movies have been disappointments. King best explained why on "The Larry King Show" (April 10, 1986), when asked if he considered his books to be the modern-day equivalent of the old-time radio dramatization:

> Sure. I think that one of the nice things about the novel is that you never see the zipper up the monster's back. In books the special effects are all created by your mind, the same way they were [with] the old-time radio.

Most should be available at your local video store for rental ($2 or so) in VHS format. Depending on the inventory, the tape may be available for sale at a price far less than full retail ($15–$20 is typical).

1. "The Boogeyman," 30 minutes, available on videocassette as one of two "mini-features" in *Stephen King's Night Shift Collection,* 1985. Produced in 1982 as a student film on a budget of $20,000 by Jeff Schiro, then a student at the New York University Film School, "The Boogeyman" went on to win an award at the NYU Film Festival. In 1985 Granite Entertainment Group acquired the rights to package "The Boogeyman" with "The Woman in the Room" as a videocassette, with a retail price of $59.95.

2. *Carrie*, United Artists, 97 minutes, released in 1976. Directed by Brian DePalma, produced by Paul Monash, screenplay by Lawrence Cohen. The lead role of Carrie White is played by Sissy Spacek. Available from Magnetic Video (20th Century), $69.95. (This movie was instrumental in King's success, bringing his book to the attention of a large audience; fortunately, this is one of the best movies made from his books.)

3. *Cat's Eye*, MGM/United Artists Entertainment Company, 94 minutes, released in 1984. Directed by Lewis Teague, produced by Martha Schumacher, screenplay by Stephen King; executive producer, Dino De Laurentiis. Like *Creepshow I* and *Creepshow II*, *Cat's Eye* has three segments: "Quitters, Inc.," from *Night Shift*; "The Ledge," from *Night Shift*; and a new segment, "The General." Available from Key Video (CBS/Fox Home Video), $79.95.

4. *Children of the Corn*, New World Pictures, 93 minutes, released in 1984. Directed by Fritz Kiersch, produced by Donald Borchers and Terrence Kirby, screenplay by George Goldsmith. Based on the short story "Children of the Corn," from *Night Shift*. Available from Embassy Home Entertainment, $69.95. (This is generally considered to be the worst film adaptation of King's work.)

5. *Christine*, Columbia Pictures, 110 minutes, released in 1983. Directed by John Carpenter, produced by Richard Kobritz, screenplay by Bill Phillips. Major characters: Arnie Cunningham is played by Keith Gordon, Dennis Guilder is played by John Stockwell, and Leigh Cabot is played by Alexandra Paul. Available from RCA/Columbia Home Video, $79.95.

6. *Creepshow*, Laurel Show, Inc., 120 minutes, released in 1982. Directed by George A. Romero, produced by Richard Rubenstein, screenplay by Stephen King. An homage to E.C. Comics, with a tie-in graphic album (color comic book in magazine format), the movie consists of four segments: "Father's Day," "The Lonesome Death of Jordy Verrill" (played by Stephen King), "The Crate," and "They're Creeping Up on You." Available from New World Video, $69.95.

7. *Creepshow II*, New World Pictures, 89 minutes, released in 1987. Directed by Michael Gornick, produced by David Ball, screenplay by George A. Romero. The movie consists of three segments: "The Raft" (from *Skeleton Crew*), "Old Chief Wooden Head," and "The Hitchhiker" (in which King makes a cameo appearance). (Sequels rarely equal the original, which is the case with this movie.)

8. *Cujo*, Warner Communications, 120 minutes, released in 1983. Directed by Lewis Teague, produced by Daniel Blatt and Robert Singer, screenplay by Don Carlos Dunaway and Lauren Currier. Major characters: Donna Trenton is played by Dee Wallace, Victor Trenton is played by Daniel Hugh-Kelly, Tad

Trenton is played by Danny Pintauro, Steve Kemp is played by Christopher Stone, and Joe Camber is played by Ed Lauter. Available from Warner Home Video. (King has said that of the movies made from his work, this is one of his favorites.)

9. *The Dead Zone,* Paramount Pictures, 103 minutes, released in 1983. Directed by David Cronenberg, produced by Debra Hill, screenplay by Jeffrey Boam. Major characters: Johnny Smith is played by Christopher Walken, Sarah Bracknell is played by Brooke Adams, and Greg Stillson is played by Martin Sheen. Available from Paramount Home Video.

10. *Firestarter,* Universal Pictures, 115 minutes, released in 1984. Directed by Mark Lester, produced by Frank Capra, Jr., screenplay by Stanley Mann. Major characters: Charlie McGee is played by Drew Barrymore, Andrew McGee is played by David Keith, Vicki McGee is played by Heather Locklear, and John Rainbird is played by George C. Scott. Available from MCA Home Video, $79.95.

11. "Gramma," an episode from the CBS television show "Twilight Zone." The 19-minute episode aired on February 14, 1986. Directed by Bradford May, produced by Philip de Guere, teleplay by Harlan Ellison (who also was the show's creative consultant). Not available on videocassette. (Ellison, a talented writer and veteran screenwriter, did an excellent job on this adaptation.)

12. *Maximum Overdrive,* MGM/UA, 95 minutes, released in 1986. Directed by Stephen King, produced by Martha Schumacher, screenplay by Stephen King, with soundtrack by the rock band AC-DC. The movie is based on "Trucks," a short story from *Night Shift.* Available from Karl–Lorimar Feature Films. (When it was announced that King would write the screenplay and also act as director, there was speculation that, finally, a King story would be effectively translated to the screen; unfortunately, the optimism proved premature.) Available from Karl–Lorimar Home Video.

13. *Pet Sematary,* Paramount, 1989. Directed by Mary Lambert, produced by Richard P. Rubinstein, screenplay by Stephen King, based on the novel of the same name. Major characters: Dr. Louis Creed is played by Dale Midkiff, Jud Crandall is played by Fred Gwynne, Rachel Creed is played by Denise Crosby, Gage Creed is played by Miko Hughes.

14. *Return to 'Salem's Lot,* "based on characters created by Stephen King." A Larco Production, 101 minutes. Distributed by Warner Brothers, released in 1987. Directed by Larry Cohen, produced by Paul Kurta, story by Larry Cohen, screenplay by Larry Cohen and James Dixon. (This one's a dog. Drive a stake through it.)

15. *Running Man*, Taft Entertainment Pictures and Keith Barish Productions, 101 minutes. A Linder/Zinnemann Production. Major characters: Benjamin Richards is played by Arnold Schwarzenegger, and Dan Killian is played by Richard Dawson (of "Family Feud" fame, a TV gameshow). Available from Vestron Video.

16. *'Salem's Lot*, a made-for-TV miniseries for CBS that aired on November 17, 24, 1979. 210 minutes. (The videocassette version runs only 120 minutes.) Directed by Tobe Hooper, produced by Richard Kobritz, teleplay by Paul Monash. Major characters: Ben Mears is played by David Soul, Richard Straker is played by James Mason, Mark Petrie is played by Lance Kerwin, Susan Norton is played by Bonnie Bedelia, Barlow is played by Reggie Nalder, and Father Callahan is played by James Gallery. Warner Home Video, $89.95. (A powerful novel, one of King's best, *'Salem's Lot* lost much of its impact because of the restrictions inherent in producing anything for the television medium. Also, James Mason was a poor choice for Straker, and the Nosferatu-like vampire was comical.)

17. *The Shining*, Warner Brothers, 143 minutes, released in 1980. Directed by Stanley Kubrick, produced by Kubrick, screenplay by Kubrick (with Diane Johnson). Major characters: Jack Torrance is played by Jack Nicholson, Wendy Torrance is played by Shelley Duvall, Danny Torrance is played by Danny Lloyd, and Dick Hallorann is played by Scatman Crothers. Warner Home Video, $69.95. (Eagerly awaited by Kubrick fans, King fans, and a general public anxious to see Nicholson, this movie was more Kubrick than King. A major flaw: Nicholson, a brilliant actor, is a poor choice for this movie. Likewise, Shelley Duvall bears almost no resemblance to her character in the novel.)

18. *Silver Bullet*, Paramount, 95 minutes, released in 1985. Directed by Daniel Attias, produced by Martha Schumacher, screenplay by Stephen King. Major characters: Marty Coslaw is played by Corey Haim, Uncle Red is played by Gary Busey, and Reverend Lowe is played by Everitt McGill. Paramount Home Video, $79.95. (Based on *Cycle of the Werewolf*, the screenplay by King is available in *Silver Bullet*, published by NAL.)

19. "Sorry, Right Number," an episode from the television show, "Tales from the Darkside." The 30-minute episode aired on September 1987. Directed by John Sutherland, produced by Richard P. Rubinstein, George A. Romero, and Jerry Golad. Teleplay by Stephen King. Not available on videocassette.

20. *Stand by Me*, Columbia Pictures, 110 minutes, released in 1986. Directed by Rob Reiner, produced by Andrew Scheinman, Bruce Evans, and Raynold Gideon; screenplay by Gideon and Evans, based on "The Body," a novella in

Different Seasons. Major characters: Gordie Lachance is played by Will Wheaton, Chris Chambers is played by River Phoenix, Teddy DuChamp is played by Corey Feldman, and Vern Tessio is played by Jerry O'Connell. (To the numerous disappointing adaptations of King's work to the screen, *Stand by Me* is a refreshing exception. Because King is not perceived, nor is he marketed, as a mainstream writer, and because his name was not used to promote the film, the public saw the film free of any preconceived notions. Many people, in fact, were surprised when told that it was based on a King story! In *Stand by Me,* an intensely autobiographical movie, Gordie Lachance comes of age in the fifties as he and his three buddies go off to look at a dead body and, in the process, lose their innocence and become adults. King's authorial voice, wonderfully preserved in this movie, goes to show that, despite what everyone believed, King's work can be successfully adapted to the screen.)

21. "Woman in the Room," 30 minutes, available on videocassette as one of two "minifeatures" in *Stephen King's Night Shift Collection,* along with "The Boogeyman" (see entry 1). Produced by Granite Entertainment, available only as a videocassette, this short adaptation was directed by Frank Darabont, produced by Gregory Melton, with the screenplay by Darabont. Main characters: John is played by Michael Cornelison, and mother is played by Dee Croxton. A videocassette with a retail price of $59.95.

22. "Word Processor of the Gods," based on the short story of the same name, published in *Skeleton Crew.* A Laurel Entertainment, Inc., release, produced for the television show "Tales from the Darkside." The episode aired on November 19, 1985. Directed by Michael Gornick, produced by William Teitler, teleplay by Michael McDowell. Major characters: Richard Hagstrom is played by Bruce Davidson, Lina Hagstrom is played by Karen Shallo, Mr. Nordhoff is played by Bill Cain, Jonathan is played by Jon Matthews, and Seth is played by Patrick Piccininni.

Future Film Projects

The mercurial world of Hollywood makes it impossible to provide firm details on specific projects, especially on King's books, most of which have been optioned. (King's shorter works, too, have proven to be fertile ground. With the exception of "Jerusalem's Lot," an epistolary story, *all* the stories in *Night Shift* have been optioned, according to King. *Skeleton Crew,* of course, provides much material, some of which has been adapted to the screen.)

According to Christopher Spruce, three books optioned are "all hanging fire": *Misery, The Stand,* and *The Talisman* (reported in the July 1989 *Castle Rock*).

Miscellaneous Material

"American Express: Stephen King," VHS format, produced by Ogilvy & Mather Audio Visual. Not for sale, this is a recording of the campy ad King had done to promote the American Express Card.

"Stephen King at the Pavilion," VHS format, produced by the city of Virginia Beach, Virginia. The recording of King's talk at the Virginia Beach Pavilion in September 1986 is professionally done, with excellent sound and high picture quality. Not for sale; *not* available through interlibrary loan.

"Stephen King Commencement," VHS format, produced by the Department of Public Affairs at the University of Maine at Orono. A recording of King's commencement address, given in May 1988, not generally available.

"Stephen King's World of Horror," VHS format, Front Row Video, 45 minutes, 1989. $17.95. An overview of recent horror films with commentary by King. A Baruch Television Group presentation of a Simmons/Fortune Production, produced and directed by John Simmons, exclusively distributed by Front Row Video, Inc. Available from Front Row Video (154 Northfield Avenue, Bldg. No. 410, Edison, N.J. 08837) or Overlook Connection (P.O. Box 526, Woodstock, Ga. 30188) for copies. Also, some K-Mart stores are stocking this videotape.

"He Who Writes Will Be Remembered," an interview conducted by Martin Coenen for Belgian Television's monthly literary program. An estimated 10 million people viewed this interview, not shown in the U.S. VHS format, 50 minutes, air date unknown (perhaps 1988 or 1989). Not for sale and not available in videocassette.

TV Projects

In the 1989–90 season, *It* will air as a two-part miniseries on ABC. The six hour miniseries will be shown in two installments.

Appendix 4
Audiocassettes

1. "Apt Pupil" (from *Different Seasons*), #84065, Recorded Books, Inc. An unabridged recording read by Frank Muller on five cassettes; 7 ¹/₂ hours. Available for purchase ($34.95) or rental. (Note: All Recorded Books tapes are rented for 30 days; this tape rents for $11.50.)

2. "Ballad of the Flexible Bullet" (from *Skeleton Crew*), #85330, Recorded Books, Inc. An unabridged recording read by Frank Muller on two cassettes; 3 hours. Available for purchase ($15.95) or rental ($7.50).

3. "The Body" (from *Different Seasons*), #84064, Recorded Books, Inc. An unabridged recording read by Frank Muller on four cassettes; 6 hours. Available for purchase ($26.95) or rental ($10.50).

4. "The Breathing Method" (from *Different Seasons*), #84066, Recorded Books, Inc. An unabridged recording read by Frank Muller on two cassettes; 3 hours. Available for purchase ($15.95) or rental ($7.50).

5. *The Dark Tower: The Gunslinger,* NAL, 1988. An unabridged recording read by Stephen King on four cassettes; 6 hours, 16 minutes. Credits: Produced by Nancy Fisher, Creative Programming, Inc., New York; engineers, Mark Wellman, John Ciglia, and Marcelo-Gandala; cover illustration by Michael Whelan; photograph by James Salzano; handlettering by Ed Rouya (credited to "Es Rouya"). ISBN 0-453-00636-1, Book Number: H636; $29.95.

    Also, a limited edition was produced: $100 (perhaps numbered, but signed by King).

6. *The Dark Tower II: The Drawing of the Three,* NAL, 1989. An unabridged recording read by Stephen King on eight cassettes; 12 hours. Credits: Produced and edited by Mark Wellman of Marketing, Media & Wellman; engineer, Mark Wellman; cover illustration by Phil Hale; photograph by James Salzano; handlettering by Ed Rouya. ISBN 0-453-00643-4; Book Number: H643; $34.95.

    Also, a limited edition was produced: $125 (perhaps numbered, but signed by King).

7. "The Mist" (from *Skeleton Crew*), ZBS Foundation. A dramatization recorded in 3-D sound utilizing the Kunstkopf binaural recording method; 1 hour, 20 minutes. Credits: Directed by Bill Raymond; story adaptation by M. Fulton; assistance provided by Dennis Etchison; musical score by Tim Clark. (Included is a 15-minute documentary demonstrating how the special sound effects were created using the Kunstkopf system, "The Making of 'The Mist'.")
   a. real-time chrome cassette, $15
   b. normal low-noise with Dolby B, $10 (O.P.)
   c. high-speed duplication, $9.95, the ZBS 3-D version licensed to Simon & Schuster Audioworks; ISBN 0-671-62138-6

8. "The Mist" (from *Skeleton Crew*), #85230, Recorded Books, Inc. An unabridged recording read by Frank Muller on three cassettes; 4$^{1}/_{2}$ hours. Available for purchase ($19.95) or rental ($9.50).

9. "Prime Evil: A Taste for Blood" (from *Prime Evil*), Simon & Schuster Audioworks. An unabridged recording read by Ed Begley, Jr., on two cassettes; 150 minutes, with an introduction by editor Douglas E. Winter. $14.95. Three stories: "The Night Flier" by Stephen King, "Food" by Thomas Tessier, and "Having a Woman to Lunch" by Paul Hazel.

10. "Rita Hayworth & Shawshank Redemption" (from *Different Seasons*), #84063, Recorded Books, Inc. An unabridged recording read by Frank Muller on three cassettes; 4$^{1}/_{2}$ hours. Available for purchase ($19.95) or rental ($9.50).

11. *Skeleton Crew: Book One* (from *Skeleton Crew*), #85210 (the set), Recorded Books, Inc. Unabridged recordings read by Frank Muller on six cassettes; 9 hours. Available for purchase ($37.95) or rental ($12.50). Stories include:
   • "The Man Who Wouldn't Shake Hands" and "Word Processor of the Gods" (#85320).
   • "Morning Delivery," "Big Wheels," "For Owen," and "Survivor Type" (#85250).
   • "The Jaunt" and "Beachworld" (#85260).
   • "The Raft" and "The Reaper's Image" (#85280).
   • "The Monkey" and "Cain Rose Up" (#85290).
   • "The Reach" and "Uncle Otto's Truck" (#85330).

12. *Skeleton Crew: Book Two* (from *Skeleton Crew*), #85220 (the set), Recorded Books, Inc. Unabridged recordings read by Frank Muller on five cassettes; 7$^{1}/_{2}$ hours. Available for purchase ($34.95) or rental ($11.50). Stories include:
   • "The Ballad of the Flexible Bullet" (two cassettes, #85240).
   • "Nona," "Paranoid—A Chant" and "Here There Be Tygers" (#85270).
   • "Mrs. Todd's Shortcut" and "The Wedding Gig" (#85310).
   • "Gramma" (#85340).

13. *Stories from Night Shift* (from *Night Shift*). From Warner Audio Publishing, available as a boxed set and, in some instances, separately. These recordings were also licensed to Waldenbooks for the Waldentapes series (O.P.). A small booklet, reprinting the introduction by John D. MacDonald that appeared in the book, is enclosed with the boxed package. Price: $34.95. Running time: 6 hours. Stories include:
    - "Jerusalem's Lot" (sides 1 and 2), read by Colin Fox.
    - "I Am the Doorway" (side 3), read by Fox.
    - "Night Shift" (side 4), read by David Purdham.
    - "I Know What You Need" (sides 5 and 6), read by Deidre Westervelt.
    - "The Last Rung on the Ladder" (side 7), read by Purdham.
    - "The Boogeyman" (side 8), read by Purdham.
    - "Graveyard Shift" (sides 9 and 10), read by Purdham.
    - "One for the Road" (sides 11 and 12), read by Fox.
    - "The Man Who Loved Flowers" (side 12), read by Purdham.

14. *Stories from Skeleton Crew* (from *Skeleton Crew*). From Warner Audio Publishing, available as a boxed set and, in some instances, separately. These recordings were also licensed to Waldenbooks for the Waldentapes series (O.P.). Price: $34.95. Running time: 6 hours. Stories include:
    - "The Monkey," read by David Purdham.
    - "Mrs. Todd's Shortcut," read by Purdham.
    - "The Reaper's Image," read by Purdham.
    - "Gramma," read by Gale Garnett.

15. *Thinner* by Stephen King (writing as Richard Bachman). From Durkin• Hayes Publishing Ltd. (incorporating the original publisher, LFP, Listen for Pleasure), LFP 7127, an abridged recording read by Paul Sorvino on two cassettes; 2½ hours. Credits: abridged by Sue Dawson, produced by Graham Goodwin. $14.95.

Miscellaneous Material

"The Author Talks: Stephen King," #87380, Recorded Books, Inc. One cassette, 1 hour, $5.50 (for purchase only; no rental available). A sampler, this has a short reading by King of "Mrs. Todd's Shortcut," and readings by Frank Muller from *Skeleton Crew* and *Night Shift*, interspersed with an interview with King, conducted by Muller, and a short overview of King's writing career.

"Stephen King," from "The Larry King Show," April 10, 1986. Lion Recording Service (P.O. Box 962, Washington, D.C. 20044). One cassette, 2 hours, $4.95. (A fascinating, illuminating interview, this recording is flawed by the poor sound reproduction, perhaps because it was a high-speed duplication.)

Appendix 5
Book Collectibles by Stephen King
A Price Guide
by George Beahm with Barry R. Levin

In the January 1985 issue of the *Wall Street Journal,* an article by Mark Zieman informed the public what rare-book dealers and science-fiction fans had known for years: Stephen King's books are highly collectible. The title to Zieman's article said it all: "When Buying Rare Books, Remember: Go for Stephen King, Not Galsworthy."

Despite speculation in some circles that the boom in King collectibles will be followed by a bust, it's hard to imagine that happening in the short term; long term, however, the possibility exists.

The reasons:

1. King appeals not only to a popular audience—which snatches up a million hardbacks and three million paperbacks of each new King horror novel—but also to a cult audience.

2. Interest in King collectibles remains high, according to the dealers who sell King books, including the limited editions. (If you've got the money, they've got the book, or can find it for you.)

3. King is prolific and has many more books in him, waiting to be written.

This price guide is intended only as an overview to what's been published and what the current market values are. I am greatly indebted to Barry R. Levin, who provided all the prices and many of the bibliographical points for this guide. To a huge extent, this is more his work than mine. (I do, however, take all the blame for any errors.) In addition, King specialist Michael Autrey reviewed this price list and made several suggestions.

The prices listed assume that the book in question is graded as "fine" in condition. This means the book looks "as new," the same condition in which you would expect the book to be if you bought it at a store when it was first published. The prices also assume that the book is available as issued—with a dust jacket (a printed paper, tissue paper, acetate, or plain paper cover).

As you would expect, the print run, the condition of the book, and its rarity determine the current market value of the book. And, of course, the law of supply and demand and market fluctuations bear considerably on the value of a book.

Definitions

The best source of definitions for book collectors is John Carter's *ABC for Book Collectors,* currently in its sixth edition, revised, published by Alfred A. Knopf ($18.95, hardback, 211 pages).

Limited edition: Generally, a book limited to a *stated* number of copies. (There are books designated limited editions and sold as such that are nothing of the kind; they are in fact *unlimited* editions because the print run is not stated.) Often published before the trade edition by a small press, the limited edition is normally signed by the author. (Often, a publisher may issue a limited-edition book in both signed and unsigned editions.)

First edition: The first impression (printing) of a book. Additional impressions (or printings) are normally noted on the copyright page. (John Carter defines it thus: "Very, *very* roughly speaking, this means the first appearance of the work in question, independently, between its own covers.")

True first edition: In cases where both a trade edition and a limited edition are published, and each is marked "first edition" on the copyright page, the edition *published first* is the *true* first edition.

Advance reader's copy: Sometimes before the hardback is published, a small run in trade paperback is printed and distributed to important reviewers and bookstores. Not for sale, and marked "advance reader's copy," these books normally have on the back cover publishing information: the size of the first printing; the budget allocated for advertising, promotion, and publicity; the publication date, number of pages, price, and trim size; and the ISBN code number (a standard numbering system used in the book trade).

An advance reader's copy is considered by collectors to be the first issue of the first edition. For instance, *Carrie* and *Thinner* had advance reader's copies available to the trade.

State: As defined by John Carter: "When alterations, corrections, additions or excisions are effected in a book during the process of manufacture, so that copies exhibiting variations go on sale on publication day indiscriminantly, these variant copies are conveniently classified as belonging to different *states* of the edition." (For instance, the first edition of *'Salem's Lot* has different states of the dust jacket: a first state, a second state, and a second printing.)

Issue: As defined by Carter: "When similar variations can be *clearly shown* [italics mine] to have originated in some action taken *after* [italics mine] the book was published, two (or more) *issues* are distinguishable." (For instance, when advance readers' copies are published, they are the first issues of the first edition. See *Carrie* or *Thinner.*)

Scope of This Price Guide

As this book is for the general reader, the items listed are primarily restricted to the first editions, and some states and issues of the limited edition.

Prices in parentheses indicate the publisher's price (the notation "not for sale" is self-explanatory). The price after the colon is the market value as of 1989. *"Identification"* indicates how to identify the edition.

Conforming to standard bibliographic practice, entries are listed by priority of issue, then the rarest states to the more common states.

Buying Recommendations

Buy from a reputable dealer (see herein "Specialty Dealers," page 121). If there's a specific title you want, send a "want list" to a specialty dealer.

1. *The Bachman Books: Four Early Novels by Stephen King*
   New York: NAL, 1985.
       a. first edition, hardback issue, with dust jacket ($19.95): $85–$150. *Identification:* On copyright page, "First (Omnibus) Printing, October, 1985."
       b. first edition, trade paperback state ($9.95): $20–$25. *Identification:* On copyright page, "First (Omnibus) Printing, October, 1985".

2. *Carrie*
   Garden City, N.Y.: Doubleday, 1974.
       a. advance reader's copy, trade paperback [not for sale]: $950–$1,500. *Identification:* On back cover, "SPECIAL EDITION NOT FOR SALE".
       b. first edition, hardback, with dust jacket ($5.95): $450. *Identification:* On copyright page, "First Edition". [Print run of 30,000 copies.]

3. *Christine*
       a. New York: Viking Press, 1983. True first edition, hardback, with dust jacket ($16.95): $35. *Identification:* On copyright page, "First published in 1983 by The Viking Press".
       b. West Kingston, R.I.: Donald M. Grant, 1983. [Barry R. Levin has indicated that there is a lettered state, but the number of copies is not known. Not for sale when published, these copies now sell for $850–$1,000.]
       c. West Kingston, R.I.: Donald M. Grant, 1983. A limited edition of 1,000 numbered copies, with dust jacket and slipcase ($65): $350. *Identification:* On limitation page: "This special edition of CHRISTINE is limited/to 1,000 copies, signed by the author and artist. This is copy _____ [hand-numbered 1–1,000]".

4. *Creepshow*

   New York: New American Library/Plume, 1982. First edition, trade paperback ($6.95): $20. *Identification:* On copyright page, "First Printing, July, 1982".

5. *Cujo*

   a. New York: Viking, 1981. True first edition, hardback, with dust jacket ($13.95): $35. *Identification:* On copyright page, "First published in 1981 by The Viking Press".

   b. New York: Mysterious Press, 1981. A lettered state, perhaps limited to 26 copies (lettered A–Z). Not for sale when published, these copies now sell for $850–$1,500.

   c. New York: Mysterious Press, 1981. A limited edition of 750 copies, with mylar (clear plastic) cover and slipcase ($75): $250. *Identification:* On the limitation page: "Of this special limited/edition of *Cujo,*/750 copies have been/numbered and signed by/the author./[DS]This is copy no. [hand-numbered 1–750]".

6. *Cycle of the Werewolf*

   a. Westland, Mich.: Land of Enchantment, 1983. The true first edition issued in at least five states:

      (1) A presentation state, eight copies, with handwritten limitation notice, stating, for example, "Presentation copy 1 of 8": $1,000–$1,200.

      (2) A collector's state with a piece of original art by Berni Wrightson tipped in: $850.

      (3) A deluxe state of 250 copies, issued with a Wrightson portfolio: $500.

      (4) A deluxe state without the portfolio: $250.

      (5) A trade state of 7,500 copies: $75.

   b. New York: New American Library/Signet, 1985. Trade paperback ($8.95): $20. *Identification:* On copyright page, "First Signet Printing, April, 1985".

   c. as *Silver Bullet:* New York: New American Library/Signet, 1985. Trade paperback ($9.95): $25. *Identification:* On copyright page, "First Printing, October, 1985". [This edition is composed of the complete edition of *Cycle of the Werewolf,* an introduction by King, a photo section, and King's screenplay.]

7. *Danse Macabre*

   a. New York: Everest House, 1981. True first edition, hardback, with dust jacket ($13.95): $45. *Identification:* On copyright page, a code number "RRD281" with no other markings to indicate it is the first edition.

   b. New York: Everest House, 1981.

      (1) $3,000 for the lettered state.

(2) A limited edition of 250 copies, with plain tissue dust jacket and slipcase ($65): $650 for the numbered state, *Identification:* On limitation page: "This special edition of/DANSE MACABRE/is limited to 250 copies numbered 1 to 250,/and 15 for private distribution lettered A to O,/signed by the author./No. [hand-numbered or -lettered]".

c. New York: Everest House, 1981. A publisher's state, limited to 35 copies (not for sale): $750. No limitation notice, no frontispiece, no tissue dust jacket, and no slipcase.

8. *The Dark Tower: The Drawing of the Three*

a. West Kingston, R.I.: Donald M. Grant, Publisher, Inc., 1987. Levin indicates that two additional states exist: a lettered state, perhaps 52 copies double-lettered (A–Z, AA–ZZ): $1,000; and a publisher's state, 50 copies: $1,250.

b. West Kingston, R.I.: Donald M. Grant, Publisher, Inc., 1987. A limited edition of 850 copies, with dust jacket and slipcase ($100): $350–$500. *Identification:* On limitation page: "This special first edition of THE DARK TOWER II:/THE DRAWING OF THE THREE is signed by/author Stephen King and artist Phil Hale. The Edi-/tion is limited to 850 copies of which 800 are for sale./[3 spaces] This is copy _____ [numbered or lettered]".

c. West Kingston, R.I.: Donald M. Grant, Publisher, Inc., 1987. A trade edition (30,000 copies), with dust jacket ($35): $45–$85. *Identification:* On copyright page, "FIRST EDITION".

d. New York: NAL, 1989. Advance copy in trade paperback, not for sale.

e. New York: NAL, 1989. Trade paperback ($12.95).

9. *The Dark Tower: The Gunslinger*

a. West Kingston, R.I.: Donald M. Grant, Publisher, Inc., 1982. Levin indicates that two additional states exist: a lettered state ($2,300 and up), and a publisher's state ($2,500 and up).

b. West Kingston, R.I.: Donald M. Grant, Publisher, Inc., 1982. A limited edition of 500 copies, with dust jacket and slipcase ($60): $900–$1,200, and up. *Identification:* On limitation page: "This special edition of *The Dark Tower: The/Gunslinger* is limited to 500 copies, signed/by the author and artist./[2 spaces] This is copy _____ [numbered]".

c. West Kingston, R.I.: Donald M. Grant, Publisher, Inc., 1982. A trade edition (10,000 copies), with dust jacket ($20): $400–$700.

d. West Kingston, R.I.: Donald M. Grant, Publisher, Inc., 1984. A second edition (10,000 copies), with dust jacket ($20): $200. *Identification:* On copyright page, "Second Edition".

Barry R. Levin: A Profile

"After being a collector and bibliographic student of rare and first editions of science fiction, fantasy, and horror for thirteen years," says Levin, he "founded Barry R. Levin Science Fiction and Fantasy Literature on January 1, 1973. Our showroom is presently located at 726 Santa Monica Boulevard, Suite 201, Santa Monica, California 90401, telephone (213) 458-6111; our hours are 10 A.M. to 3 P.M., Monday through Friday, open Sunday by appointment. In addition, we have a separate warehouse to store the majority of our 15,000-volume stock of first editions."

"The firm deals exclusively in rare and first editions, proofs and manuscripts of science fiction, fantasy and horror, seventeenth through twentieth century, and services a worldwide clientele of the elite collectors in the field. We also offer our services as science-fiction, fantasy, and horror film consultants."

A member of the Antiquarian Booksellers Association of America and other associations in the general book field and the science-fiction and fantasy fields, Levin has authored "numerous rare-book catalogues" and was an assistant on R. Reginald's *Science Fiction and Fantasy Literature: A Checklist 1700–1974*. Levin also publishes an informative newsletter for his customers.

In 1988 Barry R. Levin instituted the Collectors Award. The first awards were presented in January 1989 to Dean R. Koontz (for "most collectable author of the year") and to Alex Berman of Phantasia Press for the deluxe lettered state of *The Uplift War* by David Brin ("most collectable book of the year").

"The Collectors Awards," explains Levin, "will be presented annually in January at our showroom in Santa Monica, California, for the science-fiction, fantasy or horror author and book deemed 'most collectable' by the firm's prestigious clientele. The award takes the form of a solid travertine sphere (representing a planet) which rests on a Lucite pedestal—and what could be a more fitting award for an author or publisher who spends an entire career creating worlds for others."

e. New York: NAL, 1988. Advance copy in trade paperback, not for sale.

f. New York: NAL, 1988. Trade paperback ($10.95). *Identification:* On copyright page, "First Plume Printing, September, 1988".

Note: A number of copies were printed with a variant cover that was identical in design to the NAL audiocassette package. The design had "The Dark Tower" in small letters at the top and "The Gunslinger" in large letters at the bottom. But later, because NAL realized the book was generally known as "The Dark Tower," the cover was redesigned to emphasize the more familiar title. It is not known how many copies were printed of the variant cover.

10. *The Dead Zone*
New York: Viking, 1979. First edition, hardback, with dust jacket ($11.95): $85. [Note: Levin informed me that there are at least two states and perhaps a variant; consequently, the quoted price will be superseded by new prices once the bibliographic nuances are determined.]

11. *Different Seasons*
New York: Viking, 1982. First edition, hardback, with dust jacket ($16.95): $45.

12. *Dolan's Cadillac*
Northridge, Calif.: Lord John Press, 1989. Published in perhaps as many as *nine* states. [Note: Originally serialized in the King newsletter, *Castle Rock*, this 64-page edition marks its first appearance in book form. The book went out of print soon after publication.]

The colophon, at 1 1/2 spacing, reads:

This first edition of
DOLAN'S CADILLAC
is limited to One Thousand numbered copies,
Two Hundred and Fifty deluxe copies quarter bound
in leather and Twenty-Six lettered copies,
specially bound and slipcased, all of which
have been signed by the author.

The paper is Caress Eggshell Text and the
type CG Plantin.
Designed by Robert Schneider and printed by
Carl Bennitt of Pace Lithographers, Inc.
Binding by Marianna Blau.

Notes

1. There may be as many as nine states of this book: two (or maybe three) states of the advance proof, the lettered state, the deluxe signed state, the

limited signed state, and three presentation states. The presentation states are differentiated from the other states by Cadillac-motif endpapers. It appears that the presentation states follow the binding of the lettered, deluxe, and limited states.

2. Proofs are not listed by priority of issue; priority not yet established.
    (1) Advance proof, not for sale. Printed in gold on front cover, "ADVANCE PROOF". Bound in blue paper covers: $400.
    (2) Advance proof, not for sale. Printed in gold on front cover, "ADVANCE PROOF". Bound in gray paper covers: $400.
        • There is perhaps a third state of the advance proof (not yet seen).
    (3) Presentation state of individually designated copies for the author, publisher, binder, et al., with the recipient's name set in type on the limitation page, signed by Stephen King (not for sale): $1,500 and up. (Perhaps following the binding style of the half-leather bound, lettered copies [not seen].)
    (4) Presentation state of an indeterminate number of copies following the binding style of the deluxe, quarter-leather bound state; set in type on the limitation page, *"Presentation copy"*, signed by Stephen King (not for sale): $750.
    (5) Presentation state of an indeterminate number of copies following the binding style of the limited, quarter-cloth bound state; set in type on the limitation page, *"Presentation copy"*, signed by Stephen King (not for sale): $400.
    (6) Lettered state of 26 copies, lettered A through Z. Half bound [leather with marbled paper] and slipcased, signed by Stephen King: $1,500.
    (7) Deluxe signed edition of 250 numbered copies, quarter bound [with marbled paper], signed by Stephen King ($250): $375–$400.
    (8) Limited, signed edition of 1,000 numbered copies, signed by King. Quarter cloth with printed boards, signed by Stephen King ($100): $150–$200.

13. *Eyes of the Dragon*
    a. Bangor, Maine: Philtrum Press, 1984. The true first edition, a limited edition of 1,250 copies: 1,000 numbered in black ink, for general distribution, and 250 numbered in red ink, for private distribution. *Identification:* On limitation page, "THE EYES OF THE DRAGON/was printed and bound in Lunenburg, Vermont,/by The Stinehour Press. This first edition was de-/signed and cared for by Michael Alpert. One thou-/sand two hundred fifty copies were printed in the/fall of 1984. One thousand copies are for sale and/are numbered in black, 1 through 1000. Two hun-/dred fifty copies are reserved for private distribu-/tion and are numbered in red, 1 through 250./[2 spaces] This is copy [numbered in black or red ink]".
        (1) Levin indicates that there are two lettered states: lettered in red ink,

no more than 26 copies, these were for familial presentation (not for sale): $2,000 and up; and lettered in black ink, no more than 26 copies, these were for presentation to close friends (not for sale): $2,000.

(2) Numbered 1–250 in red ink (not for sale): $1,500–$2,000.

(3) Numbered 1–1,000 in black ink ($120): $750.

b. New York: Viking, 1987. First edition, hardback, with dust jacket ($18.95): $25.

14. *Firestarter*

Note: The same printing plates were used for the limited edition and the trade edition. The limited edition is the true first edition.

a. Huntington Woods, Mich.: Phantasia Press, 1980. True first edition, hardback, with dust jacket. A limited edition of 725 copies, with dust jacket and slipcase ($35): $450 if limitation sheet is dated July 5, 1980; $350 otherwise. [King signed the limitation sheets over a period of four days; however, because he *dated* them, the first day, July 5, 1980, has priority of issue over subsequent days and therefore is more valuable.] *Identification:* On limitation page, "This first edition of *Firestarter* by Stephen King/is limited to seven hundred twenty-five copies,/all of which have been signed and numbered by the author./[2 spaces] This is copy [numbered]".

b. New York: Viking, 1980. First trade edition, hardback, with dust jacket ($13.95): $45. *Identification:* On copyright page, "First published in 1980 by The Viking Press".

c. Huntington Woods, Mich.: Phantasia Press, 1980. An asbestos-bound edition of 26 lettered copies (A–Z), signed by King on July 8, 1980: $3,000.

15. *It*

a. *ES* [*IT*], Munich, Germany: Edition Phantasia, [May] 1986. The true (world) first edition was published in a limited edition of 250 numbered copies. Bound in leather and encased in a red velvet slipcase, this German-language edition is a unique collectible: $600. (Levin indicates that there may be a publisher's presentation state.)

b. New York: Viking, 1986. First American edition [first English-language edition], hardback, with dust jacket ($22.95): $25. *Identification:* "First published in 1986 by Viking Penguin Inc."

16. *The Long Walk* by Richard Bachman [pen name for Stephen King]

New York: NAL/Signet, 1979. First edition, mass-market paperback ($1.95): $100.

17. *Misery*

New York: Viking, 1987. First edition, hardback, with dust jacket ($18.95):

$35. *Identification:* On copyright page, "First published in 1987 by Viking Penguin Inc."

18. *My Pretty Pony*
    At this writing (July 1989), only the Whitney Museum edition has been published. It is safe to say that, because of the fact that it is the most expensive King limited edition to be published and because copies are being sold in another market, the art world, this edition may escalate rapidly in value.
    a. New York: Whitney Museum of American Art, 1989. A limited edition of 280 copies of which 150 were offered for sale to the public. Numbered, and signed by artist Barbara Kruger and writer Stephen King, this book is the sixth in the museum's Artists and Writers Series ($2,200): current market value to be determined.
    b. New York: Alfred A. Knopf, 1989. The first trade edition, limited to 15,000 copies ($50). [For a trade book by a major publisher of a popular author, the first printing, set by King, is very small when compared to King's routine printings in hardback of over a million copies. Just as the first and second printings of Grant's edition of *The Dark Tower: The Gunslinger* went quickly out of print, this Knopf edition sold out prior to publication date. It is not known now whether any subsequent printings will be authorized by King.]

19. *Nebel [The Mist]*, [Linkenheim, Germany]: Edition Phantasia, 1986. A limited edition of 500 numbered copies; fewer than 50 copies exist, according to Barry R. Levin. Of this unauthorized edition, most copies imported into the U.S. were confiscated and destroyed by U.S. Customs officials at port of entry. *Identification:* On limitation page, a blank line with a handlettered number with a printed number, thus:

    [handlettered number]/printed number

    The text on the limitation page:

    Dieses Buch erscheint in einer einmaligen/ auf 500 numerierte Exemplare limitierten Auflage.

    Dieses Exemplar trägt die Nummer

    Die römisch I bis XXX nummerierten Exemplare/gelangen nicht in den Handel.

20. *Night Shift*
    Garden City, N.Y.: Doubleday, 1978. First edition, hardback, with dust jacket ($8.95): $750. *Identification:* On copyright page, "FIRST EDITION".

21. *Pet Sematary*
    Garden City, N.Y.: Doubleday, 1983.

    a. advance reader's copy, trade paperback [not for sale]. *Identification:* "Promotional Copy—not for sale".

       (1) A photocopy state from King's original typescript, of which about 50 copies survived: $500 and up.

       (2) A typeset state, $200.

    b. first edition, hardback, with dust jacket ($15.95): $45. *Identification:* On copyright page, "FIRST EDITION".

22. *The Plant*

Note: A self-published pamphlet, from King's Philtrum Press, mailed out as a Christmas greeting.

    a. Bangor, Maine: Philtrum Press, 1982. The first installment, *The Plant: the opening segment of an ongoing work.* Numbered copies 1–200, signed by King, $1,500–2,000. [Levin indicates that a lettered state may exist, but no copies have been seen.]

    b. Bangor, Maine: Philtrum Press, 1983. The second installment, *The Plant—Part Two.*

       (1) Twenty-six lettered copies, A–Z, signed by King (not for sale): $2,000–$3,000.

       (2) Numbered copies 1–200, signed by King, $1,500–$2,000.

    c. Bangor, Maine: Philtrum Press, 1985. The third installment, *The Plant—Part Three.*

       (1) Twenty-six lettered copies, A–Z, signed by King, $2,000–$3,000.

       (2) Numbered copies 1–200, signed by King, $1,500–$2,000.

       Note: Levin indicates that there are out-of-series copies of the first two installments; these were not numbered, not lettered, and not signed by King (some designated designer's copies): $500 and up. The out-of-series copies of the second installment are slightly more rare than those of the first installment. No out-of-series copies of the third installment have yet been seen.

23. *Rage* by Richard Bachman [pen name for Stephen King]

New York: NAL/Signet, 1977. First edition, mass-market paperback ($1.50): $100–$150.

24. *Roadwork* by Richard Bachman [pen name for Stephen King]

New York: NAL/Signet, 1981. First edition, mass-market paperback ($2.25): $100–$125.

25. *The Running Man* by Richard Bachman [pen name for Stephen King]

New York: NAL/Signet, 1982. First edition, mass-market paperback ($2.50): $100.

26. *'Salem's Lot*

Garden City, N.Y.: Doubleday, 1975. First edition, hardback, with dust jacket:

prices vary depending on the state. *Identification:* On copyright page, "First Edition".

Three states exist with minor variations of the dust jacket: the first state, the second issue of the first state, and the second state (a new dust jacket printed; in effect a second printing of the jacket).

1. The first state ($8.95): $2,000, with the dust jacket having a retail price of $8.95 and "Father Cody" mentioned in the copy on the front jacket flap.

2. The first state, second issue ($7.95): $750, with the $8.95 price clipped and a printed price of $7.95, and "Father Cody" mentioned in the copy on the front jacket flap. [This is in fact a canceled state of the first issue.]

3. The second state [a second printing of the dust jacket], ($7.95): $400, unclipped price of $7.95 and "Father Callahan" mentioned in the copy on the front jacket flap.

27. *The Shining*
    Garden City, N.Y.: Doubleday, 1977. First edition, hardback, with dust jacket ($8.95): $250. *Identification:* On copyright page, "FIRST EDITION".

28. *Skeleton Crew*
    a. New York: G.P. Putnam's Sons, 1985. The true first edition, hardback, with dust jacket ($18.95): $20–$25. *Identification:* On the extension page constituting the copyright page, a list of numbers appears at the bottom of the second sheet: "1 2 3 4 5 6 7 8 9 10." Also on that page is the notation: "A limited first edition of this book has been published by Scream/Press."
    b. Santa Cruz, Calif.: Scream Press, 1985. The first edition thus, with an additional story, "The Revelations of "Becka Paulson," from *The Tommyknockers,* which does not appear in either the trade hardback edition from Putnam or the NAL mass-market paperback edition. A hardback with dust jacket, slipcase, with a laid-in full color plate by artist J.K. Potter, who illustrated the book.
       (1) Bound in a zippered leather binding, 17 presentation copies, numbered: $2,750; and 52 copies, double-lettered A–ZZ in the blank space ($350): $1,250–$1,500. [Autrey indicates that the 17 presentation copies were the result of a binding overrun; these otherwise out-of-series copies were designated presentation copies, thus creating the rarest state of the book, of which 8 copies were offered for sale to the public.] *Identification:* On limitation sheet, a pair of square brackets and, centered in the space between the tops of the brackets, a number, a slash, and the capital letter "P"; in the center of the brackets, the word "presentation"; and centered in the space between the bottoms of the brackets, the word "copy".

(2) A "Limited first edition" of 1,000 copies, numbered in silver ink, signed by author and artist ($75): $300–$350. *Identification:* On limitation page, "STEPHEN KING'S/SKELETON CREW/[3 spaces] This volume is one of one thousand copies, signed on/the facing page in silver ink/by the author and artist."

29. *The Stand*
New York: Doubleday, 1978. The first edition, hardback, with dust jacket ($12.95): $250. *Identification:* On copyright page, "First Edition".

30. *Stephen King*
Note: An omnibus collection, in order of appearance, *The Shining, 'Salem's Lot, Night Shift,* and *Carrie.*
  a. New York: Octopus Books; and London: William Heinemann, 1978. The first edition, hardback, with dust jacket [no stated price]: $50–$65.
  b. Peerage Books, 1986. Slipcased with *Isaac Asimov* and *Robert Ludlum, Stephen King* is sold as part of the Modern•Classics•Collection (printed on the three sides of the slipcase); bound in two-piece bonded leather with printed marbled endpapers and gilt edges (suggested retail, $75).

31. *The Talisman*
  a. New York: Viking and G.P. Putnam's Sons, 1984. The true first edition, hardback, with dust jacket ($18.95): $25. *Identification:* On copyright page, "First published in 1984 by Viking Penguin Inc."
  b. West Kingston, R.I.: Donald M. Grant, Publisher, Inc.
    (1) The "artist's presentation state," a lettered state, in two volumes, slipcased; signed by both authors and 10 illustrators: $1,500. *Identification:* On limitation page, a letter is hand-printed in the space in which a number is indicated. "This presentation copy #_____ of 70 copies of this special/illustrated first edition of The Talisman is signed by the/participants in the edition and is not for sale." [The number of lettered copies is not known.]
    (2) The "artist's presentation state," a numbered edition of 70 copies, in two volumes, slipcased; signed by both authors and 10 illustrators: $1,000. *Identification:* On limitation page, a number [1–70] is hand-printed in the space in which a number is indicated. "This presentation copy #_____ of 70 copies of this special/illustrated first edition of The Talisman is signed by the/participants in the edition and is not for sale."
    (3) "Deluxe edition" in two volumes with slipcase of 1,200 numbered copies, signed by King and Straub ($120): $400–$500. *Identification:* On limitation page, "This special illustrated edition of *The*

Talisman is/limited to 1200 numbered copies signed by the authors./[2 spaces] This is copy _____ [numbered 1–1,200]".
(4) "Trade edition" of 1,200 copies in two volumes with slipcase ($65): $100.

32. *Thinner* by Richard Bachman [pen name for Stephen King]
New York: NAL Books, 1984.
    a. advance reader's copy, trade paperback [not for sale]: $125–$150.
    b. first edition, hardback, with dust jacket ($12.95): $35.

33. *The Tommyknockers*
New York: Viking, 1987. First edition, hardback, with dust jacket ($19.95).
    a. First state with "permissions to come" on the copyright page, $45–$75, with two states of the dust jacket: King's name printed in red foil lettering, and in gold foil lettering.
    b. Second state with "permissions to come" deleted, $20, with two states of the dust jacket: King's name printed in red foil lettering, and in gold foil lettering.

```
┌─────────────────────────────────────────────────────┐
│                                                     │
│              Appendix 6                             │
│              Resources                              │
│                                                     │
└─────────────────────────────────────────────────────┘
```

The information in this appendix is subject to change without notice. Before ordering anything, I recommend you write and get the current price, and enclose a self-addressed, stamped envelope (SASE) for a response.

1. Art

- *Graphic Collectibles* (P.O. Box 683, Staten Island, N.Y. 10302) is a good source of prints by Berni Wrightson; its Frankenstein prints are outstanding values.
- *Glass Onion Graphics* (P.O. Box 88, Brookfield, Conn. 06804) is the best place to get prints by King illustrator Michael Whelan. Send $2 for its current catalogue, in color.
- *Glimmer Graphics* (137 Fulton St., Trenton, N.J. 08611) is a good source of prints by King illustrators Thomas Canty, Berni Wrightson, and Jeffrey Jones, and others.
- Specialty dealers like *Bud Plant, Inc.*, and *Dreamhaven Books and Arts* stock prints by science-fiction, fantasy, horror, and comic-book artists. See pages 120–122 for more information.

2. Mainstream Bookstores

Any mainstream bookstore (the local independent store, B. Dalton Bookseller, Waldenbooks, et al.) is your most likely bet for getting in-print King books in hardback and paperback. If it doesn't have it, it can check to see if its distributor or jobber has it, and special-order for you. (Ingram, a large distributor, is where many independent bookstores get their stock; be prepared to wait 2–3 weeks, and you may have to pay in advance.)

On new titles, the chain stores sometimes offer discounts for advance orders. Many of King's novels have had 25–30 percent discounts, if you buy two or three months in advance.

If you want first editions, get the book as soon as it is published; otherwise, you may get a second printing. On Doubleday books, the copyright page will state, "First Edition." (Later printings are almost always identical to the first edition, with changes in the price and the deletion of the "First Edition" notice.) Viking books normally state on the copyright page, "First published in [year of publication]." NAL books normally state on the copyright page, "First printing," followed by the month and year of publication.

If you want to check which printing you have of the book, look on the copyright page; the row of numbers, usually at the bottom of the page, typically looks like:

1 2 3 4 5 6 7 8 9

The *lowest* number indicates which printing of the book you have.

3. Specialty Booksellers

Because it's impossible for a bookstore to maintain a stock for all its customers, specialty stores have filled the gap with books and products for specialized tastes. If you are interested in science fiction, fantasy, or horror, check the yellow pages of your local phone directory under "bookstores" and look for listings that indicate specialized merchandise like science-fiction books or comic books.

Some established stores that are worth your attention are:

- *Avenue Victor Hugo Bookshop*, 339 Newbury St., Boston, Mass. 02115. Phone: (617) 266-7746.
- *A Change of Hobbit*, 1853 Lincoln Blvd., Santa Monica, Calif. 90404. Phone: (213) GREAT SF.
- *Dangerous Visions*, 13563 Ventura Blvd., Sherman Oaks, Calif. 91423. Phone: (818) 986-6963.
- *Forbidden Planet*, 821 Broadway, New York, N.Y. 10003. Phone: (212) 473-1576.
- *Moonstone Bookcellars*, 2145 Pennsylvania Ave., N.W., Washington, D.C. 20037. Phone: (202) 659-2600.

If you don't have a retail specialty store nearby, you will have to get your books by mail. The mail-order dealers on pages 120–122 sell mostly to collectors. Since most of them are also collectors, they take special care in wrapping books so that they arrive safely. (Provide your street address when ordering; UPS is much safer, faster, and more reliable than the postal service.)

The specialty stores are also the best place to get out-of-print books and limited-edition books; the prices for these collectibles can be somewhat expensive. (To get an idea of what some of the King books are worth, see Appendix 5.)

Mail-Order Booksellers

- *Michael Autrey* (13624 Franklin St., No. 5, Whittier, Calif. 90602). Specializes in Stephen King and Clive Barker collectibles.

- *Bud Plant, Inc.* (P.O. Box 1689, Grass Valley, Calif. 95945). Best mail-order catalogue for the comics field.
- *L. W. Curry* (Elizabethtown, N.Y. 12932). Good source for out-of-print books.
- *Dreamhaven Books and Arts* (1300 Fourth St., S.E., Minneapolis, Minn.
55414). Greg Ketter offers a good selection of art, books, prints, etc.
- *Barry R. Levin Science Fiction and Fantasy Literature* (726 Santa Monica Blvd.,
Suite 201, Santa Monica, Calif. 90401). Retail establishment and mail-order
company. Best source for one-of-a-kind collectibles, and the most collectible
books and states. Newsletter published.
- *Overlook Connection* (P.O. Box 526, Woodstock, Ga. 30188). Good source for
horror books in general. Catalogue issued.
- *Vagabond Books* (2076 Westwood Blvd., Los Angeles, Calif. 90025). Good
source for American first editions, especially for popular authors who do signings at the store. Catalogue issued.
- *Robert and Phyllis Weinberg* (15145 Oxford Dr., Oak Forest, Ill. 60452). My
personal favorite as a choice for the all-around mail-order bookstore in the
science-fiction, fantasy, and horror fields. Catalogue issued.

4. Conventions

Conventions for science-fiction, fantasy, and horror fans are held throughout the
world. The biggest of these, the World Science Fiction Convention, is worth
attending if you would like to see what fandom is all about. (Early in his career,
King was a frequent attendee at numerous conventions.) The best way to see
what's scheduled and when is to subscribe to *Locus* (see under "Periodicals" in
this appendix), the monthly newspaper of the field.

- *Horrorfest 1990,* the con for Stephen King fans (Horrorfest '90, Attn: Ken Morgan, P.O. Box 277652, Riverdale, Ill. 60627-7652).

5. Films

Films by King usually get extensive coverage in film-related magazines, periodicals, and book collections of film criticism.
- *Cinefantastique,* published five times a year, covers the horror, science-fiction,
and fantasy fields thoroughly. If you can't find it locally, you can subscribe, of
course; current subscription rates are 4 issues, $18; 8 issues, $34; 12 issues,
$48. (Foreign and Canadian subscriptions are higher.) Write to: *Cinefantas-
tique,* P.O. Box 270, Oak Park, Ill. 60303.
- *Harlan Ellison's Watching* by Harlan Ellison, from Underwood–Miller, is a collection of Ellison's film criticism, including pieces on King. Highly recommended. Trade hardback, $29.95, 536 pages. (Order directly from the
publisher.)

- *Joe Bob Goes to the Drive-In* by Joe Bob Briggs is a collection of his movie reviews. Introduction by Stephen King. Trade paperback, $8.95.
- *Leonard Maltin's TV Movies & Video Guide,* a 1,222-page paperback, is a Signet reference book, $5.95. Periodically updated. Minireviews of more than 18,000 films.
- *Roger Ebert's Movie Home Companion,* 832 pages, a trade paperback, from Andrews and McMeel, $11.95. Full-length reviews of 825 films.
- *We Are the Weird,* the "last uncensored publication in America," is the newspaper of Joe Bob Briggs, who has reviewed many of King's movies, sitting in his Toronado under the open skies, watching flicks the way God intended, as he puts it. Joe Bob's too modest to tell you to check it out, so consider this my unqualified recommendation. $6 for 6 issues, check payable to the Paladin Corporation; mail to Joe Bob Briggs, P.O. Box 2002, Dallas, Tex. 75221.

6. Periodicals

- *Castle Rock,* edited and published by Christopher Spruce, is an indispensable source of information on the comings and goings of Stephen King. Published monthly as a tabloid newspaper, 6 issues for $12, 12 issues for $20. (Foreign subscriptions are slightly higher.) Send check to *Castle Rock,* P.O. Box 8060, Bangor, Maine 04401.
- *The Harlan Ellison Record Collection* is the newsletter for Ellison readers, with information on his forthcoming books and current projects. 4 issues for $6. Order from the Harlan Ellison Record Collection, P.O. Box 55548, Sherman Oaks, Calif. 91413-0548.
- *Locus* is the newspaper of the fantasy and science-fiction field. Indispensable reading for anyone with more than a casual interest in the field. Published monthly; 12 issues for $28. Order from Locus Publications, P.O. Box 13305, Oakland, Calif. 94661.
- *Midnight Graffiti* is an attractive magazine that specializes in dark fantasy. A yearly subscription is $24, which includes first-class mailing. (Its special Stephen King issue, spring 1989, is $4.95, plus $2 for postage. The issue contains, among other things, the first appearance of a short story by King, "Rainy Season." Publisher James Van Hise is an old pro at putting together attractive specialty publications, and it shows in his latest effort.) Order from: *Midnight Graffiti,* 13101 Sudan Rd., Poway, Calif. 92064.
- *Whispers* magazine, published by Stuart D. Schiff, is well worth the attention of anyone interested in the horror field. (Its Stephen King issue, long out of print, is a typical example of its publishing excellence.) Published as double-issues, *Whispers* is well worth your time. For current subscription rates and back issues, write to Whispers Press, 70 Highland Ave., Binghamton, N.Y. 13905.
- Other specialty magazines—mixtures of art, fiction, interviews, book reviews, and author profiles—are usually available through specialty booksellers.

7. Audio Publishers

- *Durkin•Hayes Publishing Ltd.* offers the abridged reading of *Thinner.* Check your local bookstore.
- *Lion Recording* (P.O. Box 962, Washington, D.C. 20044) offers audiocassette recordings of "The Larry King Show." It has the Stephen King interview, which aired on April 10, 1986. Write for information on prices.
- *NAL* offers two boxed sets of *The Dark Tower* tapes, and King's vampire tale, "Night Flier," from *Prime Evil.* Check your local bookstore.
- *Recorded Books* (P.O. Box 409, Charlotte Hall, Md. 20622) has for rent or sale many unabridged readings of King's short fiction. Write for a free catalogue.
- *ZBS Foundation* (R.R. 1, Box 1201, Fort Edward, N.Y. 12828) offers the 3-D dramatization of "The Mist."

8. Mainstream Publishers

- *Berkley* published the paperback edition of *Danse Macabre.* Get it through your local bookstore.
- *Doubleday* has published in hardback *Carrie, Night Shift, Pet Sematary, 'Salem's Lot, The Shining,* and *The Stand.* It will publish the revised edition of *The Stand* in 1990. All are in print and available at local bookstores; if they don't have an item, it can be special-ordered for you. (Doubleday Book Club offers these, and other, King books at slightly lower prices; get its member's catalogue for current prices.) Note: Doubleday is planning on reissuing its King titles as part of a promotion for the release of the revised edition of *The Stand.*
- *G.K. Hall & Co.* publishes some King titles in its large-print editions (for the visually handicapped). You may have to special-order these through your local bookstore.
- *G.P. Putnam's Sons,* which publishes King in hardback, published *Skeleton Crew, The Talisman* (in a copublishing arrangement with Viking), and *The Tommyknockers.* You can get these through your local bookstore.
- *New American Library* (referred to throughout this book as NAL) publishes King in hardback, trade paperback, and mass-market paperback (under its Signet imprint). It publishes King audiotapes (*The Dark Tower* series), and books *about* King, including *Stephen King: The Art of Darkness, Stephen King Goes to the Movies,* and some of the Underwood–Miller book collections of articles about King. Check Appendix 1, "Books in Print," for a complete listing of what's available. You can also get these titles by mail: New American Library, P.O. Box 999, Bergenfield, N.J. 07621.
- *Viking,* King's primary hardback publisher, has published *Christine, Cujo, The Dead Zone, Different Seasons, The Eyes of the Dragon, Firestarter, It, Misery, The Talisman* (in a copublishing arrangement with G.P. Putnam's Sons). It will be publishing *The Dark Half* in 1989 and three other books in 1990–92.

9. Specialty Publishers

For more information, see pages 114–119. All of these publishers offer flyers or catalogues, or both.

- *Arkham House* (Sauk City, Wis. 53583).
- *Blood and Guts Press* (2076 Westwood Blvd., Los Angeles, Calif. 90025).
- *BGSU Popular Press* (Bowling Green State University, Bowling Green, Ohio 43403).
- *Dark Harvest* (P.O. Box 941, Arlington Heights, Ill. 60006).
- *Donald M. Grant, Publisher, Inc.* (P.O. Box 187, Hampton Falls, N.H. 03844). The première specialty press publisher of King's books.
- *Hill House Publishers* (P.O. Box 1783, Grand Central Station, New York, N.Y. 10163).
- *Land of Enchantment* (P.O. Box 5360, Plymouth, Mich. 48170).
- *Lord John Press* (19073 Los Alimos St., Northridge, Calif. 91326).
- *Phantasia Press* (5536 Crispin Way, West Bloomfield, Mich. 48033).
- *Philtrum Press* (P.O. Box 1186, Bangor, Maine 04401). Stephen King's own publishing company.
- *Popular Culture, Ink.,* (P.O. Box 1839, Ann Arbor, Mich. 48106).
- *Scream Press* (P.O. Box 481146, Los Angeles, Calif. 90048).
- *Starmont House* (P.O. Box 851, Mercer Island, Wash. 98040).
- *Underwood–Miller* (708 Westover Dr., Lancaster, Pa. 17601). The première publisher of books *about* King.
- *Whispers Press* (70 Highland Ave., Binghamton, N.Y. 13905).

10. Miscellaneous

- *Horror Writers of America,* a professional writer's organization specializing in dark fantasy. Write to Joseph A. Citro, 112 Hadley Rd., South Burlington, Vt. 05403, for information. (Yes, Stephen and Tabitha King are members.)
- Kenny Ray Linkous (141 Spring Street, Apt #4, Portland, Maine, 04101). As Kenneth Linkhauser, he illustrated the Philtrum Press edition of *The Eyes of the Dragon.* He is available for commissions and assignments.
- *Special Collection of Stephen King material,* contact Eric S. Flower, Head, Special Collections, Raymond H. Fogler Library, University of Maine, Orono, Maine 04469.
- *WZON-t Shirts* ($10 plus $1.50 postage and handling; in large and extra-large sizes only) from Mighty John's, c/o *Castle Rock,* P.O. Box 8060, Bangor, Maine 04401.

Afterword

If you have enjoyed this book and have suggestions on what you might like to see in future editions, drop me a line in care of the publisher:

George Beahm
c/o Andrews and McMeel
4900 Main Street
Kansas City, Missouri 64112

I am especially interested in any corrections to the bibliographic material in the appendices. (Try as you might, you'll never get everything right. Barry R. Levin, who worked with me on the price guide, can attest to that.)

Now, it's time for me to take my leave.

It has been fun for me, and I hope for you.

About the Editor

George Beahm has edited two books of fantasy art and authored four nonfiction books. As a principal in GB Publishing, he has published two regional books.

A former marketing director for a book publishing company, he resides in Newport News, Virginia, with his wife, Mary.

Copyright Page

The following pages constitute an extension of the copyright page.

Photos credited to the *Bangor Daily News* are reprinted with the permission of the newspaper.

Artwork credited to artists is reprinted with permission of the respective artists.

"The Author Talks" is excerpted from an interview, "The Author Talks: Stephen King," copyright © 1987 by Recorded Books, Inc., and is reprinted with permission.

The excerpts from the Stephen King radio interview that was broadcast on "The Larry King Show" on April 10, 1986, are copyright © 1986 by the Mutual Broadcasting System, Inc. All rights reserved.

Part One

Two letters from "Stephen King" were from "letters to the editors," as appeared in *National Lampoon* (respectively, September 1981 and July 1983).

"*Playboy* Interview: Stephen King." Published in U.S. *Playboy,* June 1983. Reprinted by Special Permission of *Playboy* magazine. Copyright © 1983 by *Playboy*.

"Introducing Stephen King," read by Kelly Powell, is reprinted with the permission of the Virginia Beach Public Library.

"Stephen King as Breckinridge Elkins?" by Donald M. Grant is copyright © 1989 by Donald M. Grant.

"A Girl's Dream Comes True in Mansion Fit for Kings" by Joan H. Smith was originally published in the December 8, 1984, edition of the *Bangor Daily News,* and is reprinted with permission.

"Wrought Iron" by Terry Steel was originally published in the October/November 1983 issue of *Fine Homebuilding* magazine, and is reprinted with permission of The Taunton Press, Publishers.

Part Two

"My Say" by Stephen King originally appeared in the December 20, 1985, issue of *Publishers Weekly* and is copyright © 1985 by the Xerox Corporation, and is reprinted with permission.

"Michael R. Collings: An Interview" is copyright © 1989 by Michael R. Collings. All rights reserved.

"Stephen King and the Critics: A Personal Perspective" by Michael R. Collings is copyright © 1989 by Michael R. Collings. All rights reserved.

"Stephen King Helps Spearhead Censorship Referendum Defeat" by Christopher Spruce was originally published in the July 1986 issue of *Castle Rock,* and is reprinted with permission.

"Clive Barker on Stephen King, Horror, and EC Comics" is comments by Clive Barker from interviews with him on "The Larry King Show," which were broadcast on May 6, 1987, and October 11, 1988. The interviews are copyright © 1987 and © 1988 by the Mutual Broadcasting System, Inc. All rights reserved.

"Harlan Ellison: An Interview" was conducted by George Beahm and Howard Wornom, and is copyright © 1989 by the Kilimanjaro Corporation. All rights reserved.

"Terror in Toontown" by Howard Wornom is copyright © 1989 by Howard Wornom. All rights reserved.

Part Three

"Stephen King Musical Lays Eggs on Broadway" by Dan R. Scapperotti was originally published in *Cinefantastique,* Volume 19:¹/₂, and is copyright © 1989 by *Cinefantastique.*

"Dear Walden People" by Stephen King. Published in Waldenbooks' *Book Notes,* August 1983. Copyright © 1983 by Walden Book Company, Inc. All rights reserved. Reprinted by permission.

"A Review of *Firestarter*" is excerpted from "Burned-up NOW Bimbos Can't Hold a Candle to *Firestarter,*" copyright © 1987 by Joe Bob Briggs, from *Joe Bob Goes to the Drive-In,* and is reprinted by permission of Delacorte Press, a division of BANTAM, DOUBLEDAY, DELL PUBLISHING GROUP, INC.

The two installments from "Harlan Ellison's Watching" originally appeared in *The Magazine of Fantasy and Science Fiction* and are copyright © 1984 by the Kilimanjaro Corporation, reprinted with the permission of, and by arrangement with, the Author. All rights reserved.

"ID" by Charles McGrath is reprinted by permission; copyright © 1986 Charles McGrath. Originally in *The New Yorker* (December 29, 1986).

"An Editor's Reminiscence" by Mr. Nye Willden is copyright © 1989 by Nye Willden. All rights reserved.

"Gary Hart Is Strange and So Is This Movie About Cornflake Kids" by Joe Bob Briggs is copyright © 1987 by Joe Bob Briggs, from *Joe Bob Goes to the Drive-In,* and is reprinted by permission of Delacorte Press, a division of BANTAM, DOUBLEDAY, DELL PUBLISHING GROUP, INC.

"A Coupl'a Authors Sittin' Around Talkin'" by William Goldstein was originally published in the May 11, 1984, issue of *Publishers Weekly,* and is copyright © 1984 by the Xerox Corporation, and reprinted by permission.

"Stephen King: An Interview with Waldenbooks" is an excerpt from "WB Celebrates Halloween with an Exclusive Interview with the Scaremaster Himself . . . Stephen King!" The interview was originally published in the November 1987 issue of *WB.* Reprinted with permission from *WB* #145, a Waldenbooks' Newsweekly.

Photo courtesy of the *Bangor Daily News*

Stephen King, hunched over his IBM Selectric, is in his own office, writing a book.

*In my novella "The Breathing Method," in Different Seasons,
I created a mysterious private club in an old brownstone on
East 35th Street in Manhattan, in which an oddly matched group
of men gathers periodically to trade tales of the uncanny.
And there are many rooms upstairs, and when a new guest asks
the exact number, the strange old butler tells him, "I don't know,
sir, but you could get lost up there." That men's club really is a
metaphor for the entire storytelling process. There are as many
stories in me as there are rooms in that house, and I can easily
lose myself in them. And at the club, whenever a tale is about
to be told, a toast is raised first, echoing the words engraved
on the keystone of the massive fireplace in the library:
IT IS THE TALE, NOT HE WHO TELLS IT.
That's been a good guide to me in life, and I think it would make
a good epitaph for my tombstone. Just that and no name.*

Stephen King, from Playboy *interview,* June 1983

EAU CLAIRE DISTRICT LIBRARY